D1135367

Something in India

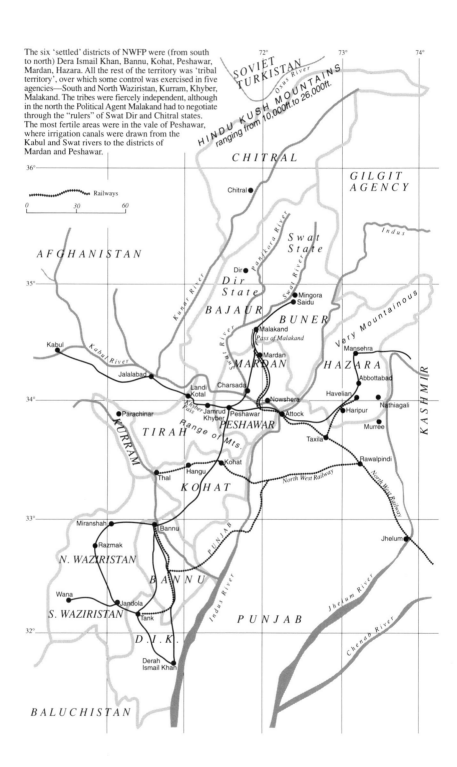

The six 'settled' districts of NWFP were (from south
to north) Dera Ismail Khan, Bannu, Kohat, Peshawar,
Mardan, Hazara. All the rest of the territory was 'tribal
territory', over which some control was exercised in five
agencies—South and North Waziristan, Kurram, Khyber,
Malakand. The tribes were fiercely independent, although
in the north the Political Agent Malakand had to negotiate
through the "rulers" of Swat Dir and Chitral states.
The most fertile areas were in the vale of Peshawar,
where irrigation canals were drawn from the
Kabul and Swat rivers to the districts of
Mardan and Peshawar.

72° 73° 74°

SOVIET
TURKISTAN
Oxus River

HINDU KUSH MOUNTAINS
ranging from 10,000ft. to 26,000ft.

CHITRAL

36°

GILGIT
AGENCY

Railways

0   30   60

Chitral

Indus

AFGHANISTAN

Swat
State

Panjkora River

Kunar River

35°

Dir

Dir
State

Mingora
Saidu

Swat River

BAJAUR

BUNER

Very Mountainous

Kabul

Kabul River

Swat River

Malakand
Pass of Malakand

Mansehra

Jalalabad

Mardan

MARDAN

HAZARA

Abbottabad

Landi
Kotal

Charsada

Havelian

Nathiagali

34°

Parachinar

Khyber Pass

Jamrud
Khyber

Nowshera

Peshawar

Attock

Haripur

Murree

KURRAM

TIRAH

Range of Mts.

PESHAWAR

Taxila

KASHMIR

Kohat

Rawalpindi

Thal

Hangu

KOHAT

North West Railway

North West Railway

33°

Miranshah

Bannu

PUNJAB

Jhelum

Razmak

N. WAZIRISTAN

BANNU

Wana

Indus River

Jandola

Jhelum River

S. WAZIRISTAN

Tank

PUNJAB

32°

D. I. K.

Chenab River

Derah
Ismail Khan

BALUCHISTAN

Something in India

A memoir of service in the Frontier Province

by

Sir Fraser Noble
ICS, NWFP, 1941–7

The Pentland Press Ltd
Edinburgh • Cambridge • Durham • USA

First published in 1997 by
The Pentland Press Ltd.
1 Hutton Close
South Church
Bishop Auckland
Durham

British Library Cataloguing in Publication Data.
A catalogue record for this book is available
from the British Library.

ISBN 1 85821 537 4

Typeset by George Wishart & Associates, Whitley Bay.
Printed and bound by Bookcraft Ltd., Bath.

Contents

Illustrations

Foreword

O ver 20 years ago, the notion that I might write a memoir of my early career arose from a request by Miss Joan Lancaster, who was then Director of the India Office Library and Records. Many former members of the Indian Civil Service responded to her invitation. The result was an invaluable book – *The District Officer in India, 1930–1947*, published in 1980.

I deeply regretted that I had been so preoccupied in my university career that I had not contributed to this volume. But I decided that when I retired I would spend no more time on committees, and would attempt to write a serious book about the development of the North West Frontier Province – established as a Governor's Province by the Government of India Act of 1935.

The Leverhulme Trust generously awarded me an Emiritus Fellowship 'to prepare a study of the NWFP in the final stages of British rule in India'. The present book reflects the efforts I made to meet my objective in the years 1982–4. At an early stage I consulted Sir Cyril Philips, the distinguished historian of India. When he learned that I had access to my letters written to my mother and my fiancée conveying full accounts of my personal experiences as a junior ICS officer, he strongly advised me to begin by 'writing myself out' of the proposed book by writing a personal memoir.

This was completed in the spring of 1984, by which time I had also assembled many notes in preparation for the proposed academic study. Unfortunately, the effects of an illness brought all those plans to an end in summer of 1984. As the years have passed, I have often reflected that I was lucky not to have published so many rather critical remarks about senior friends and colleagues. Now, in the fiftieth year after Partition, I regret that so many of them have passed on without having had a chance to put my views to the test of their experience.

I acknowledge with deep gratitude the help of the Leverhulme

Trust, the officers of the old India Office Library (especially Mr Richard Bingle), as well as the staff of the library of the University of Aberdeen and of the School of Oriental and African Studies. I will name only one of many academic friends to whose encouragement I owe a real debt – Professor M.C. Meston of Aberdeen University.

15 August 1997

Preface

Time once flown returneth never,
Idle moments gone forever,
Woulds't recall them? Call in vain.

Khushhal Khan Khatak
Translated by Sir Olaf Caroe

There was a period in my life when I found it difficult to answer the question, 'What did you do during the war?' A proper and truthful answer called for a lengthy explanation which I knew perfectly well nobody wanted to listen to. The brief reply 'I was in the ICS' really conveyed nothing to the average questioner, for within a year or two of 1947 there were all too few people in Britain who remained well-informed about the 'unequalled tradition' of that very special service of the Crown. It seemed to me that after the carnage of 1947 the British developed a guilt complex and did not want to be reminded of the decline and fall of the Raj: a totally unjustified reaction to the tragic aspect of the consequences of unusually honourable surrender of imperial power. All this was frustrating, for I was very proud of my service in India, but when faced with the question I took refuge in the vague reply: 'I was something in India', confident that in most cases that would satisfy the curiosity of my interlocutor.

At that period I was unaware of the book by Sidney Low called *A Vision of India*. Low was a journalist who went to India in the winter of 1905 to cover the tour by the Prince and Princess of Wales which went on into the spring of 1906. His despatches were developed into a full-length book of which any special correspondent would be justly proud. He travelled through India with his eyes and ears wide open with deep insight and genuine sympathy. A quotation from the book introduces the pamphlet in which in 1958 the Indian Civil Service (Retired) Association celebrated the unveiling by the Queen of a memorial in Westminster Abbey, which commemorates the work of the Civil Services of the Crown in India (the Services which Lloyd George once described as the 'steel frame' of the Indian Empire). The quotation is:

> There must be many a man now living in England to whom scenes of his active service in India will be no more than a dim memory, that may perchance steal faintly back to his brain, as he turns over the evening papers in the smoking room on some Sunday afternoon. At the Club they may have only a vague remembrance that So and So was once 'something in India'. Therein they are, indeed, not wrong. A man of this stamp was unquestionably 'something in India'.

In April 1970 Prime Minister Harold Wilson invited a group of ten British University Vice-Chancellors to a dinner at 10 Downing Street. Being prudent men, about to sup with politicians, we met for half an hour beforehand to consider our tactics for the discussion that would follow the meal – assuming that we could identify the Prime Minister's objective. We made our way to Downing Street far from confident that we had read his mind. With one or two others I was a passenger in the Oxford University car, riding with Oxford's then Vice-Chancellor, Alan Bullock (now Lord Bullock) the distinguished historian and biographer of Adolf Hitler. As we drove down Whitehall, he suddenly remarked, 'What an odd lark this is! How can anyone prepare to be a Vice-Chancellor in these days – unless he had been a political officer on the North West Frontier.' He was astonished when I laughed and laid claim to the prescribed qualification, saying that I had often told my wife that only experience of tribal jirgas on the Frontier enabled me occasionally to outguess my senate at its monthly meetings.

Alan Bullock's casual remark reminded me that the Prime Minister's best man at his wedding had been my ICS colleague Pat Duncan, who was assassinated in Waziristan by a young Mahsud shortly after I left India. I knew that at least I had a conversational gambit that might be useful at dinner. But more seriously the remark prompted reflection at leisure. Memories that had faded in the daily pressures of university expansion were stirred again. A few years later I tried without success to find time to respond to the invitation of the India Office librarian to contribute to the assembly of reminiscences of the life of a District Officer. I resolved that when I retired I would attempt to set down an account of the Frontier Province. When I set out to do that, I found that I must first clear out of the way the personal side of my experiences in the Frontier. In doing so, I have tried to keep in mind the guidelines suggested by the officials at the India Office library, so that I hope that what follows is presented in such a way as to be helpful to scholars in the future who may want to understand how events affected a British officer at the time. Although I kept no personal diary, I had written regular detailed accounts of my life to my mother and to my fiancée, and up to the time of my marriage in 1945 all those letters which had survived the wartime passage from India have been preserved. In addition, as the text indicates at the appropriate points, I have been able to draw on a miscellany of documents, memoranda, notes and oddments such as office diaries that I had kept in my possession.

I believe that an understanding of what happened in the Frontier Province in my time is essential to any interpretation of the final partition of India. That calls for a deeper, more structured analysis than I have here attempted. Although I hope that my memoir may be a contribution towards such an understanding, my personal links with some of the central factors were too indirect or tangential for me to treat them adequately in such a personal account. My main wish is that what I have written will amuse my grandchildren and in some way serve the needs of future historians. For as G.M. Trevelyan wrote: 'Every true history must, by its human and vital presentation of events, force us to remember that the past was once as real as the present and uncertain as the future.'

CHAPTER I

Nature and Nurture 1918-40

I was born on 29 April 1918 in the schoolhouse of Cromdale, Morayshire. My father was the dominie, or parish schoolmaster, and was held in great respect in the district, indeed in the whole of Speyside and the county of Moray. He had been born at Connage near Ardersier in Inverness-shire, one of a large family only half of whom survived the handicaps of rural poverty to attain mature years. My grandfather, who came from Moy, was farm grieve at Connage, but later he and his wife (a Fraser from Dunphail, between Forres and Grantown in the valley of the Findhorn), moved to a hill croft at Glenbeg, some two or three miles from Grantown-on-Spey in a little glen, since depopulated, where the ruins of the homesteads are now barely visible. Here they eked out a hard-won livelihood, and strove successfully to provide their surviving children with a basic education and a start in life. Simon, my father, the lad o' pairts in the old Scottish tradition, went to college in Aberdeen to become a teacher.

The evidence is that he had great talent and did well, but after two years he had to go home to help his parents, postponing the completion of his studies and his attainment of his degree at Aberdeen University, where he was still 'in good standing'. He took up his chosen profession, teaching first at Avoch, a lively fishing village in the county of Ross and Cromarty near the head of the Moray Firth, and then at Scone, in Perthshire. But his health broke down, his heart strained, it was said, from over-exertion at cycling in the hills, and he had to abandon his intention of returning to Aberdeen to complete his degree studies. When he recovered, after months at home, he became a teacher at the Greenock Industrial School.

In Greenock, he met my mother, Jeanie Boyd Beattie Graham, of Largs in Ayrshire. She was matron of the Home in Ann Street, a hostel for girls and young women in need of care, a charitable enterprise of the Paisley firm of J. & P. Coats. An aunt of my mother had undertaken similar work for the original hostel established by the firm at Paisley. My mother was also one of a large family. Her father was a shoemaker, but in early manhood he had served for ten years in the 59th Regiment including a tour of India. I never knew him, and cannot recall my mother ever referring to any detail of his Indian service.

My parents made their first home in Lilac Cottage in Grantown-on-Spey. My father taught in Grantown Grammar School for six years from 1907, laying the foundation of the considerable reputation which he earned in the twenty years of his public service in Morayshire. In 1913 he moved to the headmastership of the small two-teacher school at Cromdale. In 1924, he was promoted to Findhorn, a larger but then somewhat sleepy fishing community, beautifully situated on Findhorn Bay opposite the Culbin Sands on the south shores of the Moray Firth. Two years later, after major surgery in Inverness, he died at the age of 46.

This is not the place to go into detail about my father's career and personality. I was only eight when he died, too young, one might think, to remember much that is reliable. But my mother brought me up to revere his memory and example, and I believe that in some remarkable way he continued to affect my whole development. When he died his closest friend and colleague, the Rev. T.S. Cargill, published a very fine appraisal of his life and character. If I felt that I had earned a tribute half as eloquent I should die content. What emerged most emphatically from it, and from what others have said, was the belief that, considerable though his achievements were within his limited sphere of opportunity, my father 'never had work up to the level of his ability'. Though he had considerable and wide-ranging talents, a strong and striking personality, was professionally successful, notable in public debate and equally eloquent on paper, and was acclaimed for his calm, sober and moderate judgment, he was inevitably restricted in opportunity, perhaps primarily because of his record of ill health and the general impoverishment of his early days.

It became my mother's ambition to enable me to overcome such hurdles and to find the opportunities that he had been denied. For this she was prepared to make any sacrifice; and she succeeded, better perhaps than she ever realized, for all through my career I have been conscious that I was enjoying opportunities that stretched my abilities to the limit and beyond. The message she drummed into me in my boyhood was always the same. 'However hard your task, just do your best, as your father did; what happens after that doesn't matter, he would be content.' It is a challenging precept, but simple and direct and in following it I have constantly found that luck has been on my side. The opportunities have come; often I have felt that the goal has been way beyond my ability, and I have often seen others far better endowed than myself stumble and fail; I have not always done my best for there is a lazy streak in me that I suspect may have lurked in my father, nourished by his physical weakness. But more often than not I have tried, and perhaps more often than most men, I have succeeded in marshalling my resources to rise to an occasion that my instincts defined as important. What I am trying to say is that my performance and my attitudes throughout my career owed a great deal to my upbringing, and that though I had been deprived of my father's presence far too early, his influence remained strong and concentrated, through my mother's devoted care and teaching.

She had a hard time, for when we left Findhorn during the General Strike of 1926 to go to a rented home in Nairn, she had no pension, no savings, and only the small sum subscribed generously by friends in testimony to my father. Her own health was poor and her physical resources limited, but she toiled for years to keep our home together. My brother, eight years older than me, soon left school and made his own way through harsh times to a successful career in journalism. Our father, whose main private grumble about life was that the doctors denied him the chance of active service in the First World War when he had to be content as a lieutenant in the Morayshire Volunteers, would have been especially proud of his successful stratagem in October 1939 when he bluffed the doctors into passing him fit for active service, for he had been treated as a diabetic for several years. He attained the rank of captain in the Seaforth Highlanders, and having been downgraded medically on the point of embarkation for the invasion of Madagascar, subsequently served in Europe on the staff of 21 Army Group HQ.

Keeping lodgers and taking summer visitors in the late 1920s and 1930s was no joke, and far from profitable, and my mother's obsessive anxiety, inevitably, was financial. But she kept going in spite of a recurring illness involving major surgery, and I passed successfully through a plump and overweight boyhood into a fairly tall, slim adolescence. There was no stint on food and I consumed too much milk and too many milk puddings. What was exceedingly scarce was money for any kind of frill, and I learned early how to cut my coat according to the cloth. That stood me in good stead when I had to live on bursaries at the university and find my feet in India in the burgeoning inflation of the war years. I worked hard and successfully at school, and in the main enjoyed the normal activities of youth in Nairn, a small, attractive community blessed with a mild, dry climate, where there was every incentive to be out of doors. There were limitations: when the time came for the annual Scout camp it was likely to be necessary for me to withdraw because of the expense. The same thing happened when in the Thirties for the first time a small number of places were available to boys from Nairn Academy to sail on an educational cruise. When I played football for the school I wore borrowed boots that did not fit. But early on I was provided with a mixed but very adequate set of golf clubs and the seven shillings and sixpence which was then the annual boy's subscription of the Nairn Dunbar Golf Club, and I was told by my mother that she would never be worried about me if she knew that I was on the golf course. Golf and to a less extent, cycling, became my main outdoor recreations. In summer I often played informal cricket, and occasionally tennis, but I regarded these games as bad for my golf, and declined to take them seriously.

At home, there was always interesting conversation. My mother was not only highly intelligent, she was well read, and her love of literature shone through in her letters, which were very true to her personality, sensitive and perceptive and often beautifully phrased. She had quite a wide experience of life in Scotland – her work at Greenock gave her insight and understanding of social conditions and problems that would have been a closed book in those days to most people in communities like Nairn or Grantown. Her interests ranged widely, and embraced politics, for she came from a radical background deriving its philosophy from the Chartists and certainly shared my father's strong Morley-type Liberal principles. For many years our daily paper was the *News Chronicle*, partly I think to ensure that we would not become too parochially Scottish in our outlook. While my father was alive we also took the *Scotsman*. We were certainly aware of the world outside Britain, though in those days we had no radio, far less television; our first wireless set was acquired about 1935. What gave width and depth to our outlook was literature. My father's catholic tastes were reflected in the goodly stock of books that I always associate with my concept of home; to his collection my mother had brought her own preferences in the classics, including poetry, influenced in her own youth by a favourite uncle, James Meikle, doyen of the yachting correspondents early in this century, author of several books and a man of considerable stature in journalism and literary circles in the west of Scotland. He always used to send my brother and myself books from his own library for Christmas.

My love of books seemed to open doors in more ways than one. Soon I discovered that a neighbouring chum, who had older brothers and sisters, had a well-stocked library in an upper room, to which his tolerant mother allowed me access on many a rainy day. This widened – beyond our own R.M. Ballantyne collection – the range of adventure yarns to which I became addicted, and also introduced me to G.A. Henty, from whom in my early teens I learned more history than my school textbooks could convey. Perhaps in subtle ways these vicarious experiences through authors of various credentials began to stir in me the interest in backward countries and their peoples which finally emerged from my subconscious with my service in India. Curiously, though uncle James Meikle had introduced me to Kipling, his choice of a gift (*Life's Handicap*) rang no bells, and I had no real appreciation of the merits and demerits of Kipling until after I had personal experiences of India. Above all, though I had read *Kim* without properly understanding it, I certainly did not realize until long afterwards that this was one of the first, and certainly the greatest, of the genre of spy thrillers which has fascinated recent generations of readers.

Besides our good neighbours, there were others in Nairn whose shelves were made available to me. One was an avuncular grocer, whose interests were intellectual and philosophical rather than financial. His brother had become a minister, and against his will he had gone into the family business. He was a scholar manqué. My mother said he was 'a gentleman rather than a grocer', but he developed a business which a lady very senior in the Scottish aristocracy long afterwards described to me as the Fortnum and Masons of the North, and with every justification. With unusual perception, this kindly elderly bachelor presented me, round about my twelfth year, with a subscription to the Nairn Literary Institute. This society met in the Supper Room of the old Public Hall at

8 p.m. every second Friday except in summer, usually to hear a talk, preferably illustrated with slides from the 'magic lantern'. Speakers were drawn from quite a wide radius, their subjects were often of travel and adventure and only occasionally 'literary' in the more restricted sense. From time to time there would be a musical evening (certainly one towards the end of January to celebrate Robert Burns). Though I was usually the only youngster in the audience – probably the only person under the age of forty – I attended assiduously and gained much profit as well as pleasure from the experience.

Moreover, upstairs in a large, gloomy, gas-lit room was housed the Institute's library, in shelves and cupboards towering high along the walls round a parsimonious coal fire. Near enough the fire to sit at it wearing one's coat on a winter's night was a large square table and some wooden chairs, and having persuaded the grumpy hall-keeper/caretaker to unlock an appropriate cupboard, I would sit for hours browsing in strange books with accounts of Victorian excursions to exotic places. In the other corner of the vast, dark room were the artefacts that comprised the local museum, not, surprisingly, to any marked extent a record of the past history of Nairnshire – there was plenty of that in the library – but mostly a miscellany of mementoes of explorations in darkest Africa and other continents by men with some family link. The Highlander was a great explorer in the nineteenth century. In some dingy, ill-tended glass cases were skeletons and a few stuffed animals or birds, and in the corners whole sheaves of spears, swords and battleaxes. It was an odd environment for a timid boy to spend solitary hours concentrating not very successfully on books that often seemed not quite suited to his needs. It is hard to judge what good came of it, if any; perhaps some notion of another world and of the problems of its peoples, perhaps even some understanding of solitude and the importance of being able to content oneself without speech and without company.

That was to stand me in good stead in later years when I enjoyed escaping from the pressures of the office or law court and the social whirl of the Indian cantonment, to spend whole weeks on tour, camping in the hills and valleys of the Hazara District. After long days happily scrambling up and down over stony ground, inspecting fields and boundaries, listening to petitions and complaints, conversing with the villagers, semi-formally in the *hujra* in assembly, informally with individuals on the road, I found great contentment in sitting quietly by a hissing pressure lamp in the evening, at the entrance to my tent or by the blazing logs of the fire in the resthouse or dak bungalow, writing up a tour diary or communicating the day's experience in a letter 'home', or getting lost in a book to widen and deepen knowledge and understanding while my still-active brain adapted to the exhausted rhythms of my limbs, and the time came for the healthiest sleep with which a man can be blessed. Returning to base, I was invariably amused by the horror expressed by cantonment-bound friends when they heard that I had been for days on end 'alone in the wilderness', deprived, as they saw it, of the solace of speech with one's fellow men, by which they meant Europeans. The society of the villagers, who have the same facility for seeing the humour in any unlikely situation as British soldiers, the company of my camp clerk and my orderly, the stillness of the forest outside my camp, the calm assurance of the heavens above, all contributed to the refreshment of my spirit and left me content, late in the evening, to commune with my thoughts as my reading or writing led them hither and thither.

Another guide and mentor to the world of books later in my youth in Nairn was the minister of the Nairn High Church of Scotland, J.M. Little. Early in my boyhood we had attended the old Parish Church, but when my mother lay desperately ill in hospital she was comforted by this lovable man, who saw it as his duty and privilege to help all who were sick or in need, and not merely members of his own congregation. When she recovered my mother changed to his Church. We attended with moderate regularity and I came rather grudgingly to accept the notion of Sunday school and, soon, of Bible class. The latter was taken by a retired teaplanter with a gentle manner, who was more at ease talking about life in tea plantations than he was with the gospel, but the outcome was, as it should be, wholly beneficial to the modes of thought of his pupils. The customary long walk after Bible class – boys only, our inclination toward mischief restrained and tempered by our Sabbath suits – was a pleasurable relaxation, as well as being quite educational. For while solitary scholarship is a rare prize for any bright youth, by itself it is not enough, and he needs to learn in a social context outside the classroom and beyond the privacy of his own room. I realized early that I could learn from sharing the company of others of my own age or rather older than oneself who had nothing particular in mind but a walk and talk, and this sort of learning was an enjoyable process. What is more, social learning is not a matter of listening to people who are cleverer than oneself, or superior in some way in status or authority or social class. The quality of life in Nairn in those days was high because the school and church and boy scout movement embraced the whole community; one had friends equally from the east end and west end of the town.

The Rev. J.M. Little had a lot to do with the making of this environment. He won respect, admiration and love from every corner of the community, and his example must have comforted and even inspired many men and women in the stormy years of the War. It claimed him tragically as a victim for he was killed by a bus from which he had just descended in the blackout near his own manse, returning weary from a meeting of the County Education Committee in Elgin. To me at least, learning of this disaster some months later out on the Frontier, the event had appalling dark forebodings: my home in despair, saddened and bereft, and most of its young men scattered to the winds, lonely and helpless in its time of need. This digression began with a reference to those who opened doors for me to the world of books. J.M. Little's particular contribution was the gift of some of his Left Book Club books. This was made when I was already a student in Aberdeen University and beginning to be weaned away from my classical studies by a developing interest in economics and politics. This was not unassociated with my generation's preoccupation with the Spanish Civil War. I had already moved some way left of the Liberalism of Asquith, and was describing myself as a socialist. Mr Little's books in the context of their time confirmed this tendency, but I was not completely converted, nor was that his intention. What I think stayed with me from my youthful reading of the red-covered Gollancz books was an attitude of mind towards poverty and its causes, a concern for the human condition, rather than any firm belief in a particular ideology or philosophy.

No doubt my more formal education at school contributed. Its emphasis was on careful preparation and accuracy in detail, and I have no doubt that this approach is the making of self-discipline, from which emerges an educated individual. Some elements in this traditional Scottish approach to education seem to have been eroded, and new fashions in teaching practice may not always do justice to the raw material of new generations, in whose quality I retain unshaken faith. At Nairn Academy in the early 1930s I followed an excellent broad curriculum, taking 'highers' in English, Latin, French, Mathematics and History in my fifth year at the age of fifteen, and adding higher Greek in my sixth year. In addition, I had a general grounding in science, geography and art and enough music to realize that I was not entirely tone deaf – though part of the opportunity was scandalously wasted by the exaggerated pretence fashionable among the boys of being unable to attempt singing because their voices were breaking.

The school was well run by a Rector who was a strict disciplinarian, Dr J.M. Milne; his stern solemnity did not unduly inhibit the general happiness of his pupils. He was a fine classical scholar, with a sensitive feeling for languages and literature, both ancient and modern. Once trapped in study of Latin or Greek, his good pupils would have found it difficult to escape into other subjects even if they wanted to. We were so terrified of his displeasure that we spent disproportionately long hours of homework on Latin grammar and translation of tricky English sentences into Latin, as well as on set books. This imbalance was certainly a fault and unfair to other teachers, but the school discipline was so strict that we simply worked excessive hours rather than neglect such things as Maths homework. What suffered probably, was time and energy for apparently 'softer' subjects like French or English.

The school's greatest disaster however, in my time, was its head English teacher, responsible also for History, who was an eccentric, affected and often malicious creature totally bereft of discipline, at loggerheads in her vanity with the rest of the staff, who naturally suffered sorely from the inroads she made on the calm and stability of otherwise normal pupils. Although several attempts were made to remove her, it took several years before the Education Authority and the Rector succeeded in overcoming her counter-attacks, skilfully organized with the help of her brother, who was a King's Counsel with a successful practice at the bar in Edinburgh. Fortunately for me, her departure in my fourth year brought a very fine though relatively inexperienced young man, David Stewart, to her place and he worked hard to remedy the damage wrought by her neglect and misdeeds. What finally marked him out for me as my finest teacher was his readiness to give me, and others, personal attention to involve us in extra-curricular study in his subject to get our minds really working, and not just for examinations. The Rector himself, though in a less relaxed and urbane manner, continued to provide the same influences in his teaching of Latin and especially Greek, in which in the senior classes the relationship with him, though he remained an aloof and distant personality, was that of the university tutorial. All in all, though the school roll was too small and resources too limited to provide for sixth-form studies in the present-day sense, education at Nairn Academy in the inter-war years was pretty satisfactory.

I believe that that assessment applied equally to those who went on to higher education and to those who simply left school to get on with life in whatever station was open to them in the local community. Many who were fairly run-of-the-mill pupils so far as class marks were concerned, matured into successful and proficient farmers, tradesmen or skilled craftsmen. The charge that our system of education lacks relevance because it does not turn out the men and women that our modern industrial society needs has always struck me as totally remote from my own experience of school and higher and further education. Perhaps things have changed in schools even more drastically since the 1930s than I believe. Certainly the system that I knew drew its strength from the community and served the community well. If some pupils were bright enough to be regarded as the élite it was not because they came from a particular social class, and it did not provoke envy or enmity or interfere with normal friendly relationships between fellow pupils. Academic excellence commanded admiration and pride, but not dissension, and in me at any rate the system bred deep respect for anyone who did a job well, so that I have always found it as natural to admire a good farmer or carpenter or nurse or secretary as a good scholar or lawyer or doctor.

Soon after my fifteenth birthday I was equipped with a university entrance qualification, and in the year that followed there was not a great deal more in the way of new formal learning, save in English and Greek, that the school could do for me, though the headmaster taught me also a sense of prose style and the beginnings of accomplishment in Latin prose composition. But to my dismay the authorities indicated some doubt about the wisdom of entry to Aberdeen University at barely sixteen years of age. The Director of Education for Moray and Nairn, Dr MacLaren, visited the school and to my horror confronted me with this problem in open class. I was appalled by his suggestion that it would do me good 'to be put out to grass for a year'. To me that implied that I was a pale swot badly in need of fresh air. Fortunately I was aware that his shortcomings included an uncouth manner and a propensity for putting everything in agricultural terms, and I had deduced that for all his love of farming, and his equally great parade in this enthusiasm, he was likely to have been about as big a disaster as a farmer as he seemed to be as a Director of Education.

Rather more tactfully, the Rector explained to me privately when my outrage had subsided – it was probably ill-concealed – that the Authority proposed to send me to Robert Gordon's College in Aberdeen to join the sixth form and benefit from that great school's superior teaching endowment while maturing in readiness for university study. I was stubbornly uncooperative, maintaining that if I was ready to be allowed to leave home I would mature just as comfortably as a university student as I would ever do in the alien environment of Robert Gordon's, where doubtless I would also feel even more uncomfortable than at the university because at Gordon's College I would be alone among strangers all of whom knew each other and their masters well. At the university, in terms of relationships in our classrooms we would all start equal, even though others would be older and better schooled than I. In the end, my preference prevailed, the Education Authority treated me generously by awarding me an exceptionally large bursary for those days, and the university did not let me down. The Authority no doubt was influenced in its decision by its collective memory of my father's service and its recognition of the trust that my mother had fulfilled in bringing me up through the tribulations of her poverty and lonely ill health so as to prepare me, as my father would have wished, for the opportunity to go to university. Members of the Authority were well aware that in embarking on that ambition my mother's only resource, besides her intelligence and character, was the sum of money which had been subscribed by some of them and their predecessors, and my father's colleagues in the teaching profession and in public life in Morayshire, to mark their sympathy at his premature death.

For my part, I went to university somewhat weighed down, but not I think oppressed, by a sense of responsibility and obligation to my mother and even to the Authority, which was not a bureaucratic institution to me, but a body of public-spirited men, many of whom had known my parents, and were living characters in my mother's conversation. Inevitably, I followed a curriculum which would lead to honours in Classics, because that was what my headmaster, Dr Milne, expected and had prepared me for. It was hard going. In my first year I was a tyro at Greek compared with students from Robert Gordon's and other city schools, and indeed one of my great chums from Fordyce Academy in Banffshire. But apart from a spell of what was probably psychosomatic chronic indigestion in my first term, I survived without damage the 'problems of transition from school to university', which have been the subject of so much anxious study and discussion, and so many books and theses written in the 1960s, especially in the post-Robbins era, when the anxieties of student life became such a fashionable topic.

The university as an institution did not make a particularly active contribution to the process of my survival. So far as I know, those who lectured to me and marked my prose or my essays or class exams could not have put a name to my face if they noticed it in the quadrangle of King's College. They were conscientious and proficient, but few in number for the large 'ordinary classes' in my subjects, and there was no attempt to organize individual tutorial teaching. As soon as one passed into a more advanced stage of study and was accepted for honours work, that changed, and apparently remote professorial figures began to take a benevolent personal interest in individual pupils. In Classics, my most helpful mentor was Archie Cameron, Professor of Greek, then still a young man, at first sight slightly aloof and unassertive, but definitely stylish, with an equally stylish, very charming and hospitable wife – the honours students were entertained formally to dinner each year. Professor Cameron was a perceptive and tolerant man, with a well-developed social conscience which in the end led him into various forms of public service, both for the university and, after the War, the National Health Service. When I was on leave from India in 1945 and called on him at King's College, with no prior warning, he talked for three hours mainly about the war experience of many of my contemporaries with whom I had lost touch. He took a truly kindly and practical interest in us all.

While it was true that the university did nothing much to cosset young entrants and help them over awkward early hurdles, most of us who were not home-based lived in digs where our landladies had long experience of our problems. Many of them were every bit as helpful in a pastoral role as the academic wardens of the

Robbins era. Mine was a fine example. A modest widow with no financial resources, perhaps a shade prim in her manner but with great natural dignity and firm standards, she provided wholesome food and clean though spartan accommodation, and kept us in order more out of respect for her than in consequence of any formal regulations. Her affection for her lodgers was clear though not demonstrative, and her pride in any of our achievements rewarded the efforts we had expended, without affectation. For years she had students from Nairn, as one generation recommended her to another, but not to the entire exclusion of others, and friendships formed in her house were long sustained. This was all typical of the pre-war Aberdeen landlady, a rare breed, whose disappearance from the scene in the 1950s, when the whole business got commercialized, finally forced the university to build halls of residence.

We educated each other in our academic subjects and in the ways of life in general. The absence of residential life in Hall and of a Student's Union with catering facilities did not impoverish the social life of the undergraduate in the Thirties. Perhaps we matured more slowly, and were content with less sophisticated pleasures than the student of today, but the process of education was no less effective or rewarding. I have written elsewhere some notes on other aspects of my life at university and will not develop the account further here. But I should allude to my great good fortune in having my digs in my first two years with my wife's eldest brother Alastair, who had already graduated with first-class honours in Classics and was assistant to Professor Souter in the Department of Humanity. His experience, gently brought to bear on all our activities and anxieties, was a rich source of instruction for us and probably did more than anything to overcome the transitional problems of which I have claimed to make light. Being on the fringe of the university's teaching establishment he lowered the barriers between it and his young student friends, often delighting us with humorous glimpses of the world on the other side, but without betraying the proper dignity of authority or diminishing our respect for it.

The curriculum prescribed that a candidate for honours must read at least two courses outside his honours subject. In my first year I took English, thoroughly enjoying the unique flair of Professor Jack lecturing on Marlowe, Shakespeare and other themes, and also did Zoology, a summer term course, concentrated into three hours each afternoon, where I admired the neat and methodical description of the animal kingdom so carefully presented by Professor James Ritchie. Since I intended to do my second 'outside' subject in my second year, this was a strictly unnecessary extension of my curriculum, but it taught me something about scientific method and it was the best possible excuse for walking between Bedford Place and Marischal College with the young lady from Nairn Academy whom I was to marry in 1945.

My other outside subject was Political Economy, chosen originally because of the developing interest in politics and economics fostered during my schooldays and because of the tremendous reputation of Professor Alexander Gray as a lecturer and raconteur. In the summer of 1935, however, he went off to the chair at Edinburgh, and was succeeded by a young Oxford don from Queen's, Lindley Fraser. His approach to the subject was quite different, but just as stimulating intellectually and he seemed to bring a new Oxonian excitement to the Aberdeen Faculty of Arts and to its students. He analyzed the language of economics philosophically, and I became more and more fascinated by the subject. I did well enough in the exams to be tempted to abandon Classics in favour of honours in Economic Science. I suspect that I did not make the break in 1936 because I was still too young to make a decision which I knew would be disapproved of by my old headmaster and which could be said to be risky for in those days there were few graduates in Economics from Aberdeen and one was uncertain about the market for their talents, whereas Classics was still felt to lead safely to teaching, or the ministry, or the civil service or indeed to other administrative possibilities.

At any rate, I committed myself to two more academic sessions of honours study in Classics. In my extra-curricular activities, and in my reading and conversation, I continued to foster a general interest in Economics and Politics, but in retrospect I am conscious of the lack of a guiding hand. On vacation, there would be rewarding talks with the sensible David Stewart, my old teacher of English and History, providing an effective counterbalance to the seductive efforts of another schoolteacher, a committed Communist who lost no chance to take returning students or senior pupils for long walks. On the whole, I found his proselytizing zeal overdone. His conversation and anecdotes were interesting but seemed to go on interminably until one became exhausted by the whole process. This seemed to typify encounters with the extreme Left in the 1930s. I once met a drunk workman late at night under the lamp-post outside my digs and in his condition one might have expected maudlin ranting. In fact, he had a profound knowledge of Marxist philosophy and he was astonishingly articulate, as though the drink had loosened his recollection of all he had read and discussed over many years. But he went on too long and finally lost the sympathy I was instinctively prepared to feel for an ordinary working-class chap who had buckled down to books so as to express the better his innate beliefs and his interpretation of life's experiences.

Within the university there seemed to be little organized Communist activity. Yet the times were propitious for it, for like the Cambridge generation we were deeply moved by the Spanish Civil War and the state of the world and talked about these things a great deal. In Aberdeen there was a nasty incident in the Castlegate one Sunday evening, when the police appeared to lend support to a much disliked local blackshirt and his group, who were interfering with an open-air meeting organized by the Trades Council – they used amplifiers to 'drown' the Trades Unionist speeches. I was not present but the interest aroused by the incident helped to focus the minds of many of us. About this time, our Principal, Sir William Hamilton Fyfe, published in the Aberdeen University Review a pertinent article in which he applied to the Spanish situation the famous passage in *Thucydides*, Book IV about faction and civil war, substituting the names of Spanish politicians, then in the news, for the appropriate Greek names. This brought Greek history alive into the present day in a manner of which the lecturer in the subject was quite incapable; but interestingly enough we had a new lecturer in Roman History – Eric Turner, subsequently Professor of Egyptian Papyrology at London University – whose interpretation of his subject was a revelation. While I was still in love with Greek and Greek literature, and fascinated by the notion of the western heritage of classical civilization, I had begun to find the study of Latin pall on me, and was stimulated only by Turner's teaching and its revelation of Roman politics.

A group of students from different subjects founded a new society, in the way that students have, and I was a founder member and served on the committee. This was the Reform Club. It was affiliated to no political party and it was open to anyone to join provided he or she was interested in reform by parliamentary means. For two or three years it órganized an excellent programme of talks and discussions attracting speakers like Boyd Orr, Lancelot Hogben, Enid Charles and Hamilton Fyfe, and one summer term a study group met weekly to work through G.D.H. Cole's *Condition of Britain*. So a little self-help by students compensated for the lack of academic departments like Politics, International Relations or Sociology.

Shortly before the war, a young Assistant in Logic, H.W. Davies, organized an informal Friday afternoon seminar on political theory. Some nine or ten of us, from different courses, attended faithfully. The meetings were held in Davies's lodgings, a chummery in the Aulton popularly known as the Bothy, in which lived half a dozen or so of the young bachelor dons, including Eric Turner. Several of them became professors of mathematics after the War; one went on to become Vice-Chancellor of a big English university – Professor Sir Harry Pitt of Reading University. Sadly the war at sea claimed the life of Davies, who had come to Aberdeen fresh from a brilliant career at Oxford and was elected to a Fellowship of All Souls about the time that his generous interest in us was proving so welcome. All in all, the intellectual life of the small University of Aberdeen was far from moribund.

As my final examinations in Classics approached, I remained dissatisfied with the notion of teaching Latin all my life, and in the Christmas vacation of 1937-8 I went to Oxford as a candidate for a Styring scholarship at the Queen's College. That was an interesting but unsuccessful venture, rewarding for the company of one or two lively candidates from London schools. Apparently I did tolerably well in the written papers, but not well enough to persuade the dons who interviewed me that I had a good enough case for adding three years of PPE to my four years of Classics at Aberdeen. It was in those days not unusual for graduates in Classics from Scottish universities to move on to Greats at Oxford or the classical tripos at Cambridge, so perhaps it was the unusual switch of subjects that they were reluctant to accept. Judging from the interview they were divided in their opinions and since I had discovered that one of them was C.J. Hitch, I often wondered subsequently, when he became President of the University of California, which side he had been on. But when I met him many years later in San Francisco, when I was a Vice-Chancellor, I did not bring up the question.

Having put the exhausting experience of the final examinations successfully behind me in March 1938, I burned my boats and returned to Aberdeen in the summer term to begin working on an informal course under Professor Lindley Fraser's supervision, aiming at taking finals in Economics in June 1940. The university was very good to me. A brilliant graduate in English, Dorothy Hacket was just completing her degree in Economics and going off to the Home Civil Service, and so the Knox Scholarship, which she had held, was allocated to me. This was a major reassurance for my uncertainty about changing the path of my career really stemmed from uneasiness of conscience about the financial implications. I was still barely twenty but I knew how hard-up and worried my mother was, and I accepted my obligation to repay her sacrifice by getting into a position to support her without delay. I could only reconcile this commitment with my new undertaking because my own financial prospect immediately improved. The Knox Scholarship gave me £120, and the Moray and Nairn Education Authority again showed remarkable generosity by deciding to continue paying my bursary. At pre-war prices I was now fully independent, and indeed able to make my own contributions to the family needs.

It took me some time to settle down satisfactorily to my new studies. I suspect that young though I was, perhaps even because I had attempted so much by the age of twenty, I was tired and jaded after the physical and mental strain of preparing for finals in Classics. I had got a first but I knew that I was far from being a convincing scholar. While I had performed with some flair in some parts of my course, I had always dragged myself without enthusiasm or sparkle through a good deal of it, and often wondered whether I had been wise to stick with it after 1936 when I first thought of moving into Economics. Although I was a very fortunate young man with a first-class degree, I was left with considerable doubts about myself and was aware that I lacked the sort of self-confidence which I might have acquired if, years before, I had been less stubborn and gone to Robert Gordon's College. Yet an inner voice persisted that I had been right, that a year in the sixth form at Gordon's might have found me wanting and destroyed for ever any hope of acquiring genuine self-confidence. There was nothing for it but to buckle to, accept the position I was in and make the most of it. Gradually I grew more at ease in my new studies, began to concentrate better, and to find a new stimulus.

There was of course, another influence at work on my mind. By the summer of 1938 it was clear to those of my generation at university who had taken a lively interest in the affairs of the world that war was almost inevitable. The uncertainty of the future for us individually began to loom large. I took to reading Hansard in the lounge of the new Students' Union in Broad Street. My concern was not just for the speeches of the vapid Neville Chamberlain, but with the discussions about the introduction of conscription. Like so many others who began by fancying that they were against war and were pacifists and therefore would take the line of conscientious objection, I began to think that that was not the way of courage but of cowardice, and was torn between emotion and rationality. The group of senior economics students was very small, but both of my closest acquaintances – each a year ahead of me in the curriculum – were engaged in the work of International Student Service, the organisation which after the war became World University Service. I too became involved in this. Its committee was drawn from faculty and students. Its chairman was Principal Fyfe. I began to go to meetings of the Scottish committee, usually in Glasgow and Edinburgh, accompanied sometimes by a senior member like Professor Fraser or Professor Peter Noble, the new Professor of Latin.[1] The discussions were about very real problems, about natural disasters like floods or earthquakes that had befallen university people in places like China and India, and increasingly about the plight of Jewish students and scholars in Germany and Austria. In 1939 I took over the office of secretary of the Aberdeen committee and began with this experience to lay the foundation for my whole future career in all its varied aspects. I had to be careful and responsible, cultivate clarity of thought and expression and listen closely to the views of my seniors but speak out when I judged my opinions were worth airing.

In the affairs of the Scottish committee, and Aberdeen's part in them, I found myself in frequent detailed correspondence with a youthful economics lecturer at Glasgow University, Alec Cairncross, already well known as author of a standard introductory textbook but destined to become one of the most distinguished 'public service' academics in the next forty years. From that correspondence I learned a great deal, and it established a friendship which was revived after the War and has continued to provide lively stimuli. In 1938 and 1939 we were absorbed in arrangements to procure, with help from ISS Headquarters in Geneva, the release of students and young academics from concentration camps in Germany and Austria. The Germans could be persuaded to let them go if they saw evidence that they would leave the country within six weeks. Beyond that period, if still in Germany, they were rearrested and never heard of again, so intervention in individual cases had to be very carefully timed and coordinated by ourselves and Geneva. Our decisions depended on getting a Home Office visa of entry for a particular individual, and that could be obtained only when someone of standing accepted the responsibility of guaranteeing that the refugee would not become a charge on public funds in Britain. Since guarantors understandably had to know a good deal about each aspirant for their help, and the timing of Home Office consideration of each case was unpredictable, we had to take anxious risks with the mechanism of alerting Geneva to initiate a particular person's release.

On the September Sunday when Britain went to war, Barbara and I sat on the beach at Nairn and threw pebbles into the calm sea. As each stone sank it seemed to symbolize our falling spirits. We were sure of each other but not of our future. I had decided that by the end of the month I would volunteer for training for a commission in the Army and go before the Joint Recruiting Board at Marischal College for interview. When the day came I got into a rare tangle. I let it be known that I wanted to become a gunner officer because I was prepared to kill Germans I could not see, but would not like to have to stick a bayonet into someone who might remind me of a German I had liked. The Naval officer present was horrified, and the Army man very dubious about me; but the RAF representative thought I had the right attitude. The professors of Mathematics and Psychology, who were on the Board, were highly amused, as no doubt was Principal Fyfe, who knew me well, but as chairman had to secure a decision that did justice to the differing viewpoints. In the process I was twice dismissed from the room and recalled, after discussion, for further questioning, to the puzzlement of other candidates nervously awaiting their turn. In the end, I got my recommendation, passed my medical, was allocated a Royal Artillery number, given the King's shilling and advised to go home to Nairn to await call-up – some of this was disclosed privately to me by Sir William Hamilton Fyfe, but many years later it was recounted again with typical glee by the Professor of Mathematics, Sir Edward Wright, when I had succeeded him in turn as Principal of the University.

Throughout October 1939 I was pretty lost and bewildered. Then a letter came from the War Office advising me to continue my studies since there would be considerable delay in arranging my gunnery training, due to shortage of equipment. I took the next train to Aberdeen and asked the University Secretary for permission to matriculate late and take my finals in March instead of June. He sent me – by tram – to the home of Dr Henry Hamilton who had taken charge of the Economics Department on the departure of Professor Fraser. (Lindley Fraser had joined Sir Walter Monckton at the Ministry of Information, where he was to broadcast regularly to Germany about the evils of inflation, which he predicted would inevitably bring about Hitler's downfall, a line which he claimed was worth the equivalent of two divisions added to the British Expeditionary Force.) Henry Hamilton duly approved my request and I set to to make good lost time. About the time I took the examinations in March, the War Office communicated again, this time hinting politely but pointedly that I could get a commission much more quickly if I agreed to go to an Infantry Training Battalion, while still retaining an option for transfer to the RA. In May I joined the Black Watch whose reputation with the bayonet stood unchallenged. I would have to accept the risk that the German I might have to stick my bayonet into might be a thoroughly decent individual.

Earlier in 1940 my attention had been drawn to the advertisement of the competition for entry to the Indian Civil Service. This was during the period of the 'phoney war' when the War Office apparently had no intention of training those who had volunteered for service in the artillery. Trying to look beyond the uncertainty of the time to a more permanent career, I decided to enter my name. The search for candidates was being channelled through the universities, but there was not a great deal of information about the prospects, though on paper I had some chance, for I already had a good degree and even though I had no blue for sport or athletics, I had a reasonable all-round record and was known to be a fairly decent golfer. So perhaps I had better take out this particular insurance policy for the long term. It was not clear whether successful candidates would be sent at once to India – I believe that in the early summer of 1940 it was the intention of the British Government to defer the start of their careers until after the War, but that this intention was later changed under pressure from the Government of India.

When the order arrived for me to report to the Black Watch training depot at Perth, the British Expeditionary Force was in retreat to Dunkirk, and our forces in Norway had been defeated; survivors reaching Britain were bereft of equipment. My training company was the last to be issued with Lee-Enfield .303 rifles, and within a couple of weeks I was a lance corporal, acting/unpaid, responsible with my section for the defence of a sector of the road entering Perth from the south, and a member of the potential officers' platoon, awaiting a place at an OCTU (Officer Cadet Training Unit). Soon an invitation arrived from the India Office calling me to London for a first interview. I had to apply for leave at a time when no leave was being granted except in extreme compassionate circumstances. The Adjutant referred me to the Commanding Officer, Colonel Vesey Holt DSO, who asked me many questions then explained his dilemma. If he granted me leave he might be reducing by one man the number of new officers produced by his regiment's current intake. I was enormously impressed by the sense of fairness he displayed and learned at once an important lesson: senior colonels with distinguished records were not to be considered, generally, as Colonel Blimps. It was a lesson that was to stand me in good stead over the next six years. He granted me forty-eight hours leave and I made the all-night journey to London by train in a compartment with nine other passengers, jammed up against a nerve-shattered youngster who had just been brought ashore at Rosyth, his dried-out garments still reeking with the stench of oil, having survived his second torpedoing. My mind was a turmoil at my interview, of which I recall little.

A month or so later I was summoned to a second interview. There was little difficulty this time about the arrangements. My initial training at Perth was finished and I was due to report at Bulford on Salisbury Plain on the day after the interview, so I had to be passing through London anyway. Not knowing better, I took a room in the Strand Palace Hotel, where I felt very conspicuous in my Black Watch battledress with a lance-corporal's stripe. What was worse, the bed was so soft after my weeks on a straw palliasse that I suffered agony from a damaged rib and I eventually got to sleep lying on the floor. Again, I was hardly at my best at the interview. But two months later a signal came to Bulford transferring me to the War Reserve Class W at the request of the India Office. This was a great puzzle to everyone, for I was neither being commissioned nor being returned to my unit, and it had not occurred to them before that there was an alternative, namely, that I be provided with a railway warrant and sent home without dishonour. The most difficult person to convince was the Quartermaster, who read the regulations to me several times and demanded the return of every article of uniform. Eventually, he saw the point of my objection to travelling to the north of Scotland in my underwear and socks, and I was allowed to go in proper attire, having undertaken to hand in every item of uniform to the nearest Army unit to my home. The line at London had been damaged by bombing and at Clapham Junction everyone left the train to look for a bus. Lagging behind I heard the guard shout that the train had been given the all-clear to proceed to Waterloo and I jumped on board with a few others. At Waterloo a helpful Railway Transport Officer put me on my way for King's Cross and a train to Scotland, and the scenes on the crowded platforms of the underground, with thousands arriving from the East End to camp out, brought home the true significance of the glow in the sky which I had watched from Beacon Hill on Salisbury Plain the previous Saturday evening, a hundred miles to the west. These were the memories of the Blitz, that I carried with me to India, brief fleeting glimpses of the homeless of London that often intruded into my nostalgic dreams of home.

Note

[1] Later Principal of King's College London and for two years Vice-Chancellor of the University of London.

CHAPTER II

ICS Probationer:
Dehra Dun and the Frontier

When I got to Nairn and began to take stock of what had happened it was near the end of September 1940 and the War had been in progress for over a year. In the odd atmosphere of the first phoney six months, I had taken the King's shilling only to be thrust aside by the Army, and having been 'put out to grass' somehow contrived to turn back the pages of my books and face the ordeal of final examinations for the second time. Then in the early summer I was plunged into the strange and inhospitable world of an army at war, ill-equipped and ill-prepared for its dramatic change of tempo and the sudden threat to safety and survival that followed Germany's successful invasion of the Low Countries. Just as I was beginning to adjust uncomfortably to my new role I was unexpectedly withdrawn from it and left wondering whether I would ever again have any control over my life.

In the first three weeks of October a series of brief letters from Mr C. Iddon of the India Office manoeuvred me into readiness for embarkation. I became engaged, but in the face of his stern advice against taking a wife to India while still a probationer, I had not the courage to think of marriage. It was the middle of October before I knew that my probation would be spent in India, and not as in the past at Oxford or Cambridge. Earlier I had been asked to list my preferences between provinces, stating my reasons. I put North-West Frontier Province first, Punjab second and UP third. My preference for NWFP must have been largely instinctive. I think that a factor in my choice was a feeling of guilt at leaving the Army to become a civilian again, and some notion that service in the Frontier might equate in some way with military service to my country. But I sought advice from several people retired in Nairn and its neighbourhood from service in India. None was from the ICS; they, or their husbands, had all been either in planting, banking or in the Army, but my recollection is that they all confirmed my personal hunch in favour of one of the north-western provinces. I knew that direct posting to NWFP was not the established procedure, but some instinct made me persist, though it was only after I had got to India that I knew that a decision had been made to start an ICS NWFP cadre. I had had no contact with John Dent and Pat Duncan who were a year senior to me and had in fact only recently sailed for India, posted direct to NWFP after their year's probation at Oxford – the first entrants to the new cadre.

One of those who wrote to me about my appointment was a cousin of my father whom I had never met. This was Sir Benjamin Robertson, then living in retirement in Surrey after thirty-six years service in the ICS. He had ended his career as Chief Commissioner of the Central Provinces and was told about me by Jenny Bremner of Forres and her sister Molly Fraser, who were favourite cousins of my father and very dear and loyal friends to my mother after his death. Having said that he doubted whether recruitment into NWFP was possible, he wrote, 'I personally think the U.P. is the best province in India, but other men prefer the Punjab. Avoid, if you can, Bengal and Madras. The C.P. I should put in front of Bombay.' His advice was clearly coloured by the view that it was good game-shooting which made a district or province attractive, largely because this was the way to get to know the common people and speak their language well. He also made it clear that no matter where I came to be sent, that would be the best province in my view in years to come. And he advised me not to waste money buying tropical clothing and kit in Britain.

In fact, I had neither time nor money for large-scale acquisitions. Although he sent a note on kit, Mr Iddon firmly added that no kit advance was payable and then rather unhelpfully informed me that though newly-appointed officers were normally permitted an advance of one month's pay before leaving for India, unfortunately no details of the probationary allowance to be made during training in India had been received from the Government of India. Bureaucratic stinginess was to be characteristic of every arrangement made for their new officers by the Government of India. At this early stage before I left I was relieved from my mounting anxiety by a loan of £50 from John Bremner, and one of £25 from my mother's solicitor and friend, John MacDonald of Nairn. The latter I repaid in March 1945 when I got home on leave – he was adamant in refusing to charge interest. When I offered to repay John Bremner at the same time he brushed me aside with a typical laugh. One of the most generous of men, he made it clear that all the repayment he wanted was to see me home again in his house and hear from me about my adventures. Financial anxiety was to be a source of considerable strain and distraction in my first two years in India, and these comparatively small loans provided a great service to the Government of India and the India Office, which seemed incapable of appreciating that their investment in the careers of their probationers was put at risk by their unimaginative and ungenerous financial regulations and treatment of our 'pay and rations'.

There was less excuse for this kind of administrative deficiency in wartime than there was for the snags that bedevilled instructions about sailing for India. It was not Mr Iddon's fault that when I entrained for Liverpool early in November my passport was still not endorsed with the essential exit permit, in spite of anxious telegrams and phone calls to various authorities. This was only one of several worries that, for the inexperienced, assumed grave proportions in the uncertainties of those days. When eventually I embarked in the *City of Venice*, I found that I was not the only passenger who had been describing himself as a nervous wreck on account of similar administrative frustrations. It may even be that the tensions they had built up, and the relief that embarkation finally engendered, made it easier to cope with the very real hazards of the early stages of the voyage.

This is not the place to describe the experiences of the next two months. There is a detailed account in very long letters to my mother and my fiancée, posted at Cape Town, where we made our first landfall almost five weeks after we had sailed past the Mull of Kintyre. After steaming in convoy for five days, our ship went its own way when the proximity of a German surface raider led to the departure of the escort ships and the dispersal of the convoy. This was a week after the *Jervis Bay* convoy disaster in the same waters. Its destruction had been wrought by the same German pocket battleship which now threatened us. Our captain decided to run before a dramatic and terrifying storm which lasted nearly three days and left us bruised, exhausted and hungry, but far enough south to feel relatively safe, at that period, from U-Boat attacks. As a more comfortable ship's routine developed, the eleven

ICS probationers on board, having quickly become fast friends, organized daily seminars to prepare themselves for their new lives. We pooled information and ideas and guided each other in our reading. One of us, D.D. Satte, a Mahratta Brahmin who had just come down from Oxford, even got us started on elementary Hindustani. This gentle, quick-witted little man was universally liked and respected, and so well balanced in his reaction to our attitudes and prejudices and helpful in the insights he offered, that we must all have gained a great deal in understanding before we got to Bombay. In the letters I have referred to I gave an appraisal of all my new colleagues; on reflection, after over forty years, there is not much that I would want to change. We were a pretty good bunch and because I think without exception we all had a strongly developed sense of service to the Indian people and an open mind about the future of the Raj we were probably adaptable and well suited to the challenge of the next few years. Living in a close-knit group in that special shipboard environment for two months and going on to our tented training camp at Dehra Dun, we developed a bond which may well have been unusual for any intake to the ICS. For several years after we dispersed to our provinces, a circular letter kept us informed of each other's progress. Even after that arrangement broke down, perhaps partly because Roger West in Assam died, contacts persisted, certainly in northern India and as far east as Bengal. In 1943, my two Punjab colleagues, David Elliot and Brian Williams, spent an annual leave with me in Kashmir, and when I finally left India with my family at the beginning of August 1947, Brian Williams visited us in our compartment on the Frontier Mail at Lahore.

Most of us had contacts in Bombay and were 'shown the ropes' and taken on shopping expeditions in the two or three days we spent there before we were due at Dehra Dun. My friendly adviser was a member of the Scottish banking fraternity, prepared to devote time to me solely because of a distant link of friendship between his family and my parents in Grantown-on-Spey. This was my first experience of personal links that have continued to smooth the path of the British – perhaps especially the Scottish – traveller abroad long after the decline of the Raj and disappearance of the Empire. I was greatly impressed and heartened by it and mention it, not because it turned out to be anything unusual, but because it was so important and reassuring at the time.

For the next few months we lived in tents in the ICS Training

Camp which had been established in the grounds of the Imperial Forestry Research Institute at Dehra Dun under the supervision of L.G. Pinnell, a senior civilian from Bengal. The ten of us were joined a little later by two more from Britain, whose naval and military service commitments had delayed their departure. Dinkar Satte was joined by the sixteen Indian probationers who had been appointed in India, and by three young princes, heirs to the *gadi* in their respective states, Teri Garhwal, Jhalawar and Bundi, who were to be inoculated with British ideas of administration in our company. In some respects the groups mingled well and found common ground; in others, inevitably, they remained disparate. I do not think that there was anything worrying or exceptional about this. Within each of the main groups there were smaller associations of special friendships, and in particular activities there were often associations between the main British and Indian groups. While we all played tennis together, none of the Indians joined the three or four Europeans who played golf occasionally on the execrable Forestry Department golf course. By far the best tennis player, and athlete generally, was the Indian from the Punjab who was to come top in our examinations; but because of his arrogance and evident scorn of the underprivileged he was probably the person least liked by both the groups. All the Europeans greatly liked a shy and gentle Madrasi who was not a good rider and broke his arm taking his riding exam; but he was so reticent that none of us was able to become a close friend. Some of the Indians were lively companions and witty conversationalists; others were introspective and dull. The latter seemed more inclined to seek their social life outside the camp in Indian society in Dehra Dun. But the Europeans for their part were more likely to be caught up, often reluctantly, in the social life of the cantonment.

One of our early resentments was the instruction by the supervisor to make formal calls, by dropping visiting cards, on a number of senior hostesses who had expressed surprise at never seeing us. We were advised that they intended to offer us hospitality but could not do so because they did not know our names. No doubt we were regarded as eligible bachelors from Home by some skippers of the depleted 'fishing fleet', but we grumbled bitterly at the outworn conventions that prompted Pinnell's injunction. The only good thing about it was that it gave us an excuse to cycle for miles along pleasant jungle roads around

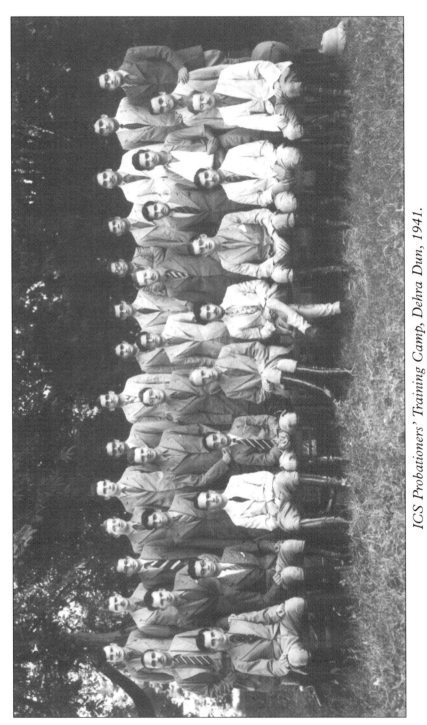

ICS Probationers' Training Camp, Dehra Dun, 1941.

the camp and that very few invitations materialized. Social life in Dehra Dun, particularly in army circles, was stilted. Yet we did get some pleasant opportunities to mix outside our camp circle. Some of these stemmed from visits by particular people to our own mess guest nights. In that way, for example, I became friendly with a young Canadian doctor, Captain Vergin, who was Assistant Civil Surgeon of the Doon, and devoted much of his time to medical work in the surrounding villages until he was posted 'on active service'. He came to my aid in April when, having contracted mumps, I developed alarming complications and had to be rescued from my uncomfortable tent and cared for in the Military Hospital.

With one notable exception, none of the local 'civilians' took much interest in us, though we saw something of our near neighbours in the Forestry Research Institute, and had much kindness from them. The exception was Hifazat Hussain ICS, the Collector or Superintendent of the Doon, the busiest and most senior government officer in the area, and a man of impressive personality and charm. He took real trouble to show an interest in us and to offer hospitality. He and his wife even had some of us to stay over a weekend in their summer residence at Missoorie, the hill station, only fourteen miles away by road, which sat on a ridge at 7,000 feet, high above our camp. Behind Missoorie lay the snowcapped peaks of Nanda Devi and other giant Himalayan mountains. On our first Sunday in camp the marvellously engineered road up to within a mile of the residential area of Missoorie had drawn us like a magnet to view these great mountains.

We were pretty self-contained in our camp. We often had distinguished visitors over the weekend. They delivered formal lectures as well as mixing with us less formally. The first of these was Sir Robert Maxwell, then the Home Member of the Viceroy's Executive Council. He seemed to be a quiet, discreet, rather dessicated man with a rather dull but not unpleasant manner. When he dined in mess we all turned up dutifully clad in stiff shirts, but no doubt to our supervisor's dismay, for he was a stickler for etiquette, Maxwell was less of a stuffed shirt than we had thought, and sat around chatting comfortably in a soft collar – changing into dinner jackets for dinner was of course de rigueur in camp. Even so our next visitor was a striking contrast. He was Sir Eyre Gordon, chairman of the Federal Public Service

Commission and therefore directly responsible for the new India-based training of ICS probationers. A burly and jovial Ulsterman, his frank and sparkling manner cheered us up; and I benefited from a personal tutorial because he wanted to play golf when only Donald Jackson, our Dubliner, and myself were free to accompany him. Donald had heard that he was to be posted to the CP, which was Gordon's own province, so he had much to ask about. What I recall is that he put the same emphasis as Sir Benjamin Robertson on the primary essential of learning the language of the ordinary people of our province. By now I knew that I was indeed to go to NWFP. There was to be no teaching of Pushtu in the camp, but in any case knowledge of Urdu was also a requirement in NWFP, and I resolved at once to make work at Urdu my first priority.

Another distinguished visitor who came early to camp was Sir Maurice Gwyer, Chief Justice of India. A big heavy man with a crippled leg, he made me think of President Roosevelt. He was witty and stimulating, and in a two-hour talk on the Sunday of his visit he had no difficulty in holding our interest. Later, we had Sir Ramaswamy Mudaliar, then one of the best known Indian members of our service. His eloquence was impressive and indeed moving. There were other senior visitors, experts in particular subjects, such as Public Health (General Jolly of the Indian Medical Service), the Cooperative Movement (Ivan Jones, ICS of the Punjab) and Education (Sir John Sargent, the Member of the Viceroy's Council responsible for the subject; my comment on his two talks was that it was refreshing to hear such cynicism about the policies of the Government of India so shrewdly expressed). There was a concentrated but interesting series of lectures on Forestry given in one week by Mr Mobbs, Principal of the Indian Forest College, which was in the grounds of the Research Institute where we lived. As probationers we were lucky to get so clear an insight into such relevant subjects as soil erosion.

Our September examinations, for which Sir Eyre Gordon would be responsible, the results of which would confirm our appointments (the alternative was far from clear), were to cover Language (in my case Urdu; there was a range of language options appropriate to different provinces), Law (Indian Penal Code, Evidence and Procedure), History and Riding. For the latter we cycled early each morning (it was bitterly cold at first) a mile or so to the Indian Military Academy, where the instructor Daffadar and his assistants put us through our paces in the same way as cadet officers in the Indian Army. This was hard going. Very few of us had previous experience of riding but it was rewarding and effective. Whether it was really necessary to put us to the ordeal of jumping quite high fences without stirrups and without reins is arguable but within a month or so most of us were sufficiently competent to take our horses hacking through the village lands and tea estates. One of our regular recreations throughout the early summer was provided by the loan to us of ten army remount horses, which were stabled at our camp.

When we got back to camp from Riding School, we bathed, breakfasted and began language classes at 10.00. Law classes began at 11.45 and took us up to lunch. Later in the day, two or three times a week there would be a lecture from Mr Pinnell, often on some aspect of our service, such as the prohibition on any participation by ICS officers in politics, or from some visiting expert. I have given some idea of the scope of their subjects above. This was a pretty tough daily schedule, and left too little time for study and reflection. By early March we were rising about 6 p.m., and we were pretty tired during our 'free time' in the heat of the afternoon when our tents became uncomfortable, with daily shade temperatures in the eighties. After exercise or games, formal dinner at 8 p.m. did not allow much opportunity for reading or writing before bedtime. We began to complain, without making much impression on 'Jumbo' Pinnell, who had slipped contentedly into the role of headmaster.[1] David Elliot of the Punjab cadre, who was later to become Professor of History at the prestigious Californian Institute of Technology, complained that he had so many summonses to answer and lectures to attend that he could not fit in the calls of nature – we were indeed absorbing the language and culture of the country. Roger West one day cycled some miles to the Doon School, on official instructions, to have breakfast with the Headmaster and learn about the school and its organization. When he arrived back at camp, perspiring, for General Jolly's lecture at 10 a.m. on Public Health he found the door had been closed and locked – to keep the flies out!

Pinnell was a kindly, well-meaning man, full of paper schemes and an efficient bureaucrat. But he had not properly grasped the implications of a course of training and study for men who had already passed through the system of higher education; and perhaps he had not bargained for the bunch of pretty hard-bitten entrants from the UK, with their experience of military service and group solidarity they had established on the long voyage. In language and law, the method of teaching was pretty crudely didactic; the language teachers were variable in quality and more used to army officer's requirements than the probing minds of young graduates. Law was taught by a retired policeman who had been Prosecuting Inspector in a district of Bengal in which Pinnell had been Collector. He was an experienced practical man, but had no philosophical understanding of his subject. While there was real advantage in being taught through his approach, there was also something missing.

On balance we probably gained a good deal from being trained in India rather than at Oxbridge, but that was because we were able to make more progress with the language, there being no language laboratory teaching in the universities of Britain at that time, and because as a close-knit group of about thirty we really did learn a great deal from each other. It was not because we saw anything of the real work in the villages of a district officer, though there were things to be learned from our specialist lecturers which we could interpret with our own eyes as we rode across country or walked through the bazaars. We made some very helpful visits to a magistrate's court, but personally I learned more from experience of a case in which I was involved as witness, and victim of a theft.[2]

As for Indian History – we were left to our own devices, with little leisure time in which to pick our unguided way through the textbooks. Later, we had some lectures from learned Indian professors which I found unhelpful. In the end, in this subject there seemed too big a demand on our time and resources; almost certainly, Oxbridge would have done better by us, but one has to ask whether the formal study of History on the syllabus prescribed really mattered very much? It would have been more relevant to us to hear more about the attempts at constitutional reform and the reactions of the Indian political parties. But who would have taught such matters? Pinnell occasionally talked discreetly about his service during the campaign of terrorism in Bengal when he was Secretary to the Governor, Sir John Anderson. But that was clearly 'outside the syllabus'.

By the beginning of April we were faced with a new problem. It was getting too hot to continue to live and study in our tented camp and during the later monsoon rains it would be uninhabitable. It had been arranged that when the Doon School closed for its long vacation, we would occupy it, and that was eminently satisfactory. The Doon School was organized like an English public school, and had fine buildings and facilities. We would each have a spacious study/bedroom. Our problem was how to spend the period of about six weeks between the break-up of the camp and the move into the school. Mr Pinnell wrote to our provinces, but most of the probationers in the end had to fend for themselves at least for most of the time. The difficulty was that this was inevitably expensive, and we were all financially hard-pressed. Most of the Indians could go home to their families, but one or two groups of the Europeans decided to rent bungalows and gain experience of running a 'chummery'.

I was the lucky one. My province responded to Pinnell's communication by extending its welcome to me, and generously undertook to meet all my expenses. Since our experience so far had been of government stinginess, this spontaneous gesture endeared the Frontier to me and sealed my pleasure at having made it my first preference. In the outcome, the hospitality I received and the careful thought and planning that were put into the arrangements for my visit transformed my whole outlook on my future in India. From then I was in the Scots term 'thirled' to the Frontier, to the officers who served in it and to its Pathan people.

Before I describe this visit, however, I should explain why financial anxiety had become so obsessive. We all thought that the Government had treated us meanly in bringing us out without pay or kit allowance. We had all had an expensive month in Britain before embarkation with no remuneration. We had not even been advised of the terms of our employment before we arrived in Bombay. Our allowance was fixed at Rs405 *per mensem*, payable in arrears. We were given an advance of about a month's pay in Bombay, and repayments were deducted from that barely adequate allowance. It took about six weeks for the Government of India to settle our claim for travelling expenses incurred between Bombay and Dehra Dun. In camp, no library was provided and we had to organize a club subscription to supplement the basic furnishings of our mess. We paid for our accommodation and food, so far as we could judge at full economic rates. My month's mess bill came to Rs120 – none of us drank anything but soft drinks – to which was added Rs40 for my personal bearer and share of other servants such as the dhobi and about Rs40 for other essentials including hire of bicycle. That left quite a generous Rs130 after other deductions from pay, but this had to meet all personal expenditure, e.g. on riding gear or sports equipment or visits to the cinema. Outlay on clothing, including household items like blankets and tablecloths, was considerable in our first months, because we had to prepare for the hot weather. All this was happening at a time when wartime inflation was driving up prices and wages – but the Government had not begun to adjust allowances, or take account of our particular predicament. Yet early in April we were for the first time advised that we had to pay arrears of fees for tuition and for our use of the IMA Riding School! Had I not had the cushion of the personal loans provided before I left Scotland, I would have been an embarrassing bankrupt from the Government's point of view. But I was determined to fulfil my obligations, especially to my mother, and made an arrangement through the bank to remit a fixed allowance monthly to her from April onwards.

These complaints may seem trivial and unimportant, but that is not how they appeared to me and others at the time, and in retrospect I think it is justifiable to record them as a significant element in a formative period in our service. It may even have confirmed me in my sympathies for the underprivileged, and in relation to the attitudes of Government it taught me the need to replace rigidity and impersonal regulation with flexibility and adaptability in response to changing human and social circumstances and needs.

As soon as I had recovered from my illness and been given the all clear by Captain Vergin, I set off on my Frontier adventure. I was eager to start, and had been apprehensive that my illness and subsequent weakness would cause the plan to break down. The change came at the right time. By the fourth month much of the excitement of new experiences had begun to pall and I was getting stale. It should be remembered that circumstances were abnormal for us all. No previous intake of recruits to the service had spent the first months in India in the confines of a closed society of trainees being rather inexpertly prepared for examinations whose significance was allowed to loom too large – partly under the influence of the majority of the Indian probationers who had been educated in Indian universities and regarded factual information and examination places as paramount in education. Very few, if any, of the European probationers could long forget the circumstances of the War and the plight of their families. We listened anxiously and regularly to the news on All-India Radio. Our spirits rose or sank, according to the turns of fortune in the Middle East which we saw as securing the lifeline between us and our homes. Several like me had got engaged before leaving home and were exercised by the question of how and when to bring our fiancées out to India, assuming that after a long parting they wanted to come, which in the event some did not. One of us, David Alexander of UP, had actually been married a few days before sailing, hoping that her status as his wife might ease the way for his bride to get an early passage. Another, David Elliot, was engaged to an American girl and full of hope that she would be able to cross the Pacific to join him before the end of the year. All our hopes were to be thwarted by various twists of fate; none of us was ever particularly confident, but it was just as well that we could not guess, in the early summer of 1941, that almost four more years would pass before any of us would be reunited with those we loved. Thanks again to the understanding sympathy of the NWFP's senior officers, I was to be the first, by some time, to be so privileged in February 1945.

I still remember the excitement of starting from Dehra Dun on my first journey to the Frontier. On the overnight train to Lahore I shared a compartment with a Gurkha captain who was on his way to Quetta. A man of mature years who in peacetime had been a box-wallah – a businessman in jute – he was wise in the ways of India and kindly in his attitude to a novice. At Lahore, where he left me, I breakfasted well and for four rupees bought myself a place in an air-conditioned compartment on the Frontier Mail. I was thankful for this, for up to Rawalpindi, whenever the door was opened, a blast of hot air from the furnace of the Punjab rushed in on us, and the external door handles scorched our hands. All day the ridge of mountains to the east crept slowly nearer through the dust and haze of heat, but by evening they stood sharp and blue and so clear and close that one could speculate on the easiest routes to the peaks. My companions left me at Pindi, and on through Taxila westwards and northwards as the evening cooled my excitement grew. The track twisted and the train jolted slowly through the hills till suddenly in the evening light we emerged into the great gorge of the Indus at Attock and crept over the dramatic rail and road bridge into a new land. Across the bridge the train turned slowly through the cuttings and I glimpsed the great water barrier of the Indus before it narrowed to enter the gorge. Upstream its expanse was greatly widened by the debouching waters of the Kabul River sweeping down past Nowshera with its bridge of boats. Across the Indus, along the bank of the Kabul River, we rattled towards Peshawar and the Khyber Pass – what British youngster could fail to be stirred by the experience? I began feverishly to speculate on the encounters that lay ahead, and, mindful of the indoctrination of Pinnell's regime, showered in the air-conditioned luxury of my compartment's separate washroom and put on a suit and tie. Peshawar came more quickly than I expected and I jumped down hastily to the platform, vaguely aware in the gloom that it was strangely deserted round my carriage. A friendly railway official called out to me and it took me an age to understand that he was telling me to climb back on board. I had got off at Peshawar City Station – the Cantonment terminus was another mile or so further on. I realized that I had indeed got a lot to learn, and had better take it all slowly and carefully. Peshawar City Station was no safe place for a solitary unescorted European ignorant of Pushtu to be stranded after dark.

Minutes later I was being greeted by a cheerful figure at the Cantonment station. This was the ebullient and irrepressible Roger Bacon, Political Agent for the Khyber tribes, who was to be my first host. The Chief Secretary, Ambrose Dundas, who had made all the arrangements, had departed a day or two earlier for Nathia Gali, the hill station to which 'Government' in the Frontier traditionally repaired for the hot weather. Within half an hour Roger had me sitting on the lawn at the Peshawar Club, drinking 'chota pegs' with a couple of senior army officers. I was astonished first at their informality of dress and bantering manner, and secondly at my own indulgence in the drink. It was the first time I had drunk whisky and soda in India. It did me a power of good and the talk was fascinating. It was about the War and about the state of the Frontier and it seemed to me for the first time that I was being allowed to share privileged information. These men were in fact privy to news not published in the press; through their contacts with their friends and regiments overseas they could interpret and comment on the military and political events of the Middle East. For the first time I understood properly how what happened in Syria, Iraq and Persia affected India, and learned that anti-tank defences were being prepared in the Khyber, the Kurram and the Tochi. These passes and valleys were the historic routes taken by invaders of India. Now they were to be defended against Germany.

Next day Roger took me up the Khyber Pass to Landi Kotal and Torkham, on the Afghan border, and I watched him in conversation with Afridi *maliks* and listened to his exchanges with the officers of the Landi Kotal brigade in their mess. This was the new world of which I was to be a part, and nobody more appropriate than Roger Bacon could have been its first interpreter for me. A frank and lively soldier, his easy and jovial manner gave him a good rapport with his Afridis and I was to come to know him as a shrewd and capable political officer whose weakness might be a tendency to flippancy or even to risk-taking and just a shade too much sympathy and fellow-feeling for his tribesmen even when things got rough.

Two days later, I was sent off from the PA (Political Agent) Khyber's house in an open Chevrolet tourer on my first journey through the Dara, the pass through the tribal salient through which the road winds on its way to Kohat. The spectacular descent through the Pass to the plain with its glimpses of the city and cantonment remains vivid in my memory from that first of many experiences of the route; but I have little recollection of the first impression made by the Adam Khel gun 'factories' in the roadside villages which have become even more famous in recent years. In 1941 their speciality was a replica of the Lee Enfield rifle; nowadays their range is far wider and more sophisticated, but their role as a chief source of arms to a turbulent and unruly race living on either side of the Durand Line remains unchanged.

At Kohat I was picked up by A.P. Low, then Assistant Commissioner Hangu, who was to be my next host. With him was John Dent, who belonged to the the 1939 entry to the ICS and had come out to India a month or two before me, having done preliminary training at Cambridge, and with Pat Duncan had been posted direct to the Frontier. John was then on a training assignment with Low, just as Pat was, in the post in which I was to succeed him in Abbottabad, with Gerald Curtis, DC (Deputy Commissioner) Hazara. From Kohat we did not proceed straight to Hangu, but drove high into the mountains of the Orakzai country behind the Samana range. Disappointingly, it rained steadily for hours, so that I was deprived of some spectacular views and I recall how I shivered in what seemed a raw chill air after the heat of Peshawar, as we huddled over a picnic 'lunch' in the shelter of a rocky overhang. Dressed in the grey 'Muzri' shirts and shorts which were to become my own official uniform, John and Alastair looked the part of the 'political' on tour and a little further on, when the rain stopped and the sun shone on a favoured mountain valley and we sat in a village *hujra* in the shade of some apricot trees, the nature of the role they played began to get clearer for me. While Alastair talked with the *maliks* and other men of the village John explained quietly to me what he understood of the topics of discussion. It was my first experience of traditional Pathan hospitality, restricted by Low's courteous but firm request to tea, with boiled eggs, fruit and nuts, which were the produce of the village itself. My first impression, never subsequently shaken, was of the sincerity with which the hospitality was extended and of the natural dignity with which our hosts attended to our needs, as they conceived them. As the new recruit, special attention somehow seemed to be given to me, but without embarrassment. There was a natural, relaxed warmth about the proceedings which made me feel at home. In the next five years, *chae* in the *hujra*, and Pathan *tikala* in varying environments were to be frequent, though never commonplace, experiences. They remained a constant renewal of a bond of friendship, even when I was acutely aware of the reasons for the protecting bodyguard posted by my hosts around the guest house.

The next two days in Hangu continued the learning process. For the first time in the Lows' family circle I saw what life might be like in a lonely Frontier outstation. It was quiet and relaxed, totally free from tension; congenial company was at hand, if few in number, at the Hangu Police Training College. The Sunday outing was a family excursion by car along the road toward Thall at the foot of the Kurram Valley, to visit a village which had been suffering from drought. We walked the rock-strewn path along which the women carried on their heads water from the nearest well two miles away – a few muddy pools in a dried-up river bed. The village normally relied on the contents of its 'tank'. The people had dug deep in search of a spring – they showed us how the end of their massive labours had come when they struck solid rock. This village impressed me; it was the first Pathan village in a settled area that I had seen at close quarters, typical with its strong protecting wall encircling all the houses, each with heavy double doors of solid timber, and most provided with a tall watchtower equipped with loopholes to give all-round vision and field of fire, and parapets round the roof platform. The walls of the house were constructed skilfully of small round stones like a Scottish dry-stone dyke, but every third or fourth row of stones was strengthened by a layer of timber. Apart from its water problem the village looked in good shape, yet its crop had failed because of drought. There was not a young man to be seen. All of them, some 120 in number, were in military service and the village's relative prosperity derived from their monthly remittances.

The Lows were great conversationalists, though less irrepressibly lively than Roger Bacon, and Alastair's rule was to read quietly for an hour after dinner – equally he had a rule that office work stopped for the day before dinner. Monnie Low was the first Frontier wife to proffer me excellent advice on future domestic plans, the first of many, for I was to find wise friendship in plenty of Frontier family circles. There was a marvellously reassuring quality in the Frontier sodality. Alastair's disposition was distinctly intellectual and his interests wide-ranging, if his manner occasionally was a little pedantic, and he soon began to unveil some of the mysteries of the Pathan way of life.

More insight came when I moved back to Kohat to stay for some days with Captain Robin Hodson, the Assistant Commissioner. Robin was a fairly recent recruit from the Army to the Political Service – a transfer arranged after a disabling leg injury – which was the result of brake failure on his truck on a road in North Waziristan. Not much older than myself, he was a deservedly popular young political, struggling a little to establish himself in the routine of administration and judicial work, and after living with the pundits for a week it was encouraging to be with a near contemporary who was wholly unpretentious, frank, congenial and engagingly honest about his own ignorance.

The genius with which Ambrose Dundas, the Chief Secretary, arranged my programme was becoming clearer day by day. The next move was back to Peshawar, to stay with Sir James Almond, the Judicial Commissioner, whose wife and family had been torpedoed on a voyage home, but survived after many days in a lifeboat. James was a fine musician, a keyboard player and a man of great sensitivity; beloved by everyone, not for his powers at games, for which he had no natural gifts, though plenty of enthusiasm, but for the way he combined warmth and dignity, wisdom and common sense. Greatly awed, I sat by his side as he settled civil cases, as the final court of appeal in the province, patiently explaining the main issues to me, dealing politely but firmly with the advocates and their witnesses. Totally devoid of pomposity but well able to laugh at himself and inclined even to deprecate his own merit, he retained great natural dignity and authority. Everything he did officially was marked by a sense of style and a decisiveness illuminated by intellect. One was aware of style too, in the arrangement of his household, in spite of the absence of Lady Almond. Even the servants had the mark of quality. Yet it was a comfortable and relaxing place in which to be. High standards were expected and observed, the conversation sparkled on a high plane, there were musical scores to read, if one wished, as well as books – but over everything presided this warm, genial chubby little man, full of reassuring benevolence. I was lucky too that he had two other guests who each fitted in splendidly, both to the Almond household and to the picture of the Frontier, which my programme was building up for me. One was Colonel Wilson, the Inspector General Frontier Corps – the various regiments of tribal militia like the Khyber Rifles, the Kurram Militia, and the Tochi Scouts. The other was Gerald Curtis, DC Hazara, who was on temporary special duty in Peshawar preparing plans for Civil Defence and allied matters for the provincial government.

One day James Almond sent me to sit with his senior Indian colleague who was reviewing a murder case. The case was a typical Frontier story, with revenge (*badal*) as the motive. Two years earlier A had been accused of murdering B, but acquitted. Now three of B's brothers were on trial for the murder of A, indicted by A's sister, an eyewitness. Typically, she weakened the value of her own case by involving D and E as well as the principal accused, C. There was no evidence to corroborate the allegation that they were all present at the incident. The case against C was strong. The police evidence was that he had blood on his clothes and wounds on his body and his counsel's plea was one of self-defence, but he himself gave evidence denying that he had been present, though he could offer no alibi. All the witnesses kept contradicting themselves and some told stories quite different from the evidence they had given in the lower court or to the police, but when I privately asked the judge why none of them was prosecuted for perjury he informed me quietly that this was never done because of the workload such a policy would impose on the judicial system!

In his court, and in my earlier sessions in Robin Hodson's court at Kohat, I was beginning to catch the special flavour of the Frontier – the family feud, the force of customary law, the frequency of such charges as the harbouring of outlaws, the theft of rifles, abduction of women and so on.

But perhaps the special importance of my day in the High Court at Peshawar was that it was the first time I had been brought into contact with an Indian officer in a senior role, except for the VIP visitors performing at the lecturer's rostrum at our training course and the informal conversations with Hifazat Hussain, Collector of the Doon, on his occasional visits to our camp. There was a bit of a danger that I would be dazzled by the virtuosity of the British officers I had been consorting with, and led to disregard the capacity of Indian officers in similar roles. A few days later I had another startling experience to help redress the balance.

I had gone out to Charsadda to stay with the sub-divisional officer, Major George Cole, whom everyone referred to as 'Batty' Cole. He was, I believe, an excellent revenue officer who was inclined to get excited and lose his judgement in some 'political' situations. Like everyone else he was very kind and helpful to me, and on the Sunday evening he took me to Utmanzai village for supper with Khan Abdul Ghaffar Khan. I never knew whether that was his own idea or an arrangement contrived by the Governor himself. A.G.K. was of course the British Government's chief Pathan thorn in the flesh. Leader of the Red Shirt movement – the Khudai Khidmatgars – and a close associate of Gandhi, his influence both on the All-India Congress Party and on the fortunes and policies of the Congress Party in the Frontier was very considerable. His brother, Dr Khan Sahib, had been Chief Minister of the Frontier Ministry which had recently resigned, in keeping with the policy of the Central Congress Party at the involvement of India in the war. Abdul Ghaffar was at that time one of only a handful of Indian politicians whose name was familiar to ordinary citizens of the United Kingdom. To be the guest of this colourful personality, on his own ground, in his own Pathan village, the heartland of the notorious Red Shirts, was a considerable surprise for an aspiring political officer, and one to which it was hard to know how to adjust in a fitting manner.

I remember the excitement and apprehension of the drive by tonga – a small, wheeled pony trap, the common mode of conveyance on Frontier roads in the settled districts – out to

Utmanzai from Charsadda through the lush fields irrigated by the great Swat River canal system. The guest's problems of course, as always, were solved for him by the code of Pakhtun hospitality. The old rascal treated us not as political opponents or despised imperialists, but as honoured guests who deserved to share not only his table but his philosophical reflections. We sat in his garden in the starlit silence of the countryside, distracted from his musings only by the evening chirpings of the frogs and crickets and the fascinating fly-past of a myriad fireflies. He made no concessions, then or ever, to the English language, but spoke in eloquent Pushtu which George Cole was well able to follow and indeed from time to time to interrupt with comment or question. My ignorance of the tongue was quietly and courteously catered for by one of his sons, Abdul Ghani, who sat close to me and explained the gist of the discourse. A younger son, Abdul Wali, later to become important in the political life of Pakistan, seemed less well-versed in English and sat for the most part silently observing the scene and ensuring that I did justice to the meal.[3]

I was never again to have such an opportunity to sit at the feet of A.G.K. Nearly two years later he was arrested in Mardan and brought to Abbottabad jail in an attempt to defuse the agitation in the Frontier in support of the Congress 'Quit India' campaign. Hearing that he intended to start a protest fast, I went to see him to enquire for his health and well-being. He received me politely but firmly declined conversation, though with a kindly glint in his piercing eyes.

From Charsadda I went on to further romantic places, following, as I saw it, in the footsteps of Winston Churchill to Malakand and the Swat Valley. I was the guest of Colonel Leslie Mallam, the Political Agent, in his dramatically-sited house at the head of the Malakand Pass overlooking the piquets and parade ground which were the scene of fierce fighting in the tribal attacks in 1897, which brought the young subaltern Churchill hotfoot to north India from his cavalry regiment in Poona to observe the campaign and prepare the despatches for the *Morning Post*. These formed the kernel of his first book, a masterpiece of critical observation, the account of the Malakand Field Force. From the gentle Mallam I learned something of the arrangements for the Frontier Government's relationships with the independent little 'states' of Chitral, Dir and Swat, and began to sense the differences between the role of political agent at the northern limits of the

Views of the Malakand Pass.

province, close to the territory on which the Great Game of the nineteenth century was played with Russia, and that of his colleague at the southern boundary, where he had to deal with the much more actively unruly Mahsuds and Wazirs and the more direct consequences of their activities on India's relationship with Afghanistan.

One unforgettable day was spent in a visit to Mingora and Saidu in Swat State, where we were guests of the Wali of Swat himself. This fierce, wiry old warrior was a most remarkable personality. He had achieved kingship by skilful intrigue, ruthless determination and courageous leadership, and he had retained it in a most unlikely environment by combining benevolence with unyielding decisiveness. Even in a few hours one saw everywhere the stamp of his policies – the good roads, the orderly agriculture, the schools and dispensaries, the fortified police posts. He seemed an old man – he was probably over sixty – but he still ran up a mountain every morning to keep fit. I saw him for only a very short time but he made a terrific impression even through an interpreter. I was left mostly in the company of his fine son, Jahanzeb, who succeeded him, and his secretary or wazir, Ataullah, a quiet, efficient courtier who would probably have made a good job running the Presidential office of the White House. They were an impressive team.

Back from Malakand, I recrossed the Indus and made my way through Hazara for the first time to Nathiagali, the summer quarters of the Provincial Government. Although by now I was becoming used to the achievements of British engineers in building roads over mountains, the bus journey from Abbottabad (about 4,000 feet) to Nathiagali (over 8,000 feet) took my breath away and left me limp with perspiration, my fists clenched in fear, mouth closed firmly to restrain any betraying cries of weakness.[4] Quite enough of these in any case were issuing from the anonymity of the voluminous *burqas* huddled close together in the row of seats behind the driver and myself. At least I had room to breathe. These poor Muslim ladies had to find consolation in the close proximity of their fellow women.

What saved me from disgrace as the journey progressed was a steadily growing admiration for the driver of Jalal-Ud-Din's mail bus, and for the cooperative teamwork of his mate or apprentice, who rode at the back step and jumped down promptly on the shout *'Pattar Rakh Bhai!'* to place a large stone behind the off-side rear wheel – from which point the driver, delicately slipping his clutch and keeping the engine revolutions up, would ease his crowded vehicle over some bumps of rock protruding through the loose gravel of the surface, round a tight hairpin bend, narrowly avoiding a thrusting outcrop emerging from the cliff to our left and threatening to decapitate nearside passengers, while those on the right stared in petrified bewilderment at the sheer drop over the precipice literally inches away from the wheels. In those days the unmetalled road was too narrow for vehicles to pass in opposite directions and gates were operated to control movement one way at a time, so that the road was open 'up' for an hour and then 'down' for a similar period. I was to make this hair-raising journey dozens of times in the next two years and I always preferred to go in the same bus with the same driver, a cheerful and witty rascal who nonetheless always stopped, got out and said his prayers near Dhamtaur village some miles from Abbottabad, before the real climb started.

After the heat and dust of my travels in Peshawar and Kohat, Malakand and Swat, a fortnight in Nathiagali in the last part of May was restful and refreshing. Before the dust haze from the plains gathered overhead at the end of the month in premonition of the monsoon clouds which produced a debilitating and disorienting effect on the residents of these mountain ridges, the air was clear, crisp and cool, and smelt sweetly of pine trees and warm sunshine, a consoling reminder of summer days in the woods of Strathspey. I sat in the garden, alternating between sunshine and shade, dozily losing myself in books from other people's libraries, chatting over coffee or tea with my hostesses and their friends, taking short strolls through the forests to seek new views on either side of the saddle between the peaks of Miranjani and Mokhspuri (each about 10,000 feet), or gazing north from the little wooden church to the great snow crest of Nanga Parbat (26,000 feet) or south from Kalabagh across the foothills of Hazara to the Indus and the plains of the Punjab. In the evenings there would be a longer walk with my host; sometimes too in the afternoons a family picnic excursion. As the night drew in, we gathered at ease round a blazing log fire, the picture of family life in the hills complete. It was early to bed to keep warm beneath ample woollen blankets, and early to sleep, for the electricity supply was generated in a little local station and was shut off at eleven o'clock.

I stayed successively with the Dundases, the Campbells and the Cunninghams. Ambrose Dundas was Chief Secretary and had much to do with the planning of the course of my career. A quiet, thoughtful man of clear intellect and firm principles, his friendship was direct and reassuring, and from the beginning of my Frontier connection provided me with a firm anchor. He conversed easily, sharing his great knowledge of every aspect of Frontier conditions, always relaxed and equable, but never leaving one in doubt about his views. His wife Mary was much more volatile and indeed could be outspoken to a fault. She was a very strong personality, characteristically Yorkshire in her bluntness with its matching kindness. I remember feeling on this first acquaintance with them that, senior though he already was, a truly great career must lie ahead. Indeed this proved to be the case: after Partition and the recall of Sir George Cunningham in August 1947 to the Governorship, when the latter finally retired in 1948 because of ill-health, it was Dundas whom the Pakistan Government chose to succeed him. He was thus the last British Governor of NWFP, and had a distinguished career in public service in Britain still to come, as Governor of the Isle of Man and Chairman of the New Town Corporation of Bracknell. But this was not what I had envisaged in 1941, when I imagined that he would become a great NWFP Governor in the tradition of Roos-Keppel and Cunningham, and could not foresee how suddenly the nature of the job was to change in 1947.

Colonel Walter Campbell was then Adviser to HE the Governor. This post derived from the curious state of the province, whose political evolution as a Governor's province had been slow, and was currently set back by the resignation of the Congress ministry in 1940. The office of Adviser was designed to furnish the Governor with the administrative help and advice which ministers in office would normally provide. Walter Campbell was a 'military political' with a great deal of experience in Indian states as well as the Frontier. A charming and cheerful Irishman, he struck me as steady and efficient rather than brilliantly assertive. He was very kind to me and there was a particularly happy family atmosphere in the household, enlivened by the presence of the two oldest daughters, then in their latish teens.

Moving from this atmosphere to the sober dignity of Government House must have filled me with apprehension. The Cunninghams had married late, and had no children. Their office carried great authority and their very beautiful residence reflected this. It was set a little apart from the other houses in Nathiagali, lower down on a saddle connecting the main ridge with the range running northwards by Miranjani (over 10,000 feet) to Thandiani, parallel to the River Jhelum, just to the east as it flowed from its junction with the Kunar River near Muzaffarabad, through Kashmir, on its way out into the Punjab. Here at this very beautiful spot, with its house wholly appropriate to the office of Governor, the Cunninghams had lovingly created a superb, quite simple garden, skilfully using the natural contours to mould the lawn and the rose gardens and beds of flowers, fruit and vegetables, subtly adding to the indigenous Himalayan trees and plants well chosen British shrubs and flowers − even, as I recall, a white Scottish broom bush which may have been unique in India. They both loved the garden and would work away quietly in it in company with the *malis* for hours on end. They made a most dignified couple, but so devoid of pomp and conceit that everyone loved them, and behind the dignity there was always a glint of mischief in the eyes, a quiet but subtle joke from Sir George, a warm deep-throated Irish chuckle from Lady Cunningham − 'Robin' to her many close friends − and invariably a little banter, a gentle teasing that never hurt. I was to stay with them often at Nathia and in Peshawar where they continued to make the much larger Government House and garden an equally welcoming and attractive focus of provincial family life, and also at St Andrews in Scotland right through their years of retirement. But I can never forget the encouragement I derived from being made to feel at home on that first visit.

Sir George was regarded by many as prone to fits of silence and a reluctant conversationalist. To my great relief I found no cause for anxiety. If he had nothing particular to say, he stayed quiet; there was no need to think that he was bored or to try to start a conversation to impress him. When he talked, he always had something interesting to say and I found that with notable economy of words he had a facility for conveying a great deal of information and elucidating complex strands of evidence. One was always learning from him, and even on that first visit I felt that he had the gift of making me feel that he was prepared to take me into his confidence and talk unreservedly about the affairs of the Frontier and indeed about the War. At that time, shortly before Hitler's invasion of Russia and six months before Pearl Harbour,

our thoughts were full of what was happening in the Middle East, and how developments in Syria, Iraq and Persia might affect the Frontier. Cunningham was a close student of world politics, a great reader of political biography and military history, and was personally acquainted with many of the service leaders whose names were constantly in the news. So for the first time in my life I began to feel that I was being allowed in on the personal grapevine that is the source of so much interesting and intriguing private gossip for a privileged circle. It probably went to my head, but it certainly gave me a lasting taste for 'getting in on the act'.

The Cunninghams and the Campbells and the Dundases, each in their different ways, made a profound impression on me. Being with them, relaxed and at leisure, after the intense experience of the previous two weeks of travel and adventure, gave me time to reflect and to digest what I had seen and heard. Each of them contributed a personal slant to the interpretation of the whole. The previous months of training began to come into perspective. The Dehra Dun course and its limitations, which had been becoming an obsession with me, no longer seemed to be the exclusive centre of my life in India. I was beginning to see it as a not wholly relevant link into a future dominated by the fascinations of the Frontier, for which it had done little to prepare me. Partly in response to their questions, but largely no doubt in the relief of unburdening myself to men who showed an understanding interest, I talked a good deal about the course and my future training, particularly to Dundas and Cunningham, and looking back to old letters after many years, in the knowledge of what happened to me, I am sure that these conversations left their mark on my subsequent career. My fortnight's holiday in Nathiagali was a vital part in my training and education – and one that I was privileged to enjoy when my fellow probationers were still having to work towards the future within the confines of Pinnel's syllabus. I still recall the twinkle in Sir George's eye when he said goodbye: 'Let us know when your school finishes so that we can get ready for you.'

My hosts were not of course the only people I met in that fortnight. A fair number of the senior Secretariat officers were in the hill station, and even more of their wives and families. There were also a few people on leave from distant parts of the province and elsewhere, and some 'weekend' visitors escaping temporarily from the heat. Amongst these was Pat Duncan, an Oxford graduate from Ireland who had joined HE's new Frontier ICS Commission with John Dent. He was Assistant Commissioner in Abbottabad under training, and as it transpired I was to succeed him there at the end of September. A charming, effervescent, lively man, so full of enthusiasm that one wondered how stable he would be. I saw less of him on his visit than I would have wished because, having been told that a panther was causing some havoc in a village some miles away in the forest below us, he rushed off there to sleep in a tree for two nights in the hope of getting a shot at it – a hope unrealized unfortunately. Soon after they had arrived in the Frontier, Pat and John had spent some time in Mardan with Colonel Edward Noel, one of the Frontier's 'original' characters and an adventurous veteran whose story began with his capture by the Khurds in Persia in the First World War, when for weeks he was handcuffed to guards and kept sane by picking lice from their hair and counting his trophies. The great thing about Noel was that he was wildly enthusiastic about innovation, technical development and agricultural improvement – and these were almost certainly things that many Frontier officers, and probably Government itself, had too long tended to neglect, through enforced preoccupation with 'political affairs', like tribal disputes, raids and similar matters. Certainly he made a great impression on Pat – and probably on John Dent also – and all the time I knew him, Pat was more concerned with exploring for minerals or working out new ways of exploiting a natural resource than with the routine of administration. He once said to me with great force and justifiable conviction, 'It is a total disgrace that the Director of Agriculture for this whole province addresses me, a junior Assistant Commissioner, as "Sir"!'

Amongst the other new friends whom I first encountered in that Nathiagali holiday were Charles and Morag Duke – he was then Secretary to the Governor – and Ian and Drusilla Scott. Ian was to have a rather unusual career over the next few years, first attached to the Intelligence Bureau which did very secret work for the Government of India in Peshawar, and then on secondment as Principal of Islamia College, before it became the University of Peshawar. Sir George understood well its importance as a training ground for young Pathans and a potential nursery of future political leaders, and his choice of Ian, at a moment of crisis in the policy of management of the college, to fill a vacancy in the Principalship was imaginative and far-seeing. He was taken from it to be Assistant Private Secretary to Lord Wavell, and remained in the Viceroy's office until Partition. Later, like Charles Duke, he had a notable career in the Diplomatic Service.

It was particularly good for me to have this chance of getting to know these officers of the ICS who were still relatively young in outlook and experience, though a good few years senior to me. I was beginning to be aware of the intellectual satisfaction that could be derived from the career that I was to enjoy. All in all, I returned to Dehra Dun greatly stimulated by my experiences, reassured by a new awareness of my prospects, and very happy in the knowledge that I already had found valuable friendships in the Frontier.

Notes

[1] My main complaint about this kindly man was that he seemed to be too lethargic to make any impression on Central Government where rules made no allowance for the special circumstances of probationers in 1940–1. Within the Camp, having drawn up the programme and regulations on the basis of prior assumptions about his objectives and our needs, the Supervisor was too inflexible and slow to make adjustments with experience.

[2] On the journey from Bombay to Delhi a thief had got into our compartment and stolen my small attaché case. He was caught, and prosecuted, and my property returned to me somewhat damaged.

[3] His silence may have been due to his role as the junior son, rather than to lack of confidence in the English language.

[4] In my first letter home after this journey, I described the road as 'an impertinence against nature'.

CHAPTER III

Last Stage from School to Covenant

Back in Dehra Dun, where I joined David Elliot (the 'Judge'), David Alexander ('Ragtime'), David Power ('Dynamite'; a recent variant had almost displaced that first nickname, viz. Dynajee) and Donald Jackson in the bungalow in Pritam Road, Dalanwala, which we had rented as a 'chummery' for the six weeks' vacation, I absorbed the news that had filtered in from various sources and took stock of my situation. My letters home show a brave enough attempt to get things into perspective; if my analysis was marked by the over-confidence of immaturity, that may be excused, for I must have seen it as a duty to convey a feeling of assuredness to those at home who were beset by uncertainty and handicapped by ignorance of Indian conditions. Like so many young men at that time, I could not help being absorbed in comparing my lot with what 'might have been'. There had been news of the death of old school friends in the Cameron Highlanders at Keren in Abyssinia. There was grave news too of chums from my Black Watch days who had been involved in fierce fighting in Crete. There was a report that the SS *City of Venice*, which had brought us to India had been torpedoed. Having spent seven pretty dangerous weeks in this sturdy old ship, conscious of our debt to her seaworthiness and the efficiency of her officers and crew, we were all shaken by that news, though it was unconfirmed.

Commenting in one letter on the pleasures of managing our own household affairs and our own daily timetable, enjoying our freedom from what I call 'Pinnellese', I ventured some observations on India and the Indians.

This is a very curious country, and however much one wants to like the Indians, and succeeds in some cases, the fact remains that there is a certain difficulty of contact, arising out of different manners and customs and so on ... There are, as I've told you, some very splendid chaps amongst them [i.e. amongst my fellow probationers

51

David Power ('Dynamite').

of the Indian entry] – John Satte, who travelled with us on the 'City of Venice' and thereby saved us from arriving with the strong anti-Indian prejudices we would have acquired if certain of the others had been in his place; H.N. Roy (from whom I took mumps, but a thorough gentleman in every other way), Brumma Kohl, a most pleasant Rip Van Winkle 'fat' boy who seldom rouses himself except to make a sly or humorous remark; and quite a number of the others who are all nice chaps with their own peculiar faults which – in sum – can be very irritating – loud voices always raised in argument or in what Arthur Askey would call ' 'earty laughter' (but few of us ever find much to laugh at in their witticisms).

I was clearly ill at ease with the few who took little or no part in the camaraderie of our training camp, but adopted 'the supercilious air of the sufferer from inferiority complex alternately with the snivelling sycophancy of the East'. Having condemned many of the things the British had done in India and lamented the

David Elliott.

omission of many things that should have been done, in this letter I expressed the view that while the Indian could get good examination results, the qualities he possessed were those of 'concentration and industry, not those of initiative, instinctive sense of responsibility and common sense', and this left him defective in matters of administration and government. I was fair enough to add that the primary duty of the British was to provide the Indian with opportunities to develop these qualities through experience, and I condemned the 'blustering incompetence' of Government in bringing about the resignation of various Congress provincial ministries by neglecting to consult Indian leaders before declaring that India was at war – even though many of them had previously declared their hostility to Nazism. I think it is to my credit that even then I saw as the worst consequence the disappearance of the ministries, 'Just when they might have been beginning to grasp the principles of responsible government'. British actions had simply fed the 'obstinate sentimental unrealism of Indian politics and politicians' and the only hope of getting them back to constructive attitudes would be the announcement of a date for the concession of dominion status,[1] though I doubted whether the Indians were sufficiently realist to accept such a move, suspecting that it would prompt them to demand that 'tomorrow' must be replaced by 'today' in our programme to provide us with the excuse to adopt 'the imperialist high-handed attitude that they make their chief grievance against us. They have, I suspect, curiously little interest in social problems. It is all nationalism and independence and bluster against our imperialism. What concern they have with economics is to attack our "exploitation" and ... they do not appear to use economic arguments constructively [to produce a programme] for their own good.'

I had begun to feel that the Congress Party line on economic policy, so far as it could be ascertained, was unrelated to the conditions of the world economy as I had studied it, and would lead the country into a hopeless tangle. The Indian capitalists who sustained Congress policies were themselves guilty of failing to improve the conditions of labour in their own factories. They had no sound ideas for the improvement of agriculture. They ignored the British achievement in providing irrigation schemes just as they ignored the consequential population explosion with its squalor and ill-health and unemployment, which the production of more food through irrigation had made possible. In my youthful view, Indian thinking at that time was a curious amalgam of book-learning combined with religious mysticism, and I could not see where the leadership for a sensible economic and social future was going to come from.

This seemed tragic to me, for:

From what I've seen of him, the ordinary common man is a fine cheery creature. Alongside the vices of crime and laziness, one finds the qualities of industry and patient cheerfulness that fights back stubbornly against incredible cruelties of nature. The best of the people live in the North [note how confidently this was said by one who had never been to Bengal or Madras], and amongst the Pathans I found incredible cruelty and unbelievable courtesy and hospitality as two leading characteristics – tendency to crime, readiness to murder and plunder, and steal other mens' wives, side by side with a magnificent sense of independence and equality amongst men, which in a more civilised state would reflect a true belief in the democratic way of living. I like the ordinary Indian: He's as cheerful and pleasant as his counterpart in most countries and I'd like to see him get a fair chance to eradicate these evil characteristics that the poverty of his environment and oppression of his rulers for thousands of years have induced in him. And nobody oppresses the Indian so much as the Indian himself.

All this may seem very smug and conceited. But it is justifiable to record it as a reflection of the feelings of a young Scots graduate reacting to India in the midst of the fog of war. Second-hand though much of the sentiment may appear, what I wrote in 1941 was what I sincerely felt.

My letters at that time did not confine their judgments to India and the Indians. There were pen sketches of my British companions, to compare with the judgments on their personalities which I had offered in letters posted from Cape Town. I had not greatly revised my opinions, except in the case of David Alexander, nicknamed 'Ragtime' because an Alexander once had a ragtime band, according to the song. I was now much more aware of his qualities and attributes, far less perturbed by his cynical pose; and very sympathetic to his bitterness, for he had just heard pretty finally that the bride whom he had married a few days before we sailed would not be given a wartime passage to India. (I had often had secret qualms of fear lest my own decision not to marry in October 1940 might be depriving us of a chance of an early reunion.) David was the 'literary gent' amongst us; he wrote very passable poetry, and had command of satire both in prose and verse. He had had pieces published in *Punch*. No wonder he seemed senior and suave to me, if not to us all. When I was ill in hospital I had composed a rather juvenile though fairly amusing skit on the camp's daily bulletin which my bearer arranged anonymously to exhibit on the official notice board.[2] It was generally believed for a long time to be the work of David Alexander, but while I was away in the Frontier the truth came out somehow. 'Ragtime' now advised me that I might take the earlier attribution of authorship to himself as the highest possible compliment to my wit! While he often contrived to annoy people with his irony, and had great delight in pouring scorn on anyone around – aided by a gift for words which was a revelation to me – I had long decided that there was no personal malice in his shafts, though they were perhaps evidence of his internal frustrations and bitter longings.

He had a well-developed taste in classical music, like David Power,[3] and their stocks of records enriched the hot, restless hours of the day in the chummery. We had rented the camp's radiogram, and were glad to be able to supplement the regular doses of Deanna Durbin songs to which All-India Radio seemed addicted. One of the great favourites in the bungalow was a recording of passages from the Messiah, owned by 'Ragtime', and it is interesting that one of my letters reports how frequently this was being played. Amongst the lighter music, I mentioned several recordings which provided nostalgic links. One was the Cameron Highlanders' Pipe Band playing Strathspeys and Reels, and Marches including 'Hieland Laddie' which fed my pride in the Black Watch. Our sentimental Irishman, Donald Jackson, was addicted to Paul Robeson's version of the 'Eriskay Love Lilt'. Poor Donald, with his airs and graces and Irish charm and kindly heart, had now, after months of doubt, learned that he had been jilted by the girl he had believed might marry him – and jilted, too, for a Catholic man he didn't know, though the young lady, like Donald, was Protestant. His emotional life was certainly disturbed, but somehow we knew he had great powers of recovery, and we were less worried about him than about dour, quick-tempered Robin Ross, with his extraordinary persecution complex, in his own brooding mind either being chased by women, apparently even by some who were still in Britain, or sinned against by men. Later that summer Robin played in a rugby match in Dehra Dun – against our concerted advice that the ground was far too hard for such a game – and suffered a serious back injury which plagued him throughout the next few awful years in Bengal. His success in his career, both in India in the face of such adversity, and subsequently in Canada, as Registrar of the University of Toronto for many years, is a tribute to his great qualities of character and intellect. By contrast, the equable Roger West, huge like Robin, but bluff and optimistic – his constant phrase was 'All right, chaps, it will all pan out in the end' – sadly succumbed to some tropical ailment in Assam. There was much more in Roger than the amiable short-sighted fool which was the role he professed to play, and I would have guessed that temperamentally and physically he was much more likely than the equally likeable Robin to succeed in East India, but fate decreed otherwise.

I had little to revise in my earlier opinions of the genial Brian Williams, his chubby face permanently lit by a cherubic grin and who did very well in the Punjab,[4] or his inseparable companion and fellow mathematician, Peter Boyce, who most unfairly had a hard time in Bihar during and after the Congress disturbances of 1942 – a frank, outspoken, wholly straightforward man; or of Harry Downing, who was to have an interesting career in Madras, and later in the diplomatic service. For some reason most of us treated Harry rather protectively like a younger brother, perhaps

The Author with Brian Williams.

because he had some nervous mannerisms. He would visit me often in my tent 'for a quiet seat and chat', and then spend all the time rapidly pacing in quick jerking movements from one side of the floor to the other.

David Elliot retained the unruffled, competent, commanding air of confidence and control that had impressed me on first acquaintance. Perhaps from his year in America, or from the American girl to whom he had got engaged, he had acquired a bit of a Yankee drawl, and with it contrived to produce an air of superior knowledge and certainty, which no doubt explained the nickname of 'Judge'. Like David Alexander and myself, David Elliot was often preoccupied with the problem of securing a passage to India for his fiancée. A year or two later, in the hope of expediting the possibility, they were married by proxy. The tensions preceding the Japanese attack on Pearl Harbour had

Donald Jackson, David Power, the Author,
David Alexander ('Ragtime').

prevented her from completing the journey to India, which she had actually begun. In the end, they were reunited and married 'properly' in Lahore Cathedral in the same week in November 1945 in which my wife arrived in Peshawar from Britain. After the war, David settled in America where he has long held a full professorship in history in the prestigious Californian Institute of Technology in Pasadena.

There were two recent British arrivals on our course who by now we were coming to know pretty well. Jimmy Tomkins had been on active service with the Dover Patrol, so his release from the Royal Navy had been delayed. Though he was hearty and genial and ready to fight anyone who hinted at insults to the Navy or the ICS, nobody would have known that he had won the DSC if I had not remembered a naval officer wearing the medal ribbon at the India Office on the day of one of my interviews. With some reluctance, Jimmy 'the Tonk' conceded that he had been the man I had seen; he was promptly christened 'the Admiral'. It was appropriate for he walked as though he had been born on a boat.

In fact his mother was Orcadian, he was born in Orkney and he seemed to me to behave very like Eric Linklater's Orcadian characters, or indeed like some of my Orcadian acquaintances at university.

The other newcomer has left me with no clear impression. His name was Bagshawe and most unfairly we burdened him with the title 'Mrs Bagwash', inspired no doubt by Tommy Handley's ITMA character. He was a nice man, handicapped from my point of view by a rather affected lah-de-dah manner, and though I learned to look deeper than that, he remained the probationer whom I felt I knew least.

The next couple of months saw us all 'back at school'. In fact, the Doon School was a most acceptable habitat. We were more comfortable and protected from the vagaries of the monsoon, but the climate was not conducive to concentration on study and exam fever was spreading. Personally, I was concerned at the ground I had lost when I was ill. In some ways, however, the day-to-day routine was more relaxed than it had been in camp. Perhaps Mr Pinnell was now feeling less anxious about his responsibilities. Some of us began to see more of him as a private person although I began to feel that he had been intensely shy with us. In my personal acquaintance with him, developed on occasional long walks, I became aware of a warm kindness and well-informed judgment of the ways of the world. We were still, however, worried by financial difficulties apparently caused by administrative ineptitude. While I had been 'saved' financially by the generosity of the NWFP Government during my long vacation, most of us had had an expensive time. Now we learned that we would have to vacate the Doon School at the beginning of September and find our own accommodation for the period up to the examinations in the third week. That meant still more expense. The timing of the riding exam worried us as it was to be held when we were out of practice at jumping because of weather conditions. We felt that it should have been organized when we were all at the peak of our training and performance. All in all a general feeling of staleness and apathy about the course grew throughout the summer. Things got no better when in August we were subjected to a bombardment of boring lectures on history, morning after morning, from a series of academic visitors mainly from Delhi.

An interesting and refreshing break in our programme came early in August when I spent several days at the UP Police Training

College at Moradabad with seven other British probationers. This was a well-planned exercise which provided valuable insight into the attitudes and training of young police officers of the rank of Assistant Superintendent. We had several special lectures and seminars on the relationship between ICS and the Indian Police. There was a particularly clear and valuable talk by Geoffrey Haig, the Deputy Commissioner of the district. We were comfortably housed in a large loft in a sort of barn, and spent a lot of our time with the members of the police course, watching their training, riding with them and of course enjoying the amenities of their well-found mess, of whose traditions they were naturally and very properly proud. Amongst their numbers were a considerable representation of officers from the police forces of several Indian States, including Hyderabad and Kathiawar.

These young Indian policemen were friendly and hospitable, and we found most of them to be agreeable and pleasant companions even though some of them were noticeably less 'bright' than the majority. Our group without exception were happy and got on extremely well with them. As we learned when we got back to Dehra Dun, this was very fortunate because another group of eight, all Indian probationers, who had returned from Moradabad just before we arrived, had been involved in some unpleasantness. We were in no doubt about the cause. The self-appointed 'leader' of this group was a very able but arrogant and uncooperative Punjabi from a wealthy landowning family, greatly given to bragging and intolerant of anyone disposed to compete with him in such a pastime. His reactions to the young policemens' pride in their mess traditions and pastimes had been thoroughly objectionable. The other Indians in his group were all too overshadowed by his overweening personality to attempt to redress the balance. As it turned out, the first party to go to the college from our camp had, like us, thoroughly enjoyed themselves and got on very well with the policemen. This group consisted of the other four British probationers, our old friend 'John' Satte, a very sensible and able Indian called A.S. Naik, and the ebullient and likeable Maharaj Kumar of Bundi, a wealthy young prince. It seemed to me somewhat ominous that it was the all-Indian group of ICS probationers which could not make or preserve a good relationship as guests of their fellow countrymen, who were members of the 'inferior' service.

There was another break in the routine of a different kind, but

A.S. Naik and the Author at Missourie, January 1941.

no less welcome. Hifazat Hussain, the Collector, had throughout our time in the Doon shown a genuine and kindly concern for us all. We liked him so much that we invited him to our chummery at Pritam Road. One Friday at the end of August he invited us – Elliot, Power, Alexander and myself – to join him and his wife in their Mussourie house for the weekend. That gave me at any rate three refreshing nights' rest in the cool mountain air, a welcome tonic at the end of the humid summer. Even more important, the hospitality of the Hussains widened our experience of Indian society and introduced us to the companionship of a number of well-educated and enlightened Indian ladies. The charm of their good looks and their conversation was a revelation. Even though

Founders' Day tea party at the Doon School.

the social setting was artificial and contrived – we went, for example, to a fashionable ball, organized to raise funds for some good wartime cause, to which various princes and maharajahs brought parties of house guests – it was good to discover that in such a context it was possible to have a lively conversation about social or political matters with intelligent and articulate Indian ladies. Some of them were accompanied by husbands whose business links brought a new insight to our education about the country and its ways. There were plenty of British ladies in our neighbourhood at the ball, but it was openly commented that the four young ICS men paid attention almost exclusively to the Indian ladies! In my case there was one exception, for I was buttonholed for half an hour by Lady Young, a well-known globetrotter, whose son Desmond was then the Government of India's chief Press officer and war correspondent.[5] I hope that I was diplomatic in my remarks to this talkative old lady. Another member of our party turned up late and sadly drunk. This was Lieutenant Prem Baghat, the Indian Army's first VC of the war. This brave man was being lionized wherever he went and often waylaid by not very sensible well-wishers. When he eventually turned up, he was sobered very quickly by the severe dressing-down administered by both our hostess and his stepmother, who was another guest; he took his medicine well and seemed a decent enough fellow at heart.

It was Hifazat Hussain himself, however, who probably taught us most that weekend, though he was so busy that we saw little of him except on the Sunday evening, when he devoted himself to regaling us with tales of our service and the deeds of some of its current characters. This urbane insight, from a senior Indian colleague who was still young enough not to be 'out of sight' of our age group – he was in his mid-thirties – was just the morale-booster that we needed at that stage.

An interesting element in Hifazat Hussain's account of his own responsibilities was the effect of war conditions on his work. The Doon of course was, like Abbottabad in NWFP, an important military centre, and the army population had grown rapidly and was mobile. There was a continual toing and froing which brought news from the various war fronts. A 'special Dehra attraction' in the social entertainment of Dehra Dun was an encampment housing a remarkably large number of Italian generals, whose resplendent uniforms were to be seen from time to time in mysterious circumstances. The score in generals at the time was nearly a hundred, and of course there were many more of lesser breed, like colonels and majors. Two who had escaped were recaptured, although not in uniform, in Peshawar, thanks to keen observation by a Pathan hotel keeper. They were well on their way to Afghanistan, where the Italian embassy, in Kabul, like the German one, was actively engaged in stirring things up in Waziristan.

This news and many other incidents kept focussing our attention on NWFP, and my proud expectations of my future career were well sustained by the arrival of letters from Ambrose Dundas about my posting and from Charles Duke about finding an army remount from one of the cavalry regiments for me to ride. I was to go to Hazara, to be trained by Gerald Curtis in Abbottabad, and nothing could suit me better. My letters home throughout the summer showed how keen I was about the prospect of service on the Frontier, my enthusiasm sparked by the excitement of the tour which had been organized for me with such foresight. I was absorbed in speculation about the course of the War, and kept on discussing how new developments might impinge on the Frontier. By that of course I meant the North-

West Frontier; at that stage few of us probably thought much about what might happen on the North-East Frontier. The German invasion of Russia had sharpened everyone's awareness of the possibility of an enemy army driving south through the passes, such as the Khyber. When the Americans sent a Minister to Kabul with full diplomatic weight to bring to bear against the Germans, and the British Government appointed Sir Francis Wylie to be Ambassador there, these matters rated comment in my letters as reflecting significant developments in the strategy of the War. In the case of Wylie's appointment I was worried about speculation reported that Sir George Cunningham would succeed him as Adviser to the Viceroy on Foreign Affairs, but was reassured by the news that a remarkable petition, apparently endorsed by everyone who mattered both in settled districts and in tribal territory in NWFP had been sent asking the Viceroy to extend his period as Governor – which in fact was done.

All this preoccupation with the Frontier did not close my mind to the wider questions of war strategy, I was constantly pontificating in my letters about what Churchill should do and I was clearly impressed by the fact that Greenwood, Attlee and Morrison, as well as Eden and Halifax, were making speeches about Britain's long-term objectives. I was fully persuaded that we were justifiably fighting, not just to save our skins, but for the future of civilization, and in one letter dated 20/8/41 to my mother I wrote:

> We have had to set in motion forces that will overwhelm us unless they are controlled when the bombing stops – forces of power production, of the control of employment, of regimentation of our staple industries, of food production and distribution, in fact forces that control our way of living alike with our means of living. The moment war production ceases, these forces must be directed towards a successful peace economy; and we must know beforehand on what principles we are to run our new economy – what aims we have for social welfare, and what schemes we will need to adopt to attain these aims, and have these schemes ready to put into action at once, and the people educated to believe in them and trust in them and finally to cooperate with them. There is no need to be afraid of a social revolution, rather we must recognise its inevitability and its necessity, and we must prepare for it and guide it, otherwise we will either have a revolution leading to anarchy and disaster, or a useless attempt to return to the conditions of 1918 or 1818, and that would mean more war, more insecurity.

Perhaps these animadversions were more than a trifle jejune, but they are reproduced here for whatever light they shed on the way young men were thinking, who were about to start an ICS career in 1941, instead of continuing in military service. In another letter written in August, I came back to the expectations which I had of the Frontier:

> I am convinced that I am going to the very best place in India. It just suits me down to the ground to go to a place where routine and red tape are not everything. Nobody claims that the Frontier is the best administrative place in India. It cannot ever be that, from the very nature of its problems. The Punjab people crow over us and say they can lick us for efficiency of administration: we don't even argue.[6] I think there is far more in good government by common sense and individual humanity than there ever can be in the book of rules and in masses of office files and paper schemes.

While I was keenly aware of some of my defects – a proneness to silent introspection, a 'certain amount of natural timidity to overcome, maybe to some extent a need to sharpen my reactions to sudden emergencies' – I felt that my short army experience had begun to show me how to grow out of these weaknesses, and I felt some confidence that my natural talents such as they were would be better suited to the needs of the Frontier than to any of the other provinces. 'I am a good solid Scot, with plenty of Highland blood in my veins to allow me to understand the ways of the clansmen of the hills and valleys, and enough good Lowland commonsense to enable me to see the other point of view and strike a balanced outlook ... I can avoid extremes and pitfalls, and that ought to count for far more than sheer genius, which I haven't got.' This letter was written just after I had been rereading some of D.K. Broster's novels, by which I had been

> struck by the similarity of conditions and characters in Jacobite Scotland and in our Highlands with the conditions in NWFP and the character of the Pathan clansmen today. The pride quick to wound, the spirit of independence, the inability to forgive, the persistence of family feuds, the intense individualism and belief in equality of all men merging into clan loyalty and blind obedience, the readiness to fight for freedom, and the dour stubborn ability to combat nature in the fight for mere existence – all these things are reproduced identically out here.

In this state of knowledge, and with this attitude of mind, I prepared for my probationers' examinations. By 20 September they were over and I packed up in the Royal Hotel at Dehra Dun where I had spent nearly three weeks, ready for a final stop of two days in Delhi. There we were given oral examinations in our various languages before I entrained for Taxila and Havelian. The party was over; the twelve British musketeers were separating, reluctantly because we had felt a strong bond of friendship, expectantly because we were each embarking on a new and more important stage in our careers. Apart from Donald Jackson who later joined the Political Service and came for a time to the Frontier, the Punjab men (Elliot and Williams), Ross of Bengal and very recently Downing of Madras, I have never seen any of them again, and after a few years the exchange of letters ceased and the flow of information began to dry up. I was glad to have Brian Williams's company to Amritsar. I can still remember how my spirits began to lift as the note of the engine changed with the pull up the incline around Taxila and the echo of the beat in the cuttings and the hills, after the flat endless plains of the Punjab, reminded me of Scottish trains. All day the mountains had lain a great way off to the north; now they crept nearer as the sun got lower. The whole atmosphere seemed to change. Pat Duncan met me at the railhead at Havelian and drove me to the DC's bungalow in Abbottabad. My bearer followed with all my *saman* (luggage) in a taxi. By nine o'clock the smell of wood fires was in my nostrils again. I was excited but content.

I was to take over from Duncan as a supernumerary Assistant Commissioner. He had nearly a year's service and was about to be gazetted with first-class magisterial powers. I would have to be content for a while with third-class powers, and strictly speaking should not exercise these till I had signed my covenant with the Secretary of State for India. That would depend on the examination results and we expected the formalities to be cleared by mid-October. In fact the exigencies of war and the difficulties of communications with London delayed the matter till well into November; once again, because of the common-sense attitude of my superiors in the NWFP the only real effect on me was that the delay produced some personal anxiety. But other probationers in more formally regulated provinces were left twiddling their thumbs and feeling useless and helpless as well as anxious until their covenants arrived with the Secretary of State's signature.

My bearer, William Umar Masih.

Notes

[1] In another letter a month later I returned to the question of dominion status (my fiancée was then reading a good deal about India, and had referred in one of her letters to reports of Indian criticisms of British policy). I made the point that India was not comparable to the new dominions, which were largely new countries peopled mostly by British emigrants, with small indigenous populations. India was an old country which had never been 'occupied' or colonized by Britain. Its people were steeped in the past, clung to a medieval way of life and outlook and its society's structure was based on an 'outworn religion which cannot stand alone in the present economic conditions of the world. It seems to me that they can't have the new [way of life and

government], till they give up the old, and this so far is what they seem never likely to do.' I am aware how immature and overconfident these comments show me to have been; their significance lies only in what they may reveal of contemporary attitudes amongst young British ICS officers.

[2] A copy in manuscript is preserved with my letters, but the detailed references would mean nothing to anyone who had not been a member of the Training Course.

[3] In the same letter I described David Power as constantly 'radiating a series of good-natured explosions'. He was a volatile, very clever little man. He worked hard at Law and Language, neglecting History even more than most of us – on the ground that the History syllabus was irrelevant to our future needs. For this he suffered, because he did not get a pass mark in History in the examinations. But after an exciting career in places like Mymensingh and a disastrous first marriage, he married a Muslim lady, stayed on after Partition, became a Muslim, and a senior and highly-respected judge, serving East Pakistan faithfully and well for many years.

[4] Brian became a schoolmaster after Partition – after being a housemaster at Repton he became headmaster of Brigg Grammar School in Lincolnshire.

[5] Desmond Young became quite well known for his biography of Rommell and other works. At the time of my meeting with his mother he had been in the news in the Middle East by walking into Damascus a day ahead of British troops, and getting captured by the French defenders of the city.

[6] No doubt 'Judge' Elliot had been laying down the law that day, but of course the rivalry with Punjab went back half a century.

CHAPTER IV

Early Months in Hazara

Being posted in Hazara was a great stroke of fortune. It provided a wonderful range of experience and almost ideal conditions in which to live and learn. The district is a large one, with a population of about three-quarters of a million. It stretches from the low hills and plains of the Punjab border, north of the site on which Islamabad, capital of Pakistan, now stands, to the Babusar Pass at the head of the Kagan Valley, on the borders of Indus Kohistan and Chilas. The western boundary runs near Taxila and Hassanabdal in the Punjab to the broad sweep of the Indus River, some miles upstream from where the river narrows at the deep Attock gorge, across which a single great iron bridge carries both the main railway and the grand trunk road westwards from the Punjab into the Frontier Province, and towards Peshawar. From there the great river completes the western boundary of the district, as one proceeds upstream as far as Amb, a little princely state which in my time was quietly and efficiently ruled by the Nawab of Amb. His benign influence and loyalty to the British helped to keep quiet and peaceful the potentially turbulent tribal areas of Buner and the Black Mountain along whose mountain ridges the border creeps north-eastward to Babusar, encompassing peaks of 13,000 feet as it skirts the Kohistan. Coming south from Babusar close to the majestic heights of Nanga Parbat, the boundary runs high first on the east bank of the Kunhar River, and then above the west bank as the Kunhar turns to meet the Jhelum River. Following the precipitous track high above the great river one looks east into Kashmir, till the river swings away east of the mountain saddle near Murree, where the road from Rawalpindi and Islamabad in the Punjab climbs over into Kashmir. The line of the boundary swings down gradually over the ridges above and to the south of the Harroh River, towards the starting point of this description.

The district has three tahsils. Haripur Tahsil to the south is the least mountainous and in winter by far the mildest. Its summer heat is tempered by the fresh breeze near the Indus water – but nowhere else, except on the Gandhar mountain range near the western border where the Mishwanis live. They are an isolated Pathan tribe, in a district in which there are few genuine Pukhtuns or Pathans. No finer or more attractive specimens of their race can be found anywhere.

Hot though most of Haripur Tahsil can be at the height of summer, it is less trying than most parts of the Punjab or of the southern end of NWFP; and so too, still more, is Abbottabad Tahsil, in the centre of the District, lying generally just a thousand feet or so higher. The headquarters town lies on the edge of the Rash plain at about 4,000 feet, encircled by mountains, which to the east loom commandingly along the range from Thandiani and Nathia Gali and on towards Murree at heights of from 7,000 to 10,000 feet. Much of this range, from about 6,000 feet to 9,000 feet, is densely afforested and very beautiful.

Beyond the Rash plain, the district's central road climbs and twists over more hills before entering the Pakhli plain, on which stands the headquarters of the third, northernmost tahsil, the subdivision of Mansehra, from which roads go on north-west, north and east to lovely valleys – to Oghi in the Agror Valley, to Baffa and on by the Konsh Valley to beautiful places like Ahl and Battal on plateaus near the Kohistan border, to the Bhogarmang Valley and to the Kagan itself, as well as by Garhi Habibulla to Domel and Muzafarabad in Kashmir.

To walk the border of this great district would take a fit man many weeks. It could not be done in winter, when the whole of the northern arc is deep in snow and many of the passes at the head of the valleys cannot be traversed. Many of the higher villages in Mansehra and Abbottabad Tahsils, particularly in the Galis range, are under snow for weeks at a time. In summer, long hot marches in the southern arc are a severe test of stamina and temperament. But over this vast tract of mountain, valley and plain one can tour in comfort by matching one's route to the season – in Haripur during the winter months, in the highest mountain tracts of Abbottabad and Mansehra during the summer. On rocky tracks and mountain paths one went on foot. On easier ground one could use sturdy local ponies. One could move out from headquarters in Abbottabad by car or bus and within an hour or two at most arrive at a suitable starting point for a tour of two or three days, or any period up to several weeks, and one seldom went far without some spectacular view unfolding.

My first three months in Hazara were exciting and eventful. Every experience was new, and I felt enriched and refreshed. I was soon given the chance to glimpse the wide range of a district officer's duties and became aware of a new challenge to my personality and capabilities different from any examination-based challenge of the past. I did not feel afraid of it because it sprang from circumstances and an environment in which I felt instinctively that I could be at home and at ease. But I was apprehensive for I quickly realized that to meet the challenge adequately I must serve an apprenticeship of training which would be demanding and ought probably to last several years, while all the signs were that responsibilities would arrive before the training was complete. Everyone, from the Chief Secretary to the Deputy Commissioner and his Indian colleagues of the Provincial Civil Service, told me that, because of the war, the district and the province were seriously short of experienced officers, and I must expect to have to carry the burdens of a real job soon.

I do not think I was worried by the prospect of hard work, but I felt some diffidence about having to tackle responsibilities which called for technical knowledge and administrative experience for which I had not yet been prepared. Looking back, I feel that to some extent this diffidence was a reflection of my Scottish upbringing and education. I needed to know about something before I was prepared to discuss it or express an opinion about it, and for me 'to know' meant to have read about it in print, to have heard an expert lecture about it, to have tested my understanding in some sort of examination. I do not know whether a product of the English public school system and Oxbridge would have felt the same diffidence in similar circumstances; perhaps not. That may indeed be why the mixture of the two cultures or nurtures, 'Scots and English', somehow produced the chemistry of a pretty successful form of imperialism over many generations.

After the communal life of the previous year I found a new comfort and privacy in Abbottabad. On advice from the Governor, the DC arranged for me to live with the Army. I had a large bed-sitting room in the bungalow of the officer commanding the 10/13th Frontier Force Rifles, with a private entry through a back door. I took my meals in the officers' mess of Regimental

Headquarters, a quarter of a mile away. Several of the older bachelor officers were delightful, quiet, kind and fatherly towards us youngsters. Many of the more junior were birds of passage, soon to be posted to battalions overseas. Nobody seemed to think that the junior 'Political' who turned up in mufti for meals was in any way odd. The Regiment had a tradition of service with political officers 'on the Frontier'.

But I was not stuck in Abbottabad all the time. Ambrose Dundas told me that the central purpose of my training was to inculcate an aversion to cantonment life and the knowledge that my real home was in the villages. Within a week I was on tour for the first time. This was in the high villages of the Galis, to the north of Nathia Gali, the summer headquarters of the Provincial Government. I was to accompany Gerald Curtis for a week, scrambling on foot up and down steep mountain paths, visiting some of the most impoverished hill cultivators of the district. We were delayed for a day in starting by news that Gerald was to be transferred to a Deputy Secretary's post in Delhi. The tour would have been abandoned if Gerald Emerson, the Assistant Commissioner in the subdivision of Mansehra, had been available to relieve Curtis. But he was absent in some inaccessible place in the tribal mountains of Indus Kohistan, seeking to assure himself that no harm had come to Aurel Stein, the explorer who was about eighty years old and had been travelling in Kohistan for some months. The Curtises were in no hurry to leave for Delhi. They (and their small children) loved Hazara, and had no wish to leave their delightful bungalow in Abbottabad to begin life in a tent in overcrowded Delhi.

I was unhappy, for I had been posted to Hazara specifically to be trained by Gerald Curtis, who was reputed to be an outstanding district officer. Already I knew that I liked him, and I admired the way he combined the dignity of his role as 'father and mother' to the people (*man bap*) with a relaxed good-humoured freedom of manner towards them. He and his wife were both wise and kind, and having felt that my future was in good hands I was shaken from complacency by this reminder that the future is unknown. But life in the open air soon adjusts to such shocks, and the next few days were exhilarating. On that first tour Gerald put down some important markers for my future life as an Assistant Commissioner. He was truly a brilliant revenue officer, then in his prime, steeped in knowledge of his district and its ways. Most of the week was spent between 5,000 and 8,000 feet. The villages were really clusters of hamlets, each of two or three households. Their fields were tiny, laboriously built up into little terraces, the stones cleared to form rough retaining walls for the soil, holding the rainfall on a few square yards of relatively level ground. Land was very scarce, and the pressure of population considerable, so that subdivision of holdings was inevitable, bringing continual quarrels about field boundaries. On this tour there were plenty of disputes to settle. I was given rigorous practice in the interpretation of the revenue records and the checking on the ground of the *Patwari's* cloth map of each circle of villages, on which every tiny patch of ground was marked and numbered.[1]

Not unnaturally, the people were poor and quarrelsome, and the importance of a visit by the DC himself was soon evident. The *sirkar* had come to the people; disputes which had festered for months or years would now be settled by real authority – and for a few months there would be a chance that fractiousness would be replaced by peace and harmony. The importance of being decisive was brought home to me. We would arrive at a spot, breathless and sweating from the strenuous scramble on steep and stony paths, and sit amongst a crowd of very noisy *zemindars* (cultivators) with all the children and some of the women hanging around on the fringes. The DC would put his questions and listen carefully to the outbursts they provoked. It was rare indeed for a statement by the *lambardar* (village headman) or by a particular owner or tenant to go unchallenged. Suddenly the DC would shout '*Chup!*' (silence!). Instantly the throng was quiet, and Gerald would pronounce his verdict. Invariably this was accepted without question, often with acclaim. What had been needed was a decision and one that had been given by the *burra sahib* after such a hearing of all sides was bound to be wise and just.

Occasionally a troublemaker would be stubborn. In one village, we were told of problems caused by illicit cultivation of the *guzara* (village forest held in common, but subject to restriction on grazing rights, and protected by Government regulation from cultivation, in order to prevent soil erosion). In this case after much argument and pulling of beards, the DC achieved a compromise, but an ancient scallywag stubbornly held out for his 'rights'. Curtis adjourned the hearing for his daily *tamasha* (entertainment, fun and games). It was his practice at the end of an afternoon's field work to organize foot races on the biggest area of flattish land he could find. Starting with the children everyone had to compete in an appropriate category. The successful children would be rewarded with an anna, while the grey-bearded elders, whose beards were usually dyed red with henna, might get three or four annas, appropriate to their *izzat* (izzat is a marvellous word for the concept of self-respect and standing in the community, a most important factor in Muslim rural life). On this particular day, as the races got under way, the DC beckoned to the elderly recalcitrant in the *guzara* case, and told him that as he was the odd man out in the dispute he would have to run a solo race, unless he agreed to sign the settlement with the others. Before this appalling shame could befall him, faced by the chuckles of his friends and neighbours, the old fellow conceded his case, and put his thumbprint on the document to shouts of *'angootha lag gya'* (he has signed!), and *'shabash!'* (bravo!).

By way of training, I was given my own taste of decision-making. Sent out with the Patwari to investigate a dispute, I could not make head or tail of the arguments, volubly expressed, though more soberly translated for me by the official. So I had him produce his map and read off the measurements and the attribution of ownership on the records. As he read, I paced hither and thither, marking corners with stones and finally stepping out along a line which I announced was the new boundary. Immediate acclamation greeted this feat of justice. Privately, I was puzzled. I knew that my pacing had been far from scientific. But what mattered was that I had heard the arguments, I had checked the records and, having made my own measurements, I had made a decision. Honour was satisfied and justice was done; and even if the decision was made by the *chota sahib* (the little gentleman, or junior officer), it was the Government's decree, and accepted by all.

Although Gerald Curtis left Hazara almost immediately after the tour, his example had given me a real taste for life in camp in the district. In the next two months I made several tours with Nawabzada Sher Afsar Khan, an officer of the Provincial Civil Service, who held the post of Revenue Extra Assistant Commissioner (REAC). This meant that he was responsible to the Deputy Commissioner (DC) for the oversight of the work of all the revenue staff – the *tahsildars, naib-tahsildars, kanungos* and *patwaris* – putting them in descending order of importance. In theory he was the person best placed to train me, not only in

matters relating to the assessment and collection of land revenue
– the tax on the land on which our whole system of government
was based – but also in the general social and economic problems
of the villages. He was, in fact, absolutely first rate in his job, an
excellent teacher and with him I felt that I was learning fast. He
came from a well-known family in the district of Dera Ismail Khan
(D.I.K.) in the far south of the province, and he taught me much
about the Frontier as a whole, not just about cis-Indus Hazara. As
a companion he was lively and witty, I thoroughly looked forward
to our regular excursions and greatly enjoyed them.

The first of these took us to Khanpur, a grubby little township
on the banks of the Harroh River, in the south-west of the district
near its boundary with the Rawalpindi District of the Punjab, and
no great distance from Taxila, the site of the marvellous
excavations of the Buddhist civilization. This was the land of the
Gakhar Rajas – despite the name they were Muslims. It was quite
different from the stony mountain terrain which I had toured with
Curtis. We were able to ride a good deal, on ponies borrowed from
one of the Rajas. Our base was the rest house about half a mile
from Khanpur, situated on a little hillock on a bend of the river. I
shall always remember it for the strong cool breeze that blew
downstream from the mountains for half an hour or so before
sunset every evening, bringing instant relief from the heat of the
day. It was still very hot at Khanpur in mid-October, but it has a
fine winter climate and the visitors' book in the rest house bore
witness to its popularity over many years with European officers
and their wives.

Later, when I graduated to the status of magistrate with first-
class powers, one of my *haqs* (privileges of one's post or status) as
Assistant Commissioner Hazara (ACH) was to be in charge of the
Khanpur *thana* (the area served by the police station there). That
meant I had to try all criminal cases emanating from local police
enquiries and keep a generally benevolent eye on the welfare of
the populace, so I could tour there regularly during the cold
weather when the more mountainous areas around Abbottabad
could be too chilly for comfortable camping. In the hot weather,
Khanpur cases could often be brought to Abbottabad, while I did
my touring in the highlands, and in particular to Dungagali, where
the police station was opened for the summer season when the
population of the Galis grew.

Khanpur was a fine fruit growing area. Not many miles away an expatriate Yorkshireman had established a successful fruit farm run on Californian lines. It produced the finest oranges and grapefruits that I had ever tasted. Touring was thirsty work. Boiled water from a water bottle was unappetizing and, to say the least, lukewarm, though often very necessary. Village tea, drowned in boiled milk and sugar, was welcome if not very thirst quenching. Best of all at Khanpur was fresh fruit. In season, I would get through a dozen big oranges on a day's march or ride.

Round Khanpur many of the tracks were sandy or gravelly, and remarkably smooth, so it was possible to make some excursions by tonga – a small two-wheeled pony trap. On my first tour with him, Sher Afsar took me to Taxila in this way. Although he had a car petrol was scarce and rationed even for government officers. When I was on my own I would go from Abbottabad to Haripur by public bus, and then take a tonga for the long drive to Khanpur. It was no different from the practice in the old days. When Winston Churchill went to Malakand to cover the 1897 campaign he travelled by tonga from the railhead. My frequent practice was to finish a tour by taking a tonga to Taxila and have a look at the excavations or the museum while waiting for the evening train up to Havelian, which was about twenty minutes by taxi from Abbottabad.

Petrol rationing discouraged me from thinking of acquiring a car, which in any case I could not afford. When touring on my own I normally made a preliminary stage by public transport, which often meant a charcoal-driven lorry, and then I would strike out on foot or horseback, away from the main roads. For a few months I kept my own horse, but I soon found that I had little use for him. The mountain tracks were normally too stony and precipitous for a horse and where they were suitable for hill ponies these could easily be hired or borrowed locally. Mostly in the forests and mountains I preferred to walk. A day's stage averaged between twelve and eighteen miles, not counting detours to 'inspect the spot' involved in some dispute or crime, or some agricultural experiment or development. My retinue consisted of my camp clerk, orderly and personal servant or bearer, who did the cooking. When I stayed in an official rest house – mostly these were run by the Forestry Department or the Public Works Department – there was usually a caretaker who might expect to do the cooking (execrably). If I was hearing formal civil or criminal cases, I sometimes took my 'reader' or *munshi* (the clerk of court). This was a dear, gentle old chap called Sita Ram, who seemed so out of place in wild country that I often left him at headquarters, where he had plenty to do, and got my much tougher, very efficient camp clerk, Ram Dutt, to take care of all the paperwork. It was a little curious that both my principal officials, in a largely Muslim district, were Hindus. But Ram Dutt was capable of anything, anywhere, a most loyal and efficient servant of the Crown – and a faithful friend to me.

On most tours, I would be joined at the appropriate places by junior local officials, like the *patwari*, who kept the records of land ownership and tenancy of several villages and recorded the state of the crops at harvest or any damaging events like floods or hailstorms. Sometimes it would be necessary to have his supervising officer, the field *kanungo*, or *girdawar*, or – even more senior still – the *naib-tahsildar*. Sometimes, too, we would have two or three police constables, and if we were touring the higher ranges a forest ranger or even a divisional forest officer. If we were camping in tents, the amount of gear to be transported increased, and with it the number of porters and orderlies. Mules had to be carefully handled on precipitous pathways.

Rest houses were normally wooden bungalows with two, three or even four bedrooms and a verandah, plus probably a kind of living room with a blazing log fire in the cold weather, in front of which I often took my bathtub rather than shiver in the bathroom, though the water, brought in large kerosene tins which had been heated over wood fires, was so hot it always had to have cold water added even if snow or sleet was falling. Most rest houses were beautifully sited, but the finest and best-managed were those belonging to the Forestry Department. Many of them were at high altitudes, 7,000 or 8,000 feet – delicious in summer. When I had charge of Dunga Gali sub-thana, on many summer weekends I would take my bicycle on the roof of the Friday after-lunch bus to Nathia Gali, cycle on the good roads along the saddles and ridges to Dunga Gali or Khanspur or Changlagali on the road to Murree in the Punjab, try cases into the dusk of the evening and again on Saturday till about teatime, and after a refreshing rest over Sunday, cycle downhill early on Monday morning before the motor traffic was allowed to start uphill through the police controlled gates. I used to be in my office twenty-five miles away before 9 o'clock. The road was steep, narrow and unmetalled, so traffic could move only one way, and there were defined periods

*A typical Forestry Department rest house
between Nathia Gali and Thandiani.*

for uphill and downhill movement. The main physical stress came
from the effort of applying both brakes continually. I was cautious,
always dismounted at the steepest parts when the wheels locked
and skidded on the loose shale and could boast that I never fell.
The Superintendent of Police gave me a permit for this mode of
travel which no Hazarwal had attempted. After some time the
Settlement Officer, Phil Tollinton, thought that he should save his
bus fare in the same way, but having omitted to ask for the
requisite *chitti* (a letter or certificate) from the SP, he had quite an
argument with the constables at the top gate. Overriding their
protests he set off, only to fall and graze his limbs to their
considerable satisfaction before he had gone very far. Apart from
saving a bus fare, my system had the advantage of enabling me to
get in a full day's work on the Monday, as well as extra work in

the Galis over the weekend. There was no downhill passenger bus in the mornings. The system was probably also good for justice which could be seen to be done in the villages, rather than in the law courts of Abbottabad. Since only two or three of the Abbottabad *vakils* (pleaders, advocates) liked the idea of going up the hill to work, their clients were deprived of their aid. But that left me more of the work of cross-examination to do, and rightly or wrongly I was convinced that the cause of justice was better served.[3]

Other favourite excursions were by the mountain paths along the chain of forest rest houses between Nathia Gali and Thandiani, with spectacular views over the Jhelum valley into Kashmir, or in the other direction over the lower hills and plains of Hazara to the Indus. Recollecting them, I can smell the pines and the pure clean air of the Himalayas, and picture the monkeys in the trees, the flowers and the butterflies, the dozy lizards on the sun-drenched rocks – and once again I am aware of the stillness and silence and peace of the far mountains, clear and clean and sweet-scented above the heat and dust and turmoil of the Indian plains.

One of the attractions of these early tours was the variation of scene and people which they provided. Within my first two months, besides touring in the Galis and around Bagnotar, and at Khanpur, I had gone with Sher Afsar to Tarbela and Ghazi, down the valleys of the Dor and Siran rivers to the banks of the great Indus itself, and had made a diversion to visit the Mishwani tribe in their mountain pastures in the Gandgar range. Most of them live on a plateau rising over 4,000 feet from the Haripur plain, overlooking the Indus, close by on the other side. The Mishwani are an isolated Pathan tribe, south of the Indus where Pushtu – and the Pakhtun code – has survived only in a few pockets. Very few of the *quaums* (tribes) of Hazara can lay any claim to be Pathan; several which call themselves Pathan speak little Pushtu, but use the local variant (Hindko) of the Punjabi dialect, which is almost universal in the district. But the Mishwanis retain the Pakhtun characteristics and in many ways remain in my memory the finest of all Pathan clans. In the struggle with the Sikh tyranny in the mid-nineteenth century they became the staunchest allies of James Abbott, the remarkable political officer who at last brought peace and security to the people of Hazara. He has remained the great hero of Mishwani folklore. They maintained a proud tradition of military service throughout the period of the

British Raj. When I got to know them, their knowledge of the War's events and understanding of its nuances took me by surprise, till I appreciated that most of the men around me, who were so friendly and hospitable, had many years of past military experience. Even thus early in the War – the winter of 1941 – the number of young men left in their village was small, so many were in voluntary service in the Army. On my first visit, one of them, Sher Zaman of Lalu Gali, a retired cavalry captain, told me that golf and tennis were games for a memsahib; the sahib's games were hockey and football, but things were no longer what they were when General Auchinleck was his platoon commander and played hockey with his men!

Talking to the villagers about the War was an important element in the work of the touring officer. In those days wireless sets were rare and rumours were rife. Enemy propaganda spread through various channels though it was received generally in the Frontier with more scepticism than All-India Radio or the BBC's news. People were eager to learn what was happening and ever ready to pass opinions. Many of them had close relations away on service – an increasing number of them overseas, some from Hazara even in Billayat (England). I was astonished one day to have direct news of a man from the village I was visiting who had been encamped at Aviemore near the Cairngorms with a mule company of transport troops, and had moved from there thirty miles to a field just outside my home town, where I imagined him being served with tea by my own fiancée at the church canteen. At that time the war news was gloomy and discouraging. Even the most remote villages knew it and must have wondered what was happening to the powerful *sirkar* which had ruled over them for generations. In Hazara – and perhaps even more so in the rest of the province amongst the Pathans – the people did not welcome the prospect of a British defeat. They regarded the Germans as *zulm* (cruel and hard), and the Japanese as rubbishy Hindus of a sort. Remembering the folklore of subjection to the Sikhs, from which James Abbott had released them, they did not want to contemplate rule by Hindus under the mantle of the Indian Congress Party in alliance with the Japanese, and it was difficult, though important, to try to get them to appreciate how serious the menace from the East might become. They had no difficulty in understanding the threat from the side of the Caucasus or Persia which was posed by the German thrust against Russia. Yet Soviet Communism was the natural enemy of Islam, and they found it hard to understand why the British, who only a few months ago had been faced by an alliance between Germany and Russia, should now wish them to regard the Russians as allies and friends.

Just two months after my arrival I made my first week-long tour on my own, in the inaccessible and neglected tracts of Boi and Bakot. From Garhi Haribullah on the road from Mansehra to Domel and Muzaffarabad in Kashmir, we climbed the narrow track along the ridge high above the west bank of the Kunhar River, as it cut its way through deep gorges to join the Jhelum on its way to the Punjab plains. Our way continued high above the great river for four or five days' march to Bakot. West of the track the slopes of the range between Thandiani and Nathia Gali rose steeply. At times the path was almost non-existent and our mules with their burdens of tents and office boxes had to pick their way round projecting rocks above precipices, not always without damage to their loads. None of them fell down the *khud* but the damage was caused in crossing the rocky beds of flooded streams. Just before the tour started the weather had been very bad and the sound of rushing torrents and the wind in the trees reminded me of Scotland. In the background on all sides there was snow – above us on the Galis range, across the river in Kashmir, and away to the north on the great mountains around Nanga Parbat. In the tents at night it was very cold and the warmth of the sun in the morning was doubly welcome.

This area was so remote that the annual visit of a British officer attracted great attention, and I was accompanied everywhere by groups of inquisitive villagers. Their sense of hospitality made them accompany me on departure until the welcoming party from the next village met us. At one place, where there had been a serious dispute about a well, two hundred came two miles to meet me, to ensure that I had the complete story before I reached 'the spot'. As I made my way along the narrow path it was an extraordinary sight to look back on this crowd following in single file, the road being too narrow for any alternative. At this stage I was still in difficulty with the language. My Urdu was improving, but in those remote parts, apart from the very occasional big landowner, nobody really spoke Urdu and I was beset by a babel of voices clamouring in the local version of Hindko, a variation of the Punjabi dialect. On this tour I had only a *kanungo* to translate for me. He was a very stout, cheerful chap, who submitted happily enough to my teasing when he arrived panting behind me at the top of a slope knowing that yet another climb lay half a mile ahead. One of the merits of frequent touring was that I was forced to learn to communicate with the people of the countryside far quicker that if I had been sitting all the time in court at Abbottabad – where what every witness said was immediately translated in several versions by opposing advocates and by my court clerk.

This tour ended with a disappointing day. From near Bakot we had to descend steeply to the footbridge over the Jhelum to Kohala in the Punjab. At that season there was no way up the mountain to the Galis road on the other side – nor was that road open for public transport to Abbottabad. The way home was a circuit of over 100 miles through the Punjab via Murree and Rawalpindi, then back into Hazara by the main trunk road. We had arranged for a lorry to pick us up at Kohala at 6.30 a.m. but the driver had funked the darkness and the dangers of the mountain road, and we had to wait for him for well over an hour. Labouring up the hill to Murree his vehicle ran out of petrol and in frustration I set off for a six-mile walk, intending to catch a proper bus at the normally busy hill station. As it turned out, it was pretty deserted, though there were vehicles going up to Kashmir, and my own lorry caught up with me just as my irritation was boiling over. The driver had scrounged some fuel from a truck passing on the way to Srinagar. We proceeded to Rawalpindi by the outrageously unsafe method of travelling in gear with the ignition switched off for long downhill stretches when the driver thought he could control the vehicle with the brakes. As we came to the gentler decline, in the neighbourhood of the future site of Islamabad, I looked northward to the Khanspur range and thought how much simpler everything would have been if I had gone to Khanpur for a few days instead of exploring Boi and Bakot. But a stop for lunch at Rawalpindi enabled me to seek out a dentist for I had lost a vital filling in an eye tooth. He said it could be crowned, for which there was no time, or extracted, and, distrusting him in the knowledge that Curtis's predecessor as DC Hazara, 'Jumo' Ross-Hurst, had died after a dental operation in Murree, I went home wearily to Abbottabad. The tooth survived to be crowned in Scotland years later. Perhaps sugar rationing, a diet of fresh fruit and unleavened bread and an outdoor life are the best treatment for dental decay.

Another tour by myself in mid-January was a real test of stamina. Starting at the railhead at Havelian (about 3,000 feet), I marched in long stages into the hills below Dunga Gali and Murree, inspecting the police stations at Lora and Nara near the sources of the Harroh River. I set out in ill humour in pouring rain, the government contractor having failed to provide mules to carry the party's gear. It was 11.00 a.m. when I got away, orderlies having been despatched with my bearer to hire other mules, and after walking through a steady downpour of cold sleet I arrived at the forest rest house at Jabri at 5 o'clock. The caretaker had lit a huge log fire, and in desperation I ate some chapattis and a half-cooked chicken; but it was 10 o'clock before the baggage party arrived, my bearer still nervous from the difficulties of the track after nightfall and fear of a notorious outlaw who had recently terrorized the neighbourhood – although, unknown to Yaqub, this dacoit had recently been killed so the track was now safe from his exploits.

The succeeding days' marches were dry overhead, though cold, but the roads, normally appalling, were almost impassable because of damage by rain and snow and all the rivers and streams were in spate. Where I was not walking in mud or water I was on the hardest and roughest imaginable stones. But the scenery was magnificent forest country, with great undulating stretches of hill and valley not unlike parts of Wales. The villages had come through a rough time: many of the older people died of pneumonia and some had died when the roofs of their dried mud and stone houses collapsed under the weight of snow. They told me that some miles away at Nathia Gali the lawn of Government House lay under 12 feet of snow. But they were not totally despondent for they knew that the exceptional precipitation augured well for their spring crops. The grass was already sprouting and where winter wheat had been sown it was passing six inches tall. The onset of spring would soon bring it to ripeness. In a letter to my fiancée, I tried to give an impression of what work on tour involved:

On tour there was the usual amount of revenue work (mostly learning on my part) social uplift or rural reconstruction or call it what you will – recommending wells to be made 'pukka', roads to be repaired and a dozen other things; propaganda – for recruitment for the army, and about the war; giving news and information to hillmen Mahommedans who think the Japanese are mere Hindus from whom India has nothing to fear; ferreting information about crime and the police and the political parties. (I was waylaid by Khaksars one day and drank tea with them, to the consternation of the field Kanungo, who was sure that my action in taking tea with them would increase the local influence of the Khaksars. He was probably right, but as I took care to say to him in the hearing of a multitude, if I did not find out personally what the Khaksars were really like, how would I ever be able to judge them and know the truth for myself?) Also propaganda of various kinds, from the encouragement of bee-keeping to trying to stimulate fruit-growing – and my pet themes of foodstuffs and prices and profiteering.

Just at this time the growing shortage of foodgrains was beginning to spark its first wartime crisis in India. The Government of the Punjab had put an embargo on all movement of grain out of their province, and so the people of the Lora area were greatly perturbed at being prevented from going for their needs to their usual market at Murree, in the Punjab, and being compelled to go three times as far, to Havelian, thus incurring additional costs of transport on the difficult route that I had traversed. But I had seen no evidence of foodstuffs on the move by that route and I soon discovered that they were adept smugglers who enjoyed thwarting the efforts of the Punjab police to catch them at the provincial boundary. I fear that I rather encouraged them in their artfulness and a month or two later negotiated an understanding with the sub-divisional officer Murree about the traffic in foodgrains. He was a Punjab ICS man a couple of years senior to me, and we negotiated over a picnic lunch on a high spur on the mountain at Khanspur near the border.

Apart from all these matters my letter concluded: 'I also had a look at some schools, a veterinary hospital, a dispensary, and other things – so now you know what sort of work I do!' On the last tours I have described I was on my own, without supervision, learning on the job. One reason for this was that in three months there were three changes of Deputy Commissioner. Unlike Gerald Curtis, the new men had no time for supervising me in camp. But shortly I was sent on a couple of tours with the Settlement Officer. These experiences were much more narrowly confined to revenue work, with a stricter element of instruction and supervision. The SO was H.P. Tollinton, an able officer with about twelve years' experience, who was totally absorbed in the important task of reviewing the result of the second regular settlement of Hazara, which had been completed by Watson in 1907. Every junior ICS officer had to undergo settlement training, usually extending over many months, and I knew that if I were to feel secure and competent in a future career of district administration, I would need to go through this process with Tollinton, and that I was lucky to have him in charge of a settlement in Hazara, and not to have to go on secondment to some district in the Punjab or the UP. Six months later the whole matter became a burning issue with me, and with John Dent and Pat Duncan, but I shall return to that affair in due course. The early excursions with Tollinton were just a preliminary to the real settlement training that was to come, and they were enjoyable in every way except for the weather. The first trip was based on Balakot, low down in the Kagan Valley, and the rain was so heavy that for a good deal of the time we saw none of the beauty of the area but were confined to the dak bungalow, working on documents. On the second occasion, towards the end of February, I set out on my own to join Phil Tollinton at Ahl, high up in the Konsh Valley between Agror to the west and the Bhogarmang and Kagan valleys to the east, and only a few miles from the Black Mountain of tribal territory and the mountainous border of Buner and the Indus Kohistan. The Konsh and Bhogarmang valleys feed the upper reaches of the Siran system which debouches into the Indus near Tarbela, fifty or sixty tortuous miles away.

On the way to join Tollinton at Ahl, I spent a night at Shinkiari at the confluence of the rivers and next day went up the Bhogarmang valley to Daddar, a beautiful site in the pine forest where there was a sanatorium for Indian sufferers from tuberculosis. It was supervised by an English lady missionary who had given her life to her lonely task, seldom seeing another European. Sir George and Lady Cunningham took great practical interest in her work and saw to it that government money as well as charitable funds were directed to it. Some months after my visit, they took the Vicereine, Lady Linlithgow, there to mark the importance of the work and the development of new accommodation at the sanatorium. At Shinkiari I found three young Royal Engineer officers surveying and laying out sites for summer training camps. One was a Scots lad from Glasgow who had been overseas for only a month, was homesick and beginning to wonder if he would ever hear a Scots voice again. Confident that I would have Colonel Teague's approval, I invited them to come into Abbottabad at the weekend assuring them that if there were no vacant officers' quarters, the Frontier Force Rifles mess would pitch tents for them in the garden.

Next day the rain which had beset me cleared for a time, so I crossed the flooding river by pony and set out to walk seventeen miles to Ahl. The track was good, carpeted in *chir* (pine) needles, climbing steadily but fairly gently through most glorious country with constant views of the river rushing audibly below. The air was like a magic tonic, and I felt so invigorated that apart from one break of a quarter of an hour I kept straight on, arriving at the rest house at Ahl just after 2 p.m., a march of seventeen miles uphill in five hours. As I rested outside in the sun, the rain returned and I retreated inside to the log fire to read until my luggage arrived three hours later. Tollinton got in about 5.30 p.m., having slogged through snow across the mountain from the Agror valley. For the next two days it poured steadily, with snow falling at times, and we stayed indoors working on our papers and reading and talking. I was putting the finishing touches to a report on the supply of foodstuffs in the district for the DC and the provincial government and was well content. Phil was quiet, rather slow and even ponderous but he had a happy knack of sharing and promoting conversation. Keenly interested in politics, he had a regular supply of *The Economist* sent out from home, and I enjoyed scanning its familiar columns once more. I thought that he was less well-versed on economic themes than on politics, so we had occasional stubborn arguments, but his company was truly congenial. After Partition, having remained in Hazara throughout the succeeding years, he went home to read medicine, and devoted the last years of his life to his profession as a prison doctor, specializing in psychological medicine. On the third day we walked through a sea of mud some eight miles to the border of tribal territory, where we spent some chilly hours attesting the land records to be rewarded in true Pathan fashion by a delightful meal – huge chapattis of wheat cooked with ghee, boiled and fried eggs, fried chicken, pistachios, a cornflour pudding and tea. Once again my heart warmed to these Pathans. At that time the Black Mountain border, where the inhabitants are Pathans of Swathi origin, was quiet and peaceful, though only a few years before news of some communal trouble in Lahore had brought the tribesmens' wrath down on the Hindu shopkeepers in the market town of Battal, which we had by-passed on our way to Bai on the border, but visited on our return journey to Ahl. Quite an elaborate military operation had to be mounted from Abbottabad, but the participation of some RAF planes, flying from the polo ground, soon dispersed the marauding lashkar and restored the tranquillity of the area. I retain a vivid memory of that day because on the way up to Bai, having crossed a river about a mile beyond Battal, we climbed a fairly steep ridge to about 6,500 feet and at its crest emerged onto a circular plain, about three miles in diameter, absolutely flat but fringed by forests and surrounded by a rim of mountains, some of them 10,000 feet. I saw that plain as an ideal summer holiday resort, with golf, polo, tennis and fishing, and possibilities too of winter sport like skiing. Clearly in those days it was too near the tribal border for such a scheme but to my mind it had all the attractions of Gulmarg in Kashmir, and at a lower altitude. Even at that time, a motor road to Battal was under construction and it would be no surprise to learn that the Konsh valley today rivals the Swat valley as a tourist attraction in Pakistan.

Whenever I returned to headquarters from one of those tours, I used to be amused by the remarks made by my growing circle of friends. They clearly found it hard to believe that I actually enjoyed spending a couple of weeks in the month 'away from civilization', which to them meant Abbottabad, 'with nobody to talk to', as if humble *hazarawals* were dumb as well as ignorant. Yet Abbottabad was an exceptionally nice station, and I was always happy there. Beautifully situated at around 4,000 feet on the edge of the Rash plain and the slopes of the pine-clad Brigade Circular Hill, it was a well-wooded cantonment with pleasant gardens, a fine polo ground and passable golf course with grass greens, and a nice sense of space on every side. Only the busy bazaar area and the centre of the old town were congested. The military population and its camp followers had grown considerably since 1939. It included the headquarters and training battalions of three famous Indian regiments – the 13th Frontier Force Rifles, the 5th Royal Gurkha Rifles and the 6th Gurkhas. A few miles away at Kakul there was an artillery centre, and in 1941 the RIASC depot there expanded dramatically with the continuous passage of large numbers of British officers, taken out from home for special training before posting to various units of the Indian Army. There was also a new development – the Army School of Frontier Warfare, about which I shall say more later. Inevitably, such a military population created an active social life. At guest nights in the Piffer mess,[4] I was frequently meeting new friends, some of them officers just out from home with news of places and people that were dear to me. Twice within a month I spotted officers wearing the tartan of the Gordon Highlanders – once at the cinema, once at a mess dinner – who turned out to come from my part of Scotland and to know many of my friends. They were both golfers, and with them and various of their colleagues to whom they introduced me I had keen games on Saturday afternoons or Sunday mornings for several months, whenever I was 'in station'.

An extraordinary feature of Abbottabad was the number of military families who were there, stranded in a sense by the War. Many of the husbands were of course away in the field on active service, and only a few of them were able occasionally to rejoin their wives and children for a fortnight's leave. The Abbottabad Club was a friendly and lively place. For quite a long time I was rather toffee-nosed about it, regarding it as inevitably an English enclave of snobbery, which was the impression I had gleaned of the Dehra Dun Club, and I went there only occasionally for library books or tea and toast at dusk after golf. But every Wednesday and Saturday there were cheerful dinner dances at which the bands of one or other of the Gurkha regiments played with a lively sense of rhythm. When the 5th Gurkhas were playing the moment would come for the second in command, Major Pat le Marchant, to take the baton and put some punch in their quickstep, 'On the sunny side of the street', and everybody's spirits rose. I was often asked to join a party for the dinner dance and thoroughly enjoyed the relaxation, even learning for the first time to avoid kicking my partner's shins. The hostesses at these parties were sometimes the wives of senior army officers in the station, sometimes one or other of the numerous grass widows to whom I have referred, more often the wives of senior civilian officers of the district. Their husbands were the resident Sessions Judge, Paul May of the ICS, the Assistant Commissioner, Mansehra subdivision, about fifteen miles from Abbottabad, Major Oliver St John of the IPS, and the Chief Conservator of Forests NWFP, Henniker Gotley, whose headquarters for the whole province were in Abbottabad. They all showed much kindness to me in many ways.

I have recorded the departure of Gerald Curtis, the DC to whom I had been posted for training. Within the next three months there were three new DCs. Gerald Emerson who had been at Mansehra before Oliver St John and had to be recalled from an adventurous and unauthorized trip into the heart of Kohistan to take over from Curtis, stayed only a month before becoming Secretary to the Governor in Peshawar. His wife was in England and he was succeeded by Hugh Richardson who at that time was unmarried. Neither took any interest in the social life of the station, and they were regarded by the army people as rather aloof – but I found each exceptionally friendly and I was encouraged by both in the habit of dropping in at the DC's house for a teatime session of official and non-official gossip, from which I derived much information as well as amusement. I also became friendly with the Superintendent of Police, H.F. Scroggie, more friendly than anyone else could imagine, for he was a dour Scot, very unhappy because his wife was ill in Edinburgh, and he would talk to nobody about his private affairs. He was a fine golfer and we managed to play together occasionally – he was too busy and perhaps too reserved ever to commit himself to a firm engagement. He was a fine policeman whom I admired greatly. I caught up with him again years later in Peshawar, where he had become responsible for recruiting and training a large force of additional police. His successor in Abbottabad, Maurice Pugh, was a family man and very sociable; in my last year in Abbottabad I lived next door to the Pughs in the civil lines.

A few months after my arrival Colonel Teague was posted overseas and his successor, Jimmy James, who had a large family, was unable to let me stay on in my bed-sitting room in his bungalow. I moved into the house of the new chaplain, a C of E priest called Saunders, from Haslemere, who had been back in England for two years on sick leave and had to leave his wife behind. I continued to take my meals in the Piffer mess. But by now Richardson too had gone to a Deputy Secretary's job in Peshawar and the new DC was Major Daya Singh Bedi of the IPS. About midsummer 1942, shortly before I had been promoted from my supernumerary status to the post of Assistant Commissioner Hazara, Bedi insisted that I should occupy the bungalow allocated to the holder of that post, near his own, the SP's, and those of the Civil Surgeon, an unobtrusive Hindu called Jai Dyal, and the Chief Conservator of Forests.

In my first three months in Abbottabad my responsibilities were naturally limited and I had to spend a good deal of my time in court work. Pat Duncan had left a pile of unfinished cases, being by temperament an innovator rather than a methodical manager of routine business. I felt handicapped both by having too often to pick up a tangle of threads and by the limitations of my magisterial power. These were only of the third class which allowed me to impose only small fines or a short term of imprisonment, so the type of case that turned up endlessly was the 'assault and battery' kind of thing, or the endemic allegation of criminal trespass which often involved a large array of witnesses all giving false evidence for both sides. Occasionally there would be a bit of fun such as when a local doctor and shopkeeper fell on each other in the latter's shop. The doctor complained of the quality of something he had purchased; the shopkeeper denied that it had been supplied from his shop. Actual bodily harm followed. The doctor had the advantage of being able to rush to the hospital for immediate treatment and certification of his injuries while he still bled, while the shopkeeper had to spend time rallying his witnesses. Nothing very unusual, except that men of social standing were involved, giving the case more flavour than most run-of-the-mill examples.

The district was short of magistrates and since all the others were senior to me they off-loaded all the rubbish on the junior Supernumerary Assistant Commissioner. In fact, the Frontier Government, as always more flexible in attitude than those of other provinces, ought not to have given me any magisterial powers at all until they knew that I had passed my probationery examinations and 'signed the covenant' with the Secretary of State for India as a member of the ICS. So far as I could gather most of my Dehra Dun colleagues were having to kick their heels in their provinces and wait for clearance. There seemed to be interminable delays about the results of the examinations. It was the middle of December 1941 before the signal arrived from London and Delhi via Peshawar that I was to sign the covenant, and another month before the detailed results of the examinations came from Dehra Dun. My marks were 7th out of 29 candidates, and 3rd amongst the British 12, of whom Brian Williams was top, and David Elliot, also of the Punjab Commission, next. I was greatly pleased with this, but what really mattered was the solemn pride of being covenanted through the Secretary of State himself to serve the Crown in India. I never lost my pride in that achievement; it still ranks as high in my esteem as anything I have attained in my later career.

Once that hurdle was passed, promotion was to come quicker

than I expected – less on account of any personal merit than because of the wartime exigencies of the Service. In only a few months I was Additional District Magistrate with first-class powers enabling me to sentence a criminal to two years' rigorous imprisonment and to take the preliminary stages of a murder trial, sending the cases up to the Sessions Judge if I was satisfied that the evidence established a prima facie case against the accused. Inevitably court work at once became more interesting, particularly when the results of appeals against my judgments began to come back to me from the Sessions Judge and the Judicial Commissioner in Peshawar, the High Court of the Province. I had little clerical help as stenographers were very scarce and wrote my judgments in longhand in the evenings; this was an exercise in weighing evidence in the balance and formulating a decision which I thoroughly enjoyed.

Unexpectedly, at the beginning of December 1941 there was a complete break with this routine. Perhaps partly as a result of the lessons of the campaign in Abyssinia and partly in anticipation of campaigns to come, GHQ decided to establish an Army School of Frontier Warfare (ASFW) which was located at Kakul, about six miles from Abbottabad, at the other side of the Rash plain on the skirts of the hills leading up to the high range at Thandiani. It was a natural choice of site. British expertise in the basic principles of mountain warfare derived from long experience of campaigns against Pathan tribes. More sophisticated weapons and equipment were now becoming available, but in mountainous terrain they would bring no advantage unless the basic principles were observed. Experience was to teach bitter lessons in this regard – perhaps especially to American troops, who took a long time to appreciate that before they could drive their tanks and half-tracks forward into mountain passes the infantry must first capture the high ground on foot. The Commandant of the ASFW at Kakul was Colonel F.E. le Marchant, uncle of Pat, the 5th Gurkha 2i/c, who had been on attachment with British troops in Norway and in North Africa. He was an experienced Gurkha officer and a tremendous enthusiast, determined that if the Indian Army had to meet a German thrust from the Caucasus through Afghanistan their training would have prepared them adequately to cope.

Sir George Cunningham kept in close touch with the Army. He was a close personal friend of some of its most distinguished officers, like Sir Richard O'Connor and Sir Claude Auchinleck.

He felt that in frontier warfare close cooperation between the political officers and the military was always going to be essential in the tribal areas, even if the direct enemy were to be German rather than Pathan. Colonel le Marchant certainly agreed and when the Governor requested a place for me on the first of his courses I was accepted. As it turned out, this was a course for senior officers and I found myself spending three intensive weeks along with two or three junior staff officers of the rank of captain, in a group in which the brigadiers and colonels outnumbered the majors and lesser mortals. It was a stimulating and valuable experience. Nobody pulled rank on me or questioned my complete lack of experience of frontier conditions. Before the end of the course I had to play the role of the political officer in an exercise for which I had to write the political scenario, performing under the critical eyes of not only le Marchant but also of General Quinan, then GOC Northern Command.

I shall never forget the encouragement I derived from words of praise from the General in his summing up of the exercise. All this was happening at a time of deep anxiety in India. To all the worries about events in Europe, North Africa and on the Russian front was added at the start of our course the news of the Japanese landings in Malaya and the sinking of the *Prince of Wales* and *Repulse* when they put to sea from Singapore. My thoughts were full of what was happening to my friends – old school and university friends in various branches of the armed forces, members of my training company in the Black Watch who had gone to the Middle East, recent friends from the 13th Frontier Force Rifles who had just left Abbottabad for Malaya and for death or its equivalent as Japanese prisoners of war. My conscience was uneasy about my non-combatant status and newly secured prospects of an established career in what could be designated an imperialist role. Even though I was not in uniform it was comforting to be working so closely with men who were, to be accepted by them as having something significant to do with them and to feel that I was not in fact running away from danger. The intellectual challenge of these three weeks was quite considerable but I felt at ease with it. After all, when I was a rookie in the Black Watch I had been far happier on some tactical exercise than having to strip down and assemble the parts of a Bren gun. I went back to Abbottabad for Christmas feeling quite pleased with myself. I had been working hard and needed a break.

Christmas proved to be more enjoyable than I expected. Brian Williams had been posted to Campbellpur in the Punjab, only about sixty miles away, and he accepted my invitation to spend the holiday at Abbottabad. Hugh Richardson, then still DC, had decided to spend the period at Tarbela, writing reports and working on his Tibetan dictionary. He kindly offered his delightful bungalow to us and we were comfortable, quiet and warm – the nights were really cold and frosty. We played some tennis and Brian introduced me to the game of squash. As the week went by we got asked to more and more parties – childrens' tea parties, the Christmas night dance at the Club and the Red Cross Ball on New Year's Eve. Having begun the holiday in a quiet, nostalgic mood, both of us suffering from a severe bout of homesickness, we ended it feeling refreshed and quite merry. We were healthy and resilient at that stage in our careers.

Notes

[1] The *Patwari* is the lowest form of life in the hierarchy of officialdom, concerned with the recording of ownership and tenancy of holdings.
[2] *Sirkar* = Government personified by its senior official.
[3] Interestingly, of the advocates who were willing to make the trip, two were men for whom I formed a particular regard and friendship. Khan Sahib Chowdry Mohammed Ali many years later became Vice-Chancellor of the University of Peshawar. I last met him at the Commonwealth Universities Conference in London in 1963, when he took the chair at a session attended by the Duke of Edinburgh, whom he amused by his firmness in cutting short long-winded contributions from certain senior but self-important academics. The other, Sajjad Ahmed, became one of Pakistan's most notable judges and held the tricky post of Electoral Commissioner in 1976-7, when the validity of the results returning Prime Minister Bhutto to power was so fiercely, and successfully, challenged.
[4] The old name for the Punjab Frontier Force had been corrupted to the nickname Piffer.

CHAPTER V

Apprenticeship Completed

Early in 1942, Major Bedi took over from Hugh Richardson. I remember my apprehension. I was afraid that I would find him less impressive than any of the British DCs for whom I had worked and that my judgment would be prejudiced because he was an Indian. Apart from Sher Afsar, whom I greatly liked and respected, I had not had a great deal to do with any Indian officer. I had very little contact with Captain Allahdad of the Indian Political Service who had been AC Hazara until November. After his departure the post was vacant until I was promoted to it in the following summer.

Unfortunately, Bedi cultivated a highly polished manner, loud and jerky, rather grandly dressed, and very much the huntin', shootin', fishin' type that I could not abide amongst Englishmen. I must have made a very stout effort to discount his style for I managed to stay on reasonable personal terms with him for the next two years. He was in fact always pleasant and charming to me and most hospitable. His father often visited Abbottabad from the family estates near Rawalpindi; he was the hereditary leader of a highly-respected sect of Sikhs. His wife and family were always very pleasant, but not stimulating intellectually. There was a rather harmless, good-for-nothing son, a rather sickly fellow who seemed perpetually to be postponing a decision to join the Army or do anything useful; and two pretty and quite lively daughters in their late teens. Their family circle was very cheerful. They entertained a great deal, and through them my circle of Indian friends widened considerably. The trouble was that Bedi came with rather a poor reputation as a political officer, and within a couple of weeks I was certain that he deserved it. He was lazy and opinionated, and far more interested in getting work out of me than in furthering my basic training. As the load on me increased, I was on the horns of a dilemma. I knew that I must pass examinations in Urdu, and ultimately Pushtu, and in Revenue Law and Administration, and also acquire knowledge and practice in the field of Civil Law, as well as Criminal Law, in whose procedures I was already immersed. Lionel Jardine, the Revenue and District Commissioner for the province (R and DC) who was nominally responsible for arranging my training, and actually read my tour reports – but for many months never saw me – strongly advised me not to rush into attempting examinations, and virtually warned me that if I did I would fail. Since he was the examiner, he was therefore well-placed to prophesy; moreover he was an ardent Buchmanite, accustomed to higher guidance on all such matters. My own instinct was that I would never do anything well unless I followed the training manuals and took the examinations; and I felt that the circumstances of the war might come to make normal procedures impossible – so the sooner I applied myself to the books and tried the exams the better.

As soon as he arrived Bedi had to face up to a growing crisis over food supplies. I had talked a good deal to Emerson and Richardson about this and at the latter's request had begun to work on a survey of the position in the district, and incidentally to make frequent allusions to local conditions in my tour diaries. When Bedi called me in to discuss it, he delivered his opinion in the form of a lecture and talked such nonsense that I was in despair – he really was a bumptious chap.[1] The DC was anxious to see my completed report on food supplies. Reluctantly I agreed although Richardson had shared my view that I would do a better job on it if I took my time, all the while adding new bits of information culled on tours to different localities. In fact I completed the drafting during the rainy weekend of my tour to Ahl with Tollinton and Bedi had the thirty-page typescript the following week.

A day or two later he told me that he wanted me to take charge of food and price-control matters, which were the responsibility of one of his Extra Assistant Commissioners Abdul Manan, a member of the Provincial Civil Service. Before any formal instructions were issued, he went off to Haripur, and the next day, cycling past the municipal offices after lunch, I saw what looked like the start of a riot. Several hundred people were struggling to get in, in order to get vouchers for grain from the Clerk of Municipality. I decided to intervene and bought some time by insisting on pushing through the crowd into his office. They were respectful enough to let me enquire what was going on and to laugh at my attempts to exchange jokes in Urdu, but soon they got impatient again and I sent a cryptic message to Scroggie asking for police help. This came very quickly in the form of forty constables under proper command, and I got order restored, not only to the crowd but to the muddled system of vouchers. Two days passed as I worked on this without a sign of Abdul Manan or a message from the DC.

The crisis in the town had followed from the decision of the Punjab Government to embargo the movement of foodgrains out of their province. The large wartime growth of population in Abbottabad made the town very vulnerable to any check in the normal flow of supplies to the grain dealers. While the Army had their own stocks under control, at that stage they did not provide the needs of the large numbers of civilian camp followers who served them as bearers, cooks, dhobis, sweepers and so on – and usually had their own families living in the compounds of army bungalows or in the neighbourhood of regimental lines. When the Punjab embargo was imposed, Bedi and Abdul Manan had arranged for a municipal depot to be opened, with vouchers for purchases to be issued by the clerk, but they had taken no real steps to assess demand or guarantee supply and rumours were soon spread that the Government's own supplies were inadequate. No doubt the commercial grain dealers helped to spread the rumours in order to boost the price at which they could sell on the black market.

When Bedi returned he asked for an estimate of our needs so I sent him a draft letter to the Revenue Department in Peshawar which he sent on, having added a nought to the figure in my estimate, thus exaggerating the amount of our requisition from the centre by a factor of ten. I was so horrified when I discovered this that I decided to telephone privately to inform both Emerson and Richardson in Peshawar about the position. The crisis was not confined to Abbottabad or Hazara and it was in my view dangerous to distort needs in this way, running the risk of diverting supplies from the point of greatest need. Moreover, the important thing was to try to get the private trade working again as normally as possible. The way to do that seemed to be to ensure that adequate, not excessive, supplies were at the DC's disposal to meet an emergency, and to make these available below the formal market price, and well below the black market price. The scheme

Brigadier Willis, Commandant Abbotabad Brigade HQ
with veteran Hazarawal.

worked: within a few days stocks that had been in the district's
mandis all the time, but had gone underground, re-emerged
bringing prices tumbling down, and our emergency depot ceased
to have pressure put on it.

I was exhausted by my first exposure to something like a civil
disturbance and by the manoeuvres I had to undertake to get
things on an even keel, partly behind the back of my DC, and
wholly without formal authorization of responsibility to me. In the
course of this minor crisis I had gone to the Brigade Commander,
who was naturally disturbed both by the upset to the normal
tranquillity of Abbottabad and by the effect on the efficiency of
his units, produced by the absence from work of numerous civilian
followers who were queuing for rations and threatening to riot. We
reached agreement on conditions under which the Army would
itself make supplies available to them and a useful understanding

on various other aspects of civil-military cooperation. I was already better known to the military hierarchy than any other civilian official, largely because of the arrangements made by the Governor and Curtis to have me attached 'for rations' to the 10/13th Frontier Force Rifles and the contacts and friendships with military personnel that followed.

Partly because of this incident, partly perhaps because of my survey of the district's food problems, and maybe because somebody in Government recalled that I had a degree in Economics, from that stage I seemed to acquire a reputation for being an embryonic specialist in economic problems, and this undoubtedly helped to shape my future career in the NWFP, setting it along rather different lines from those of Pat Duncan and John Dent. In retrospect, the food shortage in Hazara before the *rabi* (spring harvest) in the spring of 1942 was a pretty ordinary affair of no real consequence. Yet in its own way it was symbolic of *taqleef* which the war had yet to bring to India. Hints of possible famine, of breakdown in normal economic arrangements, of weakness in Government's system of administration, of urban chicanery and popular unrest, were all there to be pondered. That spring was filled with unease as India watched the reactions of politicians to the dramatic constitutional prospects opened up by the mission of Sir Stafford Cripps. My own view was that the political parties would be foolish not to accept the British Government's offer, but I feared that this would be the result and that it might quickly lead either to some sort of martial law or to anarchy, and that either way that would open the door to the Japanese, who probably could not win through to the heart of India in a military thrust, unless our defence was confounded by the political situation. In one sense, I felt my conscience had been cleared by the terms of the Cripps offer for it no longer seemed possible honestly to accuse the British of selfish imperialism. In one letter to my mother, I wrote that 'nobody can reasonably say now that we are selfish or imperialistic, or careless of the fate of India, or that our motive is to split the unity of India. The division of India may result from our suggestions, but not because we intend so – only because Indians are such bad neighbours to each other.'

Uncertainty about the future of my service was acute. At the same time the atmosphere of social cheerfulness in Abbottabad was forced and false. Far too many men who had just a month or two before been familiar faces in the mess or the club were now 'missing'. The newspapers in India were full of pathetic advertisements from wives and families asking for any information that might reveal whether a husband or father was alive, wounded, or a prisoner of war. Life had suddenly acquired uncomfortable qualities; the truth had to be hidden behind unrealities. My protective mechanism was work. My responsibilities for foodstuffs and price controls were quickly confirmed and I also had to take on the role of Administrator to the municipalities of Abbottabad and Nawanshahr, a busy market town just a few miles away. All this gave me a fair load of office work in which I had two staunch helpers. Ram Dutt was my Hindu camp clerk and really my personal assistant in every aspect of my duties. He was a member of a particularly well-respected high-caste Hindu sect, though not a man of great worldly substance. By strength of character he had the respect of the Muslims of Hazara to an unusual degree for a lowly Hindu clerk. He was highly intelligent and articulate, with a cheerful sense of humour that was quite uncharacteristic of his background and for me he worked faithfully and without stint of energy till I left the district. Mohammed Sarwar Jan was the clerk to Abbottabad Municipality. At first he seemed to have the obsequiousness of manner that one associated more with a Hindu clerk than a Muslim, though Ram Dutt had none of it. As I got to know him better, he remained deferential and gentle, but showed openness and strength of purpose that proved very helpful, for he too was intelligent, hardworking and well-informed. Moreover, at a time when one knew that clerks were exposed even more than usual to the temptations of corruption, neither of these men ever caused me anxiety on that score, though there were plenty who would willingly have informed against them if they could have brought real evidence to bear in persuading me that they were unreliable.

They had a pretty good record at a time when all round them dealers and merchants were being prosecuted for infringements of our regulations, and rivalry for permits and quotas frequently led to serious breaches of the peace, as well as less overt offences. In one letter home I told how two of the leading merchants at the Havelian *mandi*, an important market at the railhead of the branch line from Taxila, then the main route for supplies not only to Hazara and its tribal areas but also to Kashmir, Chilas, Gilgit and Hunza, came to blows in the bazaar, and immediately more than a dozen of their rivals and associates joined in freely so that plenty of blood flowed. In the subsequent police case there were so many charges and countercharges and so many 'principal accused' parties that I felt hopelessly caught in their crossfire as I sat in court trying to set them to rights and restore some cooperation to the conduct of their essential business. In the letter to my mother, having named two of the best-known merchants of our home town as the supposed principals and a number of others as parties to the cudgelling and fisticuffs, I asked her to picture the scene in those terms and ask herself what hope there was for a community in which the leading personalities behaved like that.

These incidents had their comic side, but a serious aspect also. One of my concerns was to keep normal trade moving with as little disruption as possible. It was bad enough having to impose quotas and price controls, and cope with sudden shortages resulting from external causes, like Punjab politics and embargoes, but reasonable distribution would become impossible if the private trading system broke down, perhaps out of rivalry and greed for excessive profits. It was perhaps the natural tendency of the British system of administration in India to seek to enforce the law and prosecute breaches of regulations in court rather than to substitute government agencies for private enterprise. (Here I am referring to statutory regulations like the Defence of India Regulations, wartime emergency legislation rather than offences under the Indian Penal Code.) Normal procedures took a great deal of the time and energy of police and magistrates, and of course the legal profession, and the result could be unsatisfactory because the evidence was not always reliable. On several occasions I was upset and indeed shocked when the Deputy Commissioner intervened in a case before my court, ordering it to be withdrawn. I had no doubt that he did so on representation by the parties and I did not like the smell of it, though the effect of getting everyone quickly back to work was satisfactory.

At that time, a great effort was on hand to raise funds for special war purposes of which my favourite was the Indian Red Cross. I began frankly to exploit my opportunities to boost the Red Cross funds. As early as possible in the accumulation of evidence a suggestion would be made to the parties that the case could be withdrawn if a contribution to the Red Cross were forthcoming. Invariably this was at once agreed. There was a kind of tariff applied, according to the charge against the accused. They knew that it bore a relationship to the fine they might expect if they were found guilty, and paying the Red Cross meant that they even acquired some *izzat* (respect and standing in the community), and avoided the stigma of a conviction, as well as further legal expenses in the event of an appeal to a higher court. The procedure certainly saved my time, that of the police and the higher courts, while even the legal profession accepted it readily, partly because it saved their time and they were not short of work, and possibly because there was no abatement of the fees they were charging their clients in any case.

I have no doubt that this practice was a risky indulgence. It was clearly one that could be represented as open to serious abuse on my part, but I believe that I was so naive and honest that the notion never crossed my mind, and also that by now I had the sort of reputation in the district for sympathetic and honest dealing with the people that nobody at that time would have thought of complaining against me. A year or two later when the political scene in India had changed and it became commonplace to launch attacks on government servants, I might not have got away with it. For the present, the province was governed quite happily under Section 93 of the Government of India Act by the Governor through the Civil Service, and the provincial political parties kept in the background. The flow of funds to the Indian Red Cross from Hazara was exceptionally generous, and not a few of the leading merchants exploited their benefactions in their advertisement. It was surely better to advertise that you had paid a thousand rupees to the Indian Red Cross than to proclaim that you had been fined the equivalent sum for a breach of price control regulations!

For a considerable time in the spring of 1942 my new responsibilities interfered with touring and the proper pattern of my training. But there were occasional breaks from office routine. One came in connection with a big north-west Indian air defence exercise, for which I was appointed as an umpire at the request of the Army. This provided a legitimate opportunity to exercise a schoolboyish imagination in a serious purpose – scheming where to set off thunderflashes, smoke bombs and incendiaries so as to test our rudimentary civil defence arrangements, and plotting how to embarrass the Deputy Commissioner by setting particular problems in civil and military liaison. For several evenings I had great fun. To his credit, the DC not only took embarrassment in good part, but energetically set about applying the lessons of the exercise to a reorganisation of the local arrangements to deal with the possibility of attack from the air.

A real break came at the end of March when I spent several days at Haripur with the DC, officiating at a big agricultural show and *mela* or fair. Much effort was put into this event, partly for the encouragement of agriculture but also 'to show the flag' to the people of a district which was now one of the most important areas of recruitment for the Indian Army. We felt that it was time the people enjoyed something of a circus even if we had been finding it hard to supply some of them with bread. Huge crowds turned up, and certainly enjoyed themselves – and so did the good representation of army officers, some of them with their families, whom I had persuaded in Abbottabad to pay the show a visit.

I was surprised at the efficiency of the arrangements and at the quality of some of the animals exhibited. Besides having to take charge of the comfort of the large party of VIPs, (including the Adviser to the Governor, who was during the Governor's rule in effect Deputy Chief Minister of the province) and the Nawab of Amb, I found myself allocated some surprising roles. One was to judge the bees. This function for some years had been ably discharged by Gerald Curtis when he was DC, but why it should have been devolved on me was a mystery. Being totally ignorant of everything involved save one vital fact, I found my own solution to the problem. The vital fact was that I knew who was by far the best beekeeper in the district. Gerald Curtis had told me about him. He was a shy young graduate who lived near Haripur – a place of orchards and flowers – and had, so Gerald told me, pioneered the use of scientific methods in developing an apiary, an example which Curtis had tried with some success to get others to follow, including some village cooperatives. I simply took this competitor aside, told him that he had won first prize and must conduct me round the exhibit, pointing out good features and bad in the entries, and undertaking any necessary risks such as opening hives and examining combs of honey. I stuck close to his side and everyone felt that it was perfectly proper for the sahib to get someone to do the physical work for him, so that honour was satisfied all round. For the next two years I was the official judge of beekeeping at any similar event in Hazara, so surely I cannot have been a failure!

Another task was judging the tent-pegging competition. Here I

A wartime mela *at Abbotabad, March 1942.*

had the guidance of Paul May, the Sessions Judge, who was experienced at this sport – at judging the event, not at the sport itself. Paul was a natural comic and one of his eccentricities was his peculiar inability to perform naturally or gracefully any form of physical activity. He once told me what had finally convinced him that he should specialize in judicial work rather than continue as a district officer. Inspecting land records outside a village in the Punjab, he had tethered his horse to the back of his chair while he sat checking entries in the Khasra Girdawari. Wondering after a time why the villagers seemed too distracted to answer his questions, he looked round to find that the horse was chewing his way through the *jamabandi*, a large and even more important and permanent volume of records on which the whole revenue system depended. But he had applied his considerable intellectual powers to the tricky problem that confronted the judges of a tent-pegging competition and knew exactly where to place Oliver St John and myself who were the other members of his team. The skill of the competitors surprised me and their speed was astonishing. They seemed just as good as the Scots Greys and the Lancers, who used to give exhibitions at the agricultural shows of my boyhood at Nairn.

Some of the riders had other spectacular skills, like *nimbu tarashi* – cutting lemons fixed to the end of rods by a sword slash administered at a gallop, perhaps standing in the saddle or riding bareback for variation. One pensioned Indian cavalry havildar performed some remarkable feats on a country pony. When it stood still, his pony mount looked incapable of the speed and stamina which it demonstrated in action. There were other diversions exhibiting local pastimes – like the Kabbadi competition. This was a game like schoolboys' 'tag' in which one runner had to try to get from one end of the field to the other without either of two opponents laying a hand on him. Very simple, but skilful and exciting in performance and a very popular sport in Hazara villages. Equally exciting were the bullock races where the driver stands behind his bullock on a tiny board and, having goaded them into surprising pace, tries from his precarious position to steer them in the right direction as they pull him wildly over the bumpy ground. After that, horse racing and tug-of-war seemed mundane.

There were also pipe bands to entertain the crowds. One was supplied by the Patiala Regiment, at that time stationed in

Abbottabad. They were magnificent Sikh stalwarts in their colourful uniforms. But I had my own protégés – the Adolescent Convicts' Pipe Band from the provincial central jail at Haripur. I had visited this remarkable institution several times since first being taken there by Sher Afsar several months before. It had been built only a few years earlier by a provincial government enlightened by a remarkable Inspector General of Prisons – a big Irish doctor, Shelley Smith, whom everyone referred to as Haripur Smith. It housed all the province's long-term prisoners and had a big wing for boys and adolescents. It has to be remembered that some serious crimes like murder often carried a lighter social stigma in Frontier society than we attach to them in the West. This is because many of these crimes were committed as a result of blood feuds, to preserve the family's honour or avenge some family hurt, which may not only be condoned but approved in the Pathan code of honour. Committed in British India, the crimes were dealt with under the Indian Penal Code and carried 'normal' sentences, but some at least of the convicts were not vicious criminals who might be a danger to society as a whole. The jail was years ahead of its time as an institution of penal reform. The mens' quarters were comfortable and spacious, with electric fans and lighting, adequate water and sanitation, providing conditions far superior to and healthier than anything they had ever enjoyed at home. Emphasis in their regime was on training in useful skills and crafts, and the jail's workshops were better equipped and organized for a range of industrial products than any of the private manufacturing industries of NWFP at the time. There was a large element of self-discipline in the regime, senior prisoners 'of good character and behaviour' being entrusted with supervision and enforcement of prison regulations. Most of the marshalling of the huge crowds at the Haripur Show was done by them; they wore dark green uniforms and carried *lathis*, long sticks like a boy scout's pole.

On one of my earlier visits I had heard the boys' pipe band practising and made some remarks about the appropriate speed of certain tunes they were playing. I was at once nominated their patron and when I next heard them and said that they were improving, I was very popular. While we were at the show, which went on for several days, Bedi and I stayed in the excellent rest house provided at the jail for visiting inspecting officers or other VIPs. It was probably the most comfortable rest house in the province, partly of course because it was new, and all round it were the prison gardens with the flowers for which Haripur is famous.

Diversions of a different sort resulted on separate occasions from visits to Abbottabad by the Vicereine and the Bishop of Lahore. Lady Linlithgow came for two nights with Sir George and Lady Cunningham and visited the TB sanatorium at Dadar in Mansehra subdivision, to which I have already alluded. She had no major public engagements so her coming presented no great administrative problems, but the DC gave a splendid tea party for invited guests and the usual problems of protocol arose in arranging presentations and so on. Though it was the first time I had ever been in the proximity of pseudo-royalty, it was assumed by Bedi that I should naturally take charge of this sort of thing, and I had to put in a little study on orders of precedence and measure out the paces between various spots in his garden, as well as make sure that I had a decent stiff white collar. It was quite amusing to be consulted by some of the senior guests about the correct ways of bowing from the neck (men), or curtsying (ladies), for I had absolutely no faith in my ability to escape tripping over my own feet. There was some heart-burning in the cantonment about the limited number of invitations received. Quite rightly Bedi decided that since very few of the senior army people had extended hospitality to him and his family, he was under no obligation automatically to invite everyone above a certain rank to his party. He had a proper sense of pride as well as a rather false one. In the end we all enjoyed the event and I felt less awkward and less 'bolshie' than I had expected. Lady Linlithgow stood well over six feet tall, and was extremely stately and regal, dwarfing our wiry and athletic Governor as they moved around. But she was quite relaxed and affable and we all took our cue from our own Lady Cunningham whom everyone admired and loved, and acquitted ourselves well.

The Bishop came primarily to visit his C of E flock to which I did not belong, and I had not expected to meet him. My landlord Padre Saunders delegated the role of host and hostess to the Gotleys with whom Bishop Barnes stayed, but he prepared the programme. He was surprised and I suspect dismayed when a message came from the Gotleys on the second day that the Bishop wanted some relaxation from his official commitments and proposed to play golf in the late afternoon with me. I felt this was a great honour – not because I was to play with a bishop, but because this particular bishop had played for the Oxford and

Cambridge team which first went to the USA to play against an American team in an event which was so successful that it became the biennial contest for the Walker Cup. While he might have lost some of his youthful fire, I suspected that he would not have lost much of his cunning and artful skill. I was right to feel keyed up. He played splendidly and very competitively, and as happens on these occasions when one feels that one's opponent is thoroughly congenial as well as proficient, he brought the best out of me. I won by the narrowest possible margin attributable certainly to my local knowledge, and my soul derived more benefit from the good man's blessing on the golf course than it had enjoyed for many months. The game added savour to my dreams for a long time, for over the next few months I got so little golf that I lost my form completely.

A month or so later, following up a notion that I had canvassed with the Bishop at Abbottabad, I took the padre to Government House at Nathia Gali one afternoon for tea. He had now been persuaded that his voluntary helpers should organize YMCA canteens in Kakul and Abbottabad for British officers and other ranks, whose number had grown dramatically, without any regard being paid to their social needs. Many of the officers were birds of passage, attending short courses in Kakul and often housed in very temporary quarters. The number of British other ranks was much smaller – they were mainly skilled men of REME, or attached to the RIASC, or signallers at the important and very hush-hush wireless depot in Abbottabad, where signal traffic on the Russian front could be monitored. For these men especially there was a need for a canteen, for they had no recreational facilities at their units and were not eligible to join the Abbottabad Club. But the padre, now persuaded of the need, was looking for money; hence our visit to Government House. Sir George listened quietly to the plans, asked pertinent questions about who would serve on the committee of management and then promised help both from official and from private funds – 'but on condition that you serve beer and there is no grandmotherly legislation!'

This gives an inadequate and mundane impression of the wartime impact on Abbottabad of large numbers of British soldiers. Individuals who were rich in talent seldom stayed long enough to make their mark, though one met or heard of plenty of these from many professions and different walks of life. There were King's Counsel, 'failed MPs' (unsuccessful Parliamentary candidates), musicians (both classical and from music halls and dance bands), actors and artists, to give a few examples. Occasionally some of this talent could be harnessed for a week or so. There was a brave performance of J.B. Priestly's *Dangerous Corner* at the club. For a few weeks Kakul could provide a dance band of six or seven professionals, some of them from bands famous to all radio listeners in the 1930s. But it was difficult to organize such things. The men normally arrived 'anonymous' in terms of their civilian past, they were preoccupied by their training, with little free time, and unable to rely on being free at the right time to contribute to the community's recreational needs. Nor was the possession of individual talent really characteristic of the great majority of this mass of soldiery. They had been ill-prepared for life in India and many were sadly uninterested, and consequently often appeared boorish and mannerless in their conduct. It was a saddening experience to have to deal with some of their misdemeanours which caused far greater offence to the sensitive local residents than the Army readily acknowledged. Occasionally the local police, intervening in the bazaar at nights when no military police were around, were embarrassed, not wishing to handle British sahibs roughly. More than once I was rung up late at night by a sub-inspector who needed to be assured that it was in order, in the circumstances he reported, for him to handcuff an officer.

Of course it was not only British troops who might cause trouble. During a big divisional training exercise prior to departure for Burma, a large number of troops were encamped one night a couple of miles from Abbottabad on the plain. A small party of British REME personnel were carrying out welding repairs late in the evening, working on vehicles belonging to a Madrassi transport unit. Some of the Madrassis in their curiosity got too near to the welders and were slow to withdraw when ordered by the British warrant officer in charge. Some jostling led suddenly to a serious affray in which the warrant officer was killed and a sergeant severely stabbed. The civilian police had to start a murder investigation. The inspector in charge, an exceptionally able and reliable Hindu who belonged to the same martial class and high caste as Ram Dutt, my camp clerk, was baffled by the problems of identification and translation. He had no trouble with the British witnesses and their evidence: his own English was good and he was used to telling one sahib apart from another. But he could not make head or tail of the Madrassis. They all looked alike to him – they were very black – and they spoke a totally unintelligible language. We knew that they were actually quite a well-educated bunch and that most of them understood English pretty well, but they refused to acknowledge this. There were three or four British officers with the MT company; none of them spoke Tamil or Telugu, the languages of their troops and they certainly had to communicate with their men in English. The Madrassi officer who acted as our interpreter was less helpful than we thought he should be. I was called in again next day to an identification parade when the injured sergeant was brought from hospital and carried round the open ranks of the Madrassis on a stretcher. He was very angry at his friend's death and his own injury but he admitted to me that he could never identify the culprits. To him all the black faces looked alike. I was relieved when the General exercised his right, in the military circumstances prevailing, to have the case dealt with by military enquiry and withdrawn from civilian jurisdiction. The division must not be delayed on its way to the war.

In the spring of 1942 we had problems with passers-by of an entirely different kind. These were Kazaks from the high grazing lands of the mountainous plateaus of Eastern Turkestan. Historically their territory was disputed between the Chinese and the Russians. Towards the end of the Thirties the Russians seemed to get the upper hand, and a large body of Kazak nomads became restive, fearful apparently of possible conscription to the Russian Army and no doubt also of Soviet regimentation of their lives and the enforcement of taxation. They set out in their thousands on a huge trek to India – they told us that they had heard there was a just government in Calcutta. When they attempted to enter Tibet, they were turned aside by Tibetan troops, and after terrible privations a large body crossed the pass at Leh late in 1941, having lost many of its members, particularly women and children, and large numbers of its animals – goats, sheep, yaks, horses and camels.

The State of Kashmir was not very welcoming: after a conflict of arms, the Kazaks were disarmed and brought to a sort of prison camp near Muzaffarabad. In the spring of 1941 their plight became a major political issue in India. The Kazaks were – or professed to be – Muslims and Islamic opinion in India was aroused for Kashmir had a Hindu maharaja, and his Government

Scenes at Kazak refugee camp at Tarnawa near Khanpur.

was accused of oppressing these poor refugees who were followers of the prophet. During his short period as DC Hazara, Hugh Richardson took a keen interest in this controversy. He knew Tibet well and was closely associated with B.J. Gould, the officer in the Government of India most directly concerned with that part of the world. B.J. Gould came to Abbottabad for consultations, but before these plans could be confirmed Richardson was transferred. Early in 1942 Bedi was told that the Kazaks were to march through Hazara to a camp to be established at Tarnawa, not far from Khanpur. It was hoped that some would settle there, while others would be taken to other parts of India, like Hyderabad State, where the local authorities were willing to assume responsibility for them. Bedi at first showed no great interest: the orders were coming from the Government of India and he felt no direct responsibility. But when the food crisis developed in February he urged a postponement of the exercise. In the end these poor people were brought to Tarnawa early in May. They were in such a bad state that they could not march as planned, but had to be brought in lorries, which were mostly provided by the Indian Army. Their diet in Kashmir had been so inadequate that when we took them over many were suffering from scurvy. The Khanpur district was well able to supply the balance of fresh fruit and green vegetables to set them on their feet again.

Bedi properly waxed indignant when he saw the state the Kashmir Government had allowed them to get into, and urged everyone – not least his hawking cronies the Gakhar Rajas of Khanpur – to see that they were comfortably established at Tarnawa. The trouble was that Tarnawa had been chosen months before – I think following the discussions between Gould and Richardson – as the site of their encampment, when the weather was cold and the banks of the river near Khanpur ideal. Now the weather was warm and getting hotter every day. There were still several thousand Kazaks and none of them had shed a garment: they were cocooned in felts and furs and long boots, ideal for autumn on the high Pamirs. They did not wash, and the stench struck one a full mile away from the encampment. I forecast that they would die of heatstroke.

But they were tougher that I thought and perhaps helped by the several minor officials who were attached to them to supervise health and sanitation One day in the autumn I had to try one of them for the offence of being in possession of a firearm without a

Scene at Kazak refugee camp at Tarnawa near Khanpur.

licence. It was the first time they had experienced the British Indian code of law. I decided to try the case in the camp at Tarnawa, seated in the open as near as I could get to the river's edge, in the thin hope of catching a refreshing breeze. They stood or squatted around at a respectful distance, silent and puzzled, but clearly curious about the whole strange business. The accused was a venerable grey-beard, in whose tent had been found a light and beautiful elderly Russian hunting rifle. Possession had been attributed to him, though it was more likely to be used by one of several younger male members of his family. The whole party had been disarmed by the Kashmiris and nobody denied that they had been told quite clearly that they were not allowed to bring firearms into British India. Communication of course was difficult because when they arrived we could find only one man in the province who could speak their language with any fluency – a veteran *shikari* (hunter) from Chitral, who had accompanied several British officers on expeditions into the Pamirs and beyond earlier in the century.

With his help, I got on quite well. What did the old man want the rifle for? Oh, to shoot game, like *markhor* (wild goat), or even something smaller. Oh yes, he knew our laws, but he could not see what harm he had done. And so on. There was no alternative to a conviction. I announced that I was not going to fine him but sentence him to imprisonment – a shocked silence; hints of *zulm* (tyranny), of harm to a harmless grey-beard – and then I completed the verdict: imprisonment for one day, to be complete when the court rose. What did that mean, sahib? Well, I have no other case, and after I have explained a few things to you, such as the justice of the British laws and the need for you to obey them, and the virtues of the pure waters of the Harroh River for washing as well as drinking and cooking, the court will rise – and uncle here will be free, with nothing to pay. A buzz of chatter, broad Mongolian features grinning at me, presumably in relief after facing the unknown, the grateful salaam of the old man, who had taken the rap but emerged with *izzat* (respect) enhanced by what I had said about him to them all.

Within the next few months the main body in the encampment began to dwindle as parties broke away for various destinations, including the State of Hyderabad. Some who had extended invitations earlier when the Kazaks were virtually imprisoned in Kashmir became less enthusiastic about their promised hospitality. Some small groups set up in markets in various towns in the Frontier and northern Punjab, plying their crafts, primarily in leatherwork as *mochis* (shoemakers). Some went to Turkey. Theirs had been an extraordinary migration. My part in it was small, but I had been the first magistrate ever to try one of them on a formal charge in accordance with rules of evidence and procedure, so perhaps some of them remembered me. I certainly remember them, not because of their smell, but because of their courage and hardihood before civilization began to corrupt them.

I needed such diversions to escape from the heavy grind of normal casework and abnormal war-induced business like price-control – which is an optimistic generic term for a multitude of chores. I remember how Wednesday afternoons used to test my stamina and temper, just as monthly Senate meetings were wont to do for nearly twenty years at the other end of my career. That period of each week was set aside for petitions by the merchants of the district. I wanted to bring them into the open with their machinations, the better to judge the balance of the information I derived from them and to assess the relative importance and truth of their requests. I remember that the epithet I applied most frequently to them, collectively and individually was *chalak*. They were indeed subtle and cunning, and I learned some useful lessons in their art. Some emerged in stature as dependable and enterprising businessmen, head and shoulders above the average. Interestingly, one or two of these were quite young men whose fathers had sent them to college to get a degree. They seemed better able than others to see how to cooperate in the purposes of government and to be more trustworthy from my point of view. I am sure that it was helpful to talk things over in the open in this way and not to be suspected of receiving individual petitioners at the back door.

The legal profession was occasionally brought in by the parties to such negotiations, but it was best to deal straight with the merchants without intermediaries. Of course I saw a great deal of the district's lawyers and advocates in my court work. There were a lot of them and most of them were very busy with litigation. Some were very ordinary performers, of little help to me as a magistrate, but there were a few for whom I developed a great respect, not just for their forensic skill, but because of the way they genuinely tried to assist the court while promoting the interests of their clients. Among this group there were both Muslims and Hindus. On the whole they seemed to get on quite well with each other, without serious signs of communal bitterness, and the rivalries one detected derived from personality differences rather than political or communal feelings. Some of course were deeply involved with political parties, but I do not remember any of them making me feel uncomfortable because he had strong political views about British rule. One skilful advocate in Abbottabad was Sardar Bahadur Khan, from a village near Haripur, who was brother of the future Field Marshal Ayub Khan, President of Pakistan. Sardar Bahadur became a Provincial Minister within a year or two of my acquaintance with him; he was able, but not as able as several others who were his rivals at the Abbottabad Bar. One of these, Sajjad Ahmed Jan, became a senior judge in the Pakistan Federal Court. Another, K.S. Chowdry Mohammed Ali, became a distinguished public servant of Pakistan and was ultimately Vice-Chancellor of the University of Peshawar. We were overjoyed to meet as Vice-Chancellors in London in 1963 at the Congress of the Association of Commonwealth Universities. More than from any other Indian in Abbottabad, I had enjoyed hospitality in his home, sometimes dining alone with him, sometimes with a small group of his legal friends – both Hindu and Muslim. They were the only advocates who would occasionally desert the precincts of the district courts to represent clients when I chose to hear certain cases in camp, particularly at Dunga Gali, in the summer. They acquired quite a taste for the Friday afternoon trip by bus up the mountain road – but none ever ventured to accompany me on my bicycle down the mountain on Monday mornings.

The Abbottabad Bar had an active club, whose primary purpose I think was to provide tennis facilities. At that time none of them were eligible for membership of the Abbottabad Club. Some of them were very good tennis players and they loved to take on European officers who were keen and as proficient as themselves. I fell sadly far short of their class but they still generously invited me quite often to spend an hour or two with them on their tennis courts. There was a small Bar Club of the same kind at Mansehra and it must have been the practice for the subdivisional officer to be invited there in the same way, because when I was staying in the civil rest house at Mansehra for several days doing some revenue work I was twice invited for an evening's play – though naturally I was much less well acquainted with the lawyers at Mansehra than at Abbottabad. I invariably enjoyed these occasions, less for the tennis at which I often felt embarrassingly bad, than for the relaxed friendship of these men, and I am afraid that I was at times disloyal enough to the British caste system to say openly that I regretted that so few of my fellow countrymen allowed themselves the chance of getting to know Indian friends on these terms. Perhaps I was playing with fire, or letting the side down, but at any rate that was how I felt – though later, when political ugliness showed its face more openly in India I was often irritated and exasperated by politicians' attacks on British ways.

By the middle of April 1942 I was confused and anxious about my career. The Deputy Commissioner was always complaining about being overworked and short-staffed, yet was always going off for days on end – not proper tours, but to shoot with the Nawab of Amb or to hawk with the Rajas at Khanpur. I always seemed to be having the awkward jobs to do – like dealing in his absence with a lorry drivers' strike. As the weeks slipped by, I could find no chance to study the Acts and manuals on which I would have to pass examinations. Bedi came back from a visit to Peshawar with the news that, having once again failed to get the Chief Secretary to find him an experienced officer to fill the post of AC Hazara, he had readily agreed with Mallam that I should do the work – but I would have to move into the official bungalow because he had been paying the rent while it was empty to prevent the Public Works Department from allocating it to the Army. If he lost it he might never get an experienced Assistant Commissioner who was married and had a family to accept the post.

I made a bargain with him: if he allowed me to go into camp in the Galis for a month to find peace to study for exams in June, I would accept all these responsibilities. Naturally the scheme did not work out perfectly. I had to interrupt my mountain tour to put in several hard days at District headquarters, and after the provincial Government moved up to its summer headquarters at Nathia Gali, it transpired that Lionel Jardine, who as Revenue Commissioner was responsible for my training, did not entirely accept the plans of Leslie Mallam (Chief Secretary) and the Deputy Commissioner, and arranged for me to start settlement training under the supervision of Phillip Tollinton in June. Still, I had a refreshing month beginning with a week in the neighbourhood of Nathia Gali, when the Governor himself walked in on me one afternoon with an invitation to spend a long weekend at Government House. With his usual twinkle in his eye, he assured me that I would be free to study all day, provided I joined in any game of bowls he arranged before dinner. As always I enjoyed being mothered by Lady Cunningham – who thought I looked thin and strained for I had had a bout of dysentery brought on by a visit to Tarnawa and Khanpur, and long walks and lingering conversations over breakfast and dinner with Sir George as usual restored me to a more relaxed and calmer attitude to life's problems.

By the middle of May I was enjoying the solitude of the high range between Nathia Gali and Thandiani. The wooden forest bungalows at Dagri, Biran Gali and Thandiani are all beautifully situated between 7,000 feet and 9,000 feet, with views commanding scenery on a magnificent scale. Apart from Thandiani, all were lonely, isolated places, well above the highest range of cultivation, and near the tree line, above which the mountains peaked with grassy Alpine slopes to which the Gujars brought their flocks for summer grazing. The trees were superb: particularly *chir* and pine of several varieties, *deodar*, maple, chestnut, bird cherry and Himalayan oak in all their splendour. At different levels the slopes were ablaze with flowers of various kinds:

The Governor's summer residence at Nathia Gali.

glorious banks of primulas, irises, wild strawberry, columbine, mountain roses, foxglove and a host of Indian plants and shrubs whose names I did not know. On the night after my first march over the peak of Miranjani to Dagri there was a prolonged spectacular thunderstorm, the lightning flashing continuously all around above and below me, the peals of thunder frightening in their intensity, echoing and reverberating from ridge to ridge. The storm cleared the air and for a week my spirit was uplifted by the views I captured. The day after the storm I climbed through a sea of anemonies to the summit above Dagri and was astonished by the scale of the view. Ahead of my path the mountain dropped steeply some 6,000 feet to the River Jhelum in its deep gorge, beyond which stretched Kashmir. Turning slightly to the left. I looked up to the great plume of Nanga Parbat. Looking back over Dagri, a broad silver band on the horizon was the River Indus, about seventy miles away, with all the hills and plains of Hazara intervening. The air was so clear that I could count fifteen ridges, the least of which my map told me was 3,000 feet high. The light was so good that I could define the detail as easily as if I were looking at the ridges contoured on a sand model on a scale of an inch to the mile. Away to the south, a dark smudge on the sky marked the big cement works at Wah in the Punjab.

Some days later, from Thandiani, the view was even more fascinating, for I was more directly above Abbottabad – the directory said sixteen miles away; I reckoned twelve miles as the crow flies. In the clear air, without binoculars, I could spot individual trees that I knew on the golf course and tell which little white square was the church and which was the hospital; I could follow the black-bordered white thread that was the road leaving Abbottabad for Nathia Gali and Murree through the little green patch that was the polo ground and golf course – and almost imagined I knew who was playing at the 4th hole and who at the 11th. Looking down to where my friends were somehow added to my enjoyment in detachment. I had recently had too long a spell of cantonment life and needed a way to restore my sense of proportion and, as I said in a letter to my mother, 'to find a proper sense of humility again'. That came from a week in the forests and mountains speaking to nobody but the occasional simple Gujar, so far as I could follow his dialect, watching the birds and the trees and the flowers and the wonderful succession of mountains, rejoicing in the special kind of silence that one can only find in nature and realizing 'how weak we human beings really are, for, with all our strife and high explosive bombs and armies numbering millions, we can't alter all these things that I've been seeing this week one tiny jot... no man was ever consulted in their making, and not even Hitler in all his fury can ever have a say in their existence.'

Whether these weeks alone in camp promoted my theoretical knowledge of the system of land administration or the principles of civil law, they certainly did my spirit good. Perhaps it was just as well, for the next couple of months were to try it severely. I got back to Abbottabad to find the DC disgruntled because Jardine had won the battle and directed that I was to start my settlement training. There were rushed days of settling both official and private business, the latter involving the move to the Assistant Commissioner's house, equipping it, furnishing it and girding myself to accept responsibility for employing the essential household servants – besides my bearer, Yaqub Khan. That meant a *khansama* (cook), *misalchi* (dish-washer), *mehtar* (sweeper), *dhobi* (laundry man), and *mali* (gardener). I shuddered at the effect on my sorely stretched finances, even though my salary was going up, although I was not entirely taken by surprise by all this. The District Nazir (a kind of office manager in the DC's offices) had taken the trouble to send up to me from time to time official correspondence and files. This was carried up the mountain paths by a cheerful, rustic simpleton, who one day earned far more than his customary *bakshish* by wrapping a particular bundle of letters in a tangle of wild flowers, because he knew they were '*villaiyati dak*' (mail from England) which would please the sahib. One of the tribulations of those times was having to wait for months for replies from home to one's letters, knowing that they might never come because ships might get sunk or airmail lost for various reasons. Another was that letters from home often reported distressing gaps in mail from India, meaning that long letters written in the fatigue of a long day had gone astray. It was little wonder that one's spirit needed uplifting sometimes.

John Dent, who was at that time Assistant Commissioner, Kohat, was seconded to settlement training with me. He had come up to Abbottabad to sit the examination with me in that hectic week at the end of May, sleeping on the verandah of the Padre's bungalow. Jardine had instructed Pat Duncan to come too and join in the settlement work; but Pat was APA South Waziristan and he and his PA in their tribal fastness proved to have more power to resist the Revenue Commissioner's order than the DC Hazara or the DC Kohat. Sadly, the start of our new training was bedevilled by lack of clear guidance from Phil Tollinton, who had like any sensible Settlement Officer taken himself and his touring staff away from the heat of the summer to the cool and remote upper Kagan Valley. Bedi was furious for there were many loose ends to tie up and he wanted to confront Tollinton face to face – not least because he wished to ensure that my absence on training would be abbreviated. The officers at Settlement HQ in the absence of detailed directions from the SO, were determined to play the game according to the book, and follow the instructions of a Victorian manual which envisaged many months of training in one aspect of the work after another. Out of the kindness of his heart, Phil had said that we should start in the Galis, working in a group of small villages in a valley three or four miles from Thandiani, and over 2,000 feet lower down. We were to live in tents as near as possible to our villages. His kindness was in thinking that it would be cooler up there for outdoor work in this season. Unfortunately, he had not himself reconnoitred the area. There was no camp site available in the valley near the cultivation and we had to pitch the tents much higher up on a little saddle, about 1,000 feet below Thandiani and just over a mile from that summer station. We could get down to our village easily enough in the mornings but it was a sweaty pull up in the heat of the afternoon sun after a tiring day in the fields. I can still hear in my memory our cry from afar, *'Taza nimbu tayar karo'* (get fresh lemon ready), and the answering call of our servants.[3] They always had a supply of ice-cold water in a great earthenware *chatti* and a large stock of fresh lemons, which were sliced into big jugs of water with an adequate supply of sugar. It was, I think, the most delicious and refreshing drink I have ever tasted.

So far as I remember we were completely teetotal in camp. I never took alcoholic drinks with me on tour. Scotch whisky was unobtainable at that stage in the War and the Solan version distilled in India was undrinkable, though their gin was passable and the beer produced by the Murree Brewery was good. It was the common drink at the Abbottabad Club, though in the evenings, gin and ginger beer, drunk very long, was a favourite. Any social life we had at Indar Seri camp was 'centred' on the little hill station of Thandiani, so beautifully sited a mile or two away on the crest of the range. It was a tiny place with fewer than twenty bungalows dispersed over a big area. Like Nathia Gali it was quiet, peaceful and friendly and had none of the frenetic, gaiety that is popularly associated with the stereotype of the Indian hill station in 'the season'. Thandiani was relatively cheap in terms of rents and social costs and families could get by for the summer with a minimum number of servants. It was the favourite summer holiday place for the missionaries of northern India, much cheaper and quieter than Murree or Srinagar or Gulmarg. It was also a favourite place for ladies who were expecting babies in the hot weather. Provided they could get up there early enough in their pregnancy, there were plenty of quiet gentle walks along the ridge and congenial, undemanding company. There was usually a medical missionary on hand in case of need. John and I found that summer a little group of families of senior Frontier policemen, whose husbands would probably join them for a month or for two or three shorter spells of casual leave. There was also one Frontier 'political' family – that of J.O.S. Donald, who had succeeded Roger Bacon as PA Khyber. He himself was in residence when we visited and we stayed for a pleasant dinner. He was a cousin of one of my closest friends in Abbottabad, Allan Donald, who came up for a day or two with another special friend, Hugh Easton, where they were 'in quarantine' after the sad death of our chum Tony Vernon-Betts from polio. J.O.S. (Jos to everyone) was the son of one of the Frontier's most famous politicals and had a lot to live up to. Tragically he committed suicide in 1946 after being kidnapped by Mahsuds when he was PA South Waziristan.

One early evening tennis party at Thandiani had an Alice-in-Wonderland flavour. The arrival of John and myself brought the total male population to five, but two of these did not play. There were umpteen ladies, mostly in fits of giggles because of the unexpected influx of unknown males; several of them were apparently of Victorian vintage and more than a few of the others 'in an interesting condition'. They were all very sweet and hospitable and we were in great demand for mixed doubles. The highlight for me was a game in which my partner was Miss Cox, a senior officer of the Church Mission Society, who was secretary of the Thandiani Club. She was called – behind her back – 'Warrior' Cox; very stout, a terrific livewire, she served underhand and played with more vigour than I could match.

Unfortunately, John and I were soon bored with the work at Indar Seri. There was nothing really new in it for either of us – only endless repetition of procedures we had already learned, and checking Urdu handwritten *shikasta* records at night by the pitiful light from our pressure lamps on our windy ridge was no joke. On still nights we were besieged by myriads of insects attracted by the lamps; on stormy nights we were at risk of being blown down the *khud*; when it rained we had to batten down and take to bed with our books, of which we had taken a good stock from the club library. We got on extremely well together. John came from a prosperous 'county' background, with strong Highland links on his mother's side, and he had made the most of his career at Cambridge as a biologist. Tall, slim and elegant, he was a fine sportsman and wonderfully quick on the hills. I was pretty fit and had become quite a sturdy hill-walker. The next few weeks with John sharpened up my speed but I could never match him. Downhill he sometimes appeared to float without touching the ground. Some of our descents from Thandiani to Kalapani and on to Nawanshahr now seem to me to be impossibly fast, but my letters show that we kept a careful account of our times, both up and down. Our record for the descent from Thandiani to the little dak bungalow at Kala Pani (4,000 feet lower and 6.5 miles), was three minutes more than one hour; and to Nawanshahr, where we could hire a tonga, thirteen miles in exactly three hours, the last seven miles being out of the shade in the summer heat.

John's company was a great joy to me, for he was both congenial, good tempered and full of curiosity and intelligence. He too was feeling very unsettled and the boredom of the so-called training heightened our unease. I think that there was an amalgam of factors. We were both at an age where our personal plans were all-important to us and were being frustrated by the War. Its events had been distressing and sobering for many months and had brought real sorrow into our lives through the loss of close friends. There was acute anxiety about our folks at home – John's father had been ADC to General O'Connor, a close family friend, and had by a sheer accident just escaped capture with O'Connor in North Africa in April 1941. There was the constant stress of waiting for news of loved ones and finding it incomplete and out of date when it came. The forced gaiety of the social life we saw in Abbottabad when we took a weekend off was patent to both of us. I knew that of the dozen or so ladies who prepared and served the lunchtime snacks at the poolside at the club on Sunday, passing the proceeds to the Red Cross fund, half were without news of their husbands since the fall of Singapore, or were waiting for news from the battle fronts in North Africa. Speculation about the future of India, and of our service's role in it had grown with the failure of the Cripps mission and anticipation of a Congress-led revolt perhaps to be coordinated with a Japanese push by land and sea in the Bay of Bengal.

John had got his pilot's licence while he was up at Cambridge and he wanted at this time to be allowed to leave the ICS and serve in the RAF, possibly training in India with the developing Indian Air Force. We discussed these things frequently and no doubt it did us both good to argue things out. I still have a copy of the printed circular letter, dated 21 May 1942, which Lord Linlithgow, as Governor-General, addressed to the Civil Services of India. 'Yours is a brotherhood of service the like of which the world has never seen before.' It was an eloquent message of thanks and encouragement, in part directed at men like John Dent who were feeling disappointed not to be allowed to serve the country on the battlefield.

> Let none of you think for a moment that he is not fighting for his country by steadily pursuing his appointed task... there must be no interruption of your work. If you were to slacken or falter you would

betray the common cause as surely as a soldier who deserts his post; and that I know you will never willingly do... the eyes of the people are fixed on you, and their temper and steadiness, if trouble should come, will greatly depend upon your leadership and example. Be with them as much as possible. Serve and comfort them always. Put away doubts...

We had mixed feelings about the Presbyterian theology of this exhortation, as we debated it outside our tents at nightfall in our settlement camp on that high ridge. We felt we had been taken away from our people and given an irrelevant job for the moment; but I kept telling John that that was the common experience of the soldier and airman. I was certainly proud of my service and encouraged by Lord Linlithgow's words, though on the back of the print, when I sent it home to Barbara, I wrote: 'Please show this to my mother. It's rather sentimental but I'm sure that she'll like it'. By nature I was more cautious than John, partly no doubt because I had less to fall back on if my present career aborted, and even more to gain if it did not, and I made a success of it. But we were equally frustrated by the present unsatisfactory circumstances and soon began to make thorough nuisances of ourselves to Tollinton, Jardine – and even HE, whom I confronted with our complaints that we ought to get back to 'real work', when he passed through Abbottabad one weekend. By the end of June the monsoon was breaking and the weather made conditions at our camp at Indar Seri precarious. Somehow our messages got through to Tollinton on one visit home to Abbottabad. He came up the hill, saw for himself and told us to return to Abbottabad next day, but not to cease training.

We went on to Mansehra to spend a week learning measurement and surveying. A couple of hours were enough, but the change of scene was nice and we stuck it out. We joined Phil in the Kagan and for the first time got some direct personal instruction from him. Riding up the narrow track above the Kunhar river one morning, I spurred my pony to catch up the other two. The surface was good and was made jeepable about five years later when Pakistan and India went to war in Kashmir; but the roadway was narrow, with a cliff to one side and a precipice to the river on the other. My pony cut a corner and my right knee was driven hard into a projecting rock. Somehow I held on, the alternative being to pitch down into the deep, fast river. When we dismounted to climb a rough track to some distant village, I limped far behind and the sympathetic villagers plastered my injured knee with the oil of mustard seed. In due course a nasty ulcer formed, which the medical officer at the Frontier Constabulary fort at Oghi treated by bathing it twice a day in surgical spirits, thus keeping it clean but preventing healing. After about three weeks I got back to Abbottabad and reported to Dr Jai Dyal, the Civil Surgeon; he produced a new invention, sulphonamide crushed into a powder, bound up my knee and told me not to touch it for a few days. It was my first experience of antibiotics. That was the only accident or injury of any consequence that I was to suffer in several years of hard and sometimes dangerous travel.[4]

About the same time I experienced a hurt of a different sort when I heard that I had not passed my Revenue examination. John Dent had – at his third attempt, which confirmed my view that Jardine was determined to let nobody pass simply on the performance of a written paper, but wanted candidates to wait till they knew from practical experience what the subject really meant. I had never failed before in an important written examination and I had performed much better in fact that I had expected to, so I was disappointed, but not seriously wounded – I sat the exam again and passed when I was stationed in Waziristan and far less in touch with the subject either in theory or practice!

We were now about to enter the last and most interesting phase of our settlement training – learning how to reassess the level of revenue to be drawn from a particular locality. Perhaps I should briefly bring the whole process together, to make the purpose clearer. Land revenue is a tax on agricultural resources but not on the total resources of each *zamindar* or cultivator, who might often have separate income from pensions, usually from army service or from the provision of labour or services to an employer, or from trade. To estimate the agricultural resources of a circle of villages called for detailed investigation and careful balancing of many factors. One had to know how much land there was and how many different types of land – irrigated or not; rich soil or stony; how affected by climate; whether uncultivable land provided grazing and if so what quality; how many cattle would it support, to mention only a few. How many people could or did the land support? What rents did they pay to landlords? Who owned the land and who was in possession of individual smallholdings? To what extent was it mortgaged and what was the general state of indebtedness? Had the previous assessment been fair? In what ways had conditions changed? The settlement should derive from an estimate of one quarter of the net agricultural assets, adjusted by the Settlement Officer's assessment of the general ability of the people of the locality to pay at that rate. Answers to these and many other questions had to be sought in the villages and in the fields. Evidence was given orally by landowners and tenants in the presence of their neighbours and the village *lambardars* (headmen, often with a hereditary claim to leadership, who carried an official responsibility in the process of revenue administration and indirectly of government in a wider sense), and in the presence also of the permanent subordinate staff of the revenue administration – the *patwari* and *kanungo*, who resided within a smaller or larger circle of villages, with the former subordinate to the latter, or the *naib-tahsildar* or *tahsildar* in charge of a whole *tahsil* or subdivision of the district, subordinate only to an Extra Assistant Commissioner of the Provincial Civil Service or to an AC or DC. Answers given were checked and double-checked in the light of conflicting evidence, with constant reference to and correction of the remarkable written revenue records and maps, derived from the last official settlement. Some of these records were checked by a subordinate officer every year, and his work in turn was periodically inspected by a superior. Other records stood for four years and then were rewritten in the light of interim corrections and a complete fresh investigation, incorporating the results of all changes of ownership and possession or of inheritance or partition. The official jargon for such changes was 'mutations'.

When John Dent and I were at Indar Seri in the Gali hills we were concerned first with the alteration of the old *jama bandi* (the four-year record of holdings which was always the key to all major revenue work), then with the entry of mutations and finally with the preparation of a new *jama bandi*. We were also doing the preparatory work for the rewriting of certain other maps and documents (the *shajra nasb* and the *khatauni*). The key to all mutation attestation was to ascertain who was in possession of particular plots of land – possession being frequently disputed, sometimes because of doubts about definition. The *khasra girdawari* prepared by the *patwari* at each harvest often gave a wrong record of possession, which could change following sale, mortgage, or inheritance, or because a tenant had joined the Army. When we went to Mansehra we were learning to do the actual survey and measurement work which underlay all the documentation of holdings, and calculation of revenue. We also studied some of the complications that followed from partition, always a contentious and potentially litigious occurrence. When we joined Phil Tollinton in the Kagan Valley we were supposed to have learned how the Tahsil office itself worked, coping centrally with the keeping of copies of all the records and ensuring that they were up to date, and coping also with the flow of revenue, dealing with questions of arrears of payment and a hundred other things.

Tollinton showed us how he set about the final process of assessment, then reluctantly cut us loose to prepare assessment reports in Agror. He had every reason for reluctance. According to the manual, our training had been too truncated to fit us for assessment. Moreover, the preliminary and preparatory stages by the settlement staff in Agror had not yet been completed. In any case at the last minute he remembered that I had not yet learned Pushtu, which was not generally spoken by the people of Hazara but was the natural language of the people from the Black Mountain area, who were the majority of the inhabitants of Agror. He thought they 'were not very good at Urdu'. I am afraid that both John and I were rebellious. John had been for two years in Pathan areas of the province and spoke very adequate Pushtu. I had found no difficulty in communicating with the other Pathans in Hazara (the Mishwanis) and foresaw no problem with the Swathis of Agror, many of whom were ex-servicemen who spoke far better Urdu than the Gujars of Kagan where Tollinton wanted to keep us. We wanted to break free! Not because we disliked him but because we thought he was so absorbed in his work that he had lost his sense of urgency, and had become too detached from the realities of wartime district administration to which we felt the call of duty summoned us. We were young and keen, but naive. I have no doubt that Phil Tollinton's work in the Hazara Settlement is more relevant to the ordinary *zamindar* today than any legacy I left him from my work as AC Hazara. On the other hand, the writing on the wall was beginning to be legible and we were right to feel that we might not have many years to serve the people and had better get on with the business of their current needs.

At any rate, we had our way, and set off from Mansehra on our bicycles, crossing by Susal Gali into the lovely valley of Agror, dropping easily and gently downhill to the town of Oghi in the plain beneath the Black Mountain. Oghi was a place of two or three thousand inhabitants, with a sturdy little fort nearby, manned by Frontier Constabulary. After 1935, when Hassanzai and Madda Khel tribesmen from the Black Mountain raided and plundered the bazaar at Battal to the north-east of Agror, the Hindus of the valley had congregated for protection in Oghi itself which had grown in importance at the cost of another little town about three miles away called Shamdarra, which was formerly the centre of trade with the independent tribal area. The *ilaqa* had a turbulent history in the nineteenth century and twice between the world wars there had been little outbursts, the last in 1935.[5] Now in 1942 all was quiet; a large number of the young men from the villages of the valley were absent on service and their monthly remittances were helping to maintain as high a standard of living as I had seen anywhere in Hazara.[6]

Agror is delightful. The circular valley, about six to nine miles across, is ringed by hills and mountains which are beautifully afforested. Through the plain many little streams run gently, their banks often shaded by trees and shrubs. The soil is light, sandy and soft on the feet. The rivers are easily forded and we delighted in riding everywhere on FC ponies. We stayed for about three weeks in the former FC commandant's bungalow, now a civil rest house since the unit was not large enough to warrant a European commanding officer. Agror was very cold in winter but had a beautiful summer climate and the Inspector General of the Frontier Constabulary used to time his visits to coincide with the ripening of the wild strawberries. The villagers were wonderfully hospitable. John and I each took a separate circle of villages and had to begin our assessment work by preparing village reports. So each morning we rode out to our separate destinations, sitting in the village to fire off endless questions at the people, then walking round their land to check the point of some of their answers, to try to sum up the productivity of their different classifications of soil and to sense the general truth of their evidence. When the time came to rest a while, we were feasted on *pilao* – chicken, roasted and curried, with rice, eggs, chappatis of wheat and maize and quantities of tea drowned in boiled milk and stiffened by large spoonfuls of sugar. Sometimes for a shorter break we would be revived with *lassi* – a drink made with buttermilk to which sugar or powdered *gur* may be added if you wanted to walk on, or salt if you were tired and wanted to sleep under a shady tree.

The days were long and pleasant. In the evenings we were too tired to want physical recreation and we had to work long hours in our bungalow, writing up the day's village notes and preparing our calculations and judgments for our final assessment report. We were handicapped by the incomplete data made available with some of the assumptions about prices and fields which we had been told to make. There were one or two arguments with Tollinton, conducted by letter sent by special messenger, for he was at least two days' march away and far from a telephone. In the end the job got done. Though we discussed our mutual problems freely, each had to make separate reports with independent proposals because we had done the detailed work in separate groups of villages. Mine was signed on 19 August 1942; eight months later it was returned to me with the Settlement Officer's detailed comments and criticisms and a brief note of praise from the new Revenue Commissioner, J.H. Thompson, later Sir Herbert Thompson, who had succeeded Jardine. I still have it in its file, the only copy, so that part of my effort made no lasting impact on Hazara, except in so far as it may have affected the Settlement Officer's final judgments. He was so careful and painstaking that I suspect he derived little help from my report, but his general approval of it and constructive criticisms are nice to see now. I had wished that he had given more careful thought to our training before it started and been more available to supervise it when it was in progress. But he had a huge district operation to organize. Rereading the report I am astonished at how much I once apparently knew about arcane things and how technical my knowledge was. The exercise of writing it, and the preparation for it in Agror, were wholly enjoyable.

Notes

[1] Years later I was reassured about my judgment of him when I read Sir Edward Wakefield's book *Past Imperative*. Wakefield had succeeded Bedi as Assistant Commissioner, Ajmer, in the Punjab States Agency. He describes what a poor view of Bedi had been taken by his shrewd and faithful Brahmin excise assistant, who told him that Bedi preferred to spend his energies in pursuit of partridge and sandgrouse rather than of smugglers. He never changed. He would always dodge work in favour of shikar and often disappeared from Abbottabad to go hawking in the little state

of Amb with the Nawab, whose business was not really important enough to justify so much of the DC's time – and in any case was always in apple-pie order.

2 The only other occasion on which I met the Bishop was when he visited Miranshah in North Waziristan in 1944. Alas! There was no golf course there – nor would the sniping of hostile tribesmen have allowed play even if we had tried to develop one. I had to be content with accompanying him with the Political Agent and the Commandant of the Tochi Scouts to a film show in a hangar in the Air Force section of the fort. Next morning he served communion there – a quiet, dignified service which must have brought comfort to the small group of lonely men who attended.

3 Hazarawal hillmen did not yodel quite like Swiss Alpine people, but they could communicate down mountains and across valleys by modulating their voices at a high pitch.

4 In the spring of 1943 I had one close shave. After days of torrential rain I was visiting villages some miles above Bagnotar, which is on the Abbottabad to Nathia Gali road. The only way across a raging torrent in a steep ravine was a large log wedged between giant boulders. The torrent was about twenty feet wide, running about four feet beneath the log, over huge stones and rocks. I said my silent prayer and was just past the halfway mark when my golden labrador, 'Shot', slipped from my orderly's hold and charged into the back of my knees. He got to the other side ahead of me but I never really knew how I let him past, or followed him across, without dropping hopelessly into waters which would have carried me battered for miles downhill.

5 The only serious military consequence in 1935 was that an aeroplane of the RAF blew up on Abbottabad golf course and destroyed several others on the ground.

6 My estimate was about 3,000 at that stage. The Post Office at Oghi was paying out well over Rs50,000 each month in remittances to dependant relatives. The population of Agror was between 25,000 and 30,000.

CHAPTER VI

Pukka Ishtunt Sahib

Back in Abbottabad I found that I had been gazetted AC Hazara – no longer 'supernumerary' or 'under training', but the *pukka 'Ishtunt Sahib'* (Assistant Sahib), authorized to dole out his own decisions from an office of his own. I was swollen with pride and when I wrote home I said, 'it was a grand feeling'. Bedi had done well by me, persuading the Chief Secretary, and the Governor, to leave me in this promoted role for another year. By this time problems about food and civil supplies had acquired a new dimension nationally, with a large bureaucracy in Delhi struggling to exercise central controls, often in a manner which cut across local or provincial arrangements.

In my very first day there was a splendid example. A telegram arrived from the Revenue Commissioner saying that priority rail transport facilities for moving food grains had been arranged up to 29 August. When I told the leading Hazara merchants to get on with the movement of our quota of imports, they shook their heads. They had no permits to buy grain. Why not? They had applied for them a month ago to the Wheat Commissioner in Delhi. He had declined to issue them. Why? Oh, his official had told them there was no point in giving them permits because no transport was available. I rang up the Revenue Commissioner who had not heard of the problem. He rang up Delhi, which in those days was quite a feat – if one got a connection, the line was sure to be so bad that intelligent conversation was virtually impossible. He established that the Transport Board in Delhi had decreed priority transport for grain for one week without informing the Wheat Commissioner in time for him to issue permits to authorize the movement. I decided as a double insurance to telegraph Hazara's specific needs to the Wheat Commissioner, fearful that wheat intended for Hazara would be left lying on station platforms at places like Lyalpur, to be diverted elsewhere by some *chalak* merchant in collusion with railway officials. I was worried only in case Bedi would be upset because I did these things in his name without going through the usual proper channels. But he was delighted, and in general he left me with a free hand, sometimes even encouraging a naughty or over-bold initiative if he felt it might bring favourable results without the risk of him personally incurring the displeasure of higher authority. Earlier in the year, during the crisis in March preceding the *rabi* (spring harvest), I had introduced a simple scheme for licensing and controlling grain merchants in Hazara. Now I was amused to find that the Provincial Government had produced a similar scheme, but had made it too elaborate to work without a large bureaucracy.

Settling into my own bungalow caused me quite a few headaches. My new appointment had inflated my ego more than my bank balance and I could not afford the outlay necessary to equip and staff the place properly. The rent was high and the cost of hiring furniture had leapt with the invasion of Abbottabad and Kakul by over a thousand British officers. The extensive grounds had been neglected. I determined to plough for victory and get rid of the squatters in the servants' quarters and their ill-kempt cows and goats. But I must find a lodger. When Bedi first proposed that I take over the bungalow, he had let it for the summer to Fred Cunningham, Sir George's sociable brother who had escaped from the Japanese. Fred thought that the altitude of Nathia Gali would not suit his health – although some of his friends thought he just wanted to be free from Lady Cunningham's watchful eye. But after a long weekend visit to Nathia in June, Fred decided that he could stand the height after all and after a period of alternating between the two places, he left me in sole possession. I had been away a great deal but his company had been cheerful and his conversation lively – full of stories about Malaya and his links with Scotland. The Bedi family were very fond of him and almost embarrassing in their hospitable wish to have a monopoly of him. For some time I had so many temporary visitors, like John Dent, that I had to postpone my search for a permanent paying guest. Then all kinds of solutions were proposed by various friends – including the possibility of getting one or other of the numerous grass widows available to run the place for me. That was a fair enough idea, for nearly all of them were in reduced financial circumstances and needed a cheaper billet than the hotels or regimental bungalows afforded. But some had children and all had their own social lives, some admittedly less lively than others, and I was apprehensive of too much coming and going for I often had to work hard on judgments and office files in the evenings. Twice I almost had potential solutions – army officers with wives but no children, whom I knew to be quiet and congenial, but each time the husband was transferred from Abbottabad before negotiations were concluded. In the end, what I had rather dreaded happened. My main channel of communication with the Army in these matters was the Station Staff Officer, Captain Finch – a worthy, well-meaning and hard-working man in his forties, but a notorious and tiresome gossip; what my mother would have called 'a regular sweetie-wife'. He proposed himself as the answer to my need and army cooperation was so important in my official duties that I meekly accepted him. The arrangement worked less badly than it might, although largely I fear because his health was bad, he took to having his meals alone and specially prepared, and he spent long periods in hospital.

Not long after I took over as AC Hazara, I myself had a bout of ill health. It started with a foul throat which had to be treated with the new sulphonamide M & B 693. A week or so later I woke one night in severe pain. Though this cleared after my great friend Malcolm Kerr had given me a sedative mixture, two days later it recurred as I was shaving in the morning. The clerk to the municipality arrived with some files and took me in a tonga to the military hospital, where Major Kerr had me X-rayed. It was, of course, gravel in the kidney, a very prevalent indisposition in north India and quite possibly the consequence of continual dehydration while touring in the heat and dust of the summer, and of an insufficient intake of pure drinking water. Suitably doped, I slept this off over the next day or two, but for a time always felt apprehensive about setting out on one of my long tours away from civilization. Malcolm Kerr gave me some tablets to take only in dire emergency and I am glad to say that years later I flushed them away, unused.

But I have a special reason for recording this minor upset. I had been invited to spend the weekend at Government House in Nathia Gali, where the house guests at the time included General Auchinleck, who had recently been relieved of his command in the Middle East, Lady Auchinleck and Air Marshal Sir Richard Pierce. When I got home from the hospital on the Saturday morning I arranged for a message of apology to be telephoned.

Henniker Gotley, my neighbour, the Chief Conservator of Forests, was in Nathia Gali and called on HE on business just before lunch. He was invited to stay in my place and later reported to me that Lady Cunningham's enquiries over lunch about my well-being had been so solicitous that the Auk had pricked up his ears to enquire 'who this fellow was that Robin was making such a fuss about'. Missing that weekend hurt me more than the gravel in the kidney. The Auk was, and remained, one of my special heroes of the war. The others, of course, were Wavell and Slim. The Auk was a great favourite on the Frontier where he was well known and where he cut his teeth on divisional command on active service, against the Mohmands in 1935.

I had plenty of useful resilience and was quickly back at work – just in time, for Bedi, whose kindness during my indisposition matched that showered on me by a host of other friends, went to Kashmir for much needed leave and the impact of the serious unrest provoked by the Congress Party down-country in Bihar, Orissa and Bengal was beginning to be felt on the Frontier. Bedi had dealt very skilfully with incipient trouble in Abbottabad in September when he succeeded in injecting some communal divisiveness into the Congress arrangements for picketing local schools. Muslim opinion was 'outraged' by alleged threats by the pickets to the modesty of their daughters and one of the most dangerous agitators was beaten up by some Muslims. 'Divide and rule' can be a risky tactic, however, as Bedi himself would learn five years later; but in 1942 it worked for him and I took over a quiet district. I had some trouble with a threatened strike of sweepers, on whom the town's sanitation depended, such as it was, but, as so often, the real trouble was imported from outside. It followed a violent clash in Mardan between Red Shirts, the followers of Abdul Ghaffar Khan, and the police, in which there were casualties on both sides and the usual arguments about who took violent action first. Abbottabad was under threat of an organized incursion of 300 Red Shirts, intent on provoking a similar situation. The threat grew over a whole week, but the appointed day passed without sign of unwelcome visitors and everything was kept under control. Abbottabad and Hazara were never greatly moved by Congress, and as the months went by it was the Muslim League which became a potentially effective political force. Its organization however was always inept.

Although locally I was in charge in Bedi's absence, I had the staunch support and guidance of Oliver St John, AC Mansehra, who was a senior and experienced political officer and would have come into Abbottabad to take over had real trouble developed. By this time, I knew him well. He used to come into headquarters on most Saturdays, ostensibly to try motoring offences, in fact also to consult the DC and let his wife do some shopping. He invariably had lunch at my bungalow, and in more peaceful times we would slip away to golf in mid-afternoon when our court work and office chores were finished. Oliver was known to be *zaberdast* (tough, iron-nerved) and his advice taught me a lot at this time. I also had staunch and willing support from Maurice Pugh, the senior policeman, who was an old hand at these situations. The arrest at Mardan of Abdul Ghaffar Khan, the so-called Frontier Gandhi, leader of the *Khudai Khidnatgar* party ('servants of God', more commonly known as the *Surkh Posh*, or Red Shirts), caused a deal of excitement, especially when he was brought to Abbottabad jail and threatened to go on hunger strike. But the Congress 1942 disturbances in central and eastern India never really impinged on the Frontier, save through the effects on mail and transport wrought by the dislocation of communications a thousand miles away – and by the severity of that summer's floods. Much of the credit for this was rightly given to the way in which Sir George Cunningham handled the situation, as quiet and firm in dealing with the excitable pressures of the Government of India's Home Department – which overreacted to every hint that the turbulent Pathans might come down like wolves on the fold, to join in the general forces of the uprising – as he was in dealing with the local Congressite leadership.

I think that the effect of these events on me was partly to increase my confidence in my own ability to cope with the complexities of Indian politics, at any rate at a local level, and partly to strengthen the feeling that within India the objectives of Congress were incompatible with Britain's essential wartime objectives. I know that I felt bitter about that for I had had no doubts that Britain's objective in India must be to develop the country's ability to govern itself, and I felt that the chance had been there in the spring for Indian politicians to move towards their goal steadily if slowly, while accepting some compromise so as to secure the cooperation of their people in the vigorous prosecution of the war against our mutual external enemies. I regarded them as guilty of treachery, both in rejecting the Cripps offer and in organizing the August disturbances, because I was certain that the vast majority of the people of the villages, whom I had every reason to regard as the real India, were in no hurry for self-government and were deeply concerned that Britain should defeat Germany and Japan. I saw the political breakdown as a consequence of communal distrust and the disturbances as evidence of Hindu opportunism, even of treachery and disloyalty.

Four years later, Dr Khan Sahib, back in power as Chief Minister in NWFP, used to rail against the British officers of the Political Service, accusing them of conniving with the Muslim League against the interests of his ministry and of the Congress Party. I shall try to deal later with this accusation but for the present I suggest that British officers did feel in these war years that, while they served faithfully the people of India, their primary duty and loyalty were to the Crown. In the autumn of 1942 I certainly felt no inherent dilemma in that situation. The people of Hazara were not getting between me and my duty, but the machinations of Congress, as I saw them, might be undermining us both, for surely the absolute priority must be victory in the War.

In the middle of October 1942 I was apparently in the good books of the people of Abbottabad, to judge from one letter to my mother. During the month of the Ramzan fast an acute shortage of firewood had developed in the city. I arranged for a convoy of army lorries whose drivers were undergoing training to bring a huge consignment from Henniker Gotley's forests, and it was sold to the poor people of the community at two-thirds of the market price. Then there was an acute shortage of sugar just when it was most needed, for tempers were short in the long days of fasting, which could be broken only in the hours of darkness; very sweet tea was the Mohammedan stimulant. That was solved by detaining a consignment of 500 bags which arrived at the railhead at Havelian, to be transhipped under permit by lorries to Kashmir. For the last two days of the fast, I doubled the sugar ration. I was fairly sure that Kashmir had adequate stocks and in any case this consignment would not have reached there before the 'Id festival marking the end of Ramzan. But to salve any pricking of the conscience I sent a carefully worded telegram to the Government of India asking, *post hoc*, for approval. For this I was gently chided by Bedi, who would have kept the matter dark if possible, to avoid being penalized in future supplies. I saw this as an example of the difference between Oriental and European thinking; and the terms in which the reply from Delhi confirmed my action gave me satisfaction.

When the great day of 'Id came I enjoyed the spectacle of thousands of Muslims praying together in the park, with all the children in their clean best clothes afterwards running free with their coloured balloons and kites and streamers, enjoying their fill of sweetmeats. Before prayers there was a long and eloquent sermon from Mohd Ishaq, the principal local mullah, a tall, lean, stern-looking individual with a black beard, with whom I had had little clashes over various matters. He preached a long diatribe against the British for having taken violent action against the Hurs in Sind,[1] while pussy-footing in their treatment of Hindu Congressites, whom they seemed too scared even to arrest. To Mohd Ishaq, Congressites were all Hindus at heart, even if not by religion or caste. But in his prayers I was specifically mentioned personally and excluded from his criticism of the British, and for several weeks afterwards I was told that they prayed for me in the mosque. I had, after all, sent Mohd Ishaq a bag of sugar as a gift for 'Id from Government.

My busy routine as AC Hazara continued to intensify through the autumn. 'Section 93 Government' was still in force, so that all the policy as well as administrative decisions were being taken by the Governor and his senior officers. It was rightly felt to be essential to involve Indian opinion, as far as was practicable in the face of the non-cooperative attitude of the political parties. As Administrator of the Abbottabad Municipality, for example, since the formally constituted Municipal Committee had been suspended for corruption two years earlier, I drew help from an Advisory Committee, composed of leading citizens, whose political views were broadly sympathetic to the British. Presiding over their meetings, and those of a similar committee at Nawanshahr, could be both interesting and tiresome. So far as I recall the DC himself generally looked after equivalent District Board meetings.[2]

The course of my daily work had generally become more interesting because I now dealt with more important matters without having to refer them to the DC. Similarly my court work was far more interesting as well as more testing. I could send down to subordinate courts the mundane cases, and in the difficult ones which I retained I had the benefit, if that is the right word, of the best forensic skill of the district's pleaders. In several letters home I discussed the course of one complicated case, in which about twenty villagers were on trial following an armed conflict with a party of police. The village was notorious for violence – arson being a favourite pastime of certain of its inhabitants whom it was impossible to bring to book because nobody would give evidence against them. Their womens' immodesty was a menace to the police, for whenever an officer entered the village on enquiry he was accused of molesting them. One night, information having come that certain proclaimed offenders were being harboured in the village, a party of police including four officers, all armed, went to make arrests. On their withdrawal they were attacked and split up, their prisoners escaped and three of the constables were missing. One of the villagers was shot. Nearly twelve hours passed before 'peace' – a relative term – was restored and the missing men returned by the villagers. The charges, and counter-charges, were complicated and I declined to allow bail so that every Saturday for some weeks a procession of unruly prisoners was brought to my court under heavy guard, accompanied by the jeers and slogans of supporters from the village and the wailing of the womenfolk. Inside, the lawyers regularly had a field day. In one letter I described how one of the police sub-inspectors had been cross-examined for four hours. He was a steady intelligent officer and acquitted himself very well. This kind of case was a far cry from the simple type of alleged criminal trespass or bodily harm that had occupied my hours a year earlier. I felt that I was growing up and getting a flavour of 'the real Frontier'.

In the middle of November I went to Lahore, to sit the advanced examination in Urdu which all Frontier politicals were supposed to pass before sitting the compulsory Pushtu examination. I had written to Faletti's Hotel to book a room but when I got there they disclaimed all knowledge of me. Stubborn Scots persistence eventually procured for me one of apparently several dozens of tents pitched in the hotel grounds. Lahore was Mecca for hundreds of British officers on leave now that it was too cold for Kashmir or a hill station. I was most unimpressed with Faletti's even though they tried to impress me by charging exorbitantly. John Dent arrived at my tent door off the overnight train. After we had taken the exam,[3] we spent the day together but John could find nowhere to stay, so he caught a very late night train for Rawalpindi on his way home to Kohat. Bedi had kindly given me ten days' casual leave and I spent another day looking round Lahore. It struck me as an agreeable city, but I was lonely and got myself fixed up at the club with a game of golf with a banker recently evacuated from Rangoon. The Lahore course had 'browns' instead of greens[4] and I thought it distinctly inferior; I knew I had a treat in store for it had been arranged that I spend my leave in Peshawar where there were grass greens and respectable fairways. One reason for wanting to play at Lahore was to collect the monthly ration of golf balls – for which I paid about seven shillings.[5] Balls had – like everything else – become very scarce and expensive. Another bonus of my extra day in Lahore was that I found the Minerva Bookshop in Anarkali. They had some good economics books and I opened an account, resolving to keep myself up to date in my subject.

In Peshawar I was comfortably lodged at Government House for four days with little to think about except rest, read and accompany Fred Cunningham on little excursions. I remember that one afternoon we helped Lady Cunningham and Diana Thorburn to look after some wounded British soldiers who came to tea. Mrs Thorburn was a Ross of Cromarty, sister-in-law of General Sir Richard O' Connor, and an aunt of John Dent. In summer she ran the Pines Hotel in Nathia Gali; in winter she acted as Lady Cunningham's housekeeper and companion. The convalescent soldiers enjoyed themselves and those who were fit enough played bowls on the lawn. Their spokesman was an extrovert Glaswegian who thanked his hostesses eloquently in a superb Gorbals accent. Whether they understood all he said about the cakes and the bowling and the flowers and gardens did not really matter – his sincerity was perfectly clear.

The Cunninghams went off on tour, taking Fred with them, and I was transferred to the cottage near the gates of Government House, which was the residence of the Secretary to the Governor, my former DC, Gerald Emerson. Sadly, that morning I went down with some form of sandfly fever or dengue and spent three or four days in bed feeling as though I had been battered all over. On the civil surgeon's recommendation, my leave was extended for three days and I did after all enjoy several games of golf on the Peshawar golf course which I was to come to know so well a year or two later. My old partner, H.F. Scroggie, was now Senior Superintendent of Police in Peshawar and he showed me how to play the course as well as introducing me to the mysteries of the city, which is the meeting place of rogues from all of Asia.

From my letters home it is clear that once again I had fallen under the spell of Peshawar. I waxed lyrical about the beauties of the garden cantonment, but now I was beginning to appreciate the subtle sounds and smells and spectacles of that extraordinary city. Back in Hazara, there was a mass of arrears to overtake, but no big change in the pattern of life which I have already described. Shortages of supplies of all kinds still preoccupied me. Whereas at the start of the year it had been just the sack of wheat, and to a less extent maize, now I was devising schemes for the procurement and distribution of sugar, ghee (clarified butter, essential in Indian cooking), eggs, grain (mainly for animal feed), barley, charcoal, firewood and matches. Many of my problems were compounded by statutory orders and controls from Delhi. The private economy became inefficient through corruption and the government bureaucracy was ill-adapted to deal with genuine shortages, for the transport system was overloaded and ill-coordinated. I was obsessed with these shortcomings, and too self-centred, I fear, to make allowances for the enormity of the problems that Delhi had to deal with, or the loads that the railways had to carry to keep the armies supplied and efficient at the battle front.

Still, my happy-go-lucky Deputy Commissioner had a knack of forgetting about shortages. His gift for hospitality was undaunted and he celebrated the joyful Hindu festival of Diwali by giving the biggest and most lavish private party I had ever attended. It was certainly the most cheerful Indian crowd I had seen. Not long afterwards there was a big State Durbar at Darband, the capital of the Nawab of Amb's little state. This was to mark a five-day official visit by the Governor and I travelled to it with the Station Commander and his Staff Captain, Paul Fox, in the brigade staff car. There was a tremendous *tamasha*, with much emphasis on the war effort, and plenty of bread and circuses. The latter were very similar to the Haripur Show, which I described earlier, but the 'bread' was so lavish that I felt ashamed when I described the menu in detail in a letter to my mother, particularly when I confessed to having spotted, purloined and eaten a quantity of delicious chocolates whose provenance was a mystery. I compounded the offence by adding that on the way back to Abbottabad we stopped at Haripur so that I could buy a basket of a hundred oranges for the equivalent of ten shillings, which I calculated was about three weeks' supply for my own needs. All that remained now was to prepare for my second Christmas at Abbottabad.

That was marked by the arrival of Hugh Easton on sick leave from Sind. He had been very ill from malaria, jaundice and dysentery, the result of his weeks in the desert in the campaign against the Hurs. He stayed with me, resting and recuperating, gradually more able to join us in the usual round of entertainment, for most of my friends knew him well and welcomed him. I remember that after having no office work for six days I felt resentful that the office was to work on Hogmanay, 31 December, and I arranged to do a one-day tour instead of working indoors. Hugh volunteered to accompany me but may not have bargained for what he endured. We left the road about six miles out from Abbottabad and struck out on foot across the hills towards Tanawal, working back in a circle to come into Abbottabad over Brigade Circular Hill. Shortly after our early start, it rained, and all day the rain grew heavier. I had arranged for some ponies to be available for the last lap of some six or seven miles but had miscalculated the time it would take to get to that stage. Hugh was so exhausted that my orderly and I took it in turns to ride beside him, or as near as the path permitted, in case he fell off; he was really riding in his sleep for a considerable distance. We got home, soaked and weary, long after dark, having traversed eighteen miles. After a hot bath, we turned up cheerful at a dinner party and went on to the club's Hogmanay dance. I am told that about three in the morning I withdrew to an armchair in a quiet corner and fell fast asleep; I was probably feeling pretty satisfied with myself. But in a letter to Barbara written two days later I said the 'the war's bustle has jogged me out of my old, easy, self-satisfied ways.' Deep down, I am sure, that was the real truth.

I started 1943 with a bout of nostalgia and homesickness. When Hugh Easton left to rejoin his battalion I felt that all the close friends of my age at the 10/13th FFR Mess had gone forever. Though I remained friendly with several of the old hands who were 'fixtures' like 'Uncle' Young and Major Barton, the group to which I had been very close in age and temperament had begun to break up from the time of the Singapore disaster and the death of Tony Vernon-Betts. While Hugh was with me another of them turned up and stayed for a few days. He was Hugh McBlain Douglas, a Scots Fusilier from Kilmarnock who had been a commando and was now for a short time an instructor at a special course which was being run at Kakul. He had been very wild, in a very Scottish way, but now he too needed a rest and was subdued and reticent till he came out of his shell on New Year's Eve.

When they were gone I was full of thoughts of home and my frustrations. A young Signals corporal turned up who had been posted to the so-called Wireless Experimental Depot, where radio signals on the Russian front were monitored. He was Ernest Innes whom my mother had known well when he was an apprentice in a well-known draper's shop in Nairn. He came to lunch on Boxing Day and for nearly two months he came to me for dinner about once a week, exchanging news and reminiscences of our home town. Mail at that time was particularly erratic, so our evenings together made me more homesick that ever. Then he too was posted away like so many others.

I had a distinguished visitor, Risaldar Major Mohd Ashraf Khan, OBE IOM IDSM, who was on two months' leave from the UK. When I asked him where he had been stationed, he said 'Aviemore'! It emerged that he had been billeted at Revack Lodge, near Grantown-on-Spey, within a couple of miles of my father's own home. He had been in Britain since Dunkirk and was the senior Viceroy's Commissioned Officer in Europe when he came on leave. He belonged to a village near Jabri, in the hills not far from Abbottabad, and some days later I decided to walk off my troubles by trekking for a day in that direction. The weather had been bad having snowed in Abbottabad earlier in the month, but that day was splendid. I covered twenty-three miles, visited seven villages and ate tea and chapattis with hard-boiled eggs five times! It was a long day but the going was not too difficult, the hilly country was gentle and grassy and between two of the villages I was piped on my way by an old soldier, whose repertoire included all the familiar tunes like 'Cock of the north' and 'Hieland Laddie'. By 1943 one frequently came across men who had been wounded and invalided home from their units. In one of these villages, however, a sepoy came forward who was on leave from Britain. Where had he been stationed? After Dunkirk, in Plymouth, Derby, Sheffield, Glasgow – and then an unintelligible name. I asked him to repeat it. It was Nairn, my own home town. He had been one of the sepoys of the Mule Company about which I had heard so much in letters. He sang the praises of the folks of my home town – especially Provost John Mackay and Rev. J.M. Little, my own minister, who had secured for the Muslims of the Mule Company a piece of ground which they had designated as a mosque!

A day's tour like this was not mere self-indulgence. It brought me close to the people and developed my understanding of their ways and worries. Illustrating this in a letter, I described how in his own village, at his own house, one man told me in the presence of about fifty of his neighbours why he had got into a row with his brother and beaten him, to his grievous bodily hurt, over the head and arm. At three hearings of the case in court I had heard only a pack of lies and listened to lawyers throwing dust in my eyes. Getting at the truth did matter and going about the villages on foot created the trust from which the truth emerged. Even so the element of self-indulgence in a long day's walk could be justified. I no longer had time to spare from office work and court work to enjoy the four- or five-day tours which I have earlier described. When I did get out of Abbottabad, it was often to go to the bigger market centres like Haripur or Havelian to deal with 'price control' problems of one sort or another. In Abbottabad I had introduced a crude card rationing system at the beginning of January and it seemed to be working reasonably well, but procurement problems multiplied and there were shortages of foods in which Hazara was a surplus producer. Sheep and goats were being bought up in their thousands for new government canning factories where the dehydrated meat was packed for supply to the vast armies that were being trained. There was an embargo on the export of eggs from the district because our own surplus was needed for the troops in Abbottabad, but my sources told me that they were being smuggled in huge quantities to Karachi, to sell at inflated prices that matched the appetite of the arriving hordes of American GIs who did not take kindly to *dessi* (Indian) food.

The smell of corruption was growing and it worried me constantly. Though Bedi and I kept on good friendly terms, it was becoming difficult to avoid dissension when he intervened in matters of economic management. The considerable authority which I carried was, after all, delegated by him to me. There was constant apprehension that his interference stemmed from private pressures which did not always correspond with the public interest. I felt that he was weak rather than corrupt and that the proximity of his father, the revered leader of an important and powerful sect of Sikhs in the neighbouring district of Rawalpindi, put undue pressure on my DC. Others were less charitable and in the early months of 1943 rumours and innuendo about Bedi were rife, even amongst the military population of Abbottabad. I felt

B.D.S. Bedi, DC Hazara, visiting convalescent Sikh
sepoys with Loretta Hutchinson and Esme May, 1943.

that I was in a very uncomfortable position for I tried to be loyal to him but it became increasingly difficult. Although I did not respect him and disliked his conceited manner and arrogance, he was always personally kind and genuine in his friendship and never discouraged my youthful enthusiasm.

Between him and Henniker Gotley, the Chief Conservator of Forests, a serious feud developed. The wartime exploitation of timber in Hazara was a matter of great financial moment, involving the interests of powerful private contractors, and these interests were often not compatible with conservation policy, nor with the best interests of the villagers, yet these concerns in turn might not be consistent either with the pressing needs of Government for timber. This feud was none of my business officially but Bedi tried to enlist my support and help. I asked to be excused for both men were my friends and colleagues. Gotley was rather a stodgy man, though frequently irascible, but he was held in high esteem by the European community, whereas Bedi was often unfairly scorned by them. This episode was merely a symptom of my problem, but rumours spread that Bedi was to be transferred, if only the Governor could find an alternative post into which he might be fitted.

My letters show that throughout this period I turned regularly for advice to Oliver St John and Paul May, the Sessions Judge. They were, in their very different ways, pillars of strength. Oliver, who knew that he himself was going to another post, out of Hazara and not to become Deputy Commissioner as popular opinion hoped, could take a more detached view than I could. As a subdivisional officer he was less tied to Bedi in his day-to-day work, and he was both experienced and tough. Paul, of course, was completely detached as Sessions Judge – the traditional separation of the judiciary and the executive. He was also very eccentric, sceptical, amusing and in many ways a complete clown. But he had a deserved reputation as a judge and he gave me plenty of sound advice, usually delivered in most amusing terms, always calculated to keep my spirits up.

Although the popular clamour was for Bedi's transfer, and neither Oliver St John nor myself incurred disfavour, it seemed for a while as though, like Oliver, I was about to leave Hazara. The Governor told Bedi that he wanted to send me either to Bannu as Assistant Commissioner to Alastair Low, or to Dera Ismail Khan (DIK) as AC to Major Cole, whom I had met when he was AC Charsadda. I knew that in normal peacetime circumstances such a move would have been ideal in giving me experience of the differences in district administration at the southern end of the province. I was quite ready to go to either post, my only reluctance being the onset of the hot weather which transformed both DIK and Bannu into a baker's oven of discomfort. But Bedi argued strongly against my transfer and after some delay the Governor acceded to him.

I never knew how the arguments were balanced. I was conceited enough to feel that I was being left in Hazara because during the present shortage of officers HE could not replace Bedi with a more efficient DC. The Revenue Commissioner, Lionel Jardine, came on a farewell tour before moving to Baroda and told me that I had done well. Since I had stoutly resisted all his efforts to enlist my sympathies with the Oxford Group movement, I felt that perhaps this was his genuine opinion, and not merely a flash of divine guidance.[6] Young men can be vindictive about their distinguished elders' prejudices. I felt that I had done some real good when I visited two charming elderly English missionaries who had a 'Mission farm' not far from Haripur. Writing home I reported that they did not appear to be active in converting the people, but set out to provide a Christian example by encouraging their Muslim servants to lead good lives. They gave me samples of a kind of porridge meal they had prepared from wheat, as a substitute for Australian oatmeal, which was no longer obtainable. I left them happy by guaranteeing them an adequate allocation of sugar to enable them to expand their output of marmalade.

My letters around this period give plenty of signs that I was suffering from a bad dose of swollen head, and I am sure that it was a pity that I was not sent to Bannu or DIK. It is perhaps to my credit that I actually said so in letters at the time, though I was pleased to be left in Hazara which I had grown to love. Another quality of young people is their resilience and this shows through in my letters of this period: doubts and uncertainties are regularly displaced by pleasure in events and satisfaction derived from effort. This was, of course, a period during which disruption to the mail to and from India was very serious. That added stress to doubt and uncertainty, but again the record shows how the simultaneous arrival of two or three letters, written at least two months earlier, could transform one's whole outlook.[7]

Routine duties kept getting heavier but they were full of variety and interesting diversions kept cropping up. I was very fit and none of the ailments of the autumn left any ill-effects as the consequences of malaria later did. I was accustomed to long days on foot and I had learned how to stay mentally alert and resist the eroding effects of fatigue on my powers of concentration. One simply had to train oneself for this: it was the special challenge that faced all touring officers in India. It developed mental stamina in me for which I have always been grateful. My colleague, Maurice Pugh, the Superintendent of Police, who was in his mid-thirties, was also a keen touring officer. His wife remarked one day that Maurice and I looked fitter than any other European in Abbottabad and that it must have been due to all the walking we did. True – but a special kind of walking, on rough steep tracks, with many sharp questions to occupy our minds as we went along.

The other quality which this experience developed was the ability, under pressure, to switch rapidly from one subject to another, assessing information and giving decisions.

Some of the variations in routine were of a kind that I have described before, like the annual Haripur agricultural show. This year I travelled to Haripur on foot down the Siran valley, camping in tents on two nights on the way and visiting villages I had not previously seen. At Haripur, I pitched my tent near those of the Nawab of Amb, who was to provide hospitality for the principal guests on the final day. There was an unprecedented number of them, from northern Command at Rawalpindi and the Government Secretariat at Peshawar, led by HE himself. We had added to the agricultural exhibits a strong military propaganda element, with all sorts of demonstrations of weaponry, physical training and tactics. The Air Force joined in for the first time, with an exhibition of dive-bombing by American Vultee Vengeances and some breathtaking low flying by RAF Hurricanes, which added to the problems of the tent-pegging judges and the riders of startled horses. The finals of this competition were so closely contested – and disputed, in the traditional way of these equestrian events – that we had to turn the pegs sideways-on in the 'play-off' to determine the winners.

That was about the end of March. Less than two months later, at very short notice we responded in Abbottabad to an appeal by the Viceroy by celebrating the great victory in Tunis with a war *mela*. The parade ground provided a natural amphitheatre and a huge crowd came for a march past of 8,000 troops. It took an hour and since the force included battalions that were resting after active service, it displayed an army that was highly-trained, impressive and efficient, and if it moved others emotionally as it moved me, it must have had a great psychological effect on the populace. Apart from the large number of civilians watching, the crowd included as many soldiers as were actually in the parade. It must be remembered too that at that time there were 77,000 men from Hazara serving in the forces. It had been a part of my job over the last eighteen months to help to bring this about so that I felt a strong sense of commitment in the occasion, and it must have been shared by many of the spectators. After the parade the local schools had a happy morning of sport, which was followed by the traditional adults' events. In the evening, in an unprecedented gesture, the Abbottabad Club threw its doors open for a dance, held on druggets spread over the tennis courts, organized by the ladies of the Indian Red Cross – for which the district had subscribed a fund of about Rs80,000 – raised in about three weeks, Rs7,000 of which came through the Assistant Commissioner. The dance was enjoyed by a large number of people of different creeds, colour and rank, and was an enormous success.

Before then we had come through the critical period before the *rabi* harvest without a serious repetition of the previous year's crisis. The rationing system in Abbottabad was working well, allocating each household to an official food grains depot in its neighbourhood – one depot in each of ten neighbourhoods. There had been a major flurry at the beginning of April when decisions made by the Provincial Government and the Government of India looked like producing unworkable effects in Hazara, which was always a difficult district to assess in a province in which in normal times most of the trans-Indus districts would produce a surplus of food grains, given timely rainfall in Bannu and DIK. There was evidence that the incentive to produce for the spring crop in Hazara had been weakened by a shortage of labour caused by the departure of so many young men from the villages to undertake *naukaree* (service) of one kind or another, while their remittances left their elders content to buy what they were not growing for themselves, thus producing an imbalance between supply and demand that was abnormal – and of course increased by the wartime growth of urban population in Abbottabad and its environment. At any rate, after I had analyzed the probable effects of Government's allocations, Bedi sent me to Peshawar to negotiate a solution. That was done primarily with Ahmed, then Deputy to the Revenue Commissioner in charge of food supplies. He was an ICS man from the UP, related to the family of Hifazat Hussain, the Collector of the Doon, who had befriended us at Dehra Dun. I was on good terms with Ahmed, in correspondence and on the telephone, and found him quick and responsive in personal negotiation. By the end of the day in which I had also had to see the Finance Secretary (Price), the Home Secretary (Leeper) and the Development Secretary (Dring) the necessary revised orders had been signed by the new Revenue Commissioner (Herbert Thompson) and countersigned by the Governor. I have no recollection of the details but the list of those whom I had to see indicates that I was involved in weighty enough dealings, and no doubt my success in persuading them to see things my way had its effect in their assessment of my progress. Apart from Bedi and our senior assistants, nobody in Hazara knew what was going on, so there was no public crisis and the supply of wheat remained adequate to see us into the summer without panic.

I was impressed by Herbert Thompson who talked a great deal but was very quick and decisive. I had one piece of great good fortune: I met Ambrose Dundas, walking in the Mall, and accompanied him on his way back to Government House, where he was staying. He was at the time Resident in Waziristan, the senior officer responsible for the whole of that difficult tribal area, with both Wazirs and Mahsuds. He had come down for consultations with Sir George Cunningham and I asked him outright if he would try to get me transferred to Waziristan soon. I had to wait till August for the outcome but I felt that the die had been cast.

Halfway through April, I had to contend with an unpleasant strike with worrying implications. Shortage of petrol and spare parts had been seriously handicapping the operation of the large fleet of lorries and buses on which Abbottabad, and the trade with Kashmir, depended. The police had plenty of opportunity, in enforcing traffic regulations, to harrass the drivers, whose regard for road safety was often negligible. When the strike developed the political agitators seized their chance. Several active Congress workers tried to get involved, and resented the rebuffs I gave them. I would talk only to the drivers, not the politicians. The DC was in Lahore on a week's casual leave, and the SP was out on tour some days' march away. I negotiated with the drivers and succeeded in splitting them into two groups, one of which was willing to accept my assurances and return to work. The others were stiffened by the intervention of a notorious Khaksar, an extreme Muslim political group, which liked to carry spades as an emblem of their stand for the workers, and were in the habit of sharpening the spades so that they became deadly weapons in crowd disturbances. This Khaksar had recently completed a three-year prison sentence for his leading part in a murderous riot in the city of Lahore. When the drivers who had agreed to return to work tried to drive off, he lay in the road in front of the leading vehicles. I promptly ordered his arrest and that of a group of his supporters. Within hours there was much unrest, and crowds protesting against harrassment shouted angry slogans outside my bungalow till late at night. Next day, Oliver St John arrived to take over in the emergency. After hours of discussion with the strikers and hampered by the unwanted intervention of local politicians, it was agreed that the Khaksar and the picketers who had been arrested with him would be released on bail, and the strike ended. I was convinced that this would be taken as a sign of weakness on our part in the face of political agitation, and in my huff I showed what I thought of the Khaksar by fixing his bail at one anna (a penny). So much, I thought, for the *zabardast* St John and the genial, easy-going Noble. It did no harm for the public to know that I had been overruled by the tough AC Mansehra in this way.

A week or so later I was wakened by the telephone about two in the morning. The message was that the city was on fire and when I rushed onto my verandah, I could see the flames high against the dark sky. Bazaar fires in Indian cities were terrifying affairs. Much of the property was wooden; the lanes and galis were only a few feet wide, with just one or two streets broad enough for a vehicle; the houses were over-crowded. I had often been told of a disastrous fire in 1935 which had destroyed most of Abbottabad town. The enquiry had shown that it had spread rapidly because action to deal with it had been too dilatory. I yelled for Finch, who was asleep in his room, and asked if he could secure military help. Within minutes he had got to Station Headquarters, mobilized the guard and alerted the army engineers. Meanwhile, Maurice Pugh and I were charging around in the Mohallas ensuring that people were evacuated well in advance of the spreading fire which had started, suspiciously, in a Mohammedan boys' school situated in a congested area. Some of our rudimentary efforts at civil defence training began to pay off. The local fire brigade was surprisingly efficient, and was soon joined by the military one from the cantonment. The Civil Engineer was a quiet Hindu called Malhotra who now showed much good sense, indicating where demolition should be carried out to create firebreaks, happy with my unauthorized assurances that he would not personally be held liable for damages. The army engineers accepted his directives so that shortly after dawn, the spread of the fire had been halted and it was brought under control. Everyone had behaved admirably. Bedi had arrived quickly and without ruffling his impeccable turban – he was always immaculate – he spread calm and assurance around the agitated property owners, leaving it to Pugh and myself to get scorched, soaked and begrimed in our frantic dashes hither and thither.

Next afternoon a large delegation of the leading men of the city called on each of us in turn, presenting a memorial of thanks which bore all their signatures. Its quaint but sincere wording gave me real pleasure and I am still proud to have it in my possession. Nobody had been killed, there were no serious casualties and the loss of property, though very heavy, was widely accepted as far less than it might have been without prompt and decisive action. Most pleasing of all, it was widely recognized that the Army had come into the city to help, and had come quickly and effectively. Indian towns were more accustomed to the Army appearing in aid of the civil power when rioting got beyond police control.

By this stage in the War, social life in Abbottabad had lost some of its forced gaiety and had become a little more naturally cheerful. News had come through about some of the husbands who had been missing for so long, but perhaps it was too soon for all the wives to appreciate what prisoners of the Japanese were having to endure. There were more senior and middle-ranking officers in the station who wore recent medal ribbons and could base the newly-felt confidence about the course of the War on their own campaign experiences. Sepoys on leave in the villages always seemed confident that they could beat the Japanese as the horror of defeat and retreat somehow got brushed aside. Personally, I found it hard to raise my morale. I grew increasingly irritated by the attitude of so many Europeans to the Indians and to the growing economic crisis. They seemed incapable of adjusting their own consumption standards to the realities of scarcity – and army ration standards encouraged them. The prices they had to pay in the bazaar might be rising threefold but they could get many of their needs through the Army at controlled rates. I was always conscious that the poor classes could not get enough and that amongst the Indians ostentatious consumption by the wealthy remained unbridled. Reporting home that I had been one day to a wedding in a village near Mansehra which had cost the bridegroom's father about £4,000, I felt quite ashamed, remembering how I had detailed the menu at various parties and ceremonies in earlier letters, and felt uneasily conscious of the constraints of the British diet.

When May came and the provincial secretariat moved to Nathia Gali I welcomed the chance to take to the hills as often as possible, with the excuse that I was responsible for the work of the police station at Dunga Gali. In this way, most weekends I spent some time in the calmer company of people of my own service. There were several old-established summer rest camps in the forests between Dunga Gali and Murree, which in peacetime had preserved the men of British battalions from the tortures of summer in the plains. This year, two of the camps were taken over by American troops, and some of the British mothers in Nathia Gali began to get worried when their nannies disappeared for afternoon picnics in the woods. One day I ran into a big convoy on the Murree road. A jeep came dashing up, and out stepped an American colonel who recognized me from an encounter at a function at the Army School of Frontier Warfare. He shook my hand warmly and, turning to his driver, said, 'Meet Lootenant Smith.' I was astonished for beneath the forage cap were gorgeous blond curls and the figure might have been Hayworth's or Monroe's. The Yanks had come and some of them at least were in good shape to win the war.

There was a new doubt about my own future. The Viceroy decided that the consequences of the war would not justify persistence with the scheme to develop a special Frontier Commission of the ICS, to which only Pat Duncan, John Dent and I had been recruited. The original idea had been that this commission would serve in posts in NWFP, Baluchistan and the Persian Gulf, as well as in embassy posts in Kabul. Now, unless I applied for and was accepted for the Indian Political Service, I would probably be confined to NWFP itself, which I would always enjoy – but would such a narrow base serve to let me rise to one of the top jobs? And did I really want to join the IPS? I was dubious about that, for I had no particular enthusiasm for service in Indian states. I did not let these problems dwell unduly in my mind as there was plenty of time for them to be resolved – or else my time in India might run out in any case, and the end of the Raj would resolve them for me.

The latter possibility was beginning to seem serious. In NWFP the first movement back to the political arrangements envisaged in the 1935 Act took place when the Muslim League Party deliberated whether to form a ministry. They could do this only because so many of the elected Congress representatives in the Legislative Assembly (MLAs) were still detained in jail following the civil disobedience of 1942. It was still the Congress Central Committee policy throughout India not to take office or cooperate in provincial government. This tied the hand of Khan Sahib, the Frontier Congress leader and former chief minister, and left the way open for the Muslim League Party to form a minority government, though Sir George Cunningham was anxious to release detained Congress MLAs as soon as they would give guarantees of cooperative behaviour. Just before the decision to form the ministry was taken, I wrote in a letter to Barbara dated 19 May 1943, 'I personally think the Muslim Leaguers are making a mistake in taking on the Government now. They will have nasty problems to face at the end of the war and will get themselves unpopular just when the Congressites are due to emerge from jail – as popular heroes, no doubt.' That is indeed how it all turned out, except that the nasty problems were not well dealt with, the ministry was thoroughly unpopular long before the end of the War and was displaced by a Congress Ministry, in spite of the reluctant attitude of the All-India Congress Committee to such a step.

In June, Sardar Aurangzeb, the new Chief Minister, and two of his ministers made an official visit to Abbottabad and stayed for some time. There were many official 'welcome' parties, some of which I enjoyed, and I was impressed by Aurangzeb's eloquence. After a dinner given for them by Bedi, attended by all the senior civil officers of the district – Paul May, Phil Tollinton, Oliver St John, Maurice Pugh, and Lincoln, the new Superintendent in charge of additional police – I described Aurangzeb as 'a real personality, a genial mountain of shrewdness, with the nicest manners'.[8] Sadly, while his manners remained impeccable and he was always a mountain, he was not a strong enough personality politically to exert his shrewdness effectively, and in time he was badly outmanoeuvred. But that was more than eighteen months away. Meanwhile, the impression I got was that the ministers were 'holding their horses but full of good ideas' about policy.

In fact, they had to wait for by-elections in August before committing themselves very far, and, as one has come to know, politicians can talk quite impressively when they are marking time and making no decisions. For the rest of my time in Hazara, therefore, their existence made no great difference to my work or to my policies. Had I stayed on beyond September there would have been a different tale to tell. Meanwhile, apart from liking the genial Aurangzeb, I formed the judgement that his Finance Minister, Abdur Rab Nishtar, was a man of real distinction and capacity. He will crop up again in my story when he was a member of Mountbatten's 'cabinet'. His career proved his high calibre but I think it was ruined, as so many political careers in Pakistan were, by petty jealousies arising within personal factions.

These political developments gave us plenty to talk about and in June 1943 I had plenty of company. Fred Cunningham, who had stayed at my bungalow for most of May, left early in June, and the Thompsons came for three weeks. Many of the senior Secretariat officers were financially penalized by the formation of the ministry. Under Section 93 rule, they were officers 'required' by the Governor to be at provincial headquarters in Nathia Gali during his official residence at his summer home. Once a ministry was formed, they became 'recessing' officers, and were entitled to no more than two months at Nathia Gali. This affected their household arrangements for even senior men could not lightly commit themselves to the expense of a full season's rent at Nathia Gali while maintaining a household in Peshawar at the same time. The Thompsons, only recently arrived in the province, compromised by coming as paying guests to my Abbottabad house where the temperature was tolerable for Mrs Thompson – Peshawar in June, July and August was no place for a woman. She took over the management of the house for me and dealt firmly with a *chalak* cook whom I had neither the time nor experience to deal with. Herbert Thompson was a fascinating conversationalist and they were fine company. Finch was in hospital for several months, eventually being forced to give up his room in order to go elsewhere for medical treatment.

About the middle of June, David Elliot came up from Lahore on a fortnight's leave and I put him up in a tent in my garden. During his spell, Brian Williams came for a week from Campbellpur, and we went up to Dunga Gali for my usual Friday and Saturday case work. They greatly enjoyed the hospitality they received from my numerous friends both in Nathia Gali and in Abbottabad, and we talked a great deal about our lives, careers and our future plans. There was one important outcome – we agreed to take a fourteen-day leave together in Gulmarg in Kashmir in mid-September, when 'high season' hotel charges would have abated somewhat, and we sent an invitation to Martin Fearn, an old St Andrews friend of David's and a year senior to us in the Punjab service, to join us to make up a four at bridge and golf. I had been unsure of what to do about a holiday away from Hazara although I knew that I needed to get away and that it was not enough to go to a rest house in the Galis or Thandiani, where I was far too close to my usual work and my own people. The Gotleys and St Johns, who had just had a new baby, had tried to persuade me to go away with them to a bungalow they were to share at Gulmarg in July. This was a kind and tolerant suggestion as they were probably seeing quite enough of me at home, and Bedi was good enough to offer to let me be away at the same time as Oliver St John – but the new proposition to go in September with David and Brian was far more sensible.

I was getting rather exhausted and looking back to my letters home, I can see why. I reported that in June I had tried and disposed of fifty-two criminal cases involving police evidence and defence lawyers – full hearings, some of them on serious charges involving complicated circumstances. This number excluded cases which I dismissed or dealt with summarily, or by achieving a compromise between parties – these averaged six or seven a day. Phil Tollinton at this time wanted the Governor to appoint me as Assistant Settlement Officer. In his overtures, which I firmly resisted, he told me that that caseload by itself was a full month's work and that I was overworked on ephemeral matters, but it was only a fraction of what I had to do. When my *Urz* box was opened every afternoon, it would contain as many as fifty petitions, some of which had to be attended to personally, as well as the *mulakats* who wanted an interview. I still had all the range of so-called 'price control' work. I used to say that policemen brought bail warrants or warrants for arrest to me to sign when I was in my bath. Because the DC was a Sikh, one of my functions was to be Christian Marriage Registrar for the district. With so many British soldiers around, I had several distinctly odd knots to tie. One that was blessed in June was the union of a 28-year-old British gunner, on leave from Syria, with the 38-year-old widow of an Italian who had five children. A day or two later I went to the christening of the baby of a Roman Catholic army officer. I was amazed at the thoroughness with which the officiating priest baptized the child's anatomy and was thankful that I could simplify the ritual of my Registrar's duties to suit my own inclination to be unobtrusive. I was still fit enough to climb six miles (and 3,500 feet) from Kala Pani to Thandiani in one hour and thirty-two minutes at breakfast time one morning. Waiting for my orderly and clerk to arrive with the files, I took off my shirt and lay in the sun – and paid for it, for at that height (8,800 feet) the ultraviolet rays are not filtered

Murder case outside rest house at Dunga Gali, June 1943.

Outside rest house at Dunga Gali with David Elliott, June 1943.

by the dust of the atmosphere, and I burned in a way that rarely happens in the dusty plains of India. Altogether, life in Hazara was full of adventure and new experiences, and one could never feel bored.

But if my career was to develop, it was time for a change. In the first week of August I was writing home rejoicing that I had been notified officially that I was to go to Miranshah early in October as Assistant Political Agent, North Waziristan. This was far more exciting and desirable than being made Assistant Settlement Officer, Hazara, though that would have been a post that any junior officer would have jumped at in pre-war conditions. The surprise was that the posting was to North Waziristan. I had not thought of it as a possibility, whereas I felt there was a good chance I might be sent to South Waziristan to replace Pat Duncan. In the last few years the Mahsuds of South Waziristan had been relatively quiet, and the main political and military problems had been created by the Wazirs of the North Agency, disturbed by the hostile activities of the Faqir of Ipi. The Political Agent in charge was R.H.D. Lowis – 'Jack' or even more commonly, 'Lotus' Lowis. Like his counterpart in South Waz, he was responsible, through the Resident, to the Governor in his capacity as Agent to the Governor-General of India, the Viceroy wearing his other hat. The chain of command was quite distinct from that laid down in the Government of India Act 1935 for the 'settled' districts, in which in normal times responsibility would rest with elected provincial ministries. Indian politicians were kept firmly out of action in the tribal agencies of the Frontier. By mid-August, I was sending home excited descriptions of life as it would be for me in my fortress deep in the wild tribal zone near the Afghan frontier. The account was highly romanticized and must have frightened my mother and Barbara out of their wits. I had not yet been south of Kohat or west of Hangu. But I had read a great deal about the Frontier problem, and talked for hours about the way of life to men who knew it well, both in the Army and in my own service. Experience was to prove that my descriptions were not far from the harsh realities, which made the romantic frills in which I wrapped up the story wholly otiose.

During the summer, Bedi was often unwell suffering from recurring bouts of asthma, and consequently I was kept busy with the unexpected. Just before I went on leave to Kashmir, I had to deal on his behalf with one of those cases of abduction which caused so much trouble in the Frontier. In Mansehra, a young Hindu girl eloped with a Mohammedan. Communal feeling was deeply roused and everyone recalled the details of the notorious case of 'Islam Bibi' in Bannu in 1936, the outcome of which had set the Faqir of Ipi on the hostile course which led to several major campaigns before the war, and which still preoccupied us in Waziristan. After much legal argument in the civil court, the decision was that the Mansehra woman was over sixteen and could do what she wished. She promptly went to stay with a Muslim family in the town of Nawanshahr, five miles from Abbottabad, of whose municipal committee I was president. This was a busy little market town, full of rich, influential Hindu merchants. Within the Muslim family, the young lady came directly under the protection of the leading Khaksar of the district – the same man who had been convicted for his part in the responsibility for the death of the Assistant Superintendent of Police in Lahore some years before, and had been arrested for his part in our lorry drivers' strike a few months earlier, being released on a bail bond of one anna. Naturally, the Hindus of the whole district were highly indignant. The Khaksars were bitter, often violent, opponents of Hinduism and of the Congress Party. They came to the DC in a large demonstration, arguing that the lady was really unwilling and was being coerced. Bedi decided that quick action was essential and despatched me at once in his car, accompanied by a leading member of each of the Hindu and Muslim committees involved. Naturally, I dubbed them my chaperones, in the circumstances, and we had an agreeable conversation in the car as we discussed my problem. She was brought before us in the house of her protector, completely concealed below her *burkha*. My plan was to get her to look me straight in the eye, which was normally a forbidden and unacceptable intimacy, and answer my questions; her Muslim protectors were agreeable, the circumstances being rather special. There was really not much that I could see but I judged that her reply was firm, freely given and honestly spoken without fear: it was that she was not being coerced. My Hindu chaperone raised no protest at my decision although I had a strong impression that both he and the Khaksar representative had been more eager than I to see what sort of face this lady might show. So far as the evidence presented, her appearance convinced me that she was certainly more than sixteen, was probably no great beauty and I sensed that both my chaperones agreed.

In the outcome, all was peaceful but I recalled the incident early in 1947 when a repetition of the circumstances fanned the flames of communal violence in Abbottabad at an early stage in the serious disturbances in northern India before Partition. At the time, what was most important to me, judging from a letter to my mother on 24 August, was a remark made to me by the leading Khaksar who was one of the fiercest critics of the Government in the district. I regarded him as 'the biggest twister of the lot' which was perhaps incompatible with Pandit Nehru's views that all British officers on the Frontier were hopelessly biased for the Muslims against his Congress party. He remarked that 'he and his friends were sorry that I was about to leave Hazara, but they were sure that I would get on well on the Frontier, because he had never heard of me letting my tongue get out of control.' This may very well have been deliberate and subtle flattery, but at the time I felt encouraged, for I had come to think that the secret of dealing with the Pathan was that however severely one had to 'lay down the law' to them, one must both hold firmly to a consistent line and, as I put it in my letter, 'finish with a grin, for they know that [with such an officer] there isn't likely to be injustice in his anger. They are so unjust to each other that they sense it very quickly and hate an unjust officer with a very bitter hate.' I went on, in what nowadays would probably be denounced as racial prejudice, to argue that the British as individuals were more popular with the ordinary Indian countryman than members of the future ruling class in India – the politicians who hated us so strongly because they were aware that our individual popularity was out of their reach. This may have been a far-fetched piece of sophistry, but I record it now because I recorded it in 1943, as evidence of what the young Turks of the ICS, with their commitment to the concept of self-government for India, felt about the prospects. In any case, what the Khaksar said was certainly good advice to a young man about to work in Waziristan.

The fortnight's leave in September in Gulmarg with my three ICS friends from the Punjab was a memorable success. We lived in neighbouring chalets which were an annex of Nedou's Hotel; our waking hours were spent on the golf course, eating and playing bridge. We ate substantially of pretty ordinary fare while the golf at that altitude was none too good: the courses were beautiful and full of tricks, but we swung too fast in the rarefied air. The bridge was friendly though keenly contested and we lived as frugally as we could, scrounging an occasional gin or beer from senior colleagues from the Punjab and the Frontier who were on leave, but generally confining our own consumption in the club to coffee and tea with teacakes. The hotel was expensive and we were all hard-up. Wartime inflation was hard on the heaven-born. Our holiday was marred only by the discomfort and delays of travel by road in defective vehicles, short of adequate maintenance and necessary spare parts. But I at least resumed work greatly cheered and refreshed, and eager for my move.

There was a good deal to tidy up in preparation for handing over to Khan Bahadur Faizullah Khan, a senior member of the Provincial Civil Service, who had been Assistant Commissioner in Charsadda, a subdivisional post in Peshawar District. Unexpectedly, I found on my return that the Provincial Ministry were in a panic about food supplies. They had now taken over the reins of government, endorsed by the results of by-elections and the cooperation of some MLAs who did not belong to their own party organization. They were, of course, already subject to local pressure that district officers had learned to discount, but I could not see how, at the time of the *kharif* (autumn) harvest, the supply position could have deteriorated so dramatically since I went on leave. When I checked with our grain dealers and my assistants, I was fairly confident that Hazara'a markets could cope well for the present. The Chief Minister convened an urgent provincial conference, Bedi was again unwell with asthma and at the last moment I went to Peshawar in his place. All the other Deputy Commissioners were there, except for Alastair Low, who was on leave while Bannu was represented by John Dent, his Assistant Commissioner. A great deal of nonsense was talked, principally by the ministers, and when they expressed particular anxiety about Hazara, the least fertile district, I offered information and arguments to allay their fears. The real cause of the crisis was Peshawar itself, where tempers always frayed towards the end of Ramadan (or Ramzan), the month of fasting, and there seemed to be a lack of reliable information about the true stock position. When decisions affecting Hazara had been made, I asked permission to leave in order to return to my preparations for handing over to my successor. Aurangzeb turned to the R and DC, Herbert Thompson, who was himself on the verge of leaving for Australia, and protested vigorously that I should not be going to Waziristan where I could do no good, but should be brought into the Secretariat to help them with their food problems. I smiled helplessly, and withdrew, glad to get away at last from the 'price control and civil supplies' arena. But the Chief Minister's intervention signalled that my escape would only be temporary.

Farewells in Abbottabad were sincerely regretful on both sides. It was still the month of *roza* (fasting) and that saved me from much overindulgence, for I could decline many Hindu and Sikh invitations when my Muslim friends were being prevented by the fast from entertaining me. But ways of thanking me were found, with the traditional kindness that is so marked in the Indian people, and I was garlanded and photographed and embarrassed by endless speeches from different groups. In my two years amongst them, I had begun to grow up and leave my precocious youth behind. I was truly grateful to them and to my many European friends who had contributed to the growth of my maturity.

Notes

[1] The Hurs were a fierce tribe of Muslim dacoits, who had indulged in a guerrilla campaign of terror against rail communications in Sind and generally caused much distress. A special force of the Indian Army was organized to deal with them and the campaign went on for many months. My closest friend in the 10/13th FFR, Hugh Easton, became second in command of his battalion during this campaign – with the rank of Major, aged twenty-three.

[2] The District Board was the equivalent of a British County Council, nowadays Regional Council.

[3] Three months later I learned that both John and I had passed the higher standard Urdu exam with credit.

[4] i.e putting surfaces of gravel or sand treated with oil, and not grass surfaces.

[5] The following June I reported that the price of golf balls had doubled to about one pound sterling in rupees. I was still playing with three balls which I had acquired in November 1942, with three new balls in paper, in reserve – sadly it turned out that new balls kept through hot weather in paper perished, so that when they were struck the paint came off, taking part of the cover with it.

6 It was widely rumoured in Peshawar about this time that the Jardines had been more successful in recruiting the Bedi family to their circle. It is most likely that Bedi had not committed himself, but had allowed Jardine to get the wrong impression. When he retired from India, Lionel Jardine became one of the leading figures in the Moral Rearmament Movement, playing an active part for many years both in Britain and internationally. He kept his links in India.

7 Two letters from my mother arrived in May, having been six months en route. This was becoming an exceptional delay, but the total loss of letters still occurred frequently.

8 This was in a letter dated 30 June 1943.

CHAPTER VII

Waziristan: A Second Apprenticeship

A stone's throw out on either hand
From that well-ordered road we tread
And all the world is wild and strange.

Kipling

Getting to Waziristan with all my luggage was quite a feat of organization. First I was delayed in Abbottabad by the late arrival of my successor. When I handed over to him, two days behind schedule, a telegram from Jack Lowis instructed me to stay where I was until he could get some local trouble sorted out. A mail lorry had been held up near a khassadar post not far from Isha Corner, the junction of the roads from Razmak and Miranshah on the way to Bannu. The *barampta*[1] of implicated villages had to be arranged, the khassadars suspected of complicity dealt with, and inevitably Johnny Raw, the APA, who was responsible for the Khassadars, had to defer his departure until these matters were cleared up. While fretting at the delay, I realized that I was in for a change of circumstances with a vengeance.

For some reason I did not try to travel by train via Rawalpindi, and thence by the line to Mianwali and Karachi, to the junction at Mari Indus, where one crossed the river Indus to Kalabagh and took the 'heatstroke express' on the narrow gauge to Bannu via Lakki Marwat. I went by lorry to Peshawar, staying a couple of nights at the club, and spending a morning at the Intelligence Directorate, studying maps and photographs of Waziristan and making contacts that were to prove invaluable in my work. Because bus services were disrupted by the 'Id festival, on the next stage I got no further than Kohat where I stayed a night with John Dent. From there a less hesitant lorry, charcoal driven, got me to Bannu

162

in time for lunch with the Lows. Alastair Low was well settled in to his distinguished period of service as DC Bannu. At his house I found the 3-ton Chevrolet lorry which Jack Lowis had sent with the North Waziristan PA's escort to bring me to Miranshah. At lunch Colonel J.A. Robinson, whom I had met once or twice at Nathia Gali, announced that he would be accompanying me, and so I made my entry to Waziristan seated on the bench between the Daur driver and the man who master-minded the remarkable British propaganda directed at the tribes on both sides of the international border with Afghanistan throughout the war. The justification for such propaganda was that it was vitally important to avoid large-scale military commitment in the Frontier. Any campaign on the scale of the Khaisora operations in North Waziristan in 1937–8 would have deprived the Burma front of one division or more of our best-trained troops. Major tribal unrest on either side of the border might threaten the stability of the government of Afghanistan, on whose goodwill, and behind its official neutrality, the British Government staked a great deal in its plans relating to Persia, Iraq and Turkey. The Axis powers, with embassies still active in Kabul, were equally interested in the tribal situation, but their objective was the opposite of ours. There was evidence that they were helping the Faqir of Ipi with money and had plans to provide him with material and technical aid, even, it was said, to reinforce him with German paratroops.

Robbie's effort was directed through a secret network of mullahs and other influential Islamic brethren. This network linked with another which was controlled by one of Sir George Cunningham's Pathan advisers, K.B. Kuli Khan. At the time of my arrival I knew almost nothing of all this, though Robbie managed to convey a strong impression that he was engaged in clandestine work and set himself to give me an invaluable tutorial on the nature of the Wazirs and Mahsuds. Although I had begun to learn Pushtu in the last few months in Abbottabad, I was just at an elementary stage with the pure, 'hard' Yusufzai Pushtu of the north, and could not make head nor tail of the 'soft' dialect spoken, with various corrupt local variations, by the tribesmen of my escort.

The journey, thus vividly illuminated by my mentor's commentary, made a dramatic impression on me. The road was good and almost free of traffic after we cleared the outskirts of Bannu, and as we made our way over the pass by Shinki, up the Tochi Valley for forty miles to Miranshah in the heat of the afternoon, I could sense the stark hostility of the barren rocks and the lurking danger of the ravines and overhanging cliffs, and appreciate the siting of the *sangars* that marked the piquets manned by friendly Khassadars, enjoying a field of fire that covered our flanks but equally threatening the road directly if a piquet fell into hostile hands. Every now and then we passed through an open plain, lying dry and dusty in the haze; only near the River Tochi were there stretches of cultivated land with occasional signs of irrigation. The scene might have recalled for me the English visitor travelling for the first time through a barren stretch of the Scottish Highlands; when he asked a lonely toiling crofter what on earth could be grown on such soil, the Highlander's firm reply was 'men'! I knew already that the Wazirs and Mahsuds were men of a special breed, fiercely independent, intensely democratic in their social organization, bound by a code of Pathan conduct and honour that yielded nothing to Western concepts of justice and civilization, careless of any human life that was unprotected by their code, and capable of deeds of great courage but also of cunning treachery. By teatime that day I had learned a great deal more from Robbie, to add colour to my gathered impressions and beliefs. I can remember two things that I put down on paper. The first was his eloquent explanation of the Pushtu phrase describing a whirlwind of spiralling dust rising from the bare ground a hundred feet and more in the heat of the afternoon: *da peiriano wadah* – the wedding of the fairies, presaging a gathering dust storm. The other was his precept number one for any new arrival in the agency: 'Never do the same thing in the same place at the same time on different days.' Unseen eyes noted these things and innocent pastimes or habits which became a daily routine could make one an easy target.

The Tribal Agency for which Jack Lowis was responsible was often referred to as the Tochi Agency. The Tochi River ran from west to east from the highlands of the Afghan border near Dwa Toi to the western environs of the town of Bannu, whither – joined through the stony wasteland of Jani Khel country by the underground waters seeping from the Shaktu and the Khaisora valleys, draining the high ground east of Razmak – it passed as the Gambila to its junction with the Kurram River, eventually to mingle with the Indus opposite Mianwali in the Punjab. The beds of its tributaries are usually dry and stony, like Highland streams whose waters have been diverted by pipeline to feed some dam for a hydro-electric power station. Only the Tochi regularly carries much water. Its valley is one of the important trade routes to Afghanistan, whose timber and other products are carried slowly on the backs of camels. Near the Shinki defile leading to the Bannu basin, the rugged escarpment is about 1,000 feet above sea level. From there the valley climbs steadily. Miranshah lies on the edge of the Dardoni plain at an altitude of about 3,000 feet. By the time the traveller reaches the Afghan border the surrounding mountains rise to around 10,000 feet. The adjacent provinces of Afghanistan are Birmal and Khost. The town of Matun in Khost is only about thirty miles north by air from Miranshah aerodrome. Away to the west is the much more important Ghazni, from which historically from the days of Mahmoud of Ghazni, raiders have descended on India by the Tochi route.

In 1943, the motor road from Bannu to Miranshah was excellent, though narrow and twisting in places as it climbed. Beyond Miranshah, the surface was fair for lorries, though dusty, as far as the most westerly Tochi Scout's fort at Datta Khel. Some miles short of Miranshah, at Isha Corner, the good metalled road from Bannu made a sharp left turn and wound its way steadily upwards to the important military cantonment of Razmak, lying in a plateau at about 7,000 feet, overlooked by the towering mountains of the borderland between the Utmanzai Wazirs and the Mahsuds. From this vital military stronghold, the central Waziristan road worked its way southwards through Mahsud country to Jandola, headquarters of the South Waziristan Scouts, and thence to the town of Tank, an important trading centre in the district of Dera Ismail Khan, at the head of the Derajat plain. A branch of the great road broke westwards from the Takki Zam to Wana, on its plain in the heart of the Ahmedzai Wazir country, from which one returned by the frightening Shahur Tangi defile to the central military road at Jandola. The Mahsuds, with their cousins the Urmurs, and the Ahmedzai Wazirs were the responsibility of the Political Agent South Waziristan, whose winter headquarters were in Tank. His APA was based in Wana.

Razmak, and the central Waziristan road, were a creation of the 1920s, a consequence of the serious disturbances, stretching over several years, which followed the Third Afghanistan War and the invasion of the Frontier by the Afghan Army. The establishment of the permanent military stronghold at Razmak was the symbol of the most 'forward' stage in the long history of the controversy

Author's tribal bodyguard on the road to Razmak near Isha Corner.

about frontier policy – 'close border' versus 'forward to the international frontier' arguments had always been keenly contested. Razmak was intended to be a direct threat to the back door of the Mahsuds, the fiercest and most feared of all the tribes. It was never directly used for such an attack in later years and the decision to withdraw the Army from it and leave it to Scouts and Khassadars was taken before the partition of India and Pakistan, but put into effect soon after the British Raj came to an end.

When I was in Waziristan, Razmak was still the central point of military strategy at a time when the tribes were relatively quiet and it was essential to keep them so. Yet it was very costly in manpower. The Razmak Brigade was about twice the size of a normal brigade, with the equivalent of five or six battalions and supporting artillery. To maintain it, supplies were sent twice or thrice a fortnight along a line of communication from Bannu stretching about 100 miles. To enable the convoys to get through, the entire route had to be closely picketed by troops, Khassadars and Scouts, and patrolled when necessary from the air. Apart from the Khassadars and Tochi Scouts, there were full brigades in permanent camps en route at Mirali, Damdil and Gardai. On each road open day (ROD) large numbers of men had to be deployed from each camp onto the vantage points on the ridges – a tricky and exhausting tactical exercise involving potentially explosive coordination with the local Khassadars. Hostile sniping was commonplace, ambushes far too frequent and often deadly. Though the date of each ROD was a close secret, wily tribesmen had their own intelligence system; culverts and bridges were often blown up just before the convoys began to roll – even though in those days only crude explosive devices were available and there was nothing like remote-control detonation.[2] The whole operation was, of course, a splendid exercise in mountain warfare, at which no army surpassed the Indian Army, and against the cost in manpower and money in keeping Razmak open must be set in wartime, as in peacetime, Waziristan's value as an advanced training area, in which live ammunition was used and mistakes cost lives. From the tribal point of view, also, the system was profitable for while those who wished to indulge in hostile practices enjoyed their opportunities, everyone, including no doubt numbers of clandestine snipers and bridge-blowers, could participate in the benefits of the contracts for maintaining the roads and supplying some of the troops' local needs, and each tribe provided its own contingent of Khassadars to help guard its particular section of road.

The whole of the area through which the road ran, certainly from Tall fort, near the river above Isha Corner, was cultivated only at isolated places. As the road climbed, the scrub on the hills provided grazing for sheep and goats, and in the higher reaches, approaching Razmak Narai above Gardai and Razani camps the trees thickened above hairpin bends so that any drive on any day was a nervous experience which promoted road sickness. Innocent shepherd boys made sharp-eyed lookouts for ill-disposed Bora Khel, Tori Khel or Mahsud marksmen. Nearly all the villages lay well away from the road, tucked away in little side valleys, very private behind their strong perimeter walls over which loomed the watchtowers with their loopholes, marking the status of particular *maliks*. Most of these habitations were strongly built little fortresses, constructed of dried mud and heavy timbers, the mud sometimes used as a kind of cement over large round stones. The walls were thick and solid, so that they did not easily crumble. Shells or bombs might punch holes in them but were unlikely to bring them down.

Along the Tochi river the scene was a little different. There were more clusters of visible villages and there was much more cultivation, some of the flat riverland having alluvial deposits, and being capable of irrigation by channels led off from the river. In places, the relatively level area of the valley was six miles wide. In the main valley the inhabitants were mostly Daurs, not Wazirs, and the Daurs were cultivators, not just shepherds. Historically it was partly on the request of the Daurs that the British had moved in, to guarantee their security against the marauding nomadic Wazirs, who kept threatening to encroach on what became the 'Protected Area'. Many of the Wazir tribes remained at least partially nomadic and there was an annual summer movement of Tori Khel up to the grazing grounds of the Razmak plateau where for generations there had been boundary disputes between them and the Mahsuds. A serious recurrence of this in June 1944 marked my last weeks in the agency.

It is difficult to convey in words the extraordinary feeling of this remarkable country. It was harsh, arid, rocky, weird, lonely, forbidding, threatening, rugged, misshapen, strange, alien; yet at times, in the setting sun, and at particular vantage points, it had a spectacular beauty and breathtaking colour that remain unique in my experience. One feared the ferocity of the people and abhorred their cruelty, yet one admired their sturdy manliness, respected their democratic pride and their love of freedom, and above all warmed to their hospitality and their ready wit and humour. Living amongst them, calculating their bluff and working out countermeasures, seeking out information and sifting the wheat from the chaff, was an intense and continuous intellectual exercise, which put great strain on one's emotions and above all tested one's patience and equanimity.

To discover all this took time. When I arrived at Miranshah on the afternoon of Tuesday, 5 October 1943 I was a complete tyro; yet when I left the agency in a Harvard aircraft on Thursday, 6 July 1944 I felt that I was a hardened and experienced political officer, wise to the wiles of the Wazir and capable of confronting him without being outguessed, whether in my office or in a *jirga* or in a Khassadars' piquet – or even on a *gusht* (patrol), provided I had the backing of the Tochi Scouts and the unrivalled skill and experience of their British and Indian officers. In the pages that follow I shall try to describe how this came about.

The Political Agent and his APA lived in the political quarter in the fort at Miranshah which was the headquarters of the Tochi Scouts. This corps had a fine record. Recruited entirely from

Pathan tribes with no close links in Waziristan, they were led by King's Commissioned Officers who were volunteers from the finest regiments in the Indian Army. In peacetime, service in one or the other of the Scouts militias was a great prize for an ambitious and adventurous British officer, for these lightly-armed and highly mobile forces were always in the van of action wherever it was likely to be found. At headquarters, besides the Commandant, Lieutenant Colonel P.B. Janson, or 'Jan', there were the second in command, Major Ralph Venning, who later commanded the South Waziristan Scouts, a Wing Commander, the Adjutant, the Motor Transport Officer, and two or three others. Several of the outlying forts, like Spinwam, Khajuri, Dosalli and Datta Khel normally had at least one commissioned officer; one or two of the smaller posts might be under command of an IO, a senior Viceroy's Commissioned Officer. While I was in the Tochi, I had three outstanding Muslim King's Commissioned Officers as close friends – all Pathans to whose patronymics we added the affectionate Pushtu diminutive –o or –a; thus, Sharif-o, Rahim-o and Aziz-a. Subsequently serving Pakistan, Sharif himself became a political officer, doing extremely well until like so many of his contemporaries he became a victim of Pakistani party *bazi*, the eternal struggle between rival factions. Rahim became a Major General and one of President Ayub's senior staff officers. I do not know what became of Aziz, the least volatile of the three.

The PA and I took our meals in the Tochi mess; so too did the Agency Surgeon, Major Jeff Hassett, who was succeeded by Major Morgan, and the Assistant Garrison Engineer of the Military Engineering Service; when I arrived this was a young Scottish officer, 'Jock' Graham. Our political quarters had their own walled lawn with a private gate, outside which was the political lock-up near one of the main gates of the fort. Security was tight, with a strong guard always on the gate, and the doors from our quarters into the Scouts' officers' area around the mess were kept secure. The Scouts occupied two thirds of the rest of the fort – there were normally about 1,000 men in post – and the remaining one third belonged to the Air Force.

Just before I arrived, No. 1 Squadron Indian Air Force, based in Kohat, took over for the first time from the RAF in Miranshah. The flight at Miranshah was equipped with Hurricanes which had only recently replaced Hawker Hart and Audax biplanes. They still had an obsolete Audax for 'communications' purposes, but within a month or two this was replaced by Harvards supplied under Lease-Lend arrangements by the Americans, whose restrictions in 'communications' use were calculated to prevent civilian political officers using the machines for purposes inconsistent with flying training. We used various subterfuges to overcome this piece of anti-colonial bureaucracy – and indeed could not effectively have done our job in 1944 without the facility provided by these pleasant but noisy little two-seater aircraft. The landing ground at Miranshah, just outside the RAF perimeter, was excellent – one strip of 1,000 yards and another, at right angles to the first, of 1,600 yards, adequate for anything likely to land at Miranshah. It added a nice touch of romance to know that T.E. Lawrence had served as Aircraftman Shaw at the fort, and wrote a number of his famous letters there. The aircraft which he had to service were brought into hangars inside the high walls of the fort and the screen of perimeter wire, just as was done in my days with the Hurricanes.

The Air Force and the Scouts lived their own self-contained lives, but were on good friendly terms. When a film arrived it was exhibited in a long, narrow, draughty building in the IAF section. We had to mount a ladder near the political gate and walk along the fire-step below the parapet for a hundred yards before we could descend to the safety of a hangar. Looking over the top into the dark emptiness of the Dardoni plain and the landing ground, we were always conscious of the risk that a lurking sniper would choose that moment to take a shot at the fort. Ditches which ran parallel to the landing strips made excellent cover for an unfriendly Wazir. But the knowledge that Rita Hayworth or Loretta Young or Barbara Stanwyck was about to come to life down below helped us to hasten with dignity, and on cold nights on our return we repaired to the mess to remove the chill with a glass of hot milk fortified by rum and sweetened with a large spoonful of honey. The Scouts' name for this concoction was 'zakhmi dil' – a broken heart. It was an antidote for depression as well as cold; afterwards one slept soundly, as healthy young men do after a hard day's work.

These occasional cinema evenings were rare social events in Miranshah, where life, apart from work, was quiet and sober. Only on exceptional occasions was there anything approaching hilarious rumbustiousness in the mess. Considering the strain under which we were all living, away from normal social intercourse, always on the alert, individually feeling very lonely, one is bound to record how friendly and pleasant the atmosphere was. Nobody ever made himself unpleasant. Perhaps the knowledge that at any time each might be completely dependent on the supporting self-sacrifice of the others helped to knit the small band of officers together, so that conflicting opinions could easily be expressed without offence or umbrage being taken. The Commandant set a fine example. He was dignified and could be firm, indeed sharp when circumstances called for quick efficiency, but he was relaxed and at ease with junior colleagues and had a wonderful sense of humour. The PA, Jack Lowis, complemented him perfectly in all these ways. Their easy banter gave younger men confidence for it was clear that they trusted each other completely and mutual respect and good humour spread down through the ranks. The personal charm and professional experience of the Agency Surgeon, Jeff Hassett, an irrepressible Irish bachelor, contributed a great deal to our social solidarity. He had a very sharp eye for signs of personal stress in his colleagues and a marvellous way of dealing with it. Behind his effervescence, there was a thoughtful, professional care that sustained our high morale. His reputation, too, as a healer of gunshot wounds was high throughout the agency where the tribesmen trusted him equally, as much as the Tochi Scouts.

I have said that life was sober, and perhaps I should emphasize this, for it may seem surprising how unreliant on alcohol we all were. Occasional mess nights could become pretty jolly, but nobody ever seemed to take refuge in drink.[3] So far as I recall, the private ration of whisky was one bottle of Canadian rye whisky each month, which may give some idea of the level of consumption; the mess was of course well-stocked but social drinking was generally confined to beer and was restrained and disciplined.

Indoor recreation, apart from the cinema, was almost non-existent, but most of us had few leisure hours, and these were devoted to reading and writing. On Sunday afternoons there was often a vigorously contested game of basketball between the IOs and the BOs, its version of the rules much more physical than I had bargained for. There was always keen interest in various forms of sporting contests between the different wings, each wing having some 600 or 700 men. Every now and then the IOs would entertain us and the day would end in the whirl of a Khattak dance, the dark bobbed heads of the young Scouts circling faster and faster in the dim light of the fires as their pirouettes speeded up in time with the drums.

Outside the fort, a couple of hundred yards from our gate, was the delightful political garden, designed perhaps by Sir George Cunningham himself when he was PA, back in the 1920s, or by Sir Arthur Parsons, 'Bunch' Parsons, another famous political gardener. I recall the glory of its roses in bloom in the first week of the new year. Sadly, since 1936 its attractions had been diminished by the risks of sniping and its tennis court, though still used, was certainly not in daily play. The squash court's walls provided their own protection and during the winter months we brought up a marker from the Peshawar Club – one of the Pathan family that was to provide so many world squash champions after the War. Like all these north Indian squash and tennis club professionals, he had the special talent of forcing one to raise one's game and though I was a complete tyro, I used to enjoy myself enormously trying to take a point or two from him. He could make the rallies keep up remarkably so that one felt one was achieving splendid shots – but after twenty minutes of this, as the weather warmed up in the spring, I could just collapse exhausted into a bath. In getting to and from the squash court, outside the wire of the fort and the protection of its walls, one had to nip pretty smartly, keeping in mind precept number one as enunciated by Colonel Robinson.

So far, I have sketched an impressionistic background to the life of a junior political officer in the Tochi Agency. It is time that I attempted to describe more precisely his role in the context of the Waziristan problem. The tribal agencies of North and South Waziristan lay between the administrative borders of the settled districts of Bannu and Dera Ismail Khan and the international frontier between India and Afghanistan, broadly indicated on the map, but not everywhere demarcated on the ground, in the agreement negotiated between Sir Mortimer Durand and the Amir of Afghanistan in the 1890s.[4] Waziristan differed from the other tribal agencies of the province. Moving northward, one comes next to the Kurram, inhabited by Turis of the Shia-ite persuasion of Islam. Surrounded by Sunni tribes, the Shia Turis invited the protection of the British, and for generations the agency ran relatively peacefully along agreed and comparatively democratic lines in accordance with tribal custom. To the east of them, the Orakzais were supervised in terms of 'watch and ward', but hardly governed, by the Deputy Commissioner Kohat. The main stamping ground of the Afridis, who were always potentially the hinge of tribal opinion over the whole frontier, lay in the mountains and valleys of the Tirah. In the twentieth century this territory was sacrosanct: no attempt was made by the British to set foot in it or to impose direct government within it. But for strategic reasons we had to occupy and hold the narrow line of the Khyber Pass, north of Tirah, but within Afridi country, in order to cover the only motorable route to and from Afghanistan. Through the Political Agent in charge of the Afridis, the PA Khyber, the cooperation of the Afridis in our occupation of the pass was generally secure and consistent. When they rose as a tribe to harass the district of Peshawar during the serious anti-government disturbances inspired by the Khudai Khidmatgar (Red Shirt) movement in 1930 and 1931, the key to the solution was found in the permanent establishment on the Khajuri Plain of posts held by the Army and the Frontier Constabulary. The Khajuri Plain, lying below the mountains in the settled district a few miles west of Peshawar city, was essential to many of the Afridis for winter grazing and encampments, to which they had to retreat from their snow-bound mountain fastnesses.

East of them was the territory of the Mohmands, another powerful tribe which for generations troubled the peace of the frontier, often prompted by fanatical priests. During the First World War, after successive bloody excursions into the settled district, they had to be blockaded behind a twenty-mile electrified fence for many months. Thereafter sporadic trouble with them continued for more than a decade and in the mid-thirties a major punitive campaign was directed into their territory by two of the outstanding British soldiers of the Second World War – Auchinleck and Alexander. It was a costly and not entirely victorious exercise but the Mohmands were to stay quiet from then throughout the War. Part of the problem with them, not unconnected with their propensity to throw up fanatical firebrands, was the fact that the tribe straddled the frontier with Afghanistan and was liable to cause trouble on both sides of the boundary, and to draw support from the outside. Against that, and tending to keep them quiet as the years went by, was the fact that increasing numbers of them were *dwa kor* – that is, they acquired houses and land in the settled district around Charsadda where irrigation benefited agriculture.

This reduced their restlessness and accustomed them to the laws and regulations of settled or administered territory.

Further east still the more remote Bajauris had often ganged up with the Mohmands, but in the twentieth century the British left their territory severely alone and they were often preoccupied with local struggles with powerful individuals like the neighbouring Nawabs of Dir. In fact the north-eastern tribes of Dir Swat and Chitral, which had in the nineteenth century given the British many hard campaigns, came more and more under the sway of autocratic rulers like the remarkable Wali of Swat, with whom the Political Agent at Malakand could negotiate direct, regarding his territory as a well-administered buffer state.

Throughout the Frontier, therefore, there was no uniformity of circumstances in the tribal areas; but during the Second World War it was only in Waziristan that problems of watch and ward, and threats to India's strategic security, remained patently unsolved. The Political Agents had no locally powerful tribal leaders, like the Wali of Swat, through whom they could ensure cooperation. Their tribes, the Darwesh Khel comprising the Utmanzai Wazirs, who along with the Daurs were the responsibility of the PA North Waziristan, and the Mahsuds and Ahmedzai Wazirs, for whom the PA South Waziristan was responsible, had been the focus of the bloodiest fighting against the British since the First World War. Nor was their trouble-making confined to British India; some of them, like the Madda Khel Wazirs, lived on both sides of the international boundary, and Mahsuds and Wazirs alike were always liable to get involved in the faction fighting, threatening the stability of the regime in Kabul. In the early 1920s, the struggle between the Indian Army and the Mahsuds was particularly ferocious. Its consequence was the adoption of a semi-forward policy, the reopening of posts from which the Scouts had been withdrawn during the Third Afghan War, like Datta Khel in the upper Tochi valley, and the development of Razmak as a major military base, with the improved construction of the Central Waziristan Road, and the establishment of permanent camps along its route. But in the period following the notorious Islam Bibi abduction case in Bannu in the spring of 1936,[5] the challenge of the tribes' new religious leader, Mirza Ali Khan, Tori Khel, who became notorious as the Faqir of Ipi, provoked Mahsuds and Wazirs alike into years of successive campaigns in which the British sought with no great success to punish and subdue them on the ground and from the air. A generation shocked by the enormity of the Falklands campaign of 1982 will be surprised to be reminded that 40,000 troops were engaged in these Waziristan campaigns from 1936 to 1938, and that heavy casualties were suffered on both sides – on a scale no less than in the Falklands fighting. After 1938 the disturbances were on a much smaller scale, though many troops continued to be involved, sometimes in actions by divisional 'columns', and both the Tochi and South Waziristan Scouts were frequently engaged. Waziristan was 'quiet' by previous standards throughout the war; but the Faqir of Ipi was still very active, and he was certainly encouraged by Axis Power funds and incitement. How was he kept so subdued? Perhaps my account of 1943-4 will shed some light on this question.

The distinguishing features of the administration of North Waziristan were that there was no land settlement or consequent collection of land revenue as in settled districts,[6] and the writ of law and judicial system of India gave place to *riwaj* (tribal custom) and sometimes to the prescriptions of *shariat* (Islamic law). Generally offenders were prosecuted by Government only on charges arising from acts committed on administered ground, that is in the near vicinity of a military post or on the government highway. Cases were generally tried, not under the Indian Penal Code in accordance with the statutory rules of evidence and procedure, but under Frontier Crimes Regulations. The PA or APA appointed a small group of tribal elders called a *jirga* (one of several meanings of the term) and framed central issues arising from the alleged facts on which the *jirga* was to find answers and recommend appropriate punishment where they found the accused guilty. Penalties normally had regard to tribal custom, thus for offences arising from a blood feud, there was a recognized formula of fines, or compensation, payment of which was held to cancel the excuse for continuing the feud. Frontier tribesmen are culturally totally different from the primitive animism that one commonly associates with the word 'tribe', either elsewhere on the Indian sub-continent or in many other parts of the world. Pathan tribal society is not chaotic; it rests firmly and rigidly on the basis of the Pathan code of honour, which substitutes for a centralized or institutional authority and for administrative machinery. The other essential bonds besides *Pakhtunwali* or *Nang-i-Pakhtun*, the code of honour, are belief in the sharing of a common ancestry by all members of the tribe, and the ties of a common faith (Islam).

While the Islamic faith can be very important, it often seemed to be subordinated to the Pakhtun code, and there were occasions when Wazir or Mahsud behaviour so transgressed the principles of Islam that special efforts had to be made to recall them to their faith and get them to redress their crimes, for example, in the treatment of kidnapped women, who were not normally molested as hostages.

The sharing of a common ancestor produced an intensely democratic form of society, in which each man had a right to express his own opinion, whatever his elders had said. Amongst the Wazirs, each group or subsection, each little hamlet even, had its own *maliks* (headmen), but their leadership was not a hereditary tribal one, and was often restricted to their own extended family circle, to their *kor*, or household. A *malik* who had status in a larger group had earned this by his personality and proven wisdom. Political officers frequently had to negotiate with a group of *maliks* representing a tribe or a subsection of a tribe, putting on their shoulders collective responsibility for redressing some wrong, such as kidnapping, or a raid on a village in a settled district, or harbouring outlaws, where their section was implicated. But we knew that, even if they seemed to assent to our demands, they would still have to secure the assent of the tribal *jirga* (in this case, the whole adult male population), before they could meet our conditions. There might be much hard bargaining to come. Few of them owned much land or property and the sense of individual equality was correspondingly strong – in such a society, anarchy is not far away. Curiously, this may be the logic behind the universal carrying of arms: in Waziristan no grown male moved from the protection of his house, with its encircling wall and lookout tower, without carrying a rifle and bandolier, and dagger. There has to be a deterrent, if a society marked by such equality of status is not to slip into anarchy, especially one in which one of the first principles of the code of honour is that of *badal* – the right of exchange, or revenge, for a wrong done to one's family. Another primary principle of the code is *melmastia*: hospitality and shelter must be provided to anyone who seeks it. This principle cannot be breached so difficulties regularly arise when offenders are harboured within an area for which a tribe is collectively responsible. Such responsibility, of course, also attracts payments of allowances for maintaining the peace of the area, and such allowances could be withheld, in whole or in part, until an offence had been redressed, kidnapped victims released, property restored, damaged roads repaired, and so on.

The Waziristan tribes had few actual resources to sustain them above the subsistence level and they had become increasingly dependent on cash from Government. Cultivable land was scanty and the standard of agriculture poor, constantly hampered by shortage of water and the low and erratic annual rainfall on the lower ground. The people were by nature nomadic and their flocks for generations had overgrazed the scant pasture and denuded the hillsides of shrubs and trees. The effects of centuries of soil erosion on the geological formation of these hills had produced some weird and awesome consequences – not least the exercise grounds for fleet and subtle hit-and-run guerrilla fighters. Since the tribes instinctively resisted intervention by Government, there was little that we could do to promote economic development.[7] I remember that we tried hard to find ways of improving water supplies, exploring with men who claimed to be water diviners for places to sink wells and experimenting with the Afghan system of carrying water underground by tunnel, building *karez*, an esoteric skill unknown to the western civil engineer. Such attempts were never wholeheartedly approved locally and led to disputes and sometimes fierce factional fights. Our tentative exploratory excursions were always under close protection from the local *maliks*, and usually covered by Tochi Scouts as well as the Waziri *Khassadars*, but that did not always stop warning shots from whistling overhead. There were very few schools, except for special places like Miranshah *serai*, and it was clear that until the tribes saw for themselves the advantages that would come from education, not much could be done to promote it. For one thing, teachers could hardly be found who were prepared to live in the conditions of *ghair ilaqa* (tribal territory). Yet one saw daily evidence of innate mechanical skills and high intelligence, and nobody could take part in a tribal *jirga* without realizing the deftness with which a subtle argument could be conducted by these wild people, and the eloquence that could sway opposing opinion.

Unfortunately, the historical unreliability of the Wazirs in disciplined military service prevented them from being recruited, like other Pathan tribes, for the Army. Afridis, Khattaks, Orakzai, Bangash, Yusufzai, even Mohmands were all enlisted in large numbers for service in the Frontier Militia and Frontier

Constabulary as well as the Regular Army, and during the War new channels were opened up, for example, in the additional police. By 1943 an experiment was working well with the Mahsuds, recruited to a special labour battalion, which served overseas. But the Wazirs could not even be recruited to the Tochi Scouts. In Waziristan it had long been a prime rule that the Tochi Scouts were drawn from Pathan tribes whose homeland was outside Waziristan. A scheme early in the 1920s to weld into the formation a small number of local Wazirs had long been abandoned. There was too much evidence at the time, perhaps particularly in South Waziristan with Mahsuds, that these tribes were treacherous and unreliable when serious unrest broke out. One consequence of all this was that, compared with transborder tribes outside Waziristan, the Wazirs had far less cash income from *naukaree* (service) but perhaps just as important, they lacked the influence which in the settled districts old soldiers in retirement so often brought to bear in remote places on attitudes to education, health and agricultural improvement.

The adoption of the semi-forward policy over the preceding twenty years had brought increased payments for services to contractors – on the roads and in military supplies. Many contracts went to local *maliks*, though some went to Hindus from Bannu, who of course had to pay protection money to the tribes if they were to operate across the administrative border. All the contractors had to employ local labour for work out of doors. But none of these considerations counted as much as the tribal allowances, and the payments to Khassadars. The latter were recruited for local service within the territory of each clan or subsection. They had their own officers, for whom the usual military terms like subedar and jemadar (roughly, sergeant major and sergeant) were used. They were organized by the Political Naib-Tahsildars under the general control of the Assistant Political Agent. Their primary function was to police the roads, operating from permanent piquets sited on commanding ridges or hilltops. At night they were supposed to restrain or prevent the passage of outlaws or miscreants, but throughout my command there seemed to be an endless succession of incidents in which telephone wire was cut and stolen, bridges and culverts blown, and evidence, both circumstantial and oral, was seldom lacking of complicity by the local Khassadars. Serious offences were of course investigated, and the Khassadars could be a useful source of information.

Sometimes a Khassadar company's pay would be withheld, pending restitution of some misdeed; and occasionally a particular man, or even a subedar, would be suspended or even dismissed. But discipline never could be rigid with such a bunch of carefree rascals. One was always aware that, while they might easily choose to take a shot at a passing army lorry or staff car on a road open day, they were far more likely to stop others from doing the same to me as I went along the road at any time. For I could not confine my movements to days when the road was officially open, troops were on the move and themselves picketing the hills.

I travelled either in a small Ford 'vanette' which carried seven or eight of my bodyguard, or in the 3-ton Chevrolet lorry, with at least double that number, even twenty-five or thirty, on board, many of them on the roof, and therefore awake, otherwise they might fall off. But if they were awake there was a good chance that their keen eyesight was keeping a lookout. The bodyguard was drawn from the ranks of the Khassadars. It was specially chosen to provide one or two representatives from each of the important tribal sections in the agency, and most of them were sons or nephews of respected *maliks* or *spingirays* (grey-beards, or elders). The theory was that their presence around me acted as a deterrent to a potential assailant, for if he fired at the lorry from a distance he ran the risk of hitting one of the bodyguards and therefore of incurring a bitter blood feud with influential families. The system worked admirably.

I can remember only twice being fired on when I was actually in the lorry, although soon after I left the agency, Colonel Sir Benjamin Bromhead, who had succeeded Jack Lowis as PA, was ambushed at Isha Corner and wounded in the shoulder, his Daur driver being badly hurt. In another incident a little earlier Brian Becker, the Additional APA stationed at Dosalli, was shot in the leg on the road to Ghariom. One of my predecessors in the late 1930s (Beatty) had been killed, and there was quite a high mortality rate for political officers in the twentieth century. On one of the occasions when shots were fired at me, that same Daur driver had reacted very fast, screaming orders to the escort as he accelerated towards cover, for he had seen the flash from the rifle and hoped that they could cut off the sniper's retreat. Of course, they did not. The shot had passed just behind the lorry, the sniper misjudging its speed, but he was far enough away on the other side of the Tochi river to be alarmed only by their shouted curses and imprecations as they dashed through the water in his direction. There was a reassuring *esprit de corps* amongst them and they would often sing cheerful Pushtu love songs as we sped along if the day was not too hot and dusty. The subedar of the escort was a villainous-looking Kabul Khel from near Spinwam on the Keitu river. When I first met him, his close-set eyes and wispy beard, and the dirty black turban carelessly wrapped under his chin and slopping over his face, made an impression that was anything but reassuring. He did not look half the chap that some of the athletic young warriors of the bodyguard looked, but he was nearly twice their age, certainly twice as experienced and three times as cunning, and I came to feel safer whenever Gul Behram was around. By the time I could understand his particularly vile version of Waziri Pushtu I realized that I had a fair chance of passing my Pushtu examination – a worthwhile goal, for success was to add a hundred rupees to my monthly salary for the rest of my career in posts requiring a knowledge of the language. For my personal protection he provided me with a small French automatic pistol which he had no doubt obtained through smugglers' channels. It was light and convenient but hardly likely to do serious damage to a determined tribesman at a range of more than twenty feet. Later, I acquired a standard issue Webley from the government arsenal.

I had been in Miranshah for only three days when I took part in my first *barampta*. Preparations for it had been made in such hushed tones by the PA and the Commandant Tochi Scouts that I was only dimly aware of what was afoot when we set off in the pitch darkness of Saturday morning to surround a village, Mohammed Khel, on the banks of the Tochi some fifteen miles west of Miranshah. We started in the Scouts' lorries, using sidelights only at first, then without lights for the last few miles before we debussed a mile or two from the village. For me, this was a nervous journey for the road twisted over narrow culverts and our Scouts' driver was pretty raw. Jack's temper was on a short fuse and he lost patience with the driver who was clearly falling behind schedule. When he snapped at me, 'Will you drive this bloody thing?' I had to confess that I had never attempted such a feat, and anyway didn't know the road, so he took the wheel himself, no doubt fuming that the Governor had sent him such a wet nincompoop for an APA. I was soon to discover that, while he would often blow off steam like this in awkward situations, he was as steady as a rock, and kind, fair and trusting in all his dealings with me. It was a marvellous privilege to serve with a political officer of his stature.

The Scouts from Miranshah had to join forces with another company which came downstream from the west, charged with blocking the escape routes from the village. Soon after dawn we went in, to search for men who had been involved in the mail lorry hold-up on a road open day a week before my arrival. In that incident, two men had been killed and four kidnapped and held to ransom. The Scouts went through the village thoroughly, in face of the noisy protests of the womenfolk but none of the wanted men were found. Either our intelligence work was at fault or they had got away before the exits were blocked. When we heard that an old woman had wandered out of the village in the darkness and been allowed to return after blundering into a patrol of Scouts, we suspected that she had given the signal to escape. Their route and procedure would have been thought out in advance. So we came away without them, but we took forty hostages, and arrested nine men wanted for other offences, while several houses belonging to proclaimed outlaws were destroyed. As we withdrew over flat ground separating the village from the road, half a mile away, some shots were fired from across the river. A Scout havildar about ten yards away from me had a remarkable escape. Inside his *pugree*, resting on his shaven head, he carried a flat cigarette tin through which a bullet passed, the shattered tin just grazing his head enough to draw a trickle of blood. Once we were in our lorries, on our way home, there was some more sniping but our flanks were well protected by the Khassadars, the air cover was noisy and the hostiles kept too far away to be a real nuisance. So I had my baptism of Frontier action – in Scouts' parlance, a 'show'. It involved a force of twelve platoons, backed up after dawn by armoured cars and aircraft; nothing less would have been safe in such an area, to deal with such a large village. Next day the Dardoni *jirga* brought into Miranshah the four kidnapped men unharmed. They had no doubt had to pay the ransom money, but would have their own method of avenging this on the gang.[8]

A couple of weeks later, we drove past the same village of Mohammad Khel on our way to Datta Khel, the furthest west of the Scouts' posts in the Tochi valley. This was an entirely different sort of outing, undertaken with a small escort. Datta Khel was then a name familiar to the British public for it had often been attacked and pillaged because of its proximity to the international frontier, and since 1936 the Tochi Scouts' post there had been besieged for several months on end, in several successive years, by Ipi's hostile gangs. The last 'siege' was in 1942. The names of the Scouts' officers thus confined to quarters on short rations had been familiar to newspaper readers in Europe and curiously had attracted various offers of marriage – now framed in the mess – from ladies touched by misconceived notions of the romance of the Frontier. We had a RAF group captain with us whose task was to survey the emergency landing ground at Datta Khel; I never knew exactly why. It seemed to me to make no sense to think of landing big aircraft out there in the wilderness when there was a decent aerodrome so close at Miranshah. But I supposed that the Air Force wanted to think of every contingency in case the Germans broke through the Caucasus and came on through Afghanistan, and we now know that there was a German plan to drop paratroops in places like Datta Khel to link with Ipi's forces in the rebellion that Subhas Chandra Bose had assured them was ready to break out in India. One interesting by-product of that visit was that later, when we made several attempts to plan irrigation works in that neighbourhood, many of the tribesmen were convinced that we were really preparing to build an aerodrome to attack Afghanistan, and would have nothing to do with our schemes to improve their cultivation.

But the group captain's mission was only a subsidiary purpose of our excursion and next day he was escorted back to Miranshah, while Jan, the CO, Jack Lewis, Peter Manson, the acting Adjutant, Rahim, later to be a general in the Pakistan Army, and I set off to climb Vezhda, the highest mountain in the neighbourhood, a 7,700 feet summit deep in the heart of the Manzar Khel country. This was real excitement. We took with us only one Tochi Scout signaller with his heliograph equipment and relied entirely on the protection of one of Waziristan's most famous characters, a veteran subedar of Khassadars called Darim, who had served in France in the First World War and won the IOM and the Croix de Guerre. It was said that during one of the sieges of Datta Khel fort he had knocked on the gate at the dead of night and announced to the Tochi Scouts' sentries that he had come to join their side; which he did. Two years before our adventure with him he had taken Charles Duke then the PA, on to Vezhda on a similar outing.[9] On that occasion some hostile characters bullied one of Darim's sons

On the top of Vezhda (7,500 ft) in Manzar Khel country under tribal escort.

Peter Manson, Tochi Scouts.

into letting them get close enough to shoot up the party. Having
ensured that Charles would stay behind a big enough rock, Darim
went off with his Khassadars to drive away the enemy, then turned
in a fury on his recalcitrant son and shot him in the foot to teach
him a lesson in the principle of *Melmastia* central to the Pathan
code of honour. We had no such alarm, but a thoroughly enjoyable
outing, capped on the summit by a glorious view and a 'snack' of
boiled eggs, biscuits, sultana cake and green tea – which was
supplemented by a huge lunch of mutton and chicken *pilao* with
all the trimmings when we got to Darim's *kot* at the foot of the
mountain.[10]

Next day I went on the mail run operated by No.1 Squadron
IAF on Sundays from Miranshah. I had already seen quite a bit
of the Tochi road, and I had traversed the road linking the Tochi
and the Kurram which ran from Mirali by Spinwam on the Keitu
river to Thall on the Kurram river at the junction of the Kurram
Agency and Kohat District. But I had not yet been on the road to
Razmak or seen the other outlying Scouts' posts and the brigade
camps at Gardai and Damdil. So I had asked the Air Force to take
me round all the posts when a plane was dropping mail. This
entailed being strapped to a parachute and fitted into the tail
gunner's seat in an ancient Hawker Audax biplane, trying to read
the map while travelling with my back to the engine and the pilot,
with whom radio communication was so noisy as to be almost
unintelligible. But the trip was from my point of view a complete
success and I think we dropped all the precious little packets of
mail inside, or near enough, all the appropriate destinations –
Boya, Kharkamar, Datta Khel, Gardai, Razmak, Ghariom, Biche
Kashkai, Mirali, Spinwam, and home over Darweshta, the twin-
peaked mountain that stood on its own in the east of the agency,
so like Benachie in Aberdeenshire. Apart from the pleasure of
identifying from the air these places which had hitherto for me
been just names from the romance of Frontier history, and waving
to their occupants as we swooped low in a shallow dive to drop
the little mailbags, the flight taught me a great deal about the
military geography of the area. By good luck, that Sunday was a
ROD (road open day) so I saw the troops on the move, and
understood why it was essential for them to hold certain vantage
points, and how the contribution of the Khassadars complemented
their defence of the convoys on the road. For the Khassadars also
were on duty, their white flags readily identifying their positions,

and I gained a new perspective on my responsibilities for their conduct and efficiency.

Much of my day-to-day work related to these matters. Although my office paperwork was much lighter than it had been in Hazara, I had to come back to it most evenings in Miranshah. Many of the daylight hours were spent on the road – inspecting different Khassadar companies, paying their allowances, gathering their information and coping with their complaints. Well before dusk I aimed to reach home – nights away from Miranshah were rare: one or two nights each month at Datta Khel, and also at Spinwam, where the Scouts had a strongly-held post on the banks of the Keitu river to cover the area between the Sheratullah plain and Thall on the Kurram river. Occasionally I would make a special excursion to escort a particular visitor – in my first month I went to Thall to bring my old golfing friend, Bishop Barnes of Lahore, 'by the backdoor' into Waziristan. His arrival, like any other, was kept secret, in case the rival bishop got to hear of it. That was our code name for the Faqir of Ipi, a useful way of referring to him in wireless telegraphy signals,[11] the medium on which we largely depended for internal communication, as well as for urgent messages to the Governor. Our telephone service was unreliable because the tribesmen spent so much time cutting the wires, and stealing it, for export to Afghanistan, to be traded for ammunition.

I had to look after about 1,100 Khassadars – roughly half the number employed in the agency. The others were under the charge of Brian Becker, an army officer who had been appointed Additional APA. He was based at Dosalli, a big Scouts' fort on the central road between Tall Bridge and Razmak. This appointment enabled the APA at Miranshah to allocate more of his time to the executive and political side of the PA's office. That included subjects with which I had become familiar in Hazara, like 'civil supplies', as well as a considerable caseload under Frontier Crimes Regulations. Mostly these cases were tried in Miranshah, but sometimes I heard them at places like Mirali and even Idak. They involved no 'pleaders' or lawyers, and had little of the tedium of courtwork in settled districts. It was for the *jirga* to investigate the evidence and establish the facts, and provided I had framed the issues right the burden of the work was not excessive. But it took me a long time to adjust to the style of *jirga* findings and accept their guidelines reflecting the Pathan code. I was never happy about accepting that a murder could be assuaged by getting half a dozen members of a clan to swear something on the Koran, provided the conventional blood money was paid.

My Khassadars liked every now and then to entertain to a *tikala*, and provided they had not got into hot water for some misdeed or sin of omission, propriety required me to accept their invitation. The PA and I had to be careful about other invitations: there were times when it was helpful to lunch with a particular *malik*, but other times when such a gesture might be misinterpreted by some rival group in his tribe. There was no personal reluctance on my part to participate in these *tikalas*. The food was delicious and the conversation always interesting, often quite hilarious – Pathans have a keen sense of humour. For all the sparsity of grazing, some element in these hills bred the finest quality of mutton, and it was served with rice piping hot, so tender that large fistfuls of meat crumbled in one's mouth. It was not easy, at the time of the Bengal famine, to reconcile that tragedy in one's letters home with accounts of some midday feast in a crowded little stone fortress perched on rock a couple of hundred feet above the road. My mouth waters still when I think of the mutton pilao, the liver and kidneys 'kebab', the wheat and maize chapattis, followed by local oranges, Kandahar grapes, and Kabuli walnuts, all washed down with green tea.

Early in January the PA and I walked downriver from Tall Bridge with Sir George Cunningham to be entertained in this way at Spalga, the home of an old Tori Khel *malik* called Shahzar Khan. He had been one of Sir George's most notable sparring partners when HE had been political agent many years before. Now he was on his deathbed and the Governor made the special journey to pay his tribute to the old warrior who had been paralyzed and bedridden for several years. In his diary, Sir George described how he went into the horrible dark room in which Shahzar lay, the only light coming in by the doorway. 'He talked quite sensibly of old times, and got in a request for a Bannochi outlaw that he was harbouring. Then he presented me with a robe of honour – a black choga with gold embroidery, old and stained, which turned out to have been given him by King Amanullah of Afghanistan for his services in 1919!' When HE joined us in an upper chamber after the interview with Shahzar, we enjoyed a splendid meal, capped by platefuls of delicious oranges from Shahzar's garden which Sir George said were the best he had ever tasted in Waziristan. When he enquired of Shahzar's sons about the outlaw, they pointed quietly to the man who had passed round the plate of oranges. Sir George said nothing – but later he assured the sons that he would do what he could to help the old man's '*hamsayah*' (literally, 'one who sat in his shade', to whom he had granted sanctuary), because he wished to respect Shahzar's dying request. The *choga* was quietly entrusted by the Governor to the eldest son for safekeeping as a symbol of the friendship between Sir George and his father. It is worth mentioning that our party made the journey on foot to Spalga without escort – along with ten Wazir *maliks*, we were guests of Shahzar and safe in the traditions of Pakhtun hospitality. In Shahzar's *ilaqa* there would be no act of treachery that day.

That kind of diversion added variety to the daily routine but in any case it was never boring. It was never sunk in paper, but rather absorbed in speech, with a procession of would-be informers hoping for *kharcha* (literally, expenses for the cost of their journey, i.e. a reward for loyalty to Government!). Slowly, as I improved my Pushtu, I became more able to draw together threads of different stories and more familiar with the interrelationships of the tribes and their subsections, their territorial influence and the names and standing of their various *maliks*. On occasions, usually at bedtime, the arrival of cypher telegrams originating from the Foreign Office in London reminded us that a few miles away lay the territory of an independent foreign state in whose affairs our tribes meddled almost as freely as in our own. We were even asked to account for some alleged breach of Afghan airspace by British bomber planes, presumed to have been hunting for the caves inhabited by the Faqir of Ipi and his permanent gang near Gorwekht close to the border. Since Jack Lowis had a tendency to forget to make the periodic change of key to the cypher code we never enjoyed these external intrusions on our sleep and sometimes ignored the 'immediate' tag on the requests of the 'bloody bureaucrats'. But if these were artificial emergencies there was no shortage of the real thing, and I came to realize that the strain of life in Waziristan came from the fact that we lived on a diet of wireless signals any one of which might call for a decision on which mens' lives depended. As I put it in one letter home, there was a feeling of being on permanent stand-to.

Generally at that time Waziristan appeared to be less disturbed than for several years – indeed, since 1936. There was a story abroad that Ipi was short of ammunition and some evidence that the help he had had from the German embassy in Kabul was not effective or reliable. To help to spread the notion that we now had the Germans beaten we breached all normal security rules one night and took Gul Behram and three or four Wazir *maliks* into the fort and across to the IAF quarters to see the film *Desert Victory*. We got a squadron of American Vultee Vengeance dive-bombers to put on a display by practising bombing on a proscribed area which lay between the Dardoni plain, on which Miranshah stands, and the northern slopes of Darweshta. There were also army manoeuvres on the plain with Stuart tanks combining with the Scouts, and we hoped that watching eyes were suitably impressed so that the right messages about British military might would be carried back to Gorwekht.

Early in December I went to Peshawar to sit the examination in Revenue Law. Although by now I had forgotten much that I knew when I sat the exam in Abbottabad, I passed with little apparent difficulty and was finally convinced that my earlier failure had simply been decided as a policy measure by Lionel Jardine, rather than by inadequate preparation on my part or by poor performance on paper. I had three days' leave in which to make the tedious journey back by road, but the Air Force said they would find a place for me in an Anson on the Wednesday morning, so I got a long weekend off, getting back to Miranshah just in time to participate in the Scouts' *tamasha* celebrating the festival of Eid-ul-Juha, with contests at pistol and rifle shooting, and a *tikala* provided by the IOs (Indian subedars and jemadars). The PA and I were always involved by them in such activities, being treated just as they treated their own officers. They were a truly splendid cadre, full of lively good humour and most impressive at their job and I was always very proud that the relationship between the Scouts and the political officers was so close and warm.

All this time, though the tribes generally were peaceful and Ipi was quiescent, there was a continuous crop of bothersome incidents – wire-cutting, bridge-blowing, a kidnapping near Khajuri Scouts' Post on the main road, an ambush of the 14/14th Punjab's on 'Sugar Loaf', a hill near Asad Khel,[12] a chase across the Dande Plain with the Scouts pursuing Kharoti and Ghilzai smugglers taking bales of tea and cloth to Afghanistan – we captured four men and ten camels, with their loads. Then on 13 December there was a very serious incident, characteristic of Waziristan, though fortunately it involved the PA South Waziristan and not ourselves. Pat Duncan was officiating in that post which was about to be taken up by Gerald Curtis who was delayed in Delhi by illness. The CO of the 2nd Gurkha battalion at Razmak had been keen to carry out a training exercise on the slopes of 11,000 foot Shuidar, a mountain a few miles from the cantonment to the north-west, in Mahsud territory. Although his APO was reluctant, Pat sanctioned the manoeuvre, and all might have been well had a sniper not caused a fatal casualty at a late stage in the withdrawal, near Tip Ghar. Unfortunately, though there was not much daylight left, the CO was determined to bring the body down the mountain, and this necessitated reinforcing his rearguard. More casualties were incurred and more delay; the shooting increased and inevitably attracted more tribesmen from the general neighbourhood – barren hills sprouted men whenever a show like that started. Another battalion was sent out from Razmak to reinforce the Gurkhas. When darkness fell, there was confusion; the gates of the encampment had to be closed while there was considerable uncertainty about how many men were still outside the wire. In the final tally next day, it was established that there had been about fifty casualties, half of them fatal, and many of them the result of hand-to-hand encounters in the falling darkness. In the circumstances, it was unlikely that the Mahsuds would have suffered many casualties.

While this was in a sense an isolated incident, it was symptomatic of the risks in our situation and worrying because it seemed to mark the end of a period of relative quiet, when some new signs of tribal disaffection were being reported. Amongst these were indications of trouble in Khost, across the border in Afghanistan, and there was no knowing how that might affect our Wazirs and Mahsuds. I was beginning to think that the Wazir was totally unimpressed by our display of tanks and dive-bombers, and concerned only to improve his own armament, for one of his objectives in these ambushes was to secure modern rifles and Bren guns from the Army's casualties – and in these 'quiet' months far too many weapons of this sort were lost in this way. In one shocking incident from the Army's point of view, a couple of Wazirs who had been lurking in a ditch below a culvert surprised some Mahrattas whose jeep stopped beside them. Though they were in full view of the army camp 200 yards away, they made a rich haul of weapons.

Incidents like these, particularly the Razmak one, were eventually reported in the Indian press and attracted investigative journalists to Waziristan. They came under permit, were pretty strictly confined to Miranshah and its environs and it was not easy for them to understand what was happening. Around this time we had visits from *The Times* correspondent in India, and a well-known broadcaster, A.P. Ryan, who had done distinguished work in wartime for the BBC. After his visit to Miranshah I know that my mother heard him broadcast a month or two later. I wished I had heard him for on the night he stayed with us he sat quietly in a corner of the mess writing, while I was getting 'into a flap' because the PA had been out all day in the Mirali area and had not returned. For obvious reasons, we did not normally stay out after dark and by the time of dinner I decided that real anxiety justified arranging a *gusht* (patrol) by Scouts to search for Jack. As this was being laid on, Ryan betrayed not the slightest sign of interest or understanding. Some miles down the road we met Jack and the bodyguard, their lorry limping home after mechanical trouble, but with no more serious reasons for delay. The reporter's taciturnity and phlegm proved to have been more appropriate than our flap and fuss. Another visitor, a month or so later, was Cecil Beaton, the photographer, who was discharging a special commission for the War Office. I spent a morning with him, taking him to places which I thought would be photogenic. What he really wanted was to photograph people and he seemed far more satisfied with pictures of individual Wazirs who were waiting to see me at the gate of the fort. He got most excited when I took him to the 'cavalry' lines, where the small section of the Scouts who were mounted had their horses. Years afterwards I saw in one of his books a photograph of a Scout at his mount's head, but as far as I know Cecil Beaton never acknowledged the hospitality he got by sending a print to the Scouts, for all the film he used. His languid manner did not make a favourable impression on his rough and ready hosts.

Jack Lowis took me off to Bannu, where his family was, for a Christmas break which I greatly enjoyed, though I knew far fewer people there than at Abbottabad on the two previous Christmases. On the 27th I returned leaving him to take a longer rest over the New Year, and, though he was within easy recall, I felt that I was getting 'the feel of the show' holding the fort in his absence.

Notes

[1] In this context Barampta implies entry to the village by troops, or more likely by Tochi Scouts, to search for wanted individuals or stolen property. The village would have to be surrounded at night to minimize the risks of a contested entry. The word was also applied to action against a particular tribe or subsection of a tribe, for example an attempt on a particular day to arrest any member of it, let us say in Bannu city at the time, in order to put pressure on the tribe to release kidnapped victims, or to produce proclaimed outlaws who were members of the tribe.

[2] A favourite method of blowing up bridges was to light a fire under an unexploded bomb, or shell, dragged laboriously by night to the site. It was an operation as dangerous to the tribesmen as to the bridge.

[3] Sadly, a year after I left the agency, I heard that one of the officers, who had stayed there too long and missed the chance of service in Burma, having been jilted, if that is a fair term, by the fiancée whom he had not seen since his last home leave five years earlier, had taken to the bottle in his misery. Perhaps by then supplies had become more copious.

[4] The terrain generally does not lend itself to precise demarcations so it may not be unfair to Sir Mortimer Durand to record this story. Soon after the turn of the century he became British Ambassador in Washington. The effervescent President Theodore Roosevelt took him on one of his famous walks. On their return, Roosevelt declared that Durand was 'a bad walker, and wholly unable to climb'. Sir Mortimer recorded 'we drove out to a wooded valley with streams running through it. He then made me struggle through bushes and walk for two hours and a half, at an impossible speed. My arms and shoulders are still stiff with dragging myself up by roots and ledges. At one place I fairly stuck, and could not get to the top till he caught me by the collar and hauled at me.' Teddy Roosevelt was, of course an anomaly and a phenomenon. In my day, Americans tended to be jeep-bound, and were no match for Scouts or political officers on the hills.

[5] A young Hindu girl in Bannu eloped with, or was abducted by a Mohammedan student. Trying the case, the Assistant Commissioner, I.D. Scott, found that she had been converted to Islam without undue pressure, but the furious Hindu fraternity appealed against his decision, and it was overturned. The furore

191

in Bannu and the neighbouring agencies was unimaginable. Some six months later, on further appeal to a higher court, the girl's status as a Muslim was confirmed, but the damage had been done. The Faqir of Ipi had established his cause against the British.

[6] A minor exception has to be made in respect of some of the land held by the Daur tribe, on which a light revenue was assessed, following the terms of the original treaty with that tribe, on whose request the British had moved forward into the Tochi.

[7] One of the most telling criticisms of British policy on the Frontier was that it failed to secure sound economic development in the tribal areas. True, but as Sir George Cunningham wrote in 1945, the tribesmen would rather be free and undeveloped than developed and administered. They wanted freedom from government officers, police, courts and taxation. The people of tribal territory must first be confident that Government had no intention of occupying their land before they would be ready to accept economic development. This opinion was capped by the wry comment: 'I am never sure whether the Pathan is more likely to give trouble when he is poor than when he waxes fat!' (Comments by Sir George Cunningham in July 1945 on the Report of the Frontier Committee, chaired by General Sir Francis Tuker).

[8] It is perhaps worth remarking that a note in my diary records that I attended a tea party in the house of one Rasool Khan in the village of Mohammad Khel on 7 April 1944. All was forgiven! *Inshallah.*

[9] Later, Sir Charles Duke of HM Diplomatic Service, who had a distinguished career as an ambassador in the Middle East at the time of the Suez crisis.

[10] Sadly, Darim in the end paid the penalty for his friendship towards the British. About two years after I left Miranshah, he was himself murdered.

[11] It was also wise at times to use such a code in conversations which might be overheard by tribesmen, or by servants who might communicate information, perhaps inadvertently, to ill-disposed people. It was possible to conceal the identity of the subject of conversation by using such a nickname.

[12] When Jack and I were out investigating this incident on the following Saturday, we had just got down the hill when we were told of a skirmish in progress between troops and hostiles about twenty miles up the road near Razani, on the pass approaching

Razmak. We went straight there for complicity by Khassadars seemed likely. It was long after dark before we got back and we decided to knock up the Scouts at Dosalli, where we slept the night wrapped in red hospital blankets.

CHAPTER VIII

Waziri Chess: A Bishop Checkmated?

In the next six months I had to hold the fort 'for real' on several occasions, notably for over four weeks in May and June when Jack Lowis was on leave in Nathia Gali and things really were humming. He had been very good at letting me into the secrets of the agency. He had a gift for expressing his thoughts and doubts in vivid language, just as he had a gift for conversing in Pushtu,[1] and through him I had the chance to learn how the mind of the Wazir worked, and how he responded to the moves that were open to a political agent. Over the New Year period unsettling news began to come into Miranshah seeming to confirm the impression from the pre-Christmas period that something was in the wind. The most specific worry was the rumour that the Faqir of Ipi was about to move from Gorwekht; soon it was being said that he was going to make for a remote part of the Shaktu valley, on the border between the two agencies. It was alleged that his purpose was to settle long-standing disputes involving the Mahsuds and the Tori Khel, whose territories lay on either side of the Shaktu. Some informants declared that his real purpose was to raise his standard for a general uprising of the tribes, directed against the British. The days and weeks passed nervously with no clear interpretation of these reports.

The steadying hand of Sir George Cunningham was readily available. He began an important series of flying visits to Waziristan to consult the two PAs and the Resident – sometimes flying in to Miranshah, sometimes to Jandola in South Waziristan. The new PA Mahsuds, Gerald Curtis, was bound to need time to pick up the threads; Pat Duncan, who had been in Wana as APA for two years, had just been transferred to Hangu. Jack Lowis had no trust in the Assistant Political Officer in South Waz maintaining that he was afraid of the Mahsuds, which was likely enough. In North Waz we had a strong and forceful team for our APO was

194

Mohamed Jan, a highly intelligent and articulate, very stout young man whose father Ahmed Jan was for many years the most illustrious *munshi* (teacher of languages) in Peshawar.[2] It would have been hard to compete with Lowis and Mohamed Jan in the subtle game of political analysis of tribal moves, and for some time the South Waz team was at a disadvantage.

If this sounds as if there was a kind of football match going on between two teams captained by the British PAs, almost certainly that was precisely what Ipi was aiming at. In choosing to sit for weeks on the Shaktu, in threatening posture, dragging both Mahsud and Wazir tribes by implication into his scheme to upset us, he was engaging in his own version of 'divide and rule'. There should have been a referee: that was the role of the Resident in Waziristan, the senior political officer through whom the PAs were responsible to the Governor. The post of Resident was one on which the senior army staff had insisted. Whenever there was serious fighting to do, they were reluctant to accept the judgment of a single PA, believing perhaps that he might be prejudiced in favour of 'his own tribe'. They knew that in a campaign that dealt with the tribes of both agencies, both PAs might not always speak with one voice. So there had to be a Resident senior in rank to the Political Agents to whom the General could speak. In the recent past there had been some first-class decisive Residents – until very recently, Ambrose Dundas had held the post. In 1943-4, unfortunately, the Resident was a much less decisive and less knowledgeable senior officer – Colonel John Bradshaw, of the Indian Political Service, a pleasant, good-natured but rather ineffectual man. His winter headquarters were remote in the town of Dera Ismail Khan, and though he visited us quite often, and spent quite a bit of the summer in Razmak, I never felt that he really grasped what was going on.

Perhaps Sir George was alert to this danger – indeed I am sure he was. At any rate he made himself readily available to arbitrate by flying in for frequent conferences and being accessible on the telephone whenever the system was operating – there was no radio telephone; signalling by wireless was in morse. From the start, he was more sceptical than we who were on the spot. He had sources of information not directly available to us through his link with the British Embassy in Kabul and its intelligence services, and also through his underground network of pro-British *mullahs* scattered throughout remote parts of the whole Frontier. From Kabul, he had a pretty good idea of what was happening in Khost, the administrative district of Afghanistan nearest to Waziristan. Maladministration by local Afghan officials had helped to stir something of a revolt amongst their Ghilzai and Malang tribes – the sort of 'party' in which their Madda Khel neighbours, who straddled the border, loved to join. There was a recent history of active sympathy amongst Mahsuds and Wazirs for the cause of those who would attack the regime in Kabul, and perhaps restore the fortunes of the former King Amamullah, now in Italy. Whereas the reports we received suggested that Ipi's moves were prompted by agents of the Axis powers, who certainly supplied him with cash, Sir George suspected that he might have been pressed by the Afghan Government itself to leave Gorwekht for a time to distance him from their local arguments with their tribes.

Our worry, however, was that he had moved and that he had chosen a new base for operations which threatened the maximum embarrassment to our objective, which was to keep the tribes quiet with minimum use of military force. Whenever he stayed for a night or two he brought the danger that the young bloods of that section might follow his guidance and bring their whole tribe into action – especially if we could be lured into errors of judgement or if we overreacted against the misdeeds of the minority. At the very least, we had to find means to keep the pressure on the *maliks* to move him on rapidly out of their area. This may show how subtle was his choice of the Shaktu as his new stamping ground. He could play off Wazir against Mahsud and vice versa – as one section moved him on to another; he could work up younger elements in both sections to join in some enterprise against the Army or the Scouts. He could indeed use his holy offices to settle some disputes and so unite in his debt unlikely allies in some mischievous ploy. He had money, and arms – apart from rifles and light machine-guns, he had at least two field guns capable of firing from a distance at a Scouts' post – and he had inevitably his hard corps of seasoned outlaws, some of them deserters with military training, all of them accustomed to violent action. There were not huge numbers of these men, and they often broke up into small gangs of twenty or thirty which slipped off to create trouble a day or two days' march away. But they were the nucleus round which he might raise his standard and given the right psychological circumstances, an effective action by less than a hundred of these men could rally to his cause a *lashkar* of a thousand or more in two or three days. In many ways Waziristan was like the Scottish Highlands of earlier times with the clans responding to the fiery cross.

For some weeks nothing of great note followed Ipi's arrival in the Shaktu area. Our nerves were kept on the stretch. Messages which we sent to appropriate *maliks* succeeded in persuading them to refuse to let him settle. Rumour had it that he had found the sort of refuge to which he was accustomed in Gorwekht, in caves in some very craggy and desolate country in a narrow defile called Walo Tangi. It proved to be very difficult to pinpoint a specific place on the map. The PA cross-examined dozens of would-be informers. I had a session at the Intelligence Bureau in Peshawar on aerial photographs and we twice took Gul Behram and a bunch of friendly *maliks* on reconnaissance flights in an Anson. They had never flown before and prudently turned towards Mecca to say their prayers before embarking. But once they were airborne there was no sign of nerves; they became excited when they realized within a couple of minutes that they could see further and better than even they were accustomed to with their hillmens' eyes and experience. They rushed from one side of the plane to the other in response to cries like 'There is Guljamir's *kot!*' It was clear that they were potentially useful, and after the second flight we were reasonably confident that we knew, to within two or three hundred yards, where Ipi's new headquarters were reputed to be. It looked a desolate and unpromising place, abandoned by human beings, so Sir George agreed that we might drop the appropriate warning notices announcing that it was a 'proscribed' area, liable to be bombed and machine-gunned without further warning.

Meanwhile, what was happening in the Shaktu should have been of more direct concern to Gerald Curtis than to us, for we had other diversions to preoccupy us. Several gangs based in our territory were far too active in raids in Bannu and Kohat districts and inside one period of ten days I found myself involved in different forms of *barampta*. One was a tricky daylight operation. Two Hindu girls had been kidnapped in a raid on a village in Kohat district and our enquiries established the complicity of a gang of Macha Madda Khel. This subsection of the tribe lived beyond our reach, right on the international border, but men from it often joined caravans of Ghilzai and other Powindahs who migrated between the high ground in Afghanistan and the Indian plains; at this time of the year their camels normally carried great baulks of timber on the way down. So we chose a particular day to stop every caravan on the Tochi road and search for Macha Madda Khel men. This was a touchy operation, for those Powindahs did not like any interference with their movements except at recognized posts near our administrative border with Bannu where they were accustomed to surrender their arms on the way down, recovering them on the return journey. All went well, and over the day our patrols of Scouts and Khassadars arrested twenty-seven Macha men – who would simply be detained until their tribe yielded to pressure to surrender the two Hindu girls.

The other occasions involved night '*gushts*'. There is not much to say about one of them except that it involved some incredible scrambling in the dark over uncomfortable rocks, and several times waist-deep through an icy stream. When dawn came, we saw that we were in a sort of unpleasant moonscape, a totally abandoned wasteland where God had clearly been displeased with his handiwork. Not surprisingly we made no human contact in an adventure lasting about nine hours, in the course of which I recorded that we halted only twice to sit on a rock for twenty minutes. We got back to Khajuri Fort tired and disconsolate, but in retrospect when I traced our movements on the map I was astonished at the distance we had covered and the speed of our march. That was the supreme quality of the Scouts – their rapidity of movement over difficult terrain, the reward of training and lightness of equipment allied to the instinct for movement possessed by all Pathan hillmen. In one letter I mentioned that in the last hour of that nine-hour *gusht* the Scouts covered five miles. That made it easier to believe in the account of the extraordinary marches by John Nicholson and others with their Frontiersmen during the Indian Mutiny.

The third example was rather different. I left Miranshah with Neville Williams and six platoons at 5.00 a.m. on a pitch dark morning of foul weather. The long drought had broken a fortnight earlier and that night the sleet slanted down as thick as I could remember. It was impossible to see one's own hand or to distinguish a man's shape more than two feet away. We had to make a six-mile march across flattish country broken by streams and nullahs and ditches. It had rained for two days and we plodded through water and mud everywhere. We marched in twos, each pair close on their leaders' heels; orders were whispered down the line; no light was shown. Behind us at first the searchlights from the fort blazed out and swung round, leaving us blinder than ever when they snapped out. Gradually even that occasional illumination faded behind us. At one point we halted for a time: we had lost two platoons. Within twenty minutes they had rejoined us, without a signal or any method of communication, solely because of their trained skill in night movement. Before first light at 8.00 a.m. Neville had his whole force in place right in front of the village which was the object of the *barampta*, and by dawn it was surrounded, every exit carefully blocked, before the Scouts' mounted infantry swept out from Miranshah to relieve us and let Neville's men enter the village.

That was a perfectly executed manoeuvre in weather conditions which Neville told me were the worst he had experienced in four-and-a-half years in the Tochi and South Waziristan Scouts. He already had the MC, and was a major at twenty-eight. Three months later he went off to command a battalion of his own regiment in Burma. He was killed in action, a lieutenant colonel, aged twenty-nine. The village we searched that day was Tabbai Tol Khel; it was a hard nut to crack. Some of the men we wanted had found ingenious hiding places. One was hiding in a tiny cell cunningly constructed in a nondescript heap of bricks in the corner of a courtyard. We had to threaten to use grenades on his cover before he would come out with his hands empty. A man cornered in this way often decided to run amok, with dagger or pistol, and was capable in this way of killing several of his hunters before they could stop him. In another house all seemed well except for a miserable woman lying on a cot in a dark corner covered in a sheet. She was said to be ill with fever. Jack decided to accept the story but as we were withdrawing I said, 'It's not a woman, you know – look at the hair on her hand.' I was right, although one hand was the only part of the person that was visible, but we accepted that the man had fever and left him to lie in peace. We made eight arrests, but were disappointed because we found that the gang we really wanted had left the previous afternoon with their loot loaded on donkeys, en route for Afghanistan which was just a few miles away over the hills.

Meanwhile, back in the Shaktu area there was little real evidence that Ipi wanted to settle in the unfriendly terrain around Walo Tangi, and there seemed no good reason why he might want to, except that we were still not certain where it was and probably could not harm him there even from the air if we tried. But political pressure on the Mahsuds especially was not proving immediately successful, and it was decided to use the air weapon. HE was always opposed to the use of bombs unless a specific target could be identified. This meant that we were more urgently than ever asking 'Who is today sheltering the Faqir?'

Before the end of January we were sure that Ipi was in Malikshahi country, in a hilly area higher up the valley above the junction of the Shaktu and the Sham Algad, which was a route to Ghariom Scouts' post, from which a road ran across the Sham Plain and over the Iblanke Narai at about 6,000 feet, past two prominent piquets guarding the hairpin bends which led down to the big Dosalli post on the central Waziristan road in the Khaisora river valley. This was the area on which most of the action was to be concentrated for the next three months.

We wanted air action in Malikshahi Tangi and the necessary red warning notices were dropped, but the bombs did not follow: next day the Governor decided that the targets were not specific enough. Two days later Jack Lowis flew to Peshawar to see him. I was in Miranshah, getting information that convinced me that Ipi was still in Malikshahi country; I got a signal that bombing would start in four days if there was confirmation that he had not moved on – the PA must have convinced the Governor. On 9 February, two days after the dropping of warning notices, villages in the Shaktu were bombed, about six miles away from Ghariom and several miles downstream from the junction of the Shaktu and the Sham Algad. These were Gul Zamir Kot, on the left or north bank, a Tori Khel habitation, and Trikhtalai, a Bahlolzai Mahsud village on the opposite bank. We had expected to have to follow this up with further action, probably involving Tochi Scouts, but following messages from the tribes to the political staff at Gharjom all was kept quiet for a few weeks.

The situation was now interesting enough to bring us a visit from Bernard Ledwidge, then working at the Intelligence Bureau in Peshawar – later he had an interesting career in the Foreign Service, including a spell at Kabul. Armed with new air photographs we took Mohammed Jan up in an Anson to reconnoitre the Shaktu, a hair-raising trip, flying low up and round some twisting nullahs in thick cloud from which we could emerge to bank steeply past a ridge or crest. The entry in my office calendar reads: 'We have found Ipi's caves,' but it was followed by two question marks.

In this way our game of chess with Ipi in the Shaktu went on inconclusively for weeks, but we were not lacking in other diversions and some of them were serious affairs. An account of one will illustrate our lives. Just before Christmas a gang of outlaws had entered Kohat District and set a cunning trap for the police. They contrived to get a message to them, putting them on a false trail, and prepared a successful ambush on the route the police party took. Several were killed and the gang made off with a Hindu assistant sub-inspector. In the first night they took shelter in a Kabul Khel village in our agency. Several members of the gang belonged to this subsection of the tribe. Next day they hied off to inaccessible country deep in the hills on the international border. Messages came demanding ransom for the captive. The kidnapping of a government servant of this rank was a serious offence and the ransom demanded was high. The *malik* of the subsection with which the gang had sheltered tried to play a cunning game. He came along and told us in effect, 'My people have been silly, but don't worry, I will get your man back.' Charged with official approval, he then went off and negotiated with the gang; the ransom demand was increased and his rake-off was agreed. But he was caught in his own web. The case began to look insoluble and as the weeks passed our fears for the Hindu police inspector's life grew. Tribal *jirgas* which the PA interviewed accepted that this subsection was responsible for a heinous crime, but in spite of this political pressure failed to secure the man's release.

Finally it was decided to take the risk and the subsection was warned that part of its territory was proscribed: any movement in it would be bombed. There was still no result; so two days later Hurricanes flew nine sorties over Sinda and a dive-bombing attack by Vultee Vengeance bombers damaged the malicious *malik*'s fine tower. We decided to pause for a time; I remember flying over the village in an Anson to view the damage and being fascinated by two little spurts of light that signified an angry retort by a sniper against our intrusion. Two days later, the kidnapped inspector arrived in fair shape. The tribe had decided to pay the ransom money to the gang. At the time I felt that this was a remarkably successful piece of political work by Jack Lowis, and so it was – but we were both conscious of the prolonged strain of the business, which stretched over seven weeks, and of the risks of repercussions from the bombing action. We might well be making fertile the ground that our enemy 'the Bishop' was preparing to harvest.

A fortnight or so later one of Ipi's several capable lieutenants became active with a gang not many miles from that Kabul Khel area. They operated west of Spinwam, the big Scouts' post in the Keitu river on the important subsidiary road linking the Tochi with the Kurram Agency and Kohat District at Thall. The road ran from Mirali, a permanent brigade camp, through the fairly flat and easy Sheratulla Plain for about eight miles, and then climbed gently into a weird area of rocky escarpment called Sangasara, some miles from the river and Spinwam. The rock ran in long ridges parallel to the road. Looking to the right, or south, one saw a series of little cliffs with jagged edges which provided splendid cover for marksmen whose escape route was down quite gentle slopes in dead ground so far as anyone on the road was concerned. Behind each line of rocks lay another, with curious sandy hollows between each ridge – and so on as far as the eye could see. The Khassadar piquets in this route were rather lightly manned, and the gang had little difficulty in persuading the rate of absenteeism to rise temporarily to allow them to establish a road block at a well-chosen spot. It was an effective enough ditch dug across the road with boulders rolled into appropriate places so that under fire a vehicle could not divert off the road. Here the mail lorry was held up on two successive days.

On the second day we were prepared. A considerable force of Scouts set off from Khajuri, while a *gusht* from Spinwam prepared to converge on the spot from the other side. But what made the day interesting was the keen desire of the Army to take part. The brigade at Mirali had been allocated a squadron of tanks which they wanted to try out, so I went down with my own escort to observe the show. It was a demonstration of the limitations of the modern army in mountain warfare, and the superiority of the lightly-armed militia trained to move on hills. When the tanks halted near the road block they were in no danger from the tribesmen's rifle fire. But they could find no way round and while no doubt they could have charged over the obstacle, that would not have solved the problem facing the mail lorry – or my own. The gang had to be shifted from its commanding position, so the tanks opened up with their guns and automatic weapons; the noise re-echoed from the curious rock formation. Every time the sound of a prolonged burst subsided, after a few seconds pause came the gang's reply – just one or two shots: no useless waste of ammunition. This went on for quite some time to the great amusement of my bodyguard. But the Scouts from Khajuri arrived and began to deploy while their patrol from Spinwam suddenly appeared on the flanks of the outlaws' position. Within a couple of minutes it was all over, without a shot being fired by the Scouts. The Wazir never stayed to fight a useless battle.

For the gang, this was not a defeat, but rather the contrary, and for the next week they were hanging around, up to little bits of mischief. Word came that Ipi had allocated them one of his precious field guns and that they planned to shell Spinwam. Our intelligence was that their base was somewhere behind the twin peaks of Darweshta, the big mountain that dominated that part of the agency, overlooking Spinwam from the west. So one night we set out from Khajuri with a large force of Scouts to search the mountain for their hiding place, hopeful of finding the gun in its reported new emplacement. Debussing near the scene of the earlier battle for the road block, we tramped over the rough ground onto the mountain. As we climbed the moon shone to ease our way. At about 5,000 feet the going became very rough and precipitous. Suddenly the moon went behind a great bank of cloud and we were in pitch darkness. I was suddenly conscious that I had no sense of balance or direction. Having scrambled over a rock I was aware that the man ahead of me was much higher and realized that he was climbing a vertical cliff. Following him in the chill of the night I was soaked in perspiration. I could find no foothold but my outstretched hand brushed against a root of some shrub or shrivelled tree. I cannot recall ever being so frightened. Some instinct made me haul on this root and it held; I pulled myself up and over the top, onto a narrow ledge. I became aware that there were other men crouched there, waiting, and thankfully I waited with them. An hour later, the cloud lifted, and through the darkness we could see the lights of Bannu, thirty miles away and far below. All around us was a black, empty shadow, unwelcoming and hostile. Some time before dawn, there was enough light to start moving again. My limbs ached painfully from the chill: I had been too fearful of falling at first even to risk stretching them.

Meanwhile, not all the Scouts had allowed themselves to be so motionless and many were in position to secure the first peak at daybreak. There was no sign of the enemy. Breakfast was a piece of cold toast on which was a cold poached egg, to be washed down with water from my water bottle, and was eaten on the move along the relatively easy ridge to the other peak about a mile away. The sun shone warmly and I felt comfortable and relaxed. The Scouts took the second peak and soon the word came back that nothing had been found. The decision was made to withdraw. Within minutes of the rearguard coming off the height, the sniping started. We called in the Air Force and for the first time I saw a Hurricane operating in close support of troops, its eight machine-guns blazing furiously as it dived behind the ridge just over our heads. All the way down the gang kept popping up behind us, never quite allowing the Scouts to get back behind them. Colonel Janson felt that we should get off the mountain quickly. He was anxious to avoid casualties, and aware that if anything went wrong he would have a big battle on his hands, for the gang's success would soon bring reinforcements. Jack Lowis was less fleet of foot than usual and kept dropping back. I was usually quick enough on the way down but I sensed that something was wrong with him and hung back with him, becoming alarmed after an hour or so when I realized we were getting mixed up with the rearguard. The sniping was still going on but I was aware of no near misses and comforted by the continuing active presence of our watchdog Hurricane. Then the Scouts' own field gun from Spinwam began firing over our heads, and we felt safe. The post commander sent out some ponies, we put the exhausted Jack on one and led him through the river and up into the fort where he collapsed with a high fever. We packed him off at once under escort to Miranshah, to the care of Doc Hassett. Writing home to prove that I was fit, I reported that after an hour's sleep I had a cup of tea and a biscuit and worked until 9.00 p.m.

Having stayed to clear up various matters in Spinwam and Shewa, I returned to Miranshah late the following day to find Jack really ill and under strict orders from Jeff Hassett that he was not to fly next morning to Jandola in South Waziristan for an important conference with the Governor. The Resident had sent a message that if Jack was unfit he should send Mohammed Jan, our very able APO, but Jack felt that Mohammed Jan might feel outgunned in the circumstances and asked me if I would represent him. I worked till 2.00 a.m. on the papers, having just had a briefing from the very groggy PA, and compared notes with the APO. Jack's decision to send me instead of Mohammed Jan was flattering for I had no doubt about the APO's expertise on tribal affairs. It made me quite swollen-headed and I wondered if Jack had decided that it would matter less if I felt that way than if Mohammed Jan let conceit upset his judgment.

The flight in a Harvard was fun. I was piloted by Flight Lieutenant Malse who commanded the Miranshah flight of No. 1 Squadron IAF. He had landed at Jandola on the previous afternoon to try out the runway on which a Harvard had not previously landed, though Ansons could use it in good weather, and HE was to fly in on an Anson from Peshawar. The surface was bumpy but adequate. As Jack had anticipated the meeting led to a keen debate with the Resident lining up with Gerald, tending to excuse the Mahsuds at the expense of the Wazirs. But HE's decisive vote went to me, and I was inordinately pleased till I remembered that I was just reproducing Jack's analysis, even if I had sat up late mugging it up. It was in any case likely to outweigh the other line in HE's assessment, for like Jack he was a born political officer of great shrewdness and Gerald, who had been a very fine district officer, was still new to the political game of the tribes. He had been there barely two months; inside six more weeks he was to become much more sophisticated about his Mahsuds as his papers in the India Office Library reveal. On the way home after a splendid lunch, Malse bounced me around the sky above the Shaktu in the afternoon heat like a 'fairy's wedding'. Jack felt happier and in a couple of days went down to Bannu to convalesce and recharge his batteries. I felt very important running the show for him for a few days. Privately, I prayed that Ipi's chronic asthma would help to keep him quiet. It was a judgment on me that on the day Jack returned I took to bed with flu.

Fortunately my bedroom was separated from the PA's quarters only by our guest room, from whose bathroom one of my predecessors had purloined the stately armchair thunderbox specially designed for VIP's like the Viceroy and the Governor. So I was kept well briefed on what was happening; it was just as well, for on the day I returned to duty red notices were dropped on the village of one of the Kikarai Mahsud *maliks* in the Shaktu, Mir Ghulam – and Jack was due to leave for nine days' casual leave, which could not be postponed, even for war, because he was going to ski at Gulmarg with Jeano, his wife, who was a champion skier. It was near the end of March and the snow in Kashmir would melt after the end of the month.

The day before I took over HE made one of his prudent and timely visits. A special squadron arrived to start the bombing but it was put off because we got a signal from the Political *Naib-Tahsildar*, Dosalli, who was at the Scouts' post at Ghariom, saying that Mir Ghulam had offered to surrender. Sir George replied that there would be no bombing if Mir Ghulam came in, without conditions, accompanied by fifteen of his men by sunset. He did not, so my decision the next morning was easy, although, in fact, it was not so easy as this makes it sound. The PNT Dosalli sent another message that he expected Mir Ghulam to come in and that we should again defer the bombing. I did not believe him, simply put the message in my pocket and worked to the letter of HEs earlier guidelines. But the difficult aspect of the decision-making was that the bombs were to fall, not on a Wazir village, but a Mahsud one, for which it was the PA South Waziristan, and not I, who was responsible. Jack went off; Mir Ghulam's *kot* was bombed. Afterwards Wing Commander Mukherjee,[4] the Kohat IAF Station Commander, flew me over in his Harvard to view the damage which we estimated at 50 per cent destruction of the fortified homestead and tower.

Next day there was more bombing. This time I was taken over the target by Squadron Leader Jaswant Singh,[5] who commanded the squadron. At 300 feet we reckoned that the damage had increased noticeably for there was a big hole in Mir Ghulam's tower. I decided that there would be no more bombing for the present and next day Malse flew me through thick cloud to Jandola to report to the Resident and Gerald Curtis; the day after, we heard a report that Ipi had left the vicinity of Mir Ghulam's section to go to Walo Tangi.

I have found amongst my papers a handwritten note which I had prepared on 21 March recording the information available to HE when he flew in and the decisions he left me to work to. To this I had added on 22 March an account of that day's events and an appreciation of the situation for my oral report to the Resident and Curtis in Jandola on the 23rd. The notes show clearly one of the crucial difficulties of the situation. Mir Ghulam, Ipi's main prop in the Shaktu at the time, was a Kikarai Mahsud, and the PA South Waz, not the PA North Waz, was responsible for that tribe. But the terrain made access to the area through Curtis's agency impossible, whereas from the Scouts' post at Ghariom in Lowis's agency there was a natural route. All the signs were that if Ipi took hostile action it would be directed in the first place against the isolated Ghariom post which was our responsibility. The other local Mahsuds, on whom we were relying to put pressure on Mir Ghulam and on Ipi, were talking to our officer, the Political *Naib-Tahsildar*, Dosalli, and not to any of Curtis's officials. The direct local control of air action from Miranshah by Lowis or myself was the natural thing from the air force point of view and could be organized much more efficiently than guidelines or instructions from Jandola in South Waziristan. Curtis had no local air force and no access to air intelligence unless he got it through us or came to Miranshah himself. Jack Lowis and I felt strongly that the South Waziristan officers had not involved themselves directly enough in the affair to form a balanced appreciation of its inherent dangers. Yet the air action we were having to direct from Miranshah was aimed against their tribe!

My scribbled note ends with a summary of estimates of damage caused. On the 22nd the photographs showed damage which the Air Liaison Officer estimated as one-third of the village badly damaged. The information picked up at Ghariom, from local contacts rather than visual observation, was that seven out of seventeen houses in the village had been destroyed on 23 March. I recorded that two houses had been virtually wiped out, seven badly damaged, two less badly damaged, and eight compound walls badly damaged, while there seemed to be a big hole near the top of Mir Ghulam's tower on the east side and the courtyard wall of the tower was badly damaged. My recollection is that the Hurricanes used 500-lb bombs in shallow dives to get oblique strikes. The construction of the fortified villages was very strong, and direct hits were likely to knock holes in walls rather that to cause them to crumble and fall. Damage by fire was unlikely and if it occurred it would be limited. No casualties were caused. The purpose of the red notices was to warn people to evacuate the area and our purpose was to create material damage and inconvenience.

One of the important things about the note is that it emphasises my belief in restricting action to a specific target, and one which we believed would not be an unpopular choice with the generality of the tribe involved. This was a principle which I had clearly absorbed from Sir George Cunningham and Jack Lowis but the terms of the note indicated that I had thought it out also for myself. The note also indicates the quite small numbers of personal followers who had accompanied Ipi to the Shaktu. Three locations for different parties are mentioned, giving an approximate total of 250 – almost certainly an exaggeration. But it mentioned too that Mehr Dil, one of the most active and skilful of the outlaws of the day, was 'passing through' about that time with his gang of about twenty men, and that Ipi had sent out messages calling for *lashkars* to reinforce him. If he got a response, the threat to Ghariom and indeed to our control of a part of our agency would have been considerable. We doubted whether we could hold such an outbreak with the Scouts and began to speculate what the Army might do. I remember suggesting that rather than involve the large conventional columns proceeding on foot over the dangerous ground of the Shaktu and Khaisora – the scene of so much trouble for the troops in 1936 and 1937 – if a few hundred paratroops were to reinforce Ghariom in an emergency the whole opposition would melt away.

A week or two later two senior staff officers arrived from Delhi to have a look at the position. They clearly had no faith in the ability of the paratroops to cope with the problems of Waziristan – I had shown them from the air where I thought they might safely land in the high Sham Plain, not far from Ghariom and the Shaktu. Their purpose really was to emphasize that we must continue to keep our need for military action to a minimum. The paratroops were being trained for action in Burma and no additional trained men could be spared for Waziristan, so we had to accept that we would have to cope throughout that spring and summer with no special military help.

The air weapon certainly proved reasonably effective, so long as we could direct it at specific, carefully defined and very localized targets, the choice of which could be understood and accepted by the tribes without strong feelings of resentment.[6] In summer they could repair damage to walls relatively easily without having to endure serious privation. They took a pride in building their strongholds so strong that it took quite a lot of bombing to make a mark. They got a bonus from unexploded bombs, which they put under our bridges on top of piles of brushwood, to which they set fire. One Mahsud once proudly demonstrated a land improvement project to Sir George Cunningham: he was blasting away rock for an irrigation channel with air force bombs.

The fairly continuous air action did take some toll of the Air Force. My diary notes the loss of six Hurricanes between mid-

February and mid-April 1944. Two went down after a collision in which one pilot was killed. Two came down fairly near the aerodrome in forced landings following engine trouble. Pilots were reporting that hostile fire was a cause of their difficulties but nobody seemed to believe this. It used to happen to the old slow pre-war biplanes but we argued that surely the Hurricane was too fast even for the Mahsud or Wazir marksman with a rifle and there were no reports of Bren guns being used against aircraft. Then one day I had a message that some of my Khassadars had seen a plane come down on the Kam Sarobai, a flattish plain only a mile or two from the main road near Dizh Narai, halfway between the Shaktu and Miranshah. I dashed off with the bodyguard and found the pilot safe in the hands of the Khassadars, with his aircraft relatively undamaged under their protection. The pilot claimed that his engine had overheated following a strike by rifle fire. The Khassadars had put up such a good show that I felt that the area was safe enough to get a rescue team onto the Kam Sarobai to bring the plane back to Miranshah. When it was inspected there the evidence was indisputable. The jagged hole in the coolant pipe could only have been caused by a bullet.

At the beginning of April I went to Peshawar to take my Pushtu examination. This was a thorough test, well organized, which was spread over most of two days. The written part was comparatively straightforward. Most of the time was devoted to a series of oral tests, in which the candidates had to converse, not with the examiners, but in their presence with individual Pathans from different parts of the province and different stations in life. Pathans are marvellous storytellers; their tradition is oral rather than literary. The supreme test came when a bunch of very jungly recent recruits to the Frontier Constabulary were brought in. Their Inspector General was the chief examiner. He conversed with them for some time, partly to put them at their ease – never too difficult with a Pathan, however humble his status may be – and to get them talking about their villages and their background. They came from several different tribes; some spoke 'hard' Pushtu, some the 'soft' version (*moong* means 'we' in the 'hard' version, the same word being *mizh* in the 'soft' pronunciation). After a time he got them to tell stories – these might be traditional, similar to the European fable, or an account of some actual blood feud in a man's section, perhaps extending over several generations. The candidate had to provide proof of his understanding by rehearsing in Pushtu, which the Pathans could follow the gist of their stories, by cross-examining them and by letting them quiz him. This was a hard but very fair test and I was delighted when I was told that I had passed – with sufficient credit, it appeared, for me to be appointed one of the examiners in succeeding years. Sir George Cunningham told me he believed that the Pushtu test was the only decent language examination in the whole of India. Certainly the exam in Urdu which I had taken in Lahore was academic and pedantic by comparison. Success immediately produced a badly-needed bonus of Rs100 a month on my salary (over £5). I invested the first month's amount in the purchase of an Omega watch which I found in a dingy shop in the bazaar in Razmak where it must have been lying for several years. It is still keeping perfect time, fifty years later.

I had driven to Peshawar with my friend Sharif, who had been awarded the MC for his part in the 1942 siege of Datta Khel. We did the trip in his car, accompanied by two Scouts' orderlies, in seven hours, stayed with the Dundases and felt honoured when the Governor sent for me that evening, not just for a social drink, but to talk to me in his office about the situation in the Shaktu. I began to feel that I might be going to make the grade as a political officer. Before I returned to Miranshah I was invited to RAF Group Headquarters to talk to them about Walo Tangi and work over maps and aerial photographs. Next day Group Captain Wingate piloted me home, flying an Argus Fairchild – a high wing, four-seater, American communications monoplane aircraft, which gave me a fine view of the Afridi Tirah and Darweshta, but bumped all over the place when he put it down at Miranshah in a nasty wind. Looking en route to the snows of Safed Koh and to the Hindu Kush the view was very spectacular.

Back in Miranshah news was coming in that the trouble in the Shaktu was coming to a head. Since the intense action around 21–23 March, it had subsided, but only temporarily. On 10 April, Ipi's own men moved into position near Ghariom and that night one of his guns shelled the Scouts' post. Two of the shells hit a piquet wall on the perimeter without causing serious damage, others missed. More white warning notices were dropped up and down the Shaktu the following morning, and red notices later the same day warned of impending attacks from the air on two specific targets – Shahwali and Warusta Bazina, higher up the Shaktu than before. This target was within range of 5.5-inch guns which had recently arrived in Razmak, the most powerful long-range artillery that Waziristan had ever had. Hurricane sorties with bombs and cannon were flown in the same evening, but had to be called off after an hour when heavy rain closed down on the target area. The CRA (Commander Royal Artillery) was asked to shell the target during the night.[7]

This prompt action again produced immediate, though temporary, results.[8] 'There was a report that Ipi's gun had been damaged and over successive days it became clear that his *lashkar* was divided against itself. By 16 April we were sure that it had broken up. A road block which they had established at Iblanke Narai, threatening to cut the road by which Ghariom was supplied and reinforced from Dosalli, was abandoned and the Scouts at Ghariom were able to resume normal patrols in their vicinity. The Wuzzi Khel, a neighbouring tribe which had got implicated on the charge of harbouring and encouraging hostiles, came into Dosalli to make their peace. The bad news was that two Hurricane 2Cs returning from a sortie collided near Dosalli, one pilot being killed, the other escaping by parachute.

One might have guessed that at this stage Ipi would keep the pot boiling by arranging a diversion. He chose the Keitu area near Spinwam which had worried us a few weeks earlier. Perhaps our action then had been premature, perhaps it had served to draw attention to the importance we attached to our line of communication through Spinwam to Thall. At any rate, the gun for which we had made an abortive search tried to shell Spinwam Fort on the night of Saturday 15 April, a day on which Sir George made one of his well-timed visits to meet us with the Resident at Miranshah. This gun did not function too well and two of the shells hit a nearby village instead of the fort. Two days later my Khassadars put up a good fight to protect the mail lorry from an attack. Next day, a Scouts' *gusht* was heavily fired on near Sarkalarai, no great distance from their fort, and quite a battle followed, involving the Army from Mirali as well as air support. There was aerial action next day over the mountain (Darweshta) where the gang was hiding out, and a report came in later that in one or other actions they had suffered casualties including one Gangi Khel who was seriously hurt. We wondered whether this would discourage the gang and over the next few days declined to accede to the requests from the Scouts' commander at Spinwam, Lieutenant Sydney Butterfield, for air action. His attempted justification was the continuing rumours of impending attacks on his post. Nothing happened for several nights, but on 23 April the gun fired six shots in the evening, only two of them coming near the post which enjoyed the opportunity to fire back with its own field gun.

For the moment, this diversion was also petering out and coincidentally firm news came over the border of 'real trouble' between the Afghan Government and the Zadrans. By our local reading of the situation this might easily attract the Keitu-based hostiles across into Afghanistan. As I now know, Sir George Cunningham's assessment was that Ipi's current adventures with us had been encouraged by the Afghan Government's anxiety to divert him as far away as possible from their border and their troubles in Khost. I was feeling quite pleased with myself because I had gone down to Spinwam and Shewa at the start of the Keitu trouble to tighten up the duties of the Khassadars, strengthening one or two of the lightly manned piquets and arranging for a senior and friendly *malik* to stay for a while in one of their posts. In the outcome, the Khassadars had performed unusually well. I was due some casual leave and, badly needing to get away from the relentless strain of Waziristan, I went off for a quiet fortnight in Abbottabad.

When I got back, I just had one clear day with Jack, being briefed on the situation, before he went off for a month's leave and I became officiating Political Agent. He departed at breakfast on 15 May; the same evening Ipi's gun shelled Iblanke Piquet, high up on a prominent feature within sight of Dosalli. Fortunately no harm was done by this surprise 'tip and run' attack – Ghariom was the more likely target. We had brought two of the 5.5-inch guns to Dosalli and they made a prompt response to the hostile impertinence. The noise they made probably had a salutary effect all round – I was to hear them in action at the same place some weeks later, and can vouch for the impressiveness of the noise of their shells in those hills.

That was a bad enough start to my spell as PA, but next day much worse followed. On a ROD, an Indian battalion ran into an ambush on Conical Hill near Dizh Narai. Eight men were killed and four rifles and a light machine-gun were stolen by their attackers, who had caught them at close range. When I got there to make my enquiries it was obvious that the Khassadars had performed badly, and the troops even worse. The Army's morale had taken a blow and there was a good deal of back-biting on and off for several days. In between I made a trip to Ghariom and got back to Dosalli without hindrance, which was satisfactory. At the end of the week HE came up to confer with the Resident, myself and Group Captain Wingate. Since it was a Saturday, General Bruce Scott, an old Scouts officer, and two of our 'veteran' politicals, Roger Bacon[9] and Packy (K.L. Packman) had cadged a lift on the plane. This pair of inveterate jokers never missed the chance of a party. When they all departed I went up to Razmak with Brad, the Resident, to cool off over the weekend and get some paperwork done.

On the day that I returned to Miranshah – the Tuesday – there was another bad incident involving the Khassadars and the troops near the brigade camp at Damdil. I was beginning to wonder if my record of effective cooperation with the Army was going to be permanently destroyed. Exactly a week later, on 30 May, another ambush took place, again involving the same battalion of Mahrattas, in which three men were killed and one wounded, with the loss of four rifles, only fifty yards from the fort. That took me back to Razmak for an evening of explanation and consultation with the Army. My diary recorded that the 'G1 and Brigadier Mervyn Hobbes were more amenable; other people just dull'.[10] Next day I took the GSO1 in his own staff car – accompanied by my bodyguard – safely to Ghariom and back to Dosalli, so I probably felt that I had demonstrated something to the Army about the PA's command of his territory!

At this time, the Shaktu was still my main preoccupation. The Air Force had at my request carefully reconnoitred the 'old' roads up the Khaisora and Shaktu valleys, constructed during the major campaigns of 1936-8. I wanted to know whether a column could get quickly up the Shaktu with motorized transport. Many culverts and little bridges had been destroyed – there had been no recent maintenance of these routes – but on 24 May tanks from Mirali made an easy passage as far as Biche Kashkai, a Scouts' post in the lower Khaisora, and returned. There was still plenty of evidence that Ipi was trying to rally the tribes and raise a *lashkar*, and I was convinced that the objective was an attack on Ghariom and on its line of communication. Ironically, to add to my troubles, cypher telegrams kept coming in reporting Foreign Office anxiety in London about the involvement of our tribes in the troubles across the border in Afghanistan. The Afghan Government in

Kabul was laying the blame for their problems on the machinations of the PA North Waziristan! Did the Afghans really fear that Ipi's *lashkar* was to be used in Khost against them? Or had they persuaded Ipi to move to the Shaktu to divert our tribes, and Gerald Curtis's Mahsuds, into a major show against us? I felt that these nuances were just a distraction from our real job, which was to stop the Shaktu from erupting, without involving the Army. Cypher telegrams however demanded answers – at least HE did, for he had to determine the final reply to the Foreign Office – and after the heat and dust of a wearying day when I sat down to encode a response I had no high regard for the Government of India in Delhi or the Foreign Office in London.

The days were indeed hot. For weeks at the end of May and in June the shade temperature averaged between 105° and 110°. In the escort lorry the metal dashboard reflected heat like a furnace. It was difficult not to be permanently dehydrated, short-tempered and frustrated; it was too easy for someone on whom we depended to fall asleep at his post. Down in Bannu on 24 June the recorded temperature was 119°; Miranshah, at an altitude of about 3,000 feet, was usually 5°–10° cooler, and the sharp drop in night temperature made sleeping in the open on the lawn – well protected by the fort's wall and wire! – at least tolerable. My normal working day started at sunrise at between 5 a.m. and 6 a.m. when I had a cup of tea and tried to get as much office work as possible done before the day's messages began to distract me.

After the shelling on 15 May, the next fortnight on the Shaktu was without serious incident, though as I have recorded the Army was enduring its share of disasters on the main road. Then suddenly on 28 May no fewer than seventeen shells were fired at Ghariom post – nine of them fell within the perimeter wire, four actually on the barracks. Fortunately the Scouts were very alert and nobody was hurt. This led to a bombing attack two days later on Tabai, the nearest Malikshahi village to Ghariom, and the shelling of Warusta Bazina, a Mahsud village higher up the valley, in range of Razmak's big guns. I spent much of the week visiting Dosalli, Ghariom and Razmak. The Generals and Resident were in Razmak; but though I got one cool night's sleep there, I had to keep coming back to Dosalli, or to Miranshah, to work at these damnable cypher telegrams – often full of corruptions – and talk to the air force people. On the Saturday evening, one of their liveliest pilots Randir Singh – nearly all the pilots in No. 1

Squadron Indian Air Force were Sikhs or Hindus – took me on a protracted reconnaissance of the whole Shaktu area. Before we returned I asked him to fly low over the whole route of the military roads built in the late 1930s. I was depressed to see how many culverts required repair and relieved after so much twisting and turning and craning my neck when we had worked back to our starting point near Ghariom – but he was not finished with me. Instead of gaining a respectable height and letting my stomach settle he chose to dash low up every narrow algad he could find on the journey home, pulling back violently on the stick as I was certain we were running out of air, dipping over the next ridge into the next nullah, so that I was so petrified that I was not even sick. After we landed it turned out that he had made a bet with his colleagues that I would be sick before he brought me back which would have cost me a heavy penalty in recompense – in beer – to his maintenance crew and the rest of the pilots in the flight. Instead, he had to stand me a drink in the mess.

A truly restful Sunday followed, but on the Monday night Ghariom was shelled again. Our intelligence reports kept emphasizing the complicity of the Shabi Khel Mahsuds, who kept making these audacious sallies into our territory – Ipi's game of divide and rule! When I requested the Resident to arrange more shelling of Wrusta Bazina he replied that he was thinking about it. He was not a man of action; part of the trouble was that Gerald Curtis was away at the Wana end of his constituency – where, I nastily remarked, there was no trouble. Next day the hot weather dusthaze closed down so thick that there was no question of bombing and Razmak maintained a staunch silence about shelling. The Scouts' CO, Colonel Jansen, had gone on well-deserved leave like Jack, and Ralph Venning was acting for him. Ralph was already a very experienced Scout and was soon to take command of the South Waziristan Scouts. He was less phlegmatic than Jan and at that stage in the summer our moods were in harmony. So we drove off to Razmak together to beard Brad, the Resident, on his home ground, having prepared a detailed indictment of the Shabi Khel. Gerald had returned and we had an uncomfortable couple of hours while he expostulated, probably with justification, about the onesidedness of our analysis. My diary records that the result was that 'immediate political action was to be taken', and then cynically adds, 'a jirga of Shabi Khel to be held on 12 June', i.e. five days later.

Visit by ENSA concert party to Razmak.

Ladies of the ENSA party at Miranshah with Hawas Khan.

Khassadar Havildar Hawas Khan.

Fortunately, the whole trouble was at last on the wane, though we did not know this at the time. A threatened attack on the convoy taking supplies from Dosalli to Ghariom on the Friday petered out tamely. On Saturday 10 June, Ipi held a *marakka* (open meeting) of his whole *lashkar* at Zindai in the Shaktu. Unable to get a clear directive from the Resident I acted myself that afternoon under section seventeen of the Frontier Crimes Regulations and sent off aircraft with instructions to fire at any movement near the caves at Zindai. The sortie reported seeing the caves but their guns had stoppages and so they fired only 150 rounds. Next day the Scouts' commander at Ghariom reported that the *lashkar* numbered 1,000 and included 150 Kabul Khel, which I refused to believe. He had pinpointed the site of Ipi's gun (067288) and reported that work on its improvement had been carried out over the last two days. It transpired that a little track had been made to run the gun out of the shelter of rocks to its vantage point for firing. I proposed that the area over which air action was threatened should be extended, and should include Tori Khel Wazir territory in the vicinity of the gun 'emplacement'. This was agreed with Gerald Curtis and 'white' early warning notices were dropped on the specified area on 12 June. That day I went out from the Scouts' post at Dosalli to a *tikala* given by the *maliks* of Dosalli village a couple of miles away. Everyone was in a good mood and one would never have guessed that the area was on a knife-edge between peace and war.

In fact, all stayed quiet, without the need to follow up white notices with bombs or bullets,[11] and I handed over, greatly relieved, to the refreshed PA on his return from leave on 15 June. That same afternoon we set off together for the cool heights of Razmak. There was plenty of excuse for this – at that time of year, not only were the Resident and the PA South Waz usually there, as well as the top brass of the Army in Waziristan, but a considerable proportion of the Wazir tribes migrated to their summer pastures, while some of the leading *maliks* had their *kots* not far from the Razmak plateau and liked to come into the cantonment area to see their PA. There was also a unique reason. An ENSA concert party was entertaining troops in Northern Command, India and for the first time the authorities had decided to bring them to Razmak.[12] No white woman had ever penetrated that distance into Waziristan and it was probable that none would ever again. The concert party consisted of four males and six females, and included two married couples. The Army brought them up from Rawalpindi on a ROD convoy and arranged for the ladies to step from the vehicles into a square of wet cement so that their footprints would be permanently recorded. For all I know they are still to be seen there.

The excitement engendered by their arrival was unbelievable and was an interesting reflection on the monastic life of the soldiers in Waziristan. The most boyish excitement seemed to be aroused in the most senior officers who shamelessly pulled rank in order to dominate the time of the ladies. I could hardly believe it when Brad himself, whose wife was a very motherly, loquacious person, bid fair to outdo the brigadiers and colonels with his courtly attentions. I could have wished he had shown the same activity in dealing with my signals. It was all good fun, probably the more so because the ladies and their male partners were very decent, well-behaved persons, who thoroughly enjoyed the attention they aroused and conducted themselves with complete propriety, but a most engaging sense of fun. There were endless parties at which each battalion vied with the others and with HQ Mess. But the ladies had to be omitted from the biggest event of all, so far as Jack and I were concerned, when a party of thirty British officers, including the ENSA men, went off on the Monday to enjoy a *tikala* at the village of Mirkhajan, one of our leading *maliks*. They were all exhausted by the heat of Northern India and enjoying the cool height of Razmak, while dreading the long uncomfortable journey back to Bannu and onwards by the 'heatstroke express' to Rawalpindi, when Jack hit on the brilliant idea of taking them to Miranshah and getting the RAF to fly them out in a Dakota. The RAF were willing to provide the plane so the ladies had two extra days in relative comfort on Razmak plateau at 7,000 feet. We showed off by escorting them to Miranshah with our tribal bodyguard, and the Scouts' officers got a share in the fun. We all gallantly gave up the essential comforts of our quarters for the night and 'camped out' – there was not much time anyway for bed.

For nearly a fortnight things had been so quiet 'on the war front' that I had begun to wonder if Ipi had given up. Suddenly on Saturday 24 June, a big gang established a road block at a succession of hairpin bends in the heights of Iblanke, above Dosalli, and the parade ground outside the fort was shot up. The local tribe, the Wuzzi Khel, were asked to clear the road; they tried and failed. The following day, the road block had been strengthened, and Ghariom, eight miles away across the Sham Plain, was shelled again from the old gun position, but this time by two guns. In spite of action from the air and by our two 5.5-inch guns at Dosalli, the road was still cut on the 26th, so preparations were made for a battle on Tuesday 27 June. Once again it was fascinating to see how ineffective tanks were in such a situation. This time, because of the precipitous terrain, there was no way past the road blocks for them until infantry or engineers could clear the obstacles. The position was completely exposed on very tight bends above a precipice. The 5.5-inch guns firing at the enemy snipers made plenty of noise but judging from their reaction they did not worry the tribesmen whose marksmen continued to cover the road block by accurate single shots. Once again it was a rapid outflanking manoeuvre by the Tochi Scouts, working a long way round from the east towards Iblanke, that turned the scales. To our relief the gang put up no real resistance but slipped away quickly as soon as the Scouts began to threaten their right flank and rear. By 1.30 p.m. I was again in Ghariom. An hour later I returned to Dosalli – the journey taking an hour and a half, since movement had to be cautious. By 4.00 p.m. Ipi's gunners were again firing shells at Ghariom. So there was still work to be done. Bombing of a particular target (Marghai) had begun that afternoon, and continued next day. But we had seen the beginning of the end, the last defiant fling of the summer.

The PA's attention from now on was to be absorbed by the recrudescence of an old quarrel between Mahsuds and Tori Khel Wazirs in the plateau area of Razmak. It was ironic that after stressful months of effort to keep them from uniting behind the Faqir of Ipi to fight against us, he should now have to work all summer for a settlement that would prevent them fighting each other. The role of the agent of imperialism never quite fitted the stereotype of either Marxist or American analysts. Once again, the axiom that we depended on the precept 'divide and rule' was turned on its head. By this time, however, Gerald Curtis was fully alive to the dangers and though the implications of the dispute rumbled on for months after I left Waziristan, the threat of serious conflict when the Wazirs built a new *kot* in June, in a position which threatened the security of Mahsud habitation, was kept in check. The argument had simmered for twenty years. An earlier settlement had left the Wazirs permanently aggrieved.

In the autumn, an uneasy peace was agreed, and both sides accepted that certain watchtowers should be destroyed. A special show was arranged for them because they would not believe that the Air Force could really destroy anything they had built to last. They were surprised when for the first time in the Frontier a flight of Typhoons appeared, firing rockets with unprecedented destructive effect, and took the joke against themselves in typical high glee.

The story of these six months when Ipi threatened to raise his standards in the Shaktu and involve the Army in a major campaign came to an end in June. By then the rebellion in Khost in Afghanistan was also petering out; the Madda Khel, some of whom took part in the rebellion against the Afghan authorities, had withdrawn and Mazrak, the leading rebel, came in secretly to Datta Khel one night in August to see Jack Lowis who offered him asylum in India. The British terms were not finally accepted by Mazrak until January 1947 when he and his family were settled with a pension in Abbottabad. At one time in autumn 1944 the Afghans approved British air action on their behalf on the international boundary and actually proposed targets within Afghanistan, which Cunningham declined to touch. But this is not the place for that fascinating story.

Even now I cannot be sure whether Ipi's move to the Shaktu was made in response to pressure from his Axis powers paymasters, as we had believed, or to pressure from the Afghan authorities to keep away from their trouble spot in Khost. But I have no doubt that having moved from Gorwekht he did his best to create mischief; he was a fanatical enemy of British rule though he may have had his doubts whether a German victory would improve conditions in the Frontier.[12] My account has tried to show how his efforts were contained. The events of these months are discussed in a few lines in any history I have seen of the last few years of British rule in India. Compared with the scale of military operations of the Twenties and Thirties, historians record the period of the Second World War as one of comparative quiet in Waziristan. It was important for the vital role of the Indian Army in the War that that should be so and I think that the credit should be clearly given to the political officers, of whom for a short time I was a junior member. Sir George Cunningham recorded several times his view that the political agents during the war had achieved a higher degree of understanding of the tribes than ever before and in his official reports to the Government of India on the Shaktu business he wrote that 'the PA's. have certainly been able to keep the tribes remarkably steady. Every section had asked Ipi not to use their ground as a base for action.' His own hand was always close to the tiller. On my reckoning, in my period in Waziristan he flew in on thirteen occasions, seven of them in the first six months of 1944; and he also came once or twice by road. It was little wonder that successive Viceroys and Commanders-in-Chief set such store on his contribution to the defence of India.

On one of his flights he brought someone who knew nothing about Waziristan but was the great expert at the Government of India on food supplies and their distribution. This was Sir Robert Hutchings ICS, Secretary to the Government of India Food Department from 1943 to 1947. I remember feeling bitterly disappointed when the Governor asked if I would look after him while he was in conference with Jack Lowis, the Resident and Curtis. But I enjoyed talking to Hutchings and showing him round the fort – I even took him into the Scouts' big grain store. Later it turned out that his visit and my assignment as his guide were not wholly fortuitous.

HE had become very anxious about the Frontier's food problems and was planning how to deal with the impending crisis. On 29 June a telegram from him instructed me to go to Peshawar as Assistant Director of Civil Supplies for the province. I was frankly disappointed. I loved my job for all the strain it could involve and felt that I was contributing actively to the war effort, even occasionally at some personal risk. There was a sense of shame about the idea of sitting behind a desk at the Secretariat. But there was nothing that I could do about it – or even Jack Lowis, although he went through his copious vocabulary of Pushtu curses and telegraphed his protests to the Governor. In the next week I took farewell of many dear friends and even fitted in a last trip to Ghariom – 'an early start, but a quiet day'. On 6 July it was 'good-bye to the Tochi' and off to Peshawar, on my last flight in a Harvard, at 800 feet. It has always been one of my regrets that I was never to return to that wild and strange land of Waziristan.

Notes

[1] It was said that Lowis spoke Pushtu better than any other European of his time. Twenty years later I met him one day in London and asked how proficient he now was in Pushtu. 'I'm worried,' he replied. 'I have stopped dreaming in Pushtu.'

[2] One of his pupils was Wavell. In *A Viceroy's Diary*, Lord Wavell refers to a visit by Ahmed Jan to Delhi.

[3] While this rather prolonged battle was going on, Jack Lowis was sitting frustrated in his office in Miranshah wondering what was happening. He got a pilot to take him over the site in a Harvard. Flying pretty low in tight circles Jack became sick, though he was an experienced flier with an 'A' civil pilot's licence and a very expert yachtsman. The air pockets drawn up from these fearsome rocks by the afternoon heat must have been very bumpy. Opening his canopy to lean out, he saw his watch pulled off his wrist by the slipstream. The following Christmas I was with him in the

Peshawar Club and suddenly realized that he was wearing his old watch. Several months after I had left the agency he had complained to the tribal allowance *jirga*, at which the whole business was being settled, about the loss of his watch. One of the *maliks* sent for a shepherd who produced the watch. He had found it some days later after the incident, lying by some fluke in a sandy hollow in a gap between the parallel razor-edged ridges of rock. The face was scratched but the mechanism was undamaged. When Jack was in London on leave two years later, he called at the London agents for Rolex watches and told his story. Apparently they felt that it was too incredible to publish for so far as we knew it was never used as one of the elements in their advertising, which frequently reported wonderful stories about what a Rolex Oyster could survive.

[4] Mukherjee was then the highest ranked Indian serving in the Air Force. He was to become an Air Marshal, AOC Indian Air Force.

[5] Jaswant Singh was an Indian Christian. He also had a fine career in the Indian Air Force, and he organized the training of the Ghanaian Air Force for Nkrumah. In 1945 he married Miriam Khan Sahib daughter of the Chief Minister of NWFP. The marriage aroused much communal criticism – see later in this account.

[6] As I have said a good deal about the air weapon, a few general comments may be helpful. Since it first became available in the Frontier in the early 1920s, its use was controversial, both in military and in political circles. It was criticized as barbaric, blamed for causing tribal unrest and in the days of unreliable aircraft held to put pilots unnecessarily at risk. Most senior political officers in the Frontier probably felt that it was a useful medium of control, representing force which the tribes respected without causing many casualties or involving big bodies of troops in operations. From 1928 the use of aeroplanes was carefully regulated by a Government Grey Book, which was frequently revised – the edition I used was issued in January 1941.

Air power could be used freely for purposes of reconnaissance or demonstration, and in emergency in support of a ground 'column', when retaliatory action could be taken, in close support or in pursuit of hostiles, but not indiscriminately and not against habitations. Flying within three miles of the Afghan border was prohibited. Provided the Government of India sanctioned it, specific named and topographically-defined areas of harbourage of outlaws or hostiles could be attacked or proscribed, and in defined circumstances the authority to proscribe could be delegated down given chains of command, always subject to immediate report to the central Government.

Bombing, or machine-gunning, had always to be preceded by dropping large numbers of printed warnings – first white notices, giving the name of the tribe or section involved and the reasons for action proposed against a specified village or area, advising which areas would be safe refuges and notifying conditions under which there would be a cessation of operations. White notices had always to be followed by notices printed on red paper, which were the final warning. Conventionally these were dropped twenty-four hours before action was taken; but in exceptional circumstances this 'evacuation' time could be reduced to two hours – never less.

In Indian legislatures, of course, the subject was especially controversial, but in the crisis of April 1947 Mountbatten informed Sir Olaf Caroe that after acrimonious discussion the Cabinet had agreed that there might be circumstances in which air action was essential, and had delegated powers of decision to the Viceroy. It appears that one reason for Nehru's ill-fated decision to tour the Frontier in October 1946 had been his unease about the bombing of the Shabi Khel Mahsuds after Jos Donald was kidnapped. Yet Nehru was so enraged in 1947 about a decision by the state of Travancore to sell India's rights in uranium resources there that he declared he would approve the use of air power to discipline Travancore.

[7] When these splendid new guns arrived at Razmak, Colonel Finlay, the senior gunnery officer, consulted me about a suitable practice target. He was a thoughtful, sober man who had lost an arm in action, and between us we had no disposition to take unnecessary risks. But the point was that these guns really could fire a vast distance and he quite rightly wanted to prove it, not only to the Army in Razmak but also to the Wazirs and Mahsuds. We poured over maps and questioned the junior political staff meticulously. Ultimately I agreed on a target – a specific hill top in completely uninhabited country, apparently miles from anywhere. But when the guns fired, the shells went right over the top and carried on for miles before apparently coming to earth not very far from a village deep in a valley. Whoever had recalibrated the guns after their move up to Razmak – which was over 7,000 feet – from the plains of India had got a vital sum

wrong. Colonel Finlay still had a red face when I met him months later in the Peshawar Club. In fact there had been no real harm; but the Wazirs sent in a claim for compensation, alleging that a cow and three goats had been killed and an old woman frightened out of her wits. They did not press the matter very seriously so we judged that their sense of humour was at work and their primary concern was to ensure that we did have a red face.

8 Within a few days messages reaching us emphasized that the speed of our reaction had caused surprise. The tribes had got accustomed to the gentlemanly way in which there was often a delay of a day or two before action was taken even after red notices had been dropped. For bombs to fall on the same evening must have upset their plans to send in more messengers about Mir Ghulam's impending surrender, in order to delay our action longer and let their forces build up their strength for the attack on Ghariom.

9 It was Roger Bacon who had first given me hospitality in the Frontier when I arrived on my visit from Dehra in 1941. He said he felt old when he arrived in Miranshah to find me in charge of the Tochi in the middle of such trouble when I had seemed a raw youngster only three years before – he had been in the Middle East meantime with the Mahsud Labour Battalion.

Packman some months later became Resident in succession to Bradshaw.

10 G1 – General Staff Officer Grade 1, the senior staff officer at Razmak.

11 In retrospect, this was a good outcome. To some extent the threat of aerial action had worked. But if it had been followed up, the effect might have proved counter-productive. We were in some danger of abandoning our policy of choosing only very specific, restricted targets. I have no doubts that in the end Sir George Cunningham would have stopped us from making this mistake.

12 ENSA (Entertainments National Service Association) was the organization through which during the war professional actors, singers, musicians etc. were enabled to entertain troops on active service overseas.

13 The evidence is that the Axis agents in Kabul provided Ipi with funds, but that their plotting was jejune and amateurish, and lacked any real grasp of tribal conditions and attitudes.

CHAPTER IX

Peshawar: Rationing Wallah

My first days in Peshawar in July 1944 were wretched. I felt lost and uncertain, frustrated by the humid heat and the vague lassitude it seemed to generate in everyone I contacted. In Miranshah I had known what I was and how to cope with my problems. By day the heat of action, the dust of the road, the sweat of the hills were purposeful and satisfying even though intensely uncomfortable. In the evenings the solitude of my quarters or the deeply sincere camaraderie of the Tochi Scouts' mess equally counterbalanced the fatigue and worry of the day. I had found refuge from the spiritual stress of the war and its prolonged partings in the very wildness and strangeness of that hostile land. I could readily accept the challenge of responsibility in that environment. I was reassured by the constant support and encouragement of my immediate superior, Jack Lowis, and made confident by his comradely trust. Shaken out of this assurance by a sudden transfer to 'a desk job', I felt resentful and not a little cynical and fearful. I knew too little about my new role, and nobody could tell me how the job could be done.

The Governor's telegram had said that 'the political situation has compelled the urgency of reinforcing Dring's staff' – hence the decision to transfer me as Assistant Director of Civil Supplies. It sounded terribly like going back to the frustration and drudgery of permits and licences amidst political chicanery from which I had been glad to escape less than a year before. The Muslim League Ministry had scarcely got into its stride when I left Hazara, but I had seen enough of how they worked to know that the administration of food and civil supplies would be no easier under a ministry than when I had to cope only with the trickery of the dealers and a mistrusted DC. Since then my old colleague Gerald Emerson, who had responsibility in the Secretariat for foodstuffs, had lost the confidence of both the ministers and the Governor, and a new Food and Civil Supplies Department had been formed, detached from the office of the Revenue Commissioner, and placed under the aegis of Major John Dring with the rank of Secretary.[1] He was a very able and experienced officer, suave and assured – a great personal favourite of Sir George Cunningham. He had a first-rate record as PA Mahsuds, and proved to be equally efficient in the Secretariat. His number two was Arthur Wooller, from the Bengal ICS cadre – an IPS officer some six years my senior.[2] Arthur had spent part of the war years in exhausting posts in the Persian Gulf – to the detriment of his health – and had been recalled to Bengal in 1944 to help to deal with the Bengal famine. Under Dring his assignment was to devise a rationing scheme for the Frontier.

When I arrived there was some uncertainty about my role but it was soon decided that Arthur Wooller would himself move into the Secretariat as Deputy Secretary to Dring, while I took over his embryonic office as Controller of Rationing, operating from a rather run-down bungalow which had once been Flagstaff House, the residence of the Army's District Commander. I had only been in Peshawar for an hour when I was summoned by the Chief Minister, Sardar Aurangzeb Khan. He was friendly and encouraging, conveying the impression that HE had recommended me for my tact. I knew that any such quality in me would be severely strained in the next few months but consoled myself with the feeling that I would get on all right with Aurangzeb. I did not know then quite how seriously he had quarrelled with Emerson when he was in charge of food supplies; but Gerald had quarrelled with his own father when the latter was Governor of the Punjab and Gerald, as a subdivisional officer, disagreed with his orders, so I was not surprised at the implication that he had not been tactful with ministers when he was handling sensitive issues about scarce commodities.

I soon found that the political situation was very hazardous. There was a genuine food shortage and after months of ministerial intervention in the normal executive responsibilities of district officers, public confidence in the system of distribution had been shaken. Consequently the normal channels of supply had dried up in anticipation of still higher prices and the bonanza of profiteering on the black market. The Muslim League as a party sprang from the ranks of the big landowners; the Congress Party, professing the interests of the labourer, the landless and the underdog found

227

it easy to mount demonstrations against the alleged oppression and corruption of the Ministry. Thus, at a critical period of the War, when national interest called for cooperation and efficient administration, the Frontier was faced with political dissension and the breakdown of the procurement and distribution of foodstuffs. In the previous year the Government of India had been shaken by the Bengal famine, in which many hundreds of thousands died, starving quietly by the roadside because administrative problems could not be solved in time. In the Frontier, though the scale of the problem was far smaller – the area compact, its transport facilities good, its population minute in comparison with Bengal – the political implications were frightening. The aggressive Pathan would never meekly accept starvation or bow to administrative incompetence. Serious disturbances in the volatile city of Peshawar, even with a population as small as a quarter of a million, could easily disrupt the relative tranquillity of the whole province and its tribal territories – which had been such an important factor in the successful build-up of the Indian Army and hence in the prosecution of the Indian war effort. Even the steadfast Cunningham had become nervous about the prospect in July 1944.

He came to Peshawar from Nathia Gali for a Legislative Council meeting in the week after my arrival. Apparently he had been apprised of my disgruntlement over my transfer for I was invited to dine alone with him and my old friend Oliver St John – now the Secretary to the Governor – on the Saturday evening, and Sir George took great pains to assure me of his sympathy with my feelings on being dragged away from my beloved enemies the Wazirs and confronted with more beastly problems and people in provincial headquarters. He gave me an insight into the political and economic background and his judgment of its critical balance, and – as always – sent me away with renewed confidence and a more acceptable sense of purpose.

It surprised me to be told that there was such a serious and genuine food shortage in the Frontier, for in September 1943 just before I moved from Abbottabad to Waziristan I had attended a special provincial conference about a food crisis, which I had regarded as exaggerated, contrived and fairly easily overcome. A factor in its development had been a drain of supplies away from the main Frontier *mandis* (markets), partly originated by the diversion of Punjab wheat to Bengal in an attempt to offset the rice famine, which had limited success, because Bengalis could not adapt their habits to prepare and eat wheat flour products. The measures taken after that conference had helped to get the grain trade operating again at price levels which were below those of the rest of India. Government offered to accept wheat as payment of arrears of land revenue, at a rate which was a rupee per maund above the wholesale market price. This was intended to furnish reserves to offset shortages in 1944 but throughout the spring there was great concern about supplies and policy.

In February the new Food and Civil Supplies Department had held another provincial conference about urban rationing and controls, involving wheat, maize, barley, sugar and kerosene. The Governor reported to the Viceroy that he felt that the controls operated by individual Deputy Commissioners in each district were effective, but in early April he qualified his optimism when the Food Department published a price control notification, a full month in advance of the *rabi* harvest and its fresh supplies, which in his view kept the price of wheat too low. Within the month shortages of wheat flour were reported in Hazara, Kohat and Peshawar districts, but it was thought that there were adequate supplies of maize. An official request was submitted for a large consignment of wheat from the Punjab (5,000 tons) and the Chief Secretary reported that the growing opposition to the procurement efforts of the DCs was being encouraged by an intense Congress campaign of opposition to the control system. It was even suggested that Dr Khan Sahib's fierce rhetoric exposed him to the charge of exploiting the poor, since the controls he opposed were intended to protect their interests. About this time the Governor appeared – for perhaps the first time in the long record of his fortnight reports to the Viceroy – to be getting a little rattled by this problem. 'For the first time, I have felt anxiety about public feeling in this Province.' He was appalled by the cumulative effects of petty dishonesty on the supply position. The evil connotations of the attacks on controls perturbed him – the word 'control' had entered the Pushtu vocabulary as a 'bad word'. It kept being voiced by tribal *jirgas* and Mohmands and Afridis made it an issue of complaint. What was needed was early action by the Government of India – to shift consignments to NWFP, and to control the price of maize, which was suddenly scarce because Frontier surpluses drained away, attracted by higher prices elsewhere – it was the Provincial Government's policy to control the price of maize around 80 per cent of the price of wheat. The last *kharif* maize crop (autumn) had been poor because of low rainfall, and this was intensifying the demand for wheat from the new *rabi* crop (spring) at a time when local procurement was in difficulties and imports from Punjab were well below normal levels for the season.

One factor in the Governor's alarm was clearly the inability of contractors to deliver normal supplies in June 1944 after the *rabi* harvest to the Frontier Scouts, Police, jails and hospitals. It was this which led him to make his personal appeal to the big landowners to deliver grain but he was disappointed by the result. The ministers agreed in the middle of July to make an order for compulsory registration of stocks. This had been tried, with no success, in 1943, when the limit above which stocks became liable to be requisitioned was put ridiculously low at twenty maunds. In 1944 the limit agreed by the Ministers was 150 – the Governor had proposed 200. But the opposition of the big *zemindars* was obstinate and compliance with the obligation to declare stocks was very patchy. Sir George Cunningham wrote: 'I can think of no occasion in my experience of the Frontier that has demanded more tact and firmness on the part of District Officers than will be demanded of them by these operations.' Yet it was 'imperative, and must be faced', (23 July 1944).

But the early results were poor and Sir George's view in April that the official price had been set too low was confirmed by the fact that such wheat as was coming from the Punjab cost a rupee per maund more than the official market price in NWFP. Naturally, whatever their political purpose, landowners would hold back stocks in the hope of an increase in the official rate.

Even in the peaceful Kurram Valley the Governor saw ominous signs: five villages tried to seize stocks which Government had procured. 'What a tricky business procurement might become in this part of India.' Throughout the summer, the efforts of each Deputy Commissioner were reinforced by the appointment of joint DCs, solely engaged on procurement work, but it was not till the Central Government allocated increased supplies from the Punjab in September that local procurement figures rose above target in three of the six districts. The dramatic improvement in locally procured supplies produced by a marginal shift in imports transformed the whole outlook, and the Governor argued that the

Government of India should abolish the restrictions on trade in grain between provinces. He tried to persuade Sir Bertrand Glancy, Governor of the Punjab, of this in August but met resistance. When Glancy was ready to agree, at the end of September, the Government of India strongly and effectively blocked the proposal.

It was one of the ironies of Frontier politics at this period that opposition to price control and allied measures should have been so vehemently expressed by the Congress Party, which might have been expected to regard them as designed to protect the landless and the poor, and guarantee them against starvation; while it was the Muslim League Ministry, whose political power base was supposed to lie in the landowning classes, who defended and insisted on controls – and indeed doubly offended the landowners by choosing price levels which were so low as to discourage procurement and by enforcing compulsory purchase orders against them. Their opponents, of course, accused them of simply wanting controls as an instrument of power which they would administer corruptly and exploit for their own ends. In my view much of the trouble arose because nobody adequately understood the economic problems. Policies were tried which ignored the laws of supply and demand. The instincts of the Governor were much better attuned to both the economic and the political pressures than those of the politicians of either party. Quite apart from this, neither party displayed the ability to pursue the public interest rather than indulge in internal *party-bazi* or feuding – the eternal curse of northern Indian politics.

I have tried in the preceding paragraphs, with benefit of hindsight, to set in context the situation confronting me in mid-July 1944. I think that there were three main elements of difficulty in our position. One was the procurement of adequate supplies – the task to which Johnny Dring and Arthur Wooller had to give priority. The second was the equitable distribution of these supplies; the task of devising a formal rationing scheme was allocated to me. In the first place this was to be introduced to Peshawar city. The third element involved solving the difficulties of the first two without either losing the confidence of the Ministry or finally undermining its precarious stability. Ministers would want constantly to intervene: they would want to be associated with any success the officials achieved, but they would also want to disclaim responsibility for any mistakes. All the time they would

231

be exposed to the criticisms of their political opponents and to the complaints of the consumers, as well as to pressure from producers and dealers in foodstuffs.

On the whole, I was to find that I personally had less difficulty with this third element in the problem than I might have expected. While I was setting up the Peshawar rationing system, I had surprisingly little direct interference from the ministers. The Chief Minister, Aurangzeb, kept the Food portfolio to himself and he was generally helpful and encouraging. He was rather an ineffectual man: an eloquent political speaker, mild in manner, bulky in physique and – I think – extremely lazy. At any rate, I was able to stay on good terms with him over the next six months. Sadly, he 'lost the place' in the developing political struggle, and failed properly to build on the opportunity to strengthen the provincial Muslim League Party and broaden its base.[3] It was caught unprepared, divided and leaderless when the end of the war brought Dr Khan Sahib's Congress Party into successful contention for political supremacy, thus putting the Frontier Province at the centre of the national stage in the struggle between the Congress and the Muslim League in the months before the transfer of power. In that period, mistrust and mutual criticism came to dominate relations between ministers and officials in the province, particularly over matters of distribution of scarce commodities. But that is part of a later stage in the story, some time after I had completed my work as Controller of Rationing.

The first two elements in the problem were not easily overcome. In normal times the province as a whole was generally self-sufficient, the fertile lands of Peshawar and Mardan producing enough to compensate for any deficiencies in districts like Hazara where a bad harvest could produce local shortages. But these were not normal times and the flow of grain to the *mandis* was constrained. Many *zemindars* held on to stocks which they would usually sell; motives for hoarding were political as well as economic, a fact which was to highlight problems of procurement in which I became directly involved a year later. In the summer of 1946 the Governor made a personal appeal to producers and issued instructions to all district officers that procurement was to be their first priority, superseding all other duties. In effect, because of the Ministry's inaptitude about local procurement, Dring and Wooller had to accept that they must rely on securing imports controlled by the Government of India. The source of these supplies was the Punjab and the state of Bahawalpur but both the Central Government in Delhi and the Punjab authorities were reluctant to release the abnormally large quantities of wheat and other grains which the Frontier Food Department requested. Our view was that if we could get big enough supplies early enough from outside, stocks privately hoarded in our surplus districts could soon begin to move into the markets. In fact, for some anxious weeks, all that we could secure from the Punjab had to go straight to meet the urgent needs of consumers, and we had no reserves on which to build a formal and reliable scheme of rationed distribution, or to use as a lever to get home-produced grain moving. No rationing scheme, implying a commitment by Government to provide the ration, could possibly be launched until supplies were secure, so my planning was done more in hope than in expectation.

It was the end of August before Dring and the Governor between them succeeded in getting a large enough quota agreed with the Government in Delhi. Then I had a new problem. The provincial grain dealers had decided to boycott Government's effort and were frostily non-cooperative. Since they owned or controlled the warehouses, and it was essential in the circumstances for me to control the storage of external supplies, I had to find ways of taking delivery of very large quantities, and preserving the grain in good conditions ready for timely supply to the distributing depots. Early in September I was visited by the Central Government's special adviser on storage. He was an Edinburgh University scientist called Coyne who had done an outstanding job in the Middle East for the grain supplies for Egypt, Palestine and Iraq and he was brought from Cairo to India by the Viceroy (Wavell) in 1944 to advise on similar problems. He painstakingly inspected every building that I had commandeered and examined all my arrangements. Before he left he was kind enough to show me his report to the Government of India in which he assured them of the imaginative efficiency with which the problems of storing their quotas were being tackled in the Frontier.

Two months later these arrangements were strained to breaking point. Soon after the Peshawar rationing scheme had been launched in mid-October, the Government of India released exceptionally large supplies for Peshawar and we had very short notice of their delivery. Once again I relied on my good standing with the Army. Colonel Duncan, who had been Station Commandant in Abbottabad in 1943, had come to Peshawar as Administrative Commandant, and with his support I went straight to General Bruce Scott, the District Commander, asking for the use of some empty barracks in the old fort and elsewhere in the cantonment. The request was promptly granted and with it the bonus of an offer of a special military railway siding where the exceptionally large consignments could be unloaded without delay.

This negotiation had an interesting consequence. The accommodation provided by the Army was so good that the wastage of grain incurred during the period of storage proved to be dramatically reduced below normal, and some months later the Controller and Auditor General was so surprised by the unusual figures that – instead of complimenting my staff – he suspected that they had been cooking the books. I had quite a battle with him about the technicalities of weighing grain before and after a period of storage. The effects of humidity, of weevils, and other factors, such as rodents, can all affect weight over a period and all these factors are influenced by variations in conditions of storage, as well as by season and climate. Because grain stored in military godowns was shown by our accounts not to have lost weight at the date of distribution, the C and AG held that there ought to be no loss of weight in stocks held in inferior conditions. The warehouses normally used by the grain trade were often appalling – *kacha* buildings, in which the grain was subject to all sorts of risk. After much disputation his suspicions were grudgingly withdrawn, for there was no evidence to support them, and he could not refute my technical arguments or disprove the accuracy of our records.

The attitude of the wholesale grain dealers and importers left me with no option but to operate in effect a large, official, monopolistic agency. With one notable exception, all the important Hindu grain dealers refused cooperation and waited on the sidelines for the whole enterprise to break down. The exception was a cheerful, stout and steadfast youngish contractor called Acharaj Lal, who put his knowledge and energies wholeheartedly to work to help the staff of the Rationing Department. No doubt he benefited financially from his efforts: he certainly worked hard for anything he earned. Without his knowledge of the background to our transport and storage problems and his links with the trade in the Punjab, it is doubtful whether we could have solved all our problems so successfully within the time-limits available to us.

The staff which I took over from Arthur Wooller were a pretty scratch lot and when I came to expand it I had great difficulty in getting efficient men. In the end there were about 150 in the department, a fair mixture of Muslims, Hindus and Sikhs, but the extraordinary thing was that they worked up a genuine spirit of teamwork. Perhaps there was a feeling that they were embarked together on a new kind of adventure in administration. At any rate, there seemed to be remarkably little of the petty jealousies and internal office quarrels that were so common in the subordinate ranks of government service. They were not well-paid and the system we built up was so watertight that it could scarcely provide opportunity for the private feathering of nests. A few of them were so proficient that they earned rapid promotion, but the majority seemed content with their lot as members of the team. Their loyalty to the department showed up much later, long after I had moved on, when communal rioting broke out in the city in the spring of 1947, and several of them – Hindus and Sikhs – were killed or wounded in stabbing affrays as they tried to go about their normal business. There were cases where Muslim colleagues took great personal risks in seeking to protect these victims of the mob.

My Assistant Controller of Rationing was Mohammed Nawaz Khan, a member of the Provincial Civil Service who had good general experience but no great business acumen. At first, I felt that he was a fish out of water, a man with whom I would have had complete trust working together in a tribal agency, but not in the technicalities of office work in a peculiar economic context. But he worked hard, was tremendously loyal and he was splendid in relationships with junior staff of all communities, Sikh, Hindu or Muslim. He formed a tennis club at which many, of all grades, participated in the evenings on the grass lawns of our office-bungalow, and often their speed and enthusiasm reduced me to the depths of exhaustion. Deservedly, when I went on leave in January 1945, Mohammed Nawaz succeeded me as Controller of Rationing and he continued to do a fine job.

Developing and training this staff kept me busy in the first months after my arrival. I had to build and elaborate the outlines of the scheme conceived by Wooller. In a city like Peshawar, with its polyglot population and large numbers of itinerants, formal enumeration was difficult. Many of the details of my system have long been forgotten, though no doubt they survive on files in Pakistan; but it may not be unfair to assert that the system was as

Staff at Rationing Depot, Peshawar saying farewell to the Author when he handed over to Mohammed Nawaz, January 1945.

sophisticated as any that had been tried in India, while it was simple enough to be understood and accepted by a suspicious and sceptical people. I put much stress on establishing appropriate ration depots, where service would be clean, efficient, dependable and quick. This involved careful survey of all the streets and *galis* in the various quarters of this fascinating, complex and teeming city, followed by selection of over 100 official shops or depots from almost 250 'possibles'. The final stage in the process saw me spend six successive evenings walking the streets of the city in the last week of Ramzan – always a tense period of the Mohammedan year. But the excessive heat of July by now was tempered: the daytime maximum was not much over 90°, and at night it was beginning to feel cool again, at around 70°. My spirits were raised when Dring came back from Delhi with news that the Government of India had allocated a quota of grain adequate to guarantee the feasibility of my scheme.

In his absence, and that of Wooller, who had gone on six weeks' leave, I had secured the Ministry's approval for the organization and establishment of my department and for some reshaping of the Secretariat arrangements. To my great relief, I had also found solutions to the problems of funding the whole enterprise – including the payments for imports on Government account. Such a financial operation was novel, complicated and calculated to rouse unending difficulties in the bureaucratic minds of the provincial Finance Department. But again fortune smiled on me for recently the post of Finance Secretary had been assumed by my old friend and mentor, Alastair Low, and his quick, sharp mind cut through the tangle of objections to my proposals in the friendliest manner. I was particularly glad of his help at that stage as I was feeling rather left on my own in the Food Department. I had been sent, at short notice, on a brief leave before the end of July in order to be back in time to cover for Wooller's long absence – he was married in Nathia Gali where HE declared at the wedding reception that he was now appropriately a controlled commodity. He had been given a long furlough because he had had to contend with so much ill health in Persia and in Bengal. After my return, Johnny Dring went soon after Wooller, combining leave with subsequent negotiations about quotas for the Frontier in Delhi and Simla. I was therefore in sole charge for some time. My holiday had been timely enough for I had had a rough spell in the dry heat of Waziristan, and Peshawar's July humidity and my prickly heat were very wearing. But there was no time, or money, for another trip to Kashmir, which I had hoped earlier to arrange with my Punjab friends. I was refreshed by ten days in Abbottabad, but the batteries were not fully recharged and I was lucky to get over the hump of the work by mid-September without collapsing. I had spent the first weekend of the month at Rawalpindi with a Punjab ICS colleague named Rodgers, who had been controlling food and civil supplies there for nearly three years, and was able to teach me a great deal.

No sooner had the end of Ramzan come and 'Id-ul-Fitr – the celebratory festival – brought some leisure to complement the relief from the worst of my anxiety about the scheme, than I developed a recurrent fever, which was at first misdiagnosed, so that the malarial parasite which had afflicted me got a free run and a firm hold of my system. For the next year and more I was to have an uncomfortable and debilitating sequence of recurrent malarial attacks, despite swallowing huge quantities of quinine, mepacrine and pamaquin in appropriate sequences.

Somehow one survives these aches and discomforts, and on 22 October the new rationing system was launched on an apparently complaisant city. Snags and complaints were few. This was truly remarkable, because Peshawar is a turbulent cosmopolitan city, full of footloose independent characters, and its womenfolk make themselves heard behind the protection of *purdah-nashin*. Strong opposition to formal rationing had been expressed on the grounds that the enquiries of the rationing department's staff were an intrusion into the privacy of the Islamic family. During the summer we had put a great deal of effort into the reassurance of the public. In this, my first lieutenant Mohammed Nawaz was a pillar of strength. Greatly respected by the Muslims, he was not a particularly clever or subtle man, but so patently sincere and honest that he won the trust of the people for the work of our staff. In the end that trust was reinforced by the public's awareness of the obstacles put in our way by the protracted opposition of the traders – many of whom were Hindus.

The Muslim League Ministry had directed that there was to be no private wholesale agency for foodgrains – either for importation, or for stocking and issue to retailers, or for milling flour. As I have already said, this put the Controller of Rationing in the position of managing a big trading agency. The tight regulations under which this was run, with strict accounting procedures, were anathema to the traditional grain dealers, who preferred an element of manipulation in the weighing of quantities, kept their accounts in their head and resented orders to complete daily and weekly returns under external supervision. The scheme allowed them only a very narrow margin of profit because Government was anxious to keep prices under strict control. In the middle of October the dealers were refusing to indent for stocks of grain and sugar and the launching of the scheme was jeopardized. But public sympathy was on the side of the officials, the ring was broken and supplies started moving out to the depots two days before the start of formal rationing. On 22 October, when we got going, our central reserves were enough to guarantee supplies for no more than the second week, but within a few days large consignments were reaching us by rail from the Punjab and the worst of my anxieties were over.

About a week after the scheme started the Governor made an unheralded tour of the city's ration depots with Johnny Dring and myself. He found conditions in the city vastly different from July when the people had been sulky and hungry, trade was disorganized and supplies scarce. In his diary he recorded his pleasure and relief at the success of the rationing scheme, and the reassuring responses he got from the people as he enquired about the quality of the atta, and the convenience and assurance which the arrangements provided for the public. Although I did not know it at the time, my reward was to be placed high on the list of officers who were to be granted home leave early in 1945. Ever since my transfer to Peshawar, I had been preoccupied with this possibility. I guessed that the end of the War in Europe would enable many senior officers to take long leave and that my chances would recede again if I had not got away in advance. I expected the years immediately after the War to make heavy demands on the ICS and correspondingly to create fresh opportunities for the exercise of responsibility, for the service was clearly going to be undermanned.[4] So I wanted to get home first, and – all being well – to bring back my bride to be at my side in the exciting period of post-war reconstruction and political development.

Throughout the last six months of 1944 my spirits were pretty low. My energies had taken a rude knock as a result of my persistent malaria, and although I was now sure that the War would soon be over in the West, I was thoroughly wearied by the prolonged years of anxious separation from my loved ones. I had never felt settled in Peshawar. In the hot weather, it was impossible to establish the sort of friendships that had given me strength both in Miranshah and in Abbottabad. By October and November I was restless and 'of no fixed abode'. Having been a paying guest in Dring's bungalow with Arthur Wooller, when that ménage broke up I had moved on to share a bungalow with Broughton Hay, an ICS man who had, after a long leave in Australia following a serious illness, come to be City Magistrate, Peshawar. Within a few weeks he was under orders to transfer to Nowshera and before the end of November I was looking for new accommodation. In the end I moved into a quarter in Dean's Hotel for a month before my sailing orders arrived.

During most of the autumn and cold weather I had little opportunity for recreation; though I began to get some golf, and the Peshawar golf course was a big improvement on any other I had seen in India, my form was indifferent. One problem was the unavailability of golf balls. Some remoulds sent from home for my birthday kept me going. One day, Acharaj Lal, the helpful grain dealer, presented me with three new Dunlops in their paper. He had scoured the bazaar for them and was delighted with his find. But as soon as a blow was struck at one, the paint and cover began to break off and none of the balls remained whole and spherical for more than a couple of holes. They had been stored too long and if undamaged by weevils, had suffered from temperature change even more severely than my foodgrains. At that time, this sort of problem of scarcity affected many of our pleasures – tennis balls were also scarce; photographic film was almost unobtainable; petrol for non-official purposes was severely rationed, and even for official business was hard to get; travel by bus was uncertain, depending often on the whim of the charcoal-driven engine and the mechanical skills of the driver and his mate, who were admittedly often surprisingly effective with emergency repairs. I had no inclination to take up riding again and never hunted with the Peshawar Vale Hunt. The nearest I got to that was to visit the kennels several times with Johnny Dring or Gerald Emerson when they went to supervise the feeding and grooming of the hounds.

Sir George Cunningham found a way of keeping me amused while doing something useful at weekends. He was always very close to the senior army people and he knew that a stage had been reached in the War when it was important to sustain the morale of British troops. He and Lady Cunningham always made a great effort to entertain and befriend them. He had discovered that many of them tried to take an intelligent interest in India but were confused about the country's political state and frustrated by the conventional barriers that blocked the way to a better understanding. He developed a scheme for groups of volunteers to be taken out into the districts for a weekend by one of his younger political officers, to follow a programme that would both entertain and educate.[5] The Army, or the RAF, supplied the transport and equipment, such as tents, and HE supplied the food and arranged the contacts. On my first weekend I went under the charge of Major John Steward who was then the Subdivisional Officer at Charsadda in the heart of Abdul Ghaffar Khan's country. John had been the first to lead one of these excursions and he was ideal for the purpose, having both military and political experience and a cheerful outlook on life.

In a letter home I described that first excursion. The party consisted of two British officers and fourteen other ranks – half from the RAF and the rest from the Intelligence Section of a British battalion then stationed in Peshawar. We drove out to a lovely spot on the banks of the Swat River canal some miles from Charsadda and not far from the border of Mohmand tribal territory. The men were housed in the Canal Department's rest house, while the two officers, along with Steward and myself, were accommodated in a beautiful little cottage nearby in the orchard of Ghulam Haider Khan of Sherpao – over the next two and a half years I got to know this fine man well. He was a survivor of the class of khans or leading landowners on whose loyalty the British Raj had long relied in the Frontier. Their influence had been steadily eroded by political developments and many were now associated uneasily with one or other of the political parties. Ghulam Haider was nominally a prominent member of the Muslim League, but he was far too '*sharif*' a man – a thorough gentleman – to be an important politician in the rough game of political feuding that was characteristic of the Frontier.

In the orange groves of his lovely estate at Sherpao he entertained us to a sumptuous lunch of mutton pilao and fresh fruit in vast quantities, and afterwards John Steward and his *Tahsildar* explained the system of land administration to the men and tried to answer their questions. Then we took them for a long walk through the fields to let them see how the farms worked and the system of canal irrigation operated, stopping to watch a sugar-cane press producing *gur* – the peasants' substitute for sugar. After dinner, there was a long informal session on general administrative problems. Next morning we drove to a post on the border held by Frontier Constabulary and from a high vantage point nearby explained the lie of tribal territory, describing some of the historical background and the present method of securing 'watch and ward'. Driving on from there along the canal road we stopped at a large village and called into the police station to hear a talk by a DSP (an Indian deputy superintendent of police) about the organization of the service and about characteristic duties, such as the capture of proclaimed outlaws and the surveillance of political agitators. After yet another Pathan feast provided by another landowner and a walk through the village, we returned to base for a further long discussion. Most of them had served in India or Burma for several years and they were not short of acute questions and penetrating observations. On the return journey to Peshawar next day we stopped at Charsadda to listen to cases being tried in the law courts. That was the general pattern of subsequent outings which I led myself. They were enjoyable experiences, made refreshing by the lively interest shown by the troops. On more than one occasion members of the party displayed keen political awareness, obviously fostered by long study – no doubt encouraged by the publications of the Army

Bureau of Current Affairs and in some cases by the Left Book Club and the publications of the Communist Party – no wonder I was far less surprised by the results of the 1945 General Election than the great majority of my European friends in Peshawar!

I always enjoyed my contacts with the military – in Hazara, Waziristan, and now in very different circumstances in Peshawar. These weekends reminded me of other days when I had myself been an 'other rank' in the Black Watch. Perhaps, too, there was reassurance in association with men in uniform who were more frustrated by the emptiness and futility of their present jobs than I could ever be with mine. I had always felt an uneasiness about the relative comfort and security of my life in the Frontier. I had even had pangs of conscience when I heard that autumn that Brian Becker, the Additional APA stationed at Dosalli in North Waziristan, had been shot in the leg while driving on the Ghariom road which I had traversed so frequently in safety a few months earlier.

On the weekend which I spent in Rawalpindi early in September with Rodgers, he had entertained to dinner a Scottish Presbyterian minister called Routledge whom we escorted home around midnight. Taking a short cut back through the grounds of the 'Pindi Club, we were hailed by a slim, familiar figure, sitting with a group of officers. This was my old chum, Hugh Easton, convalescing after being severely wounded in a fight behind Japanese lines near Imphal. When he described his escape – several of the other ambulances in the convoy were cut off – and his feelings of bitterness towards the enemy, I was appalled and shaken to the core. This was what war did to the body and mind of a gentle, kindly young man, and here was I, safe and smug and full of self-importance. There was a strange ambivalence in my attitudes. My early instincts for pacifism were still strong; but I enjoyed the dangerous war games we indulged in in Waziristan and I loved the contacts my work gave me with senior officers who had proved themselves great soldiers – like Bruce Scott, now GOC Peshawar District, who had been one of Slim's Divisional Commanders in the 14th Army, and in earlier days had been both a Tochi Scout and a 6th Gurkha and therefore 'brought up in' Miranshah and Abbottabad. No doubt this sounds like pompous name-dropping, but I was aware that few men of my age got the chance to meet and know such heroes of the time and I revelled in my luck.

Outside magistrate's court, Charsadda in Peshawar District.

An evening spent in the company of General Tuker, who had commanded the 4th Indian Division, was another such occasion. He had come to the Frontier as chairman of a special committee which was to seek new ways of dealing with the problems of Waziristan and other tribal areas. I was impressed by his analytical mind and fascinated by his conversation. In my own role, I had to spend a day 'under inspection' by Lieutenant General Sir Clarence Bird, the retired Master of Ordnance, who had become Regional Food Controller for north India on behalf of the Government of India. I have only a faint recollection of that experience but from my notes it seems to have been satisfactory and pleasant.

Looking back at my notes on all these encounters, I can see that I must have been getting too big for my boots and that a spell back home in Scotland to bring me down to earth was certainly now overdue. The fresh winds of the Moray Firth were needed to bring my head back to size. By Christmas 1944 I was on stand-by for orders to sail. Mysterious coded cables dropped hints of my impending leave in the ears of my mother and my fiancée. By the third week in February 1945 I had disembarked at Gourock on the Clyde and was on the overnight train north – to be met in the darkness of the early morning by the slim, dark, faithful lass whom

I had missed so sorely. On 24 of March we were married, amidst a host of old friends in the High Church at Nairn.

Notes

[1] After Partition, Dring was for some years Prime Minister in the State of Bahawalpur and later held several important advisory posts in Africa during the final years of colonial rule. He was knighted in 1952.

[2] In 1948 Wooller joined the Diplomatic Service, working mainly in commercial posts, but becoming successively Deputy High Commissioner for India, High Commissioner, Mauritius, and Economic Adviser FCO at the final stages of his career.

[3] He had been able to form his ministry without having a majority of members of the Provincial Assembly. A number of Congress MLAs had been kept in detention since the 1942 Quit India Campaign. Some Congress members defected to the opposition and Aurangzeb's enemies within the League accused him of neglecting his old friends in favour of new allies. The uneasy internal relationships within the party were typical of the Frontier, where politics were riddled by feuds and enmities. Aurangzeb lost the confidence of Jinnah who sent Liaqat Ali and other emissaries to Peshawar to investigate the position. Aurangzeb was also under constant pressure from the Governor to release the imprisoned MLAs.

[4] In one letter home I described the effects on the older ICS men of the long years of the war. It had greatly complicated their work and added to its volume, as well as creating frequent emergencies, while they had to be spread more thinly on the ground. Many showed signs of over-strain and badly needed long leave. The effects of the Bengal famine had seriously harmed the health of many dedicated officers working devotedly at full pressure for months on end. Yet the survivors would have to face new and even more demanding challenges when the War ended and political pressures mounted – and their numbers would be still further reduced.

[5] The Governor devised the scheme which I describe after a conversation with an American general who complained that the large numbers of American troops now in India were not getting any real impression of the country.

CHAPTER X

Secretariat Johnnie

There is no need to write much about the first six months of 1945. The anxiety of the long wait for news of a passage home was soon lost in the boredom of the protracted wartime voyage. I shared a cabin with a delightful senior member of the Indian Agricultural Service, A.P. Cliff, overdue for retirement and nervous about how to build a relationship with his daughter whom he had not seen for over six years. With us were two lively characters of nearly my own age from Bengal – an ICS man and a member of the Indian Police. They were so brashly self-confident that I felt that I must have been becalmed in a sleepy backwater for years. When they came on board they each carried a case of spirits. The troopship was of course 'dry' but the regulations allowed an officer to take aboard a reasonable quantity of liquor appropriate to normal consumption. This was in very small print and interpreted by those few who noticed it as entitling them to take on board an opened bottle to be finished, but these incorrigible Bengal officers boldly – and after long argument successfully – claimed that what they had was for their normal consumption and could not be confiscated. They were completely unselfish with it and shared it while it lasted with A.P. Cliff and myself on the basis of one drink each before lunch and two before dinner. After a couple of days at sea our party was the envy of the ship. We played bridge happily for three or four sessions each day, relaxed in the knowledge that there would be another ration tomorrow. When we got to Suez, we were not allowed to disembark but somehow the policeman developed contacts that enabled him to replenish supplies at Cairo with a quantity of barely potable Cyprus liquor.

We had entered the Suez Canal in a high wind and the pilot promptly swung our bows into the bank. After a few hours delay all seemed well, but in the Bitter Lakes we were anchored for several days while divers inspected the hull and everyone got anxious about missing escorts through the Mediterranean or onwards from Gibraltar. My clearest memory is of how cold the wind was as it swept over the desert and the waters of the lakes. There were a couple of nervous nights at Gibraltar, marked by occasional minor explosions which were said to be caused by Germans operating from midget submarines. Then onwards uneventfully through the Atlantic to a final, and very nerve-racking passage north of Ireland, where there was still evident reason for extreme caution in navigation through an area of hostile activity. Dawn broke slowly as we crept up the Firth of Clyde, gradually becoming aware of the snow-clad hills to the north as we approached the Tail o' the Bank. I remembered a childhood holiday at Greenock when I had spent hours watching the big liners, then so numerous, identifying their funnels and flags. My announcements of new sightings of ever larger liners used to bring from my parents the question, 'And how many funnels has the Cunarder got today then?' – a question often repeated, which subsequently became the family's gentle way of bringing me down to earth from some boast or conceit. Now on this dark, still, frosty February morning I wondered what had happened to myself in all these years when there was nobody to put that warning question to me. It was not just the cold of the Scottish dawn that got into my marrow. There was also relief – and excitement – and apprehension. After years of parting, full of unshared events and all the strange experiences of war, what would I find? And how would they find me? Had the Cunarder acquired too many funnels to be credible?

The answer for me was clear next day. I found love and care and loyalty, and soon began to view my whole career in a new perspective – much less self-centred, certainly less naive, but not, I think, any less dedicated to the idea of service to the people of India. I was intensely patriotic and like many Scotsmen who found it possible to combine patriotism with devoted service to the peoples of the Empire, I found my love of my country strengthened by home-coming to Scotland. The spring of 1945, in the last months of a terrible war, with the anticipations and uncertainties of impending victory, was a specially emotional time for a home-coming. Amidst the joy and happiness of preparation and celebration of our wedding, of renewing old friendships and picking up threads, there was an intensity of discussion and speculation about a future which we all knew contained greater uncertainty than anything we might previously have conceived, both for life in Britain and life in India. But the magic of our new life together in the present carried us happily through the next few months, until June came and a new separation loomed.

Because of all the efforts we had made, before my leave, to secure for Barbara a passage to India, we had every reason to expect that she would accompany me on my return. She had been allotted a number on the waiting list for passages for women, high enough to indicate that she would have sailed in April or May at the latest if I had not been granted home leave. In the euphoria after V-E Day, we were confident there would be no more separation. Within weeks, we were in despair: not only would I have to travel without her, but nobody would give us any information about when she might follow. The misery of the next few months linger still in my mind, for the uncertainty and lack of information about her passage obsessed both of us. Right through the hot weather of Peshawar in August and September I was distracted by my daily efforts to move somebody to do something or to say something about the situation. It was small comfort to me, and less to my wife, to know that we were not alone in our predicament. Certainly many hundreds of families were affected. We came to know, of course, of the shipping shortages, at first explained by the plans to build up our armed forces for the invasion of Japan. The whole question, however, became a great bureaucratic scandal, from which I learned one invaluable lesson – that refusal to explain or give information, or even to answer queries with a polite and friendly if unpropitious response, is the most damaging of all bureaucratic abuses and the worst outcome of the corruption of power. Like many others similarly placed, I pursued the matter indefatigably by every sensible channel of communication, in Peshawar, Bombay, Delhi and London. In India, yes even in Delhi, I constantly found a sympathetic and willing response, but from London, from the India Office and the office of the High Commissioners, nothing but delay and silence and lack of understanding. In the end, the scandal built up to such proportions that even the Viceroy became infuriated at being unable to help his distressed officers. One reads his diary recording other reasons for frustration with London over far more important issues with a sense of genuine personal sympathy. The great objection to the extension of central control in any sphere of government is the abuse of power and privilege at minor levels of authority to which it leads.

I got to Peshawar on the evening of 24 July 1945 to be met at the station by Robin Latimer and my own bearer, Mozam Khan.[1] Robin told me that I was to return to the Food and Civil Supplies Department, though not to my old job as Controller of Rationing. At present he and Arthur Wooller were in joint charge, each with the rank of Deputy Secretary, but Robin was to move across to the Development Department in place of Roger Bacon. He took me to join the 'chummery' at 9 Jheel Road, the familiar home of Sir James Almond, the Judicial Commissioner. James insisted that I stay for a week as his guest until I had found a more fixed lodging. The night after I arrived he had an all-male dinner party, at which the guests included two very senior military officers. The news of the results of Britain's General Election was the sensational topic of discussion. The senior people were surprised and appalled by Labour's victory and by what the Services' vote had done to Churchill. I was not only unsurprised, but in sympathy with the outcome and for the first time in my knowledge of him, Sir James was upset and lost his temper. I suddenly realized what the War and the impending loss of Empire meant for his decent, traditionalist generation. My generation had come to India avowedly for a different purpose, knowing that we were to assist India towards self-government. The war years had held all of us together in the service of the Crown, united willingly in the common patriotic cause, measuring the tactics of the Indian political parties against its yardstick. Now the cause was won but the retention of Empire had become irrelevant and our service to the Indian people could no longer ignore or circumvent political pressures on the ground that the villager was satisfied with a fair hearing and the fatherly protection of the sahib.

At first I was disappointed at the news that I was to work in the Secretariat. I had hoped for a subdivisional post like Hangu or Charsadda; Oliver St John had written to say there was a chance that I would go to Mansehra in Hazara. I had longed for the traditional role of the district or subdivisional officer, taking his bride with him on tour, 'where the real India is, in the villages and fields, in the mountains and forests'. But sober reflection reminded me that conditions in *mofussil* were no longer easy for a young wife. India was suffering from shortages of all kinds and the solitude of a station like Mansehra would not be conducive to learning how to run a sahib's household. There was much to be said for starting married life in provincial headquarters, with the best facilities available and plenty of friends to help in every need. But the prospect of continuing indefinitely in this artificial world of 'controls' was, to say the least, unexciting. My last job had had the excitement of a particular challenge, but I could not see any lasting satisfaction in dealing repetitively with tiresome shortages in postwar conditions. We were unlikely to be faced with the crisis of another possible famine or with riots because of a shortage of cloth.

It turned out that my main responsibility was to be for cloth. In my role as Deputy Director of Civil Supplies, one of my grandiose titles was 'Provincial Textile Commissioner'. When news of this got back home to Scotland, I had to put up with quite a bit of teasing. Asked what I was doing as a jumped-up draper, or where I had acquired expertise in negotiating for supplies of women's underwear, I protested huffily that my tormentors had no conception of how India was administered. Not much indeed now needs to be said about the work of the next few months. Besides cloth and sugar, there was a wide range of commodities over the supply and distribution of which I had some responsibility – ranging from kerosene to firewood. At first I worked as Under Secretary to Arthur Wooller who was mostly concerned with foodgrains. One of the biggest problems was the influence of the Ministry to which of course we were responsible. In the months of my leave the Muslim League's shaky hold on the reins of provincial government had finally been undermined – not least by the constant allegations that they abused the instrument of price and commodity control for their own ends. Dr Khan Sahib now led a Ministry of the Congress Party who were committed to a policy of control and intervention not so very different from that which they had so recently virulently condemned. Moreover they were much more prone to intervene in executive decisions than, in my particular experience, the Muslim League ministers had been. Whereas as Chief Minister Aurangzeb had been soft and almost sycophantic in his dealings with British officers, the Congress ministers were tough and tended to be fearless, often reckless, in making accusations of administrative inefficiency or corruption. They had pursued this line so vigorously as the party in opposition that a Committee of Enquiry into corruption had been set up. Its membership consisted entirely of officials, under the leadership of Gilbert Grace, by then the senior police officer in the province. Serious allegations of maladministration involving prima-facie charges of corruption were made against four district officers – all of them Muslim, but three of them no longer serving in district appointments in NWFP. Neither Sir George Cunningham nor Dr Khan Shaib was personally inclined to follow up such indictments with formal departmental action and the charges rested. This was probably in the long run unfortunate because over the next two years relations between the new Ministry and the officials – particularly the Muslim officials – became more and more strained, and it might have helped if the air had been cleared by formally testing the allegations made in these early cases. In particular the unresolved accusations against Sheikh Mahboob Ali as DC Kohat were clearly a factor in the charges later levied against him – and the procedures followed – when he was PA Malakand during the attacks on Pandit Nehru, Khan Sahib and Abdul Ghaffar Khan in Malakand at the end of Nehru's disastrous tour of the Frontier in November 1946.

By the time I arrived Arthur Wooller was already having trouble with the ministers. He was a strong, efficient, highly principled officer whose manner might give the impression of undue intellectual arrogance. Interventions by ministers and their cronies were often inconsistent with the Government's own policies and Arthur never hesitated to say so. He was utterly incorruptible and became the target of critics whose motives were less pure. Up in Nathia Gali, where the Provincial Government was in recess for the hot weather, the decision was made to assuage ministerial irritations by moving him from the Department, and Robin Latimer, who had left it just a week or so earlier, was brought back to head it. I was invited to spend the weekend at Government House in Nathia Gali where HE gave me the background of the trouble stirred up for Arthur Wooller. My reactions led him to insist on the ministers meeting the responsible officers in Council to agree on a firm policy from which they would not depart. Writing home on V-J Day, just after this excursion, I wrote: 'Arthur is the first victim of the Congress political campaign and they are fools to have forced him out … it's pretty sordid and makes me feel there is not really much future for any of us out in India.' Exactly a month later, in another letter to my wife I wrote: 'I am getting more certain that you won't know India for more than three years.'

Latimer and I prepared carefully for the conference with the ministers on 25 August, driving to Abbottabad from Peshawar late on the Friday evening. Next morning we had three-quarters of an hour alone with HE going over the papers, then had to wait while he and the ministers dealt with the Cabinet's other business. When we were called in there was an exhausting discussion lasting for two and a half hours. After lunch Robin and I drafted the minutes of the meeting. Later on the Saturday afternoon, the Governor having returned to Nathia Gali, Robin had a private session with the Chief Minister before himself going 'up the hill'. Having stayed the night with Rushton, who had recently become DC Hazara, I had a long session alone with Dr Khan Sahib on the Sunday morning before returning to Peshawar to prepare for an All-India Textiles Conference which I was to attend in Bombay in the first week in September.

Memory has faded, but I believe that the Abbottabad conference had a useful effect. Decisions were made that helped us to work on agreed policy lines without constantly being outflanked by individual ministers or their parliamentary secretaries. The Chief Minister himself took responsibility for our department; nobody ever doubted his integrity; it was the source of his remarkable political stature. He was uniquely incorruptible – though his judgement could be swayed by personal prejudices and pressures. A bluff, agreeable man, he could reveal flashes of Pathan temper: a much firmer, stronger character than the suave, deferential and equally friendly Aurangzeb, his Muslim League predecessor. But Khan Sahib never struck me as being sharp or particularly intelligent. He could not match in debate the lawyers who were so prolific in Frontier politics – like Qazi Ataullah, his Minister for Revenue, or Abdul Qayum who deserted the Congress Party to become the League leader, or even Aurangzeb or Sardar Bahadur, the Haripur pleader whose brother Ayub became President of Pakistan. Most impressive of all in argument in my experience was Abdul Rab Nishtar who will crop up again in my story. In August 1945 I was just beginning to know Dr Khan Sahib personally and though I was deeply suspicious of the reasons for moving the efficient Arthur Wooller from the post to which he was so well suited, I was glad that it was Khan Sahib and not one of the other ministers, to whom I was to be ultimately responsible.

I can perhaps most vividly illustrate this by recounting just one incident of the next few months. Towards the end of October my office informed me one Friday that the Finance Minister had given an oral instruction about the disposition of cloth quotas for the district of Dera Ismail Khan. DIK was the home of the minister, Diwan Bhanju Ram, the Hindu representative in the Congress Ministry. The instruction had, of course, been conveyed orally by one of Bhanju Ram's servants. I instructed the office to ignore it and to adhere to orders which I had already passed. I was quietly warned by one of my trusted clerks that I should expect further interference. For the rest of the day I kept dodging emissaries of the Minister, hoping that over the weekend nemesis would overtake him.

On the Saturday for the first time he approached me direct, on the telephone. He wished to see me that afternoon at 4. I was most apologetic: I had, regrettably, a previous engagement.

Sharply, he had the nerve to push me: 'Is it important? With whom are you engaged?'

'Sir, I have to see the Brigade Major'.

Fortunately for me, this was a personage of sufficient standing to give pause even to ministerial authority at this stage in India's political history. I guessed that the Minister was wondering whether behind the meeting with the Brigade Major there might be some important matter affecting the Brigade Commander or even Army District Headquarters, matters into which he would have no authority to pry. He rang off abruptly and I heaved a sigh of relief: I was indeed to meet Major Wilson – on the first tee of the golf course. We had a regular series of excellent weekend games.

Next morning, I was in a dilemma. I knew that even a Scotsman's Sabbath was no defence against this particular minister when he was under pressure from contractors in his home town. It was my normal practice on Sunday to work quietly in the bungalow and to write my letters home, but I felt too edgy to settle and decided to put off the evil hour of confrontation by going out without telling my servants where I might be found. Having walked to the club and sat for a long time by the pool, I returned after lunch, still hot and frustrated, to find the Minister's orderly lurking in the shade of a tree in the garden. He had a letter summoning me at once to the Minister's presence. There was now no escape. We had an uncomfortable interview in which I made it clear that the orders he was instructing me to issue to the DC DIK were not compatible with agreed policy guidelines. I was given a deadline for the issue of the letter – for some reason that now escapes me, timing was a factor in the affair, and I had been playing for time deliberately.

Next morning the revised instructions were drafted, but I sat at my desk staring at the letter awaiting my signature, pondering what I should do. Not to sign was to disobey a minister's order. I had made my objections very clear and he had gone as far as he dared to make his instruction formal and specific. I decided that there was only one possible step: that was to ask for the Chief Minister's instructions. If he took action against me for disloyalty or disobedience, that would be that. Suddenly it dawned on me that the thing to do was to ring him up: if I followed the proper procedure, which was to ask through his office for an interview, Bhanju Ram would certainly be alerted and Khan Sahib's mind would be filled with all sorts of allegations unpropitious to me. I knew perfectly well that any formal action by me would be keenly observed within my own office and undoubtedly reported to the Finance Minister or his minions. So, without preliminaries, and without going through the usual channels, I contrived to get the Chief Minister on the telephone. He sounded surprised and even a little flurried, possibly puzzled about why a youthful Under-Secretary should be addressing him on the telephone. I simply said that I required his advice as I had been given an instruction by the Honourable Finance Minister which I regarded as inconsistent with HCM's policy; I did not wish to disobey HFM but would like to have HCM's assurances that this would not be incompatible with policy, and that policy had not been changed. There was an immediate explosion of fury on the telephone – rage directed not against me, but at the Finance Minister. It was unfortunate that the latter could not hear it. 'That man is a fool, I tell you! He is corrupt! Do nothing that he tells you!' The telephone was slammed down. I had not even begun to tell Dr Khan Sahib what it was that Bhanju Ram ordered me to do. I did nothing, with a very light heart.

I heard no more on the matter from Bhanju Ram and for a long time had no interference from any other minister. Not very long after there was a Cabinet reshuffle and Bhanju Ram was dropped, being replaced by a very much sharper man, Mehr Chand Khanna, formerly leader of the Hindu Mahassabha Party in the Frontier, who had at last allied himself to Congress. The change had nothing to do with the trivial incident which I have described but perhaps I was lucky in my timing of my phone call. At any rate, the story tells a good deal about relations between the ICS and ministers in the Frontier – and even more about Dr Khan Sahib.

Later in my experiences in posts in the Secretariat there were to be other pressures from ministers and some uncomfortable encounters, but none that I recall in which there was such a strong smell of corruption. It was inevitable that as the months passed in an atmosphere of expectations of independence frustrated by mistaken tactics and the stubborn selfishness of politicians' motives, ministers should question the actions and intentions of British officers who were now clearly subordinated to their authority for the first time in the history of the province. None of them ever seriously embarrassed me by trying to involve me in dubious transactions, or suggesting that the dishonesty of others had any connection with me. Apart from Dr Khan Sahib, whose treatment of me was invariably avuncular and benevolent, the ministers I saw most were Mehr Chand Khanna and Qazi Ataullah. The former was urbane and sophisticated. Widely travelled, he cultivated a Westernized style and liked to play host at parties. These could be fascinating social experiences, but sometimes one felt uneasy in the company of subordinate officers, clearly at home in his house, whose normally constrained and courteous manners might be unexpectedly relaxed in circumstances more familiar to them than to me. I have no doubt that the fault lay more with me than with them. For all my liberal views, I was still affected by conventional British attitudes to rank, class and race, and there was something in the well-heeled pretentiousness of the Khanna household that brought my hackles up. But he was often interesting and challenging in conversation and though I always mistrusted him, I rather enjoyed my dealings with him. He was clever, in the best as well as the worst senses of the word.

Qazi Ataullah was a more frightening proposition. He cultivated the coarse homespun of the Ghandi tradition and he was closely associated by marriage to Abdul Ghaffar Khan and by politics to the latter's Khudai Khidmatgar movement – the servants of God, otherwise known as the the Red Shirts. One would never expect him to have any social intercourse with a European officer. His public career had been dedicated to the view that they were out of place in India; his manner was cold and severe. There came an occasion when I was visiting Bannu on official business and he turned up at Circuit House. I was summoned to tea and put through a most severe cross-examination about my business in Bannu, then about my work in the department in general and finally about my views on such broad issues as world socialism, and about education as the salvation of the underprivileged. At the beginning of this conversation I felt very much on the defensive but gradually it became more relaxed, as though barriers on both sides had been dismantled. His philosophy struck me as less homespun than that of AGK, more derived from books he had read but never discussed very deeply with contemporaries. Afterwards I never felt so nervous about him again, though I realized that he was a potentially dangerous opponent, and a man who would never relax in the exercise of power – altogether, a man to be wary of; but of his good intent I was now less suspicious.

It was in the nature of my new job that there would be unpleasantness in dealings with colleagues as well as with ministers. I was at the centre, responsible for taking a provincial view and controlling the distribution of supplies about which each district officer had his own views of need. The system of administration in India placed huge responsibility on Deputy Commissioners in charge of their individual districts, and in the Frontier, on political agents in their agencies. The war and its problems had complicated their lives by introducing so much more central control. Their authority had been reduced but there was no relief from their burden of responsibility. It was very important in the Civil Supplies Department to establish and keep a good relationship of trust with DCs and PAs, even though one did not always agree with their assessment of needs – or estimates of local surplus, in the case of products like wheat which we might wish centrally to procure. It was not always easy for a DC, subjected to local pressures, to take a sufficiently detached attitude so as to understand the provincial view we held at the centre, and so adopt reasonable arguments in trying to make us change our minds. Here a great deal depended on personal character and temperament – probably far more than can be conceived in the context of the Government of Britain, even in terms of the relationship between London and Edinburgh or Cardiff. It was very important for us at the centre to know and trust, and to be known and trusted by the men in the districts with whom we corresponded. We could not judge matters just by statistical calculation – not only because the data were notoriously unreliable, but also because we had to take account of particular factors in local conditions that could never be shown up by statistics.

It was almost in the nature of the job that a district officer should be an individualist, while a secretarial officer – at least under the rank of Chief Secretary or Revenue and Divisional Commissioner – should try to suppress his individuality. After all, his decisions or instructions carried the authority of his post and spoke for themselves. DCs spoke up for their districts in which they were *man bap* ('father and mother') to their people. Criticism of a personal nature, therefore, tended to be directed from the districts towards the centre and I had to expect to be at the receiving end. Over the whole period I must have been remarkably lucky for my letters recall only one instance which got under my skin, and I was young and appropriately sensitive. This trivial episode is worth recording because it both illustrates the general points I have been making and says something about the peculiarly Indian atmosphere in which we worked. Hugh Rushton, who had recently come to the Province to be DC Hazara had a sad reputation for being irascible and ill-tempered. Older officers knew this from earlier years of his Frontier service and it was confirmed in the record of his recent service in states. I knew of it only at second-hand. In August 1945 I stayed with him twice in Abbottabad and found him hospitable and charming – but almost embarrassingly so, as though he were trying quite unnecessarily to make a point of it to a junior officer who would not know what to expect from a man of senior rank. Unfortunately he did not at all impress me by what he was saying about his district and his job; after all, I thought I really knew something about Hazara, and my yardstick for the DC was whether he measured up to Gerald Curtis or Hugh Richardson – or down to B.D.S. Bedi.

Some weeks later I had a very bitter personal letter from him, protesting – if that is the appropriate word for a wounding personal attack – about an order which he had heard I had passed to the effect that certain facts were to be concealed from him. His source, of course, was a garbled second-hand account in his office of a conversation involving one of my clerks, but he had jumped on this shaky foundation to his own conclusions without taking thought. As his junior, I found it hard to know how to word my reply, which had to hit him pretty firmly without appearing to 'tick him off'. The facts were easy enough. All I had to do about them was to send him a copy of my office order. He had heard only a garbled version of half of it – and that part only half understood and embroidered by other alleged facts for which there was no basis. When he saw the whole of the instruction, he had not a leg to stand on – and to be fair to this very up-and-down man, within a week I had a very handsome written apology from him. But it was my first, and in India my worst experience of this kind of wounding. I felt that it would have been so easy for Rushton to have asked me for an explanation rather than mistrusting me and condemning me so rudely on the basis of such a piece of gossip less than two weeks after we had been getting on famously with each other on my visit to Abbottabad. However, I learned a great deal from the incident, as one does from every unpleasant experience in life.[3]

Before this happened – in mid-September – I had once again visited the Bedis and enjoyed their warm and friendly hospitality. Bedi had eventually to be transferred from Abbottabad where his inefficiency and dubious associations had led to so much public criticism, and – as so often seemed to happen! – he had been rewarded by transfer to Parachinar, the headquarters of the Kurram Agency, where the Political Agent had the most agreeable job in the province. Most of the inhabitants of the Kurram Valley were Turis, a minority Shia tribe amongst the predominantly Sunni Pathans. The British occupation of their delightful valley began in 1892 at the specific invitation of the Turis, seeking our protection from the harassment of their Sunni neighbours. The agency ran up the valley from Thall in Kohat District to the high Peiwar Kotal, the pass into Afghanistan over which General Roberts fought his way in 1879. To the south lay Waziristan, to the north the Tirah, homeland of the Orakzai and Afridi. The Kurram Agency was generally the most peaceful in the province. The valley had a favoured climate and produced a delicious range of fruit – we enjoyed the last of the peaches and the first of the new season's pears and apples. The PA's house in Parachinar, at 6,000 feet and with its lawns and gardens and orchard, was one of the most beautiful situations in the whole country. Here I went with Ambrose Dundas to spend the official holidays celebrating V-J Day on 15 August 1945. As Revenue and Divisional Commissioner, Ambrose was Export Trade Controller, responsible for the supervision of trade between India and Afghanistan; and one of the hats I wore was that of Deputy Export Trade Controller. There was some squabble between Bedi and the DC Kohat about allegations of smuggling through Kurram to Afghanistan, Ambrose suggested that we enjoy the holiday by 'visiting the spot' – a favourite pastime of magistrates investigating or trying cases. It was my first journey into Kurram beyond Thall, at the junction of the road to Spinwam and Miranshah, and I would have loved to spend the rest of my service in India there. Bedi was in his element with all the shooting and hawking and fishing he might wish, and very little pressure of work.

My job took me away on other excursions that were less of a relief from Peshawar. Early in September I went to Bombay to a Textile Conference, for the first time making a long distance journey by air. Civilian air services were just beginning to operate in close conjunction with the Air Force's arrangements. From Peshawar we flew in a converted Dakota, bumping through monsoon clouds, stopping for fifteen minutes at Rawalpindi and for twenty-five minutes at Lahore, where tea was served. Then on to Delhi, a flight of one and a half hours, compared with a whole night's journey by train. The whole of that stage from Peshawar took four hours, compared with the Frontier Mail's scheduled train time of twenty-seven hours. Part of the advantage was lost at Delhi where I had to wait overnight in the Air Transit Centre for an onward connection for Bombay, leaving at 6.30 a.m. The hutted accommodation was crowded and noisy, but surprisingly comfortable. The flight to Bombay was made in a much smaller aircraft, of American make, seating about twelve passengers. I seem to recall that it was called an Expeditor; the general standard of fittings was superior, but the range was limited, and we landed twice en route – at Jaipur, I think, and at Ahmedabad – arriving in Bombay by lunchtime. The cruising speed was about 180 m.p.h. The aircraft fought its way up above the storm clouds, giving me my first taste of serene flight in a calm blue sea above the snow-white mountains of fleece.

In Bombay I stayed comfortably with a banker called Harris whom I knew only slightly from a short period when he was manager of Grindlay's Bank in Peshawar. It was characteristic of Europeans in India that they should have been willing to extend such generous hospitality on the basis of slight acquaintance. He had a pleasant flat near Breach Kandy and it was a useful private refuge for me, for there were – inevitably – textile contractors who lay in wait at the end of each conference session from whom quick and final escape was essential for one's peace of mind. The conference was a strange experience. Presided over efficiently by Sir Akbar Hydari, who was Minister for Supply in the Government of India, the delegates sank themselves in endless oceans of words – speech after speech seemed to go on interminably. From every province and probably almost every state in India delegates delivered their pleas – often impassioned, sometimes bitter, always tedious, only very occasionally lightened by a flash of wit. Each day we sat till between 7 p.m. and 8 p.m. I had to make one speech of my own, with one or two brief interventions, and I was relieved to be well received and apparently understood. Perhaps my Scots accent was clearer and more intelligible than some of the deliverances which baffled me. I wrote home that 'it was really most interesting' – a comment which in retrospect I find puzzling, except that it was very strange to me and I was young and conscientious.

On the way back from Bombay I stopped at Delhi for about four days, partly to represent Robin Latimer at a conference about sugar. I stayed with Cecil Griffin, the Secretary of the Government of India's Political Department, for part of the purpose was to investigate the possibility of transferring to the Indian Political Service. By now it was known that the scheme to create a separate NWFP ICS Commission, to which Pat Duncan, John Dent and I had been the only appointments, would not be proceeded with. It was open to us to stay as we were – probably therefore to be restricted to posts in NWFP – or to seek transfer to the IPS. On board ship returning from leave I had become friendly with Derek Harrington-Hawes of the IPS and learning more from him about its work outside the Frontier had for the first time begun to feel seriously that I might apply for appointment to it. He was in Delhi and had kept in touch with me, helping greatly in the effort to secure information about a passage for Barbara. This was my greatest preoccupation throughout these months of August and September, and in Delhi I saw several of the officers most concerned in the Defence Department who were involved in the business of organizing passages. By this time, frustrated husbands in India had made the matter a major public scandal; even senior officers breached the code of silence to write to the newspapers complaining of official ineptitude. The officers I saw were all kind and helpful, grateful indeed for information I could give them about our own case and about others, to help them in their unceasing struggle with the real culprits back in London.

Amongst the senior IPS men whom I met were Sir Conrad Corfield, the Political Adviser to the Viceroy – who left Bombay on retirement in the same ship as we did in 1947, having put up a stout-hearted but unsuccessful struggle for a better deal for the states from Mountbatten and the Congress Party – and Sir Olaf Caroe. It was my first meeting with Sir Olaf, whom I was to get to know well. He was then Foreign Secretary, and widely talked about in the Frontier as likely to succeed Sir George Cunningham as Governor. This was mentioned in a letter to my wife dated 11 September 1945, but in it I offered no assessment of Caroe on the basis of my lunch with him, which is perhaps surprising, for he had a strong personality, and when writing home I was usually pretty ready to offer opinions about people and events. What is recorded is that I told him and the others with whom I had interviews – who besides Corfield and of course Griffin included Charles Duke, Edward Brownsdon, Derek Harrington-Hawes and Paddy Keene, who was then Under-Secretary in Corfield's department – that I was holding back from asking formally for a transfer because in the small print of the conditions of service an ICS man would forego the right to premature retirement on joining the Political. My letter records that Sir Olaf said that this point had been in their minds and referred for decision to the Secretary of State for India, and he suggested that it might be helpful if when I put in my application I requested that the question of the rights of ICS politicals in this respect be clarified. My papers do not reveal what happened subsequently. I think that Pat Duncan, John Dent and I all put in formal applications, though Pat like myself had hesitated about it, largely because we both felt so committed to service in the Frontier. The outcome was that John was appointed to the IPS while Pat and I were not. I think this information reached us not very long before transfer of power and certainly it did not seem to me at the time to have any bearing or relevance to my career.

These days in Delhi were enjoyable for the new acquaintances made and old friendships renewed. Amongst the latter was Jeff Hassett, the jovial and rather wild Irishman who had been the Tochi doctor in 1943-4. Now he was Civil Surgeon, New Delhi – a very dignified appointment indeed for a man who had been famed for his treatment of gunshot and stab wounds in Miranshah.

For several years he had seen only occasional female patients, and then under close surveillance from their heavily armed husbands. Now he was the deliverer of fashionable babies and in great demand as the post-war bulge got under way in Delhi's official circles – eight night deliveries in the last month, he told me. As always, his Irish wit reduced me to tears as he regaled me with his opinions on Delhi society.

The Sugar Conference turned out to be 'an awful bore' – perhaps because I knew so little about the subject that I had to keep silent, though after it I sought out the Sugar Controller privately to make a case for an increase in the Frontier's quota in 1946. More interestingly, I went to see the Foodgrain people, about whose subject I felt I had more competence, and through them I met Christie, who was the Director General of Food for India. Supply prospects were likely to remain unsatisfactory till at least the summer of 1946 and I recorded my talks with him and his officers as 'interesting and extremely helpful'.

Back in Peshawar, after an alarming flight – as far as Lahore in extremely stormy conditions, the last forty miles into Lahore down at 'deck level' looking for the road, a hazardous exercise with the equipment of those times – I found a bit of a crisis in the office, with Arthur Wooller having come in to lend a hand. A big consignment of *atta* (wheat flour) had been brought to Peshawar instead of being delivered to other towns in greater immediate need – an administrative blunder that was costly in money and might have been the cause of civil disturbance. The error had been made by Robin Latimer up in Nathia Gali just after he had taken over and before he had all the technicalities at his fingertips. My comment was that one could not run a Department like Food from a hill station with a couple of clerks when the main staff were inevitably in the Secretariat at Peshawar. In this case, Robin had been badly let down by his office. He naturally wanted to spend as much of the summer as the rules about recess would allow in Nathia Gali with his bride, who was newly arrived from England but bravely accompanied him to the sweltering heat of Peshawar whenever he came downhill. At least this episode showed me that all my personal problems would not have been solved if only my bride had got the passage we had hoped for in July, for she could not have endured the climatic conditions that I was still experiencing on the plains. There was no air-conditioning in Peshawar in those days. I was very sorry for Robin, who was a delightful officer to work for, highly intelligent and stimulating, consistently equable and blessed with a refreshing sense of humour. Very kindly, he announced that he would stay in Peshawar from mid-September and let me get up to Nathia Gali to cool off for a spell – Peshawar normally began to be bearable by day about the end of that month; from the end of August, the nights were gradually getting cooler, making it possible to get more rest.

The transition to Nathia Gali certainly provided climatic relief, but at the cost of increasing my personal misery. I was worn out by the worry of frustrated efforts to get Barbara out to India, and the knowledge that she was equally upset and unhappy. The joy of the months of spring and early summer in Scotland had been replaced by sour bitterness at the revival of memories of sad years of parting. The restless journeying of the last month and the pressure of work had covered the wound, but the long empty days in Nathia opened a festering despair. There was not much work – just enough to make daily office sessions a source of irritation from which one longed to escape. If only she had been there, the empty hours in that beautiful situation would have been paradise! I still remember clearly how depressed I became. There were plenty of kind friends who tried to cheer me up, but the quiet, relaxed atmosphere of the hill station was always one of family happiness and that summer I was too conscious of my family's absence. I stayed with Dudley de la Fargue, who was now Chief Secretary. I had not known him well; he was kind and cheerful in a rather sardonic way. His own family had gone home to Britain and his languid manner, which could exude charm when the mood took him, did nothing to jolt me out of my dejection. Oliver and Elizabeth St John, living down in the cottage by Government House – he was still Secretary to the Governor – did their best to cheer me up, but they were having their own trouble at the time. Elizabeth suffered from severe headaches, attributed to sinus trouble and the altitude, but in fact probably the symptom of a neurological illness that too few years from then was to be fatal.

As always, it was the Cunninghams themselves who did me most good. They truly were uniquely gifted in their handling of relationships with all the officers in the province. They brought me, the most junior, into the same relaxed circle of friendship that embraced the most senior; one was always alert to respect the dignity of their status, yet never felt patronized by them. They both seemed to have marvellous insight into one's feelings, and to know when and how to probe and when to leave alone. Lady Cunningham's Irish genius could charm secrets out of the most sullen introvert. During that fortnight I was often invited to Government House for meals, or to play bowls, or to join HE on his evening walk. Lady Cunningham learned a good deal about Barbara, and when she eventually arrived in Peshawar she was at once brought into the circle of friendship and helped and encouraged as I always was.

One of my preoccupations for some time had been to find somewhere in Peshawar for us to stay. Accommodation was very scarce because of the wartime expansion of the European population and the number of military families. My post was one of these wartime creations which did not have a bungalow associated with it. Soon I saw that the choice lay between a flat in a fairly modern and rather crowded complex or a tiny private cottage in the grounds of the Deputy Commissioner's house. This was originally orderlies' quarters but these had been converted a few years before to accommodate the wife of a political officer stationed in tribal territory. In 1945 Arthur and Frances Wooller had had the tenancy at the start of their married life.[4]

The tenancy was in the gift of the Deputy Commissioner and I had to wait for some weeks before being able to establish my claim. The new DC was to be Johnny Dring whose return from home leave had been delayed because he was bringing out his young daughters whose mother had tragically died in Britain during the war. Johnny finally arrived in Nathia while I was there and at once conceded my claim – there were others in the queue and Lady Cunningham's influence exerted on our behalf may have counted with Johnny. Soon after I got back to Peshawar, I got entry and began to furnish and equip this modest little place which was to be our first home. Almost at the same time a telegram announced that a passage had been allocated, and for almost a fortnight the daily communication by air letter between us stopped – until a further message told me that a docker's strike at Liverpool had delayed the sailing. This maddening development kept me permanently in ill humour through October and into November, when at last I knew that my wife was on her way and I could make arrangements to help her on arrival in Bombay. The best that I could wangle for myself was a coincidental trip to Lahore to deal with certain textile matters. I stayed with the Thompsons – Sir Herbert was now Resident for Punjab States – and met once again my old chums Brian Williams and David Elliot. David's American wife Nancy, whom he had married by proxy during the War in an attempt to secure a passage for her, had just that week arrived at last in Lahore and they were preparing 'to get married properly on Saturday in Lahore Cathedral'. Next morning I was on the Lahore station platform, agitatedly awaiting the arrival of the Frontier Mail, on which I was reunited at last with my Barbara. As the train rumbled through the sunlit Punjab plains and we brought each other abreast of the news of recent weeks, the wretchedness of the months just past and the revived pain of wartime years of separation began to fade. The next year brought us great happiness, and much excitement as I shared in Barbara's discovery of the Frontier about which I had told her so much. But there was sadness too and a sense of deprivation for from the start we were both aware that the prospect had changed, and that this was not to be the permanent home that we had imagined in our letters in the early years of the war.

Notes

[1] Mozam was a Khattak who had served for a time in the police service; from being an orderly, he became servant to John Steward, now AC in Charsadda. Like many Pathans in household service he proved to be more in tune with the officer than with the memsahib. Pathans tended to be smart and efficient in appearance and in 'outdoor' duties, but less responsible in matters of household management. Maeve Steward soon found Mozam's shortcomings tiresome enough for John to persuade me to take him on as successor to Yakub Khan, my Hazarawal servant who had found life in Waziristan too lonely and rough for his old age and had retired to his village near Haripur. Mozam served me excellently – but in time his domestic shortcomings took their toll. He preferred to accompany me as orderly and escort to looking after the domestic staff in the bungalow and in the end, for Barbara's sake, we replaced him, taking on an old faithful bearer from Maurice and Stella Pugh when they went home in 1946. Although I had sent no message to Mazam Khan, it was not surprising that he should be at the station. Personal servants in India had an instinct for news from Britain about those whom they served loyally.

2 Although Dr Khan Sahib liked going to Nathia Gali, like many Indians the other Ministers preferred in the hot weather to meet in Abbottabad at 4,000 feet rather than at Nathia Gali at 8,500 feet. Senior officials were allowed to recess in Nathia Gali – i.e. to work there, not on leave – between early May and the end of September, and to take a nucleus of the Secretariat staff with them. But if they were 'required' by ministers in Peshawar, they had to come down – usually, of course, temporarily, leaving their families behind.

3 Early in 1947 Rushton seriously mishandled a communal disturbance in Abbottabad, ignoring the advice of subordinates and brushing aside helpful suggestions from the military commander. A departmental enquiry produced an anodyne report and he escaped with a reprimand – but effectively his career was ended.

4 Their landlord was Iskander Mirza, then DC Peshawar – much later to be President of Pakistan. Recently, he had been transferred from the province. It was true that he had himself requested a transfer but it was also well known that Dr Khan Sahib and his ministers had been very keen that he should go. He had been DC in 1942 during their civil disobedience campaign, and had outmanoeuvred and humiliated them on several occasions. During the Muslim League Ministry, his personal links with the League's high command had become evident, and his contempt for Aurangzeb, the Chief Minister, helped to undermine his authority. When Jinnah sent a Commission to Peshawar to enquire into the provincial Ministry's shortcomings, Liaqat Ali, the League Secretary and Jinnah's First Lieutenant, stayed at the DC's house.

CHAPTER XI

Life's Miscellany: General Dogsbody

By the time we had settled together in our modest first home at 12a The Mall, Peshawar it was well into December 1945. When Arthur Wooller had the tenancy, with Iskander Mirza as his landlord, the monthly rent had been a bottle of whisky and a bottle of gin. Under our new landlord, Johnny Dring, the cost of living had gone up somewhat; but there were compensations. When we dined in the DC's house Barbara was intrigued to find some of our glasses on the table, while his finger bowls supplied a deficiency in our equipment when we entertained to dinner. There was a nice easy relationship between servants as well as between landlord and tenants.

We began with the bare minimum, but our needs were modest. Except when we had guests, we drank only soft drinks. After years of British rationing, Barbara luxuriated in the abundant and varied fruits of India. On our first Sunday the St Johns and other friends entertained us to the traditional curry lunch at the Peshawar Club and patiently bore with her as she lingered over each segment of an orange, enjoying what to us was commonplace but to her had been denied so long. Economical though we were we had a full complement of servants. Mozam Khan's son Swalikh was about fifteen and became *misalchi* – dish-washer, and apprentice waiter. We had a young Goanese *khansama* (cook) who had been 'second chef' in the Dundas household and cooked for the men during the summer in Ambrose's chummery, which had been my base in Peshawar in August and September. The bearer and the cook each earned fifty rupees a month and the young *misalchi* twenty. So did the sweeper, who besides his other duties fed and groomed the dog. The *dhobi* (washerman) got twelve rupees (less than a pound) for our share of his services.

Both Mozam Khan and the *khansama* regularly presented bills for purchases they made on our behalf in the bazaar. The cook bought the meat, cooking fat (ghee), vegetables, chickens and eggs for our table. Mozam got all the other 'messages', items which recurred regularly in the accounts including firewood (to heat water for our baths), soap (both toilet and carbolic!), thread, mending wool, aspirin, shoe polish, toilet paper (there was a great shortage of the genuine Bromo) writing paper and envelopes, matches, buttons, needles, orange squash, and a host of miscellaneous things like shoelaces (at two annas) or bicycle repairs. Generally there were monthly bills from Gulab Rai, the grocer, or Maira Brothers and from the London Book Company for newspapers, Kirpa Ram the draper, the Royal Bakery for bread, the Military Dairy for milk, cream and butter. My detailed accounts over the years contain many fascinating items. There were periods when they were less methodical than at others and the basic system of housekeeping, altering according to my way of life – sometimes running my own household, sometimes living in a mess, sometimes living as a paying guest in a chummery – was reflected in changes in the style of the accounts. The servants were forever getting advances – either as a 'float' to meet expenses, especially when on tour, or more commonly because they incurred personal debts, borrowing to meet the cost of a wedding, or sometimes of a funeral in the family. Repayments deducted from monthly wages were quite a high proportion – perhaps not surprising if they borrowed two or three months' wages. Sometimes the details in the accounts are clear, sometimes unintelligible!

Our kitchen typically was a primitive corner in an outhouse in the tiny compound behind the cottage. There was a wall of brick and mud out of which crept scorpions. One night after a wild dust storm there was a positive plague of them and when Mozam brought us our *chota haziri* he invited me to inspect his trophies – twenty-seven dead scorpions laid out on the verandah; there were two more alive in the bathroom when I went there. We learned to be careful to shake out our shoes before putting them on, but neither of us – fortunately – was ever stung. One morning Barbara went into a little shed in the garden and was startled by a snake dropping from the roof and wriggling away into the undergrowth. We never knew whether it was a poisonous one. More than a year later, when we had moved house, the *chowkidar* (watchman) killed a large cobra on our verandah – the uproar he made frightened us more than the snake. We were nervous for some days in case its mate should come into the bungalow in search of it.

At the front of the cottage there was a small lawn divided by a path leading to the road, from which we were screened by a hedge and some high trees. There was no scope for flowers to grow in their shade and no need for a *mali* (gardener) but the DC's *mali* supplied flowers from his garden. Barbara was surprised one morning to find a gang of three rough-looking characters working on the grass. One was pushing a mower in the usual way with another pulling on a rope attached to it; the third squatted characteristically to one side, supervising the others. She was a little nervous when I explained that they were prisoners from the jail, who came regularly to work for the DC's *mali*, and cut our grass once or twice a week. She soon got used to them – pleasant enough rascals, mostly convicted murderers, in jail because of some blood feud or crime committed in a fit of passion, glad to be doing their hard labour in a kind memsahib's garden. Though their services were free, our monthly wage bill was high in relation to our income.

For a month or two expenditure exceeded income, and Barbara was perturbed, but she soon got the books in balance, after the heavy initial outlay of setting up house.[1] Various special allowances or increments of salary came my way and our anxieties diminished. We had to live as frugally as possible but we had no expensive tastes and we felt no real hardship. Dietary staples were chicken and mutton, besides fruit, vegetables and milk. Culinary monotony was often relieved by presents of game – woodcock, partridge or snipe, or even splendid guinea fowl shot by the Governor, who was always generous in distributing the produce of a shoot. Occasionally Indian friends coming in from their villages would bring an acceptable gift of this kind, or maybe a huge comb of wild bees' honey, carried in the branch of the tree from which it had been cut. We acquired a live turkey which was tethered by a long rope in the back compound and fed royally on grain till the day came when Barbara reluctantly permitted it to be killed for Christmas dinner.

On Christmas morning there was a queue of well-wishers presenting compliments at the door. Their sincere greetings were usually accompanied by large baskets of fruit and flowers, and when she saw me burrowing into these with my hands while the donors were still wishing us a happy Christmas she whispered indignantly that I was being rude. The trouble was that I was searching for the real bribes that might accompany some of the fruit and flowers and so she was even more perturbed when she saw me insist on one basket being taken away – until I explained that I had found beneath the blossoms a bottle of whisky which I could not accept. The point was soon taken by our well-wishers as well as my wife and we were left with a vast quantity of gorgeous fruit and flowers, much of which was later in the day sent round to the hospital, but nothing that contravened the Government Servants' Conduct Rules. I had never before received so many generous offerings at Christmas time – they could be explained equally as genuine good wishes to my new bride and myself, and as a hint of the favours I might bestow in allocating quotas and permits as Controller of scarce commodities, like textiles and sugar.

Outside office hours, life around this period was gentle, pleasant and happy. I could usually get home for a leisurely lunch, and after a short afternoon session of work return in time for an evening walk or a few holes of golf. The golf course was built on and around the race course, just outside the high barbed-wire fence protecting the cantonment and we often had to make haste to get back through the gate before it was firmly closed for the night at dusk, which came so quickly after the sun set behind the Khyber hills. Barbara had a bicycle and got around the cantonment quite happily on that. I had a little autocycle and with the help of its engine with me pedalling, she could sail up the incline from the golf course effortlessly, holding on to my shoulder. On Saturdays at least once a month there were horse races but we had a Calvinist disinclination to join the parties which assembled at the meet to place their bets, and we stuck to our own private game of golf, pausing now and then to watch at close quarters the manoeuvering of the riders at the starting point or to observe the horses at full gallop passing close to us while we waited to pitch onto the next green. We apologized to our friends for being anti-social, arguing that we were getting the best view without sacrificing either our game or our housekeeping money. On Sundays there was often a family foursomes match – with the Latimers or the Grahams (George Graham was the Civil Surgeon) or the McReas or the Wagstaffes (Kim McCrea was a police officer in the Intelligence Bureau, Keith Wagstaffe in the Frontier Constabulary). We had quite a large circle of congenial friends, mostly younger members of the civil services but a few from the Army or the Air Force too. On the whole, the latter tended to have their own social links. Very few of the younger officers had families in Peshawar; the military people we knew socially were either senior people whose family links with the place went back to pre-war days, or one or two younger bachelors who became friends as a result of encounters at the golf course or because of mutual acquaintanceships in Scotland.

Occasionally we went to a dance at the club but because Peshawar was a much bigger European community these were not the regular 'family' gatherings that had been characteristic of Abbottabad. We did attend the great social event of the Christmas season, the Peshawar Vale Hunt Ball, held in the club. Though many of the well-to-do Muslim landowners took an active interest in following the hunt, the ball was so far as I recall an exclusively European affair. At that time, there were very few Indian members of the club, and those few were seldom to be seen. One reason, of course, was that the wives of Muslims were in purdah and did not mix socially. There were very few exceptions to this rule. By this period, however, Indians had attained senior ranks in the armed services and some of them used the club fairly regularly. I can recall, too, meeting there Mian Zia-ud-din, one of the leading barristers in the province and a senior office-bearer in the Muslim League; he was the first Indian elected to membership of the club, having been invited in gratitude for legal services he had rendered a year or so before the outbreak of war. So one could not say that a colour bar determined our social lives, especially when one remembers that we were very friendly with Indian colleagues.[2] But the history and the structuring of Muslim society as well as of our own produced something of the consequences of segregation on racial lines in social life and one can view these with regret. Barbara got few chances to know Muslim ladies, though one of her close friends was an Englishwoman married to a Muslim, the head of the Veterinary Service. Through her, one or two of the Muslim ladies would join in a tea party. Some of the younger ones also 'came out' in the intimacy of the summer community at Nathia Gali and loved to chatter eagerly with European ladies; but back in Peshawar they kept in seclusion. It was always one of my regrets that the political and social conditions in 1946 and 1947, and the nature of my work in the Secretariat, prevented Barbara from enjoying the opportunities open to the wife of a district officer, of touring in the villages and meeting Indians in their natural environment, and not only in shops or at official functions.

Barbara supervising washing of hands at a children's play group in Peshawar Cantonment, with Betty Latimer.

She did meet some Indian ladies at the Red Cross work parties which were still held regularly at Government House and she was a helper at a play school for both Indian and European children which was run on a voluntary basis. It had been started during the War to help some of the European mothers who wanted to take jobs in the auxiliary forces as clerks or nurses or in other roles. By and large, though she had no housework to do in the conventional sense, and was no longer professionally occupied as a teacher, Barbara found that she had plenty to do and never found herself bored with time hanging heavily, although she would have been hard put to it to explain her preoccupations to her friends and colleagues in Scotland. She greatly enjoyed her first months on the Frontier. Occasional excursions provided an exciting taste of its romance, like a visit to Landi Kotal in the Khyber with Betty and Robin Latimer, or a few days spent with the Lowises at Kohat – the drive through the Kohat Pass was her first experience of the atmosphere of tribal territory, combined with the thrills of the mountain roads. We went one day to a great Pathan *tikala*, or feast, provided by Sheikh Mahbub Ali in honour of the Cunninghams in his village on the Khajuri Plain, and although there was a host of guests, many of them already friends and acquaintances, and the food was mouth-watering, the sincerity and simplicity of characteristic Pakhtun hospitality made the occasion uniquely memorable for her. Even when they entertained on a grand scale like this, there was an unpretentious straightforwardness, an absence of pomposity, a cheerful frankness and infallible good manners that always marked out the Pathans as the finest of hosts.

This was one of many occasions on which their friends in the Frontier marked the approaching retirement of Sir George and Lady Cunningham. Nawab Sheikh Mahbub Ali was a Pathan, a member of an influential and well-to-do family with a tradition of loyal service to the Crown. He had been a member of the Provincial Civil Service, promoted to the IPS and had a long personal association with Sir George. HE's close relationship with Dr Khan Sahib, the Chief Minister, helped to protect the Sheikh from the criticisms and accusations of the Congress Party which by now were fairly widely known, and there may well have been a political significance in this enormous party which drew so many guests to a Pathan village. Within a year the Sheikh was in disgrace and suspended from duty, accused of conniving at or indeed promoting the assault on Pandit Nehru, Khan Sahib and Abdul Ghaffar Khan at Malakand in November 1946.[3]

Sir George's influence was no longer there to moderate the political hysteria. At the end of February 1946 he had handed over to Sir Olaf Caroe. I recall that we all felt uneasy apprehension as the undercurrent of political instability grew stronger – not so much because of doubts about Caroe as because the familiar staunchness for which Cunningham's record stood was, after so many years, no longer there to calm and settle us. Before they left, smothered in garlands both literally and metaphorically, there had been a big farewell dinner at the Peshawar Club at which Sir George made a memorably witty speech, and a smaller private one, held in Sir James Almond's house at 9 Jheel Road on 14 February, at which the 'Politicals' took farewell of their admired friend and mentor. It was an occasion of great pride for me for I was honoured to be asked to organize it, working on instructions that there should be no pomp and ceremony, and trying indeed to capture and recreate the warmth and affection as well as the dignity which we all associated with the hospitality of Government

House. Half my problem was solved by the genial nature of Sir James Almond and his generosity in putting his house at our disposal. There were none of the difficulties about protocol and precedent that one might have expected on such an occasion in India because the ties of brotherhood in the Frontier service relegated such matters to insignificance. In spite of the distances involved and the difficulties of being absent from local duties, hardly any of the Frontier officers failed to attend.

For Barbara, the evening provided a wonderful insight into all that I had told her over the years about service in the Frontier, for it was a reunion of old friends and colleagues. Besides Sheikh Mahbub Ali and Khurshid, then PA Khyber, and K.B. Shah Zaman – all of whom of course came without their wives – Bedi was there accompanied by Mrs Bedi whom I placed between HE and the Chief Secretary (Dudley de la Fargue). The other ladies, besides Barbara, were all wives of old friends – Mrs Packman, Decima Curtis, Jeano Lowis, Peggy Dredge, Frances Wooller, Betty Latimer. Quite a few of the political wives had gone home to Britain and so had some of the officers whose names have cropped up in this account at various stages. Besides Sir James Almond and Dudley de la Fargue, those who attended were Leslie Mallam (now in charge of post-war Reconstruction and Development) 'Packy' (Colonel K.C. Packman, Resident in Waziristan), Johnny Dring, Gerald Curtis, Alastair Low (still Finance Secretary) Bill Leeper (then DC Mardan), Oliver St John, Jack Lowis, Sir Benjamin Bromhead (Benjy, a baronet and an army political had succeeded Jack Lowis as PA North Waziristan), Phil Tollinton (still Settlement Officer in Hazara), Johnny Raw (then, I think, AC Tank), Arthur Wooller, Robin Latimer, Broughton Hay and John Dent. John Wilson, who had succeeded me as APA North Waziristan, seconded from the Army to the IPS, was also there,[4] and so was my old Dehra Dun friend Donald Jackson, who was training as a political officer under Jack Lowis in Kohat, and shortly to go to the Embassy at Kabul.

When the Cunninghams left, I was uncomfortably aware that my future on the Frontier was unlikely to fulfil the promise of the past. But some months were to pass before unease turned to certainty and meanwhile our lives continued in a pleasant vein. One of our leisure pursuits provided some intellectual stimulus as well as a useful initiation into the art of broadcasting. The enterprising Station Director at Peshawar for All-India Radio developed a series of programmes in English that would not have discredited the producers of foundation courses of the Open University. One of his aims was to encourage listeners to improve their understanding of spoken English, and he and his programme executives recruited the help of several of the younger ICS officers in Peshawar and their wives. Barbara and I were roped in, in the first place at the suggestion of Arthur Wooller, because apparently our plain Scots voices were acceptable and intelligible to the listeners whom AIR wished to encourage.

We found ourselves quite busy in the evenings preparing a remarkable variety of talks. The simplest, and financially most profitable, were short film reviews. For five minute talks we were paid twenty-five rupees, the same as for a much deeper fifteen-minute talk on some quite high-flown subject. English, or American, films were shown in the local cinema on three successive nights. We got free tickets for the first performance and broadcast our review the following night at 9.40 p.m., so that our effect on the attendance was minimal; but it was felt that listeners were being encouraged to develop a critical view of what they had probably already seen before they heard the talk. There was also a regular monthly review of new books in English. These were selected by the producer of the programme but over the period he provided a remarkably interesting range of titles which we were allowed to keep.

Most demanding of all was the preparation of scripts for special discussion programmes. I am amazed at the subjects which we had the temerity to tackle. Very early in our broadcasting career Barbara and I did a fifteen-minute dialogue on the theme of 'the greatest good of the greatest number' – in a series of talks entitled 'Open to Question'. Another discussion, with Norval Mitchell, was on the proposition that the right of private property should be abolished – fee only twenty rupees for ten minutes! Somehow I acquired the mantle of the expert on literature and was saddled with a range of commissions, from a talk on the character of Mr Pickwick to an analysis of recent trends in English literature in a series called 'Yielding place to New'. According to the producer, this series was 'intended to study how far our ways and manners have been modified and developed during this century, and more so during the last titanic struggle between the biggest powers of the world. Your talk is intended to deal with the revolution that has taken place in the field of literature.' I was not in the least confident that I was competent to say anything profound on such topics, but I gladly accepted the challenge. For one thing the fee, though very modest, was more than acceptable. But more important, the effort itself was rewarding. I had to apply my mind to a genuine intellectual exercise, and one that I enjoyed. Finally I began to see what would interest Indian minds in that sort of intellectual exercise, and felt that I was getting new insight which was relevant to my work and my responsibilities to the people of India.

At work these responsibilities certainly absorbed one's attention. Peace had brought no immediate relief from shortage of essential supplies. Fortified by success in the provincial elections completed in February 1946, the Congress Ministry intensified its interference in the executive decisions of the officers who had to carry out their policies or take responsibility locally for them. There was a growing lack of confidence between them and the officials, especially at the district level. At the centre, the Ministry acquired a sharper edge from the sophisticated mind of R.B. Mehr Chand Khanna, the new Finance Minister. Although he and Qazi Ataullah, the Revenue Minister, had no love for each other, their rivalry had the effect of sharpening their intellectual powers with results that could be disconcerting. I seemed to escape the worst of the unpleasant consequences, partly of course because I was Deputy Director of Civil Supplies and therefore protected by the Secretary in charge of the Department, first Robin Latimer and later Humphrey Cooke. The latter arrived in the province in the spring, fresh from a long spell in States' service. He was a pleasant, quiet and reserved ICS man who years before had lost his right arm when he fell from a railway platform while taking farewell of the bride and bridegroom after a wedding party. He developed an angular left-handed script which was quite legible when he could take his time. I liked him and got on well with him, but was conscious of a barrier of seniority that had never obtruded in my relations with Robin Latimer and Arthur Wooller. Although Humphrey let me get on unhampered with my own share of the work, I was taken less into his confidence about other subjects and was to regret this later in the summer when I was appointed Provincial Foodgrains Procurement Officer, while remaining DDCS and Under-Secretary in his Department.

Before then there was little in the daily routine worthy of record, except an interesting episode in which I had to negotiate with a minister of the Afghan Government who came to Peshawar with complaints that there was interference with deliveries of the internationally agreed quota of petroleum allocated to Afghanistan. The supplies came to Peshawar from Karachi by rail, and were kept in bond awaiting transhipment by lorry through the Khyber Pass to Kabul. The allegation was that the supplies released by us from the bonded warehouses were deficient. To my surprise, the Governor and Chief Secretary left the matter in my hands as Deputy Export Trade Controller and I had to try to convince the Afghan Minister that he would need to keep a closer eye on his own lorry drivers. He was, of course, a member of the Afghan royal family – all Ministers were – and he had had some education in France. What astonished me was that he apparently spoke no Pushtu, although that was the official language of his country and the language of most of its inhabitants. Like all Afghan aristocrats his family tongue was Persian which I did not speak. He offered to negotiate in French, but I declined; I could not trust my elementary schoolboy French in a diplomatic exchange and I could not see why I should not negotiate in Pushtu since his Government acknowledged the pre-eminence of Pushtu in his country. He was accompanied by a bright and agreeable official so we settled amicably to a conversation in which the Minister addressed me in French, I replied in Pushtu, the Afghan official translated my Pushtu into Persian, and the Minister followed up in French. I have totally forgotten the details of the negotiation and its outcome, but I have often recalled the oddity of the circumstances whenever at international meetings or conferences I have been aware of the barrier to understanding that derives from language differences.

Throughout this period the political situation in the Frontier was growing more volatile. This was an inevitable consequence of the developments in Indian politics which reached a new stage with the British Cabinet Mission's arrival in the spring and the Viceroy's attempt with them to reach agreement with Congress and the Muslim League about the formation of a national interim Government in June. By then, the Muslim League under Jinnah's leadership were playing for the highest stakes through partition, and Congress, having got to the brink of fulfilment of its wildest dreams, so lacked imaginative generosity of spirit that it confirmed Jinnah in his obduracy and in effect surrendered the hope of independence for an undivided country. Thus the way was paved for the Muslim League policy of direct action against Congress rule in NWFP on which the party embarked on 29 July.

In the Frontier uneasy months of discontent preceded this formal development. The Provincial Muslim League had been rent asunder by party *bazi* (internal feuds) ever since the collapse of Aurangzeb's ministry in March 1945. Attempts by Qazi Isa and other emissaries of Jinnah to repair the damage and create a sound party structure had been unsuccessful. When Jinnah visited the province in November 1945 he got a hero's welcome but the League still got its tactics wrong in its preparations for the general election in January and February 1946. There was a bland assumption that for the electorate the issue was clear, namely the need to keep the province out of the hands of the Hindus. At that time, it was too early to proclaim simply that to vote for the League was to vote for Pakistan, while to vote for Congress was to vote for a Hindu Raj. The implication was that Khan Sahib and Abdul Ghaffar Khan and their Muslim allies had sold out to the Hindus; after all – so the propaganda constantly proclaimed – Khan Sahib's daughter had been given in marriage to a Hindu (Jaswant Singh was in fact a Christian) and A.G.K's son had married a Parsi. By the end of 1946 this sort of argument had acquired more persuasive force as the process of communalism advanced in the Frontier. But at the start of the year the electorate was still more concerned with questions like food supplies and controls. The League Ministry had made a bad botch of their policies and abused their powers. The Congress Ministry were due more time and a second chance. Their electoral tactics were more eclectic and pragmatic than the League's which contested every Muslim constituency and did badly except in Hazara. Congress concentrated its effort better and cultivated alliances with other groups in constituencies where its chances were rated poor, so that overall its performance was convincing. This clear-cut Congress victory, in an election in which the Muslim League was confident of establishing the Frontier as an integral part of Pakistan, solid for Partition, nevertheless had a strong Pyrrhic overtone from the beginning. It set the League firmly on a communal tack, which in the end unmanned the Khan brothers and kept them uneasily on the defensive, although Dr Khan Sahib held office for a further eighteen months and his majority was unassailable in the Assembly.

From the start they were preoccupied with the food problem,

whose dimensions dominated much of the Viceroy's effort in the spring of 1946 to establish an effective Executive Council, truly representative of both political parties. In each of the last two years the Frontier had been spared the trauma and turmoil of famine and consequential Pathan rebellion only by allocations of grain from the Punjab, despatched by order of the Government of India. Yet in normal times the province was broadly self-sufficient, capable indeed in favourable conditions of producing a surplus. In each recent year, the channels of trade had got clogged and quantities of grain had gone into private hoards, rather than into the *mandis*. In 1944 the Governor personally had appealed unsuccessfully to the big landowners for supplies. They had strongly resented the efforts of the Muslim League Ministry, with which they were generally thought to be in alliance, to introduce and enforce controls. Insofar as the ministers' purpose was to abuse and exploit the power which the apparatus of controls gave them, rather than to secure the best interests of the consumer, the resentments of the landowners was understandable. It was paradoxically exploited by Congress which as the party of the poor man might have been expected to approve of 'controls'. Back in office, the Congress ministers of course adopted the system of controls which they had criticized, and systematically abused the officials for its shortcomings.

As in 1944, the main problem in the early summer months after the rabi crop was the procurement of grain, particularly wheat and barley, for government stock. In 1945 the difficulty was eased by the high yield of the harvest. The Ministry adopted, with reasonable success, a so-called monopoly purchase system which conferred the exclusive right to deal in foodgrains on government-appointed agents, licensed to operate in specific local markets or *mandis*. These licence-holders were able to supply about 14,000 tons of wheat for distribution through official depots, enough to tide the system over the period before the *kharif* crop and the arrival of allocations from the Punjab.

In the spring of 1946 the situation was less propitious. The Frontier crop was less satisfactory and the all-India food position had deteriorated ominously, so that the Frontier Government had to be warned by the Delhi Government that they must plan for a reduction in imports. It was generally recognized that the 1945 procurement arrangements might have produced a much larger total stock, but in face of the anticipated lower crop yield in 1946 it was decided to adopt a tighter, stricter form of procurement. Fixing a higher procurement target, from a poorer crop, the Ministry introduced a compulsory levy on individual *zamindars*. The 1945 Procurement Order was replaced by a Provincial Notification on 3 April 1946 introducing and defining the compulsory levy. Targets were set for the four potentially surplus districts – Mardan, Peshawar, Bannu and Dera Ismail Khan. The total to be procured was 23,000 tons, of which it seemed essential to control 12,000 tons by mid-July.

To administer this scheme, I was appointed Provincial Foodgrains Procurement Officer. It was an unhappy task for I had not been closely involved in the drafting of the regulations and I soon felt sceptical about the scheme. It was impossible with the ordinary revenue staff, untrained for this special duty, to achieve equitable assessments of the individual levy. The paperwork involved was too complicated and the degree of precision implied was ludicrous in Indian conditions. The element of compulsion on individual landholders was unacceptable and the scheme, constructed meticulously on paper, ignored many of the real-life factors that inevitably concerned the *zamindar*. Instead of lubricating the economic system, the scheme injected grit into it. Above all the ministers consistently ignored the fundamental change in the political atmosphere which made farmers more and more unwilling to cooperate with Government. Ironically the Congress Party began to reap the harvest of discontent with controls which they had sown so diligently two years earlier. Farmers, who had resented the imposition of controls by the landowners' own party, the Muslim League, saw even less reason to cooperate with inequitable measures enforced by Congress. The new communal line of propaganda developed by the League began to take more effect, particularly in the very areas in Mardan and Peshawar where large surpluses should have been available at the *mandis*.

I shall not go into the technical details here. Some ten years later I prepared a critical analysis of the scheme and its results for the new Economic Development Institute established in Washington DC under the auspices of the World Bank and the International Monetary Fund by Sir Alexander Cairncross. The document was used as a case study in seminars on planning in underdeveloped areas. Later, a version of the paper was published in Chicago in the journal *Economic Development and Cultural*

Change. The article was prepared from the report on the scheme which I prepared for the Provincial Government, writing in Nathia Gali in the last week of July 1946. I was feeling pretty disgruntled; I was disappointed with the results and not consoled by the fact that I had been pessimistic from the start about the possibilities. Humphrey Cooke had not been happy about some of my criticisms, and my suggestions that the Government was working along the wrong lines and did not understand economic principles or appreciate the reasons for its own unpopularity – or even accept that it was unpopular – were not going to be easy for him to convey to Dr Khan Sahib, Qazi Ataullah and Mehr Chand Khanna. When I wrote that report, reunited with Barbara in the cool mists and still pine forests of the Galis, I had become sure that the heat and dust of the plains and the turmoil and corruption of Indian politics were not now going to fulfil for us the promise of the career on which I had embarked nearly six years earlier.

It had indeed been a hard, testing summer for us both. I had scarcely started on my new job when it became necessary to take Barbara to Nathia for the hot weather. She was pregnant – Hilary was born in Peshawar on 13 December 1946 – and could not possibly enjoy or endure the sort of touring which I would have to undertake in May and June. She settled into a bungalow shared by Lionel Jardine, who had returned as Revenue Commissioner, his wife Marjory having gone home to UK, and Leslie Mallam who was now a widower, with little Marcus just beginning to run around. Barbara contributed a modest daily sum towards the communal housekeeping, over which she also kept a feminine – if junior – eye. Marcus had his nanny, Violet Roach, an Anglo-Indian lady who was devoted to the boy. She and Barbara got on very well together.

There was also Simba, Oliver St John's big golden retriever. Oliver had left him with us while the St Johns went home on leave. He was a staunch watchdog and a reassuring companion to Barbara on her regular solitary walks on the lonely hill paths around Nathia. Though he loved chasing monkeys down the khud, he was never far from her side when anyone approached and the hill folk gave him a wide berth. His upper lip curled in a menacing snarl which they interpreted as a warning, not aware that it was also his way of smiling when he greeted friends. He was a most welcome temporary accession to our family for we had been without a dog for a short time before he arrived. My faithful yellow

Labrador, Shot, had died when I was home on leave. He had a habit of wandering in search of illicit pleasures outside his bailliewick. I had left him with John Dent, who had a fine Labrador bitch, Rona. One morning, trotting with Rona behind John's bicycle en route for the office, the fickle Shot suddenly took himself off and when he returned nearly two days later he was so badly savaged by bazaar dogs that he had to be put down. John gave me Maia, a lovely pup which was the offspring of Shot and Rona. In our first months together in Peshawar Maia had been a real source of pleasure as we trained her and took her for walks; but one evening she was poisoned and died wretchedly. Whether some malicious person did this deliberately, or it was an accident, there was no way of discovering. So Simba's arrival, and his contribution to Barbara's peace of mind that summer, were propitious.

My procurement task was far from being an office job. I had a three-ton lorry provided with a driver by the additional police and in it I toured the whole province accompanied by one or two clerks, an orderly, and my bearer. An essential part of our equipment was an enormous earthenware *chatti* filled with drinking water. It was remarkable how cool it would keep the water although the heat of the sun was terrific. The lorry, like the one I used with my escort in Waziristan, had a roof for shade or for sitting on but it was open at the sides to allow the wind our progress created to dry off the perspiring passengers. Seated beside the driver I had to avoid touching the metal dashboard for it was scorching hot. Dust was forever in my hair, ears, nose, eyes and mouth. Some of my trips were memorable experiences because of the physical conditions. I have a vivid mental picture of the Pezu Pass, on the way from Bannu to D.I.K., the dramatic cliffs of Sheikh Budin looming over the road, shimmering under an ominous cloud of dust, lowering threateningly at the parched wayfarer. One dreaded the possibility of a breakdown, contemplating gloomily the chance of survival through the solitude of an afternoon in which any inhabitants seemed to have burrowed underground in the deep shade of caves. It was easy to feel disorientated and abandoned, mistrustful of the faithful servants dosing uncomfortably in the back of the lorry, apprehensive that the driver, bleary eyed and thirsty, would fall asleep at the wheel.

When we arrived, Dera Ismail Khan was a furnace, but an hour or two later, as the temperature suddenly dropped and a cooler breeze rose from the great river Indus, people came to life and began to move again, and as I emerged from the deadly torpor of the desert I began to feel just normally hot, dusty and thirsty. A day or two later, after a visit to Tank, I decided not to tackle the physical tortures of the Pezu road again but to take the risks of ambush by Bhittani outlaws on the seldom used military road through the Bain Pass. The surface was excellent and the risks were the familiar ones of travel in tribal areas like Waziristan – in my calculation much reduced by the timing of our journey in the midday heat and by the fact that nobody, not even the driver, had expected us to be taking that route, certainly not at that time of day. Although it offered many spots ideal for ambush, I judged it unlikely that anyone with hostile intent would be sitting on the hot rocks on the slight chance of casual prey. Apart from surprised Frontier Constabulary whom we flushed from their siesta in one or two posts, we saw nobody for many miles.

The oddest experience of the summer's travels was at Mardan. I went there for a couple of days to try to ginger up the work of the revenue staff who were so far behind with their procurement work. The Deputy Commissioner was Colonel Bill Leeper, a senior IPS man who had been a cavalry officer. I did not know him well but had found him congenial. His wife Dorothea was charming but I knew that she was now home in Ireland. He had kindly asked me to stay in his bungalow and after a simple evening meal we settled quietly to what I expected would be a fruitful discussion of the problems of procurement. It was the oddest experience. Leeper was scathing about the procurement plan, and I was embarrassed at having to defend it from his irony for I had some sympathy with his criticisms. But he transgressed all the rules for after all he was responsible to Government for carrying out their orders, and after a time I realized that he had quite deliberately ignored the whole operation. I asked him what alternative he had, for surely he could not doubt the need for Government to acquire stocks in order to feed the people, nor deny that it was from the rich irrigated lands of his district that surplus food should be drawn. At this stage he became incomprehensible. The only thing I could establish was that in the old days the Indian cavalry regiments knew how to live off the land and if we used their techniques we could get what we wanted, because the peasants respected their methods, recognized their needs and would not fail to cooperate, as they would certainly fail to cooperate in any bureaucratic scheme promoting the interests of the provincial politicians.

Throughout a long disquisition he transfixed me with a gaze as hypnotic as the Ancient Mariner's and I went to bed despondent and baffled, well aware that Mardan was an albatross round the neck of the Provincial Procurement Officer. Next day I toured in several villages, finding only confirmation of the inept way in which the district staff interpreted the scheme, and also of the unwillingness of the *zamindars* to cooperate with the Congress Ministry and its representatives. Back in the DC's bungalow, I found no trace of him but next morning a note from him was waiting for me. It told me that he had gone off on casual leave to Abbottabad and he would be pleased if I took over his court work in his absence. It was clear that Bill Leeper had a problem; but so had I. He might have been drunk but I had not actually seen him imbibe much liquor. I concluded that whatever the reason, his mental aberrations were due to some sort of breakdown and I telephoned the Chief Secretary for instructions. It was a very embarrassing phone call for a junior officer to make. Although Mardan called for an intensive effort to procure grain – the responsibility of the DC who had now abandoned it to me – I had plenty of other things to do and did not want my first formal tenure of a DC's post to hinge on inheriting this mess. I was cheerfully told to do my best, hang on for a day or two and to ensure that there was not too much chaos in the DC's office and court. I impressed on Dudley de la Fargue my view that it was essential that Doc Morgan, who was now Civil Surgeon at Abbottabad, should seek out Bill and see what should be done for him. To my dismay a day later a telegram arrived conferring on me the powers of Additional District Magistrate Mardan, and authorizing a period of leave for the DC.

The next few days were a nightmare. The office work was a shambles and the district staff, though kind and willing enough, were too confused and uneasy to be of much real help. I was so ignorant of local matters that I was pretty ineffectual on many of the cases that were presented to me. It was a sad state of affairs which did nothing for my confidence in my future in the ICS. I had never before had any suspicion that any part of our administration in the Frontier could get into such a mess. No wonder poor Leeper had thought of calling in the cavalry! After a week or so I was relieved, and in due course Bill Leeper was posted to the safe haven of the Kurram Agency. By now the critical period for procurement was almost over – the scheme had sadly failed to meet the target and the time had come for me to go to Nathia to write down what I thought of the whole exercise, in language more temperate than I was tempted to use.

At that time there was little to endear me to Mardan. At the height of the hot weather, there was little chance of building a relationship with the Guides Regiment. Casual encounters with the Army in residence were pleasant but unfulfilling. The most rewarding evening was spent with some Danish missionaries who lived a few miles out of the cantonment. I learned more about the district that evening from them than I could from the official staff. These torrid days in Mardan were the nadir of my career in India – I felt lost and in a way abandoned; I seemed to be utterly ineffectual; I could not unravel the tangle of most of the DC's pending cases; I knew that I could not get the procurement scheme to work. One part of my mind told me that Bill Leeper was just *paghal* (daft, mad: in Scots, puggled). Another inner voice whispered that it was not Bill who was mad but everybody who had been responsible for concocting the procurement scheme. That made me feel thoroughly uneasy and it was an enormous relief to get away from the madhouse to the reassuring familiarity of Nathia Gali and to rejoin the provincial 'family circle'. I had been through the sort of experience born of India that only Kipling could have understood and described. Recovering from it was like emerging from the delirium of a tropical fever. It was a relief to have done with foodgrains and civil supplies. I became Under-Secretary to Colonel Leslie Mallam in the Development Department.

I have no sharp recollection of my duties over the next few months. Leslie Mallam was putting the finishing touches to his Post-War Reconstruction Plan. I came into his department too late to be able to make any innovative contribution. I felt that the plan was highly artificial and statistically unsound but I had a real respect for Mallam's motivation and purpose and I believed that the guidelines he offered for development were worth following. Although he was rather dry and uninspiring in manner, Leslie Mallam was thoughtful and philosophical, and cared deeply for the well-being of the people of the Frontier. I think that he was happier gazing into the future possibilities of improving their welf·re than by that stage he could have been in any other role in the service. I remember a conversation with him and Lionel Jardine when I was living in their Peshawar bungalow that summer. They were discussing the trend of Frontier politics in the light of the Muslim League's formal decision to conduct a 'direct action' campaign against Government. They both had vivid memories of the unrest in Peshawar in 1930 and 1931, of the Afridi uprising and the virtual breakdown of law and order over a period of several months. Both men said that the experience and the process of coping with the chaos were the most dramatic upheavals of their lives and thoughts, and Leslie solemnly added that it was an experience which he would not be able to survive a second time, given his age and feeling of fatigue after the responsibilities of the war years. Within a few months of that conversation, younger men at the peak of their abilities, like Gerald Curtis and Norval Mitchell, were taking a similar hopeless view of the role of the ICS officer in advice which they – separately – tendered to the Governor and the Viceroy.

Meanwhile Leslie and I were happy enough, cocooned in his plan, persuading ministers to work in what we conceived to be the right direction, and negotiating with prospective entrepreneurs and industrialists. I remember that I formed an emphatic view that the Ministry was on the wrong tack in their plans to develop big hospitals. I was sure that resources would be wasted in over-centralization of specialist medical facilities, and that far more patients could be relieved if they put more resources into developing a large number of rough and ready health centres or dispensaries in rural areas, training compounders or dispensers to identify a reasonable number of endemic diseases and to prescribe for them, at much lower cost in training than was envisaged for a much smaller number of highly qualified doctors trained on European lines. This in effect was the Chinese scheme for training 'barefoot doctors' for the villages. The more highly trained the doctor – or the teacher or engineer – the less likely they were to stay in uncomfortable conditions in service of the bulk of the population; therefore in moving towards progress and higher standards, it was advisable to hasten slowly and not to dissipate resources by aiming at the start for the best, rather than spreading the second-best more widely to the general advantage.

Nobody can deny that ICS officers were prepared to tackle anything. While I was Under-Secretary in the Development Department I had to wear the hat of the Director of Industries

NWFP, a grandiose title in a province which had not really begun to industrialize. In the post-war enthusiasm for development there was great pressure for tangible evidence that new industries would improve the standard of living and there was a popular expectation that the Industries Department could produce new factories ready-functioning out of an office file. Some would-be entrepreneurs even expected a visit to the office to provide not only a licence to manufacture but also the essential raw materials for an industry which they had not bothered to identify. It was government policy to encourage belief that state control was the essential ingredient of industrial policy. The Congress Ministry's ideology was decidedly left-wing, although Mehr Chand Khanna was the epitome of the successful Hindu man of business. The ministers believed in planning and in nationalization of large-scale industry – but of course there was no such industry for them to nationalize. In a NWFP Factories (Amendment) Act passed in the autumn of 1946 they set out their intentions, particularly that of greatly enlarging the Industries Department, where a bright young Pathan officer of the PCS, Mohammed Aslam Khan Khattak, shortly took over the role of Director of Industries on a full-time basis.

It would be a mistake at this stage to go into details of my preoccupations as the first Director of Industries for the province. The provincial government's policy was based on ideas about industrialisation that were not appropriate in a backward, undeveloped economy. But I was in no position to anticipate the lessons of the future, and I will here confine myself to a single example of interest to my personal story. In a broadcast which I made in autumn 1946, I said:

A few weeks ago, a signboard was erected on a piece of land near Mardan announcing the appearance on the ground of the Premier Sugar Mills and Distillery Company Ltd. In two years' time the largest sugar mill in India will be in full operation on the site. It will have an annual output of over thirty thousand tons of sugar, about five times as great an output as the existing Takhtibhai Mill. During the war the Government of India were able to persuade the British Board of Trade to release skilled men and materials from war-work for the manufacture of specially designed machinery for this factory, and some of that machinery is at present being brought to Mardan from Karachi on specially constructed railway wagons. Soon two thousand tons of sugar cane will be entering that factory every day during the cane season, and growers will be protected from the worst effects of any future slump in the price of gur. The presence of many zamindars from the Charsadda and Mardan cane-growing areas on the list of the company's shareholders is proof of the importance of its success to the welfare of this part of the province. Their cane will be brought to the factory by locomotive-powered tramway-line from as far away as Utmanzai. The factory will produce power alcohol as well as sugar and will run a full-sized flour mill as a sideline.

My confidence in the Premier Sugar Mills was justified. Its successful establishment was a remarkable story. The enterprise was the brainchild of Rai Bahadur Ishar Dass Sawney, a quiet, gentle little Hindu businessman from Nawanshahr near Abbottabad in Hazara. I got to know him well in 1942 and 1943 and in 1946 I was glad to help to foster his plans for his sugar mill in every way I could. There were many difficulties to resolve, including problems with the Nawab of Hoti, by far the most important and wealthiest landowner in Mardan, an eccentric man whose influence was eroded as new political forces, channelled through the party organizations of both Muslim League and Congress, displaced the authority of the great landowners as powerful allies of the Raj. The biggest difficulties, of course, arose after Partition, for Ishar Dass became a refugee in India, and apparently impassable political barriers cut him off from the site of his dreams. The extraordinary thing was that, such were his determination and his respect and standing in the eyes of the new Chief Minister, Abdul Qayum, and the sugar-cane producing *zamindars*, he was enabled to retain his interest, guaranteed safe conduct to attend meetings in the Frontier and saw the enterprise through to triumphant success in the 1950s. The first General Manager of the new factory was my old senior colleague Roger Bacon, who had been PA Khyber in 1941. Years later I discovered from Ishar Dass that he had had it in mind to appoint me to that job, after Partition, but I had left India and become unavailable!

Preoccupations of this kind sheltered me to a great extent from events in the province that were to alter my future. At this stage in the long struggle for Indian independence the Frontier Province had, perhaps surprisingly, moved right into the limelight, and in a curious way events happened, seeming to be in no way connected with the destiny of the Raj, which turned out to have direct significance even for those of us who played no personal part in them.

The new political significance of NWFP in the Indian struggle was highlighted by the result of the 1946 Elections, to which I have already alluded. Within months of losing the Election, the Muslim League had succeeded in persuading the electorate that, after all, the Frontier must be aligned with the Muslims cause and must not be sacrificed to the Hindus. Congress on the other hand desperately argued that the recent electoral defeat of the League in NWFP showed convincingly that Jinnah and his party could not justify the claims they made so uncompromisingly for a Pakistan that must include all areas where Muslims were in the majority. Had the League not put that very point to the Pathan electors and been rejected? In the deepening communalism of the argument in the Frontier, the charge was increasingly made against Dr Khan Sahib and his brother Abdul Ghaffar that they had betrayed their faith and their heritage to the Hindus, just as their children had been allowed to marry outside Islam. The explosive Khan Sahib was the last man to contemplate compromise with his opponents in face of such a charge. To him, it was so ridiculous and unreal that it merely confirmed his contempt for the party that made it. He remained blind and obdurate in a developing situation which called for insight and imagination. His brother, so closely associated with the mystique of Gandhi, was unable to appreciate how unreal his mentor's political judgments had become, or how slight his influence might be in crucial decisions which the All-India Congress Party would have to take. In spite of their electoral triumph, things were not going at all well in the Frontier for Dr Khan Sahib and his colleagues. Continuing shortages of essential commodities were becoming tiresome and the Ministry's interventions through controls were becoming too partisan.

For all the Chief Minister's contempt, the Muslim League was at long last taking a grip of itself. Its appeal to Islamic susceptibilities was consistently reinforced by the energetic influence of the Pir of Manki, a religious leader who travelled tirelessly with his message in tribal areas as well as in the districts. Continuing efforts to reorganize the formal structure of the party began to bear fruit. One of the leading figures in the Congress Party, Abdul Qayum, had changed sides, and he was not alone. Excluded from the inner family circle of the Khan brothers, he had gained his political experience and stature more from participation in the work of the All-India Congress Committee, but he now found with the League new scope for his considerable talents. By July, the League's organization in the Frontier was ready to embark on a positive 'direct action' policy, and to make its efforts at non-cooperation with the Congress Government of the province increasingly effective.

External events were conspiring in the same direction. This is not the place to describe developments at the Centre following the failure of the British Cabinet Mission and the formation of the Viceroy's new Executive Council or Cabinet, at first with no League membership. But one aspect of the new Interim Government carries more significance for the Frontier story than was realized at the time. This was the attribution to Pandit Nehru of responsibility for external affairs. Conventionally, this subject included relations with the tribes of the Frontier, as well as with sovereign states overseas. The Frontier tribes were not British-Indian citizens but protected persons whose independent status was recognized in a series of formal treaties historically binding on the British Government in London and the separate tribes. The relations between the tribes and the British were therefore conducted between their *jirgas* and the agents of the Crown. The Political Agents were responsible to the Governor in his special capacity as Agent to the Governor General – the Viceroy's 'other hat'. In this capacity the Governor was completely free from any responsibility to receive advice from the provincial Ministers, whose authority covered only the settled districts. Although a few tribesmen, particularly Mohmands, had houses in the settled districts as well as in tribal territory, until 1946 tribal interest in Frontier provincial politics was slight – though tribal interest in global politics, ranging from relations with Afghanistan, Persia and Turkey, and of course Russia, to the strategies of the War against Germany and Japan, was always acute. When it was realized in the summer of 1946 that the Hindu Nehru had assumed control of the advice given at the Centre to the Viceroy about tribal affairs, tribal concern over Indian politics began to stir. The notion that there might be a Hindu master of their affairs, so long dismissed from their thoughts as ludicrous, now acquired a new significance, and the existence of a provincial Ministry controlled by the Khan brothers, who gave their children in marriage to infidels, quickened their interest in the message of the Pir of Manki. At the same time, as the Congress Ministry's experience of government under the terms of the 1935 Act matured, they became more conscious of and sensitive to the anomaly of administering a province whose people were artificially divided into separate categories by the administrative boundary. After all, the ministers were now responsible for law and order in the settled districts but the history of the Frontier showed that raids by trans-border tribesmen into the districts were a big element in the difficulties confronting the police. And how could they ignore the tribal areas in formulating plans for economic development? Inevitably, the scene was being set for a fresh questioning of the whole system.

One element in the British system for control of the tribes was the use of air power and for many years this had been the focus of criticism of British actions by Indian politicians. In fact – as I hope I have shown in describing events in Waziristan in 1944 – the use of air power, under the strict regulations of the 'Grey Book', was reasonable and effective up to a point, and never indiscriminate and inhumane, yet it had always aroused strong passions in debate in Britain as well as in India, and it is not surprising that Pandit Nehru felt uneasy about air actions against the tribes when he took over the 'external affairs' portfolio. Just when that irascible man was specially embarrassed by the indignity he brought on himself near the end of June when, ignoring the prohibition of the State Government of Kashmir, and the wishes of his closest colleagues, he went to Kashmir and got himself arrested, an event occurred in South Waziristan which was to raise the issue of the use of air power very sharply. This was the kidnapping of J.O.S. Donald, the Political Agent, by some Bromi Khel of the Shabi Khel Mahsuds. It was an almost unprecedented act of foolishness in the eyes of every other section of the tribe, even though the PA was taken by mistake for a less important government officer. I need not go into details for the fascinating story of subsequent events is relevant here only because after Donald's release it had to be decided to bomb certain Shabi Khel villages when the tribe failed to comply with terms imposed by Government, including conditions for the repayment of ransom money. The reasons for the decision were very complicated and deeply rooted in the lore and conventions of tribal ways and the 'rules of the game' between them and the political authorities. Even the Viceroy (Lord Wavell) felt dubious about the ethics of the decision to bomb – although he sanctioned it, but only after in personal conference with the Air Officer Commanding-in-Chief and Air Commodore Long (the senior air officer in the Frontier) he had satisfied himself on the ability of the RIAF to hit the chosen targets, and on the suitability of these targets.

Nehru does not seem to have been involved in the decision but it evidently weighed on his mind, for two months later, as in the case of his visit to Kashmir, he brushed aside the advice of his own senior Congress colleagues, as well as the Viceroy, not to mention the strongest representations by Sir Olaf Caroe, the NWFP Governor, and against their wishes embarked on a tour of the Frontier tribal areas accompanied by Dr Khan Sahib and the meddlesome Abdul Ghaffar Khan. Caroe himself has recorded (MSS Eur. F. 203 in India Office Archives) that an important reason for Nehru's decision to go ahead with this fateful visit in face of so much well-considered advice was that he felt upset by the aerial bombing of the Shabi Khel. As Minister for External Affairs he had felt that he bore responsibility for the action, yet he had had no control over it. In his mind, therefore, something was wrong with the system of government relations with the tribes which it was his duty to put right; so he must go and see for himself, and exercise his moral authority – no doubt over tribesmen and political officers alike.

The outcome was disastrous. Wherever they went – to the Khyber, to Miranshah and Razmak in Waziristan, to the Malakand, Nehru and the Khan Brothers met hostile questioners and hecklers, and a frightening show of violence, especially in the Khyber and in the normally peaceable Malakand. All three were quick tempered, volatile characters, and Nehru was unable to resist the taunts of Pathan tribesmen, to whom the cut and thrust of sharp debate was a natural opportunity to provoke loss of temper in an opponent – whose subsequent loss of face was their objective. The details of events are a fascinating story to be found elsewhere. I had no part in them, but like all Frontier officers I heard accounts from all sides and realized that something dramatic had happened which would change our lives. Never before in our experience had *jirgas* behaved in this way: experienced political officers who were present were appalled at the breakdown in the normal conventions of communication.

From this time it became clear that, so long as they were linked with Nehru and the Indian Congress Party, Dr Khan Sahib and his brother could not hope to retain political control of the Frontier. Even the fact that the Faqir of Ipi had already shown his hand against Congress and in favour of the League scarcely mattered, for Nehru's broad itinerary had spread the bad news far wider than Ipi's influence stretched. More that anything else, in Caroe's later judgment, Nehru's visit made Pakistan inevitable. In such interesting ways the spell of the Frontier was cast over all India. For British officers, the immediate consequence strangely was to impair their confidence and undermine their 'influence'. They were seen by the tribes to have been unable to curb the insolent arrogance of this Hindu, whose place amongst them should be no better than a suppliant *hamsaya*, dependent on their protection. They were bitterly accused by Nehru of incompetence, even of engineering the show of opposition from their subservient tribes – a charge which caused great resentment in the tribes, who took enormous pride in their freedom. These allegations left a harsh taste for in certain cases they were rashly made by Nehru against men who had in fact saved his skin, if not his pride. In Delhi, Hugh Weightman, the Foreign Secretary, patiently and courageously pulled to pieces the extravagant analysis of Frontier affairs and Frontiersmen which Nehru prepared. In the end only Sheikh Mahboob Ali, the PA Malakand, had to face serious charges of dereliction of duty. They were investigated by a British Sessions Judge from Madras who exonerated Mahboob Ali completely, though Wavell himself felt that he had been, to say the least, remiss in his arrangements for protecting his visitors at one critical point on their return journey. Gerald Curtis, whose intervention at that moment almost certainly saved Nehru's life, was so enraged by the allegations against the political officers that he wrote formally to the Governor asking to be relieved and allowed to resign, and warned that the authority of the service was being so undermined by the Ministry that the time had come for us to leave them to sort out the mess for themselves.

Throughout these events I was a distant spectator and anxious listener to the radio news, finding light relief in personal accounts of particular episodes enlivened by the wit of various raconteurs. But I could not but be aware that something very significant had happened in the Frontier, and I became more sensitive than ever to reports of negotiations – or discussions, or arguments – in Delhi and in London. There had been terrible communal rioting in Bengal and Bombay, and it was clear that there was more to come. As yet, the Frontier was free from such slaughter, but the League was building steadily on its Direct Action platform, and Abdul Ghaffar's Khudai Khidmatgars were more than ever ready to act as a private army. Their leader, sworn to the creed of non-violence, had been nonplussed by events, and had reacted with characteristic Pakhtun hot temper. They were unlikely now to be kept under peaceful control.

A few weeks later the Viceroy himself paid the province a visit, seeking to take the temperature and spread some calm and reassurance. I was too junior to be amongst the officers who had formal access to him and I did not expect to meet him privately. But as he returned by air from a couple of days in Waziristan and the south, he sent a signal that he wanted a game of golf that afternoon. The Governor's ADC caught me just before lunch – it was a Saturday – and I presented myself at Government House to drive nervously with Lord Wavell to the golf course. It was notorious that he was a silent man and for the first few holes little was said except to exchange information about the score, and an occasional indication by me of the best line to take to the green. As he played, for a time the tiredness seemed to lift from him, and suddenly he said, 'They tell me you come from Nairn. Do you know my old friend Colonel Wallace?' That started an easy and pleasant conversation which somehow led him some time later into the remark that he felt his hands were tied in all his efforts because the British had become so thin on the ground. The ICS was seriously under-manned, and many of the senior officers had been too long over-worked and had no reserves of energy left. Thinking that he implied that matters would be easier if the Government at home had not let recruitment in the UK run down and stop – the last intake to the ICS from Britain had been in 1941 – I asked what more young men of my vintage, or with even less experience, could possibly contribute to the solution of such fundamental difficulties. We went back to happier topics, such as golf. His game in fact was good, considering how tired he must have been. I beat him 6 and 5, but he had lost four holes before he got into his stride. He got round in about 82, against my 72, which was a good round for me. He seemed a good deal happier at the end of the game than he had been when we set out from Government House.

I had always admired Wavell for his military leadership and his literary and analytical gifts. After meeting him in such surprisingly relaxed circumstances I admired him even more, but I had an uneasy feeling that he was tired and despondent, and that the outlook was gloomy. Within a few weeks he was to be superseded by Mountbatten, whose charisma and confidence appeared to transform the picture. But at the time I regretted Wavell's departure, feeling that his courageous honesty and steady patience might in the end secure the agreement of the conflicting Indian politicians, and that his worst handicap was the constant carping interference by the British Government. In many ways I feel now that Linlithgow also might have got further if he had been given anything like the same freedom of action and decision that Mountbatten insisted on being allowed. But by the end of their terms of office, both Linlithgow and Wavell must have been exhausted in every way, and frustrated by the obdurate refusal of the Indian parties to compromise. At the end of 1946, as a young officer I often felt impatient with the entrenched attitudes of politicians and some senior officers with whom I worked, but I could not help being affected by the sense of weariness and frustration that many British officials could no longer conceal. If Linlithgow had seemed old-fashioned and uninspiring, Wavell uncommunicative and exasperated by the stubborn ditherings of lesser men, it was now too late for the most charismatic Viceroy to build a new future for the European members of the ICS in an independent India. The service was still honoured and respected, but its real influence with the people was being slowly undermined by the growing power of politicians jealous of its prestige, and since the end of the War perhaps its sense of purpose and motivation had been clouded and confused. Until then, through all the pressures towards national independence, we had been clear where our duty lay in service to the Crown and devotion to the welfare of the people of India. Now our right to be the interpreters of the people's well-being had been challenged by Indian politicians in a manner to which in the circumstances there was no answer.

I can remember slowly becoming aware of these changes in our circumstances. There was no sudden dawning of the light. Understanding came gradually, encouraged by conversations with colleagues who knew more and could see further. Sometimes these were incidental to a game of golf – on Sunday mornings with Kim McRea, who had a shrewd policeman's eye for underground events and a trained intelligence officer's access to secret sources of information; or with Oliver St John, who inherited from his family's generations of service in India an instinct for the nuances of the country. Perhaps most often these occasions were of games with Norval Mitchell, who had taken over from Alastair Low as

Finance Secretary. Norval was very quick at his desk work, and a keen and energetic golfer. He organized me firmly so that I cleared my files in time to get at least twelve holes before dusk, returning refreshed to tackle the files which the orderly brought home to the bungalow. Norval had much experience of central India and his powerful mind reached beyond the parochial concerns of the Frontier. He saw that his personal ambitions – very properly conceived – were to be thwarted, and there was often an edge of bitterness in his observations. Already planning for the future of his family, he was studying the practical side of hill-farming – reckoning that he could afford only to start on marginal land in Scotland – and his delightful American wife Mary was, as always, complementing his enthusiasms by learning about bee-keeping and butter-making.

I was not well enough organized to follow that sort of example, and was happily absorbed in the joys of our marriage, which made us both contentedly self-contained. Barbara came through the trials of a pregnancy in India in splendid fashion, well cared for in the later stages by a new Civil Surgeon, Andy Taylor, a thoughtful Canadian whose caring ways reminded me of my old friend Captain Vergin of Dehra Dun. Late on the evening of 12 December I took Barbara to the Lady Reading Hospital, just outside the walls of Peshawar city. Having been sent home by the sister in charge of the labour ward, I was tossing restlessly in bed in the early hours of the 13th when the lights of Andy Taylor's car shone across the little garden. He had come to tell me that Hilary had arrived safely and that all was well. Barbara remembers how throughout a difficult birth one of the dusky nurses encouraged her with regular enjoinders not to waste her labour pains – wielding all the while a fly-swat, to minimize the possible sources of infection.

Notes

[1] The Imperial Bank of India sent us a monthly statement of account meticulously handwritten by one of its countless clerks. For two months Barbara noted the rise in our balance without comment, but at the end of the third month she remarked that we seemed to be managing rather well. It was only when I pointed

out that the balance was inscribed in red ink that she appreciated the true position, and the meaning of the phrase 'in the red'.

2 But it has to be emphasized that in the Frontier Province Indians were in a small minority in the senior services. I knew Bedi well, rather less well Iskander Mirza, Sheikh Mahboob Ali and S.M. Khursheed and as all were so much senior to me that close personal friendship could hardly be expected to develop. The only youngish IPS Indian officer I had met was Allahdad Khan, whose family observed strict purdah. Nearer my age a late entrant to the Political Service was Yusaf, from the South Waziristan Scouts, with whom, as with all Scouts officers, easy, relaxed, comradely friendship was the most natural thing in the world. I have mentioned this when referring to Sharif, Rahim and Aziz in the Tochi Scouts – but I knew them in the 'family' of the Scouts mess and the comradeship of the *gasht* or the isolation of the outpost like Datta Khel or Spinwam, and I never saw their wives, though I was shown snapshots of their children. An exception was Ataullah Jan, a young political officer whom we knew for a short time in 1946. His wife was a doctor and did not observe purdah.

Friendship with colleagues in the provincial administrative service was sincere but limited in its scope by the hierarchical differences imposed by the status of their 'junior' branch of the Civil Service. This barrier affected even more sadly our relationship with Indian officers of the 'inferior' services, like the Education Service or the Agricultural Service, which were in entirely Indianised NWFP, unlike the IPS or the highest ranks of the police. I remember vividly a conversation with Pat Duncan, who was passionate in his enthusiasms for improving the life of the people. He had ideas about agricultural improvement, but felt hampered by the difficulties of getting the Director of Agriculture to discuss them in a relaxed way. 'It is scandalous,' he said, 'that in this country with its needs I should be addressed as "sir" by the province's Director of Agriculture instead of the other way round.' Somerset Maugham once said that if Waterloo was won on the playing fields of Eton, India was lost to the Empire in the public schools of England (Robin Maugham, *Conversations with Willie*, 1978, p. 96). Pat and I might well have agreed with that remark; but of course it is unfair to attribute to English notions of class differences the whole blame for the social barriers that hampered communications between the British and the Indians.

[3] After a formal enquiry conducted by a British judge from Madras, Mahboob Ali was acquitted of blame in March 1947.

[4] Shortly after this time, in addition to John Wilson in the established political post of APA North Waziristan, there were four other military officers temporarily seconded to Political posts in North Waziristan as Khassadar officers. It will be recalled that when I was in the agency, there was one such officer, Brian Becker, stationed at Dosali.

CHAPTER XII

Deepening Crisis

Barbara got home from hospital with the baby just in time for Christmas. The decision to take formal proceedings to enquire into the events at Malakand during Nehru's visit was being taken at the same time. The Secretary of the Home Department of the NWFP Government was sent to Malakand to inform Sheikh Mahboob Ali that he had been suspended from duty. The Home Secretary was Colonel Evelyn Cobb who had returned to the Frontier not long before, from Gilgit. He was an extraordinarily loquacious man about whose eccentricities stories were legion. Just before the War he had been DC Bannu, and deeply entangled in the case of Islam Bibi, which launched the Faqir of Ipi on his hostile path. Cobb's instructions from the Governor were to stay in Malakand as PA having relieved the sheikh of his post. On the same day, 8 January 1947, I was appointed to succeed him as Secretary, Home Department. This was very flattering. I was at least ten years too junior to qualify in normal times for a post of such seniority. It entitled me to a senior scale of pay and to the tenancy of the Home Secretary's bungalow at No. 3 North Circular Road – both perquisites being highly acceptable. Barbara bravely faced up to moving house before she had got properly on her feet again.

With the bungalow we took over Evelyn Cobb's paying guest, a bachelor PWD officer, Major Charles Gordon Caffin, who had only recently returned to civilian duty on the Frontier after some years with the Royal Engineers in Persia and the Middle East. Unlike Evelyn Cobb, he was a taciturn, shy man, but he had an amusing sense of humour and a nice nose for gossip. We quickly became good friends – and kept regularly in touch for many years until he died. We enjoyed his company at North Circular Road. The bungalow was big enough for a tactful man like Caffin to be able to avoid intruding on our privacy, and he was tolerant of the baby, of whom he seemed to become just as proud as we were. On the Sunday of her christening we gave a party for our many friends, and Caffin presided benevolently over the dispensing of the drinks – but failed to alert me to the mass attack on the food supplies organized by some of the attendant children. Their raids left the tables bare so that we had no way of sobering their carefree parents. My new duties absorbed me for a time, but such was my innocent confidence that they seemed lighter and less onerous than anything I had hitherto had to tackle. After a week or two I was quite blasé about writing orders on the appeals of convicted murderers who sought redress from the Privy Council. The sense of responsibility was great, but the amount of paperwork was easily manageable and its intellectual demands seemed light. I began to labour under the delusion that the higher one climbed up the ladder the easier life became. The work has left no sharp impression on my memory; it seems to have been largely routine. It may be that the office was quiet because the Ministry was so preoccupied with other things that they had no time for legislation. I was office-bound and in some danger of becoming bored, but in the middle of February I contrived a good reason for an outing to Mardan that brought me into direct contact with the dramatic political events that were developing in the Frontier as in other parts of India in that fateful year.

It was the day for declaration of the results in an important by-election, in one of the most sensitive constituencies in the province. As Secretary, Home Department, I had both the right and the duty to see that the District authorities were operating the electoral procedures in a proper manner – I had no serious anxiety about this; since Leeper had been moved, the district had been in efficient hands, first under Gerald Curtis, and then, since mid-January, under another old friend, John Steward. In the provincial elections a year earlier, the Muslim League had won the seat with a majority of 169 out of a poll of 16,539 votes. Both parties were desperate to win the by-election at this crucial period in Indian affairs. The campaign was fought on the straight issue of the League for Pakistan, the Congress for Akhund Hindustan. The League had recently formed a Provincial 'War Committee' under the leadership of the revered young Pir of Manki. Across the Indus in Hazara, there had been two months of violent communal disturbance, spreading across the district in a trail of arson and murder after raids in December 1946 by Black Mountain tribesmen on the Hindu traders in border markets round Baffa and Oghi. An army division was engaged there in support of the police and Frontier Constabulary, but in the bad weather of January it had been difficult to bring force to bear on the tribes.

The Congress Ministry had promulgated a Public Safety Ordinance which provoked the League to despicable tactics – blaming the Hindus and Sikhs for causing the troubles by black marketing, urging offenders to refuse to pay fines, and calling for *mujahiddin* to rise in opposition to the authorities – in other words, to fight a holy war. The Pir of Manki had postponed action on this call until the results of the Mardan by-election were known. During polling, at a station reserved for women voters, the wife of Yahya Jan, one of the ministers, had cause to feel that the vote was going against Congress while there was still a queue of women and half an hour to go before polling ended. She took her own direct action to stem defeat, adopting the simple tactic of sitting on the ballot box and refusing to budge, challenging the presiding officers and police to shift her bodily and incur the wrath of men and women onlookers alike, for in Pathan society to lay hands on a woman in a public place is a serious breach of the code, and a cause of great shame. This vigorous lady was a daughter of no less a champion of democracy than Abdul Ghaffar Khan, the Prime Minister's brother, so the officials present decided they had better phone Peshawar for orders, by which time the hour had come to close the polling station. So I felt justified in being present in the *Tahsil* in Mardan when counting was being done and the result declared.

Looking down on the scene from an upper room I formed a very clear impression of impending danger. The crowd milling round the *Tahsil* building numbered many hundreds, and the police seemed to have no control. Yet the people had made way for me, allowing me to enter the building without difficulty. From my vantage point above I secured a couple of memorable snapshots of this potentially explosive scene. In a way it was an exhilarating sight, for here was a free people who had been voting for their future; it was also frightening. But there was no outbreak of violence, though Mardan was one of the main centres for the Red Shirt movement inspired by Abdul Ghaffar Khan, and some of its leading landowners were now prominent in the Muslim League organization. In a total poll of 17,294 votes, the League had a majority of 558. A year earlier they had failed to convince the

Pathan voters that a vote for Congress meant a vote for Hindu-controlled India. Now it was clear that Abdul Ghaffar had lost ground, with his argument that Pathans could control their own destiny in an alignment with Hindustan, whereas within a Pakistan grouping they would be exploited and abused by the Punjabi majority.[1]

By the date of this by-election the normal *party-bazi* or faction-fighting of Frontier politics had become less significant than the blatant communalism fed by events in the rest of India. Most of the Frontier people were characteristically Pakhtun first, Muslim second; pride in their ethnic separateness kept religious fanaticism in place. Now there was a reaction to the killing of Muslims in Bengal, Bihar and Bombay – especially in Bombay, where many Pathans had flourished on the strength of their violent ways and keen nose for business, and had to pay the penalty. Communal violence had crept nearer the north-west and threatened to reduce the Punjab to chaos. In Hazara already some 150 Hindus and Sikhs had been killed. In the peaceful Galis there were some pockets of Sikh cultivators settled in their own villages, where they had lived amongst the Muslims of the region at peace since the days of Sikh rule a century earlier. Now they were burned alive in their own homes with their women and children in appalling acts of mass arson, committed by the very *zamindars* amongst whom I had toured so happily between 1941 and 1943. Some of those responsible regularly served European families in their summer bungalows.

A Sikh woman who was pregnant was abducted by a Hazara Muslim. Dr Khan Sahib, the Chief Minister, courageously intervened and brought her to the protection of his own home in Peshawar. There she swore before the District Magistrate that she wanted to rejoin her Sikh people and that her alleged conversion to Islam had been forcible. It was widely rumoured that this was false and that it was the Chief Minister himself who was coercing her to rejoin the Sikh community. Undaunted, he called in Abdul Qayum and other League leaders to hear her testimony and they were persuaded. But shortly afterwards Qayum was arrested in Mardan, a day or two after the by-election. The DC had given him permission to address a crowd gathered in defiance of an order under section 144 of the Criminal Procedure Code, on the understanding that he would direct it to disperse peacefully. Instead he urged the mob to defy the Government. His arrest was the signal for the start of the new phase of Direct Action for which the Frontier Muslim League Provincial War Council was formed on 20 February 1947 – the very day on which the British Prime Minister announced in Parliament that there would be a transfer of power no later than June 1948. On 24 February a hostile mob of several thousands penetrated the garden of the Chief Minister's residence in Peshawar cantonment, just opposite Government House. The crowd's objective was to 'free' the Sikh woman from Hazara forcibly converted to Islam, whom Dr Khan Sahib was sheltering. It was dispersed with tear gas, having first been halted by the defiant imprecations of Khan Sahib's cockney wife, for whom we all felt unbounded admiration. A new and desperately dangerous phase of civil disobedience had begun. Although both the Deputy Commissioner and the Senior Superintendent of Police were present, the police had not carried out an order to fire on the crowd threatening the Chief Minister.

The following Sunday morning the Chief Secretary, Dudley de la Fargue, called on us at No. 3 North Circular Road and over a drink in the garden told me that I was to be Joint Deputy Commissioner, Peshawar. I was none too pleased. In place of my rather grandiose status as independent Secretary in charge of the Home Department, I would not be an independent DC and though the term 'Joint' implied equality and more authority than the less unusual term 'Additional DC' the office of DC Peshawar was historically so important and prestigious that I knew perfectly well that I would have to take my orders from its incumbent. It was not that which really worried me, however – it was Dudley's direction that I was to do the normal administrative work of the DC and run his office and court in order to free him to cope with the civil disobedience campaign. That sounded dull and frustrating. In the event, over the next ten weeks I was just as heavily embroiled in problems of law and order as the DC himself, and very little 'normal' administration or court work was done before the middle of May.

The main reason for this was simply the press of events. We were not dealing with occasional isolated happenings, but with a rushing torrent of disturbances in which there was no time for ordinary business. Moreover, the Governor himself put a strange gloss on the Chief Secretary's guideline. Shortly after my new task began I was very surprised when I answered the phone at home one lunch hour to find Sir Olaf himself speaking. As if to reassure me that he had not demoted me, he said in the most confidential tones and only slightly guarded phrases that he was relying on me to keep a careful eye on what was going on, and particularly on what the DC got up to. He inferred that I was to let him personally know if I felt uneasy. When his brief message ended I put the phone down feeling very astonished. Caroe had always been kind and encouraging, but I had never had the sort of man-to-man frank conversation with him which had been so characteristic of Sir George Cunningham. What he had now said seemed to assume an intimate rapport between us that he had done nothing to create. Instinctively I felt that I had been given an instruction on the telephone that should only have been hinted at delicately, if at all, in a personal confidential interview. I was left with an uneasy feeling which I could not rationally have explained that the Governor was jittery, or at least more unsure of himself than he should have allowed a junior officer to infer.

As the weeks went by I began to understand his purpose more clearly and to appreciate the mysterious way in which he had hinted at it. The Deputy Commissioner was Major A.S.B. Shah (Aga Syed Badshah Shah) a political officer who had recently come from the post of Counsellor in the Embassy at Kabul, to succeed Johnny Dring. Dring's departure to Baluchistan had been disturbing. For months, in 1946, he had been criticized and indeed publicly attacked by ministers who alleged that he favoured the Muslim League and was actively helping them. This was a charge which the Congress Party levied fairly generally against British officers in the Frontier, but the accusations against Dring were particularly nasty. He was an old cavalry officer, Master of the Peshawar Vale Hunt, and just the type to get on well with the landlords whom Congress leaders despised, but he was a fine officer, very experienced in Frontier affairs, and I was only one of many British officers who were very uneasy at the notion that the Ministry could undermine him and get him removed. The climax came when he refused to drop a case which the Chief Minister wanted to withdraw from his court, probably to have it dealt with under Frontier Crimes Regulations. Dring rightly made an issue of this for an important principle was involved if ministers could readily interfere with the judicial process and the course of justice. There had been far too much of this in the whole province over the last year. Sir Olaf Caroe backed Dring, but he was transferred – apparently at his own request for he felt that his usefulness in

NWFP was bound to be impaired. He had recently remarried, and understandably may have wanted to get away from this kind of political *taqleef.*

I hardly knew the new DC although he had been an agreeable landlord and neighbour for about six weeks before we moved from 12a The Mall to 3 North Circular Road. He was one of the earliest Sandhurst-trained Indians to join the Political Service – the most famous of course was Iskander Mirza,[2] Dring's predecessor who had also left under a cloud, despite Sir George Cunningham's close friendship, after quarrelling with Aurangzeb, and being altogether too mixed up in Muslim League affairs. Shah was a member of a respected Peshawari family of Shia Muslims. At school and college he had been friendly with many of the men who were now prominent in the professional and political life of the district – indeed of the whole Province. Although all his recent service had been away from the Frontier, in Kabul he had been well placed to see how things were developing, and I was to find that he had mysterious sources of information which would never have been open to a European officer in the DC's post at that time. His relationship with me was pleasant and congenial, though he could be moody and sardonic with other colleagues. He was always readily accessible, but that did not mean that he was always frankly communicative. There were times when it was not easy to read his mind or follow his intentions. For three months he was under almost intolerable strain and I feel that he deserves much credit for the fact that Peshawar, the cauldron of the Frontier, suffered far less than many other places in north India from pillage and killing at such a critical period. The breakdown in law and order was serious, at times alarming, but considering the political issues at stake it might have been much worse. The events of 1930 and 1931 had shown what we might expect. The DC set himself to prevent that happening and he succeeded remarkably well.

The pot began to boil over in the last week of February. On 3 March, after a week of trouble in the city, Shah set down his thoughts and objectives in a six-page memorandum of which I have a copy. His object was to reassert the authority of Government and prevent 'political bodies from resorting to lawlessness while airing grievances against the Government of the day'. So far, he had not been wholly successful, because of the scale and the strength of purpose of the Muslim League's campaign of civil disobedience, reinforced by the repercussions of events outside the Frontier, and now increasingly attracting support from the tribal areas, in which the Pir of Manki had begun to stir a new interest in the political affairs of the province and of India. The worst handicap for the district authorities was the development of extremely bitter communal feelings. In dealing with the Congress 'Quit India' disturbances in 1942, the Frontier police had not had that handicap. Now, whenever a lathi charge was launched on a crowd of demonstrators, Hindus and Sikhs were attacked elsewhere in the city – there had been about twelve of these occurrences each leading to a crop of stabbings and arson. The police could not be everywhere, and must be reinforced, because they were becoming exhausted. They were not even adequately fed during long hours on active duty.

During the critical first three days of the trouble the military had acted helpfully and effectively in aid of the civil power, keeping the outskirts of the city and its suburbs, and the approaches to the cantonment, clear of demonstrators, but there was a limit to their usefulness and their ability to help in circumstances of general unrest. The Army was properly unwilling to be called in unless there was a specific job for them to do. So after three days they had withdrawn, leaving the police to cope, although they stood by to help on a Friday when trouble was always likely to break out after the special Friday prayers in the mosques. On that day, in particular, large crowds from the rural areas and even from tribal territory were likely to be in the city.

The DC did not shirk from calling on the Congress Government to respect and make allowances for the criticisms and grievances of the people and to take 'initiatives towards clemency and reconciliation'. He called courageously for a willingness to participate in open discussion – if only to 'allay the doubts and suspicions of those who are levelling unworthy and ill-founded charges against Government'. It must have been a difficult document to draft in the circumstances – and events were soon to show how empty an exercise it had been. I have pencilled notes of a meeting of senior officers held to review the happenings on the following Friday, 7 March. Those present, besides the DC and myself, were the Senior Superintendent of Police (SSP), the PA Khyber Agency, the City Magistrate, the Assistant Inspector of Police (in charge of training) and the Deputy Superintendents in charge respectively of the City Police and the force of Additional Police based in the district (DSP City and DSP AP). The SSP was a key figure throughout these months. He was Sardar Abdur Rashid, an exceptionally bright police officer, not many years older than myself, who in the first phase of independent Pakistan had an outstanding career, becoming a senior minister in West Pakistan, and Chief Minister in NWFP, before disappearing from the active stage in the upheavals that are endemic in the faction-fighting of Pakistan's politics. By coincidence, the City Magistrate's name was also Abdur Rashid Khan. He was a competent, hard-working civil servant, whose temperament was put to severe test in these tempestuous weeks.

The notes of our meeting are an interesting illustration of such occasions which occurred fairly regularly. The SSP began by reporting on the afternoon's processions in the city. At three places they had broken through cordons of police by adopting new tactics, namely suddenly charging without warning at the line of policemen. Although their numbers seemed smaller than on the Friday before, Rashid judged their temper to be higher, and he believed that the communal tension had become worse with news of the awful events in the Punjab. The Deputy Commissioner concluded that we must concentrate now on preventing further deterioration of the communal situation. The police no longer had the strength to cope with the purely political aspects of the unrest. They should not now try to interfere with processions, although the Government had required orders under section 144 Criminal Procedure Code – prohibiting assemblies – to be strictly enforced. Instead, the police should concentrate in three main groups, to protect the Hindu-Sikh *mohallahs* in Indershahr, Chowk Yadghar and the police B Division area. Reserves were to be held at A Division police station, and on the railway bridge between the city and the cantonment to deal with any crowds that emerged from the city and tried to get into the cantonment. Generally the police were to carry *lathis* (long poles) which was the usual weapon for dealing with unruly crowds, but maximum force, including firearms, was to be used without delay against anyone seen to be looting or attempting arson, or molesting Hindus or Sikhs. There was some argument about the use of Frontier Constabulary – who the DC wanted to take up this latter role. The FC were trained to operate, not in cities, but along the administrative border, pursuing gangs of tribal raiders, smugglers or outlaws from the settled districts. They were highly mobile, and more akin to the trans-border militias like the Tochi Scouts, than to the regular police.

When I questioned the wisdom of letting them loose in the city in the role described by Shah, he snapped peevishly, 'What does the taxpayer maintain the FC for, if I can't use them in this emergency?' Both the DSPs ventured to agree with my view and for the present it was decided not to bring the FC in with such specific instructions.

We also discussed ways of trying to reduce ingress to the city on Fridays, for it was after Friday prayers in the mosques that Muslim tempers were on their shortest fuse. It was suggested that we should: close the shops of all communities; stop the cattle fair which was held on the Grand Trunk Road a short distance out beyond a well-known warehouse; close all Government offices inside the city, like the Tahsil, the courts of the Tahsildar and Naib-Tahsildars; and simply prohibit all entry through the city's numerous gates after the start of Friday prayers. I was very nervous about most of these suggestions, opposing them partly because they would interfere with the legitimate business of many people and would cause more bad temper and fuel the rising tide of criticism of the Congress Ministry. The idea of closing shops reminded me of the notorious August public holiday which had been declared in Calcutta in 1946 and had left too many malcontents of both communities with too much time on their hands, leading to the awful Calcutta killings which had marked the earliest worsening of the communal situation after the failure of the Cabinet Mission. In my view, the best policy was so far as possible to allow business as usual, and try to protect the minorities.

A note written that evening after the meeting shows what my thoughts were.

The signs are that the spread of communal rioting in Punjab has definitely made our dangerous situation extremely delicate. I agree that we must concentrate on preventing actual communal rioting rather than on mere political demonstrations, if our police are really stretched. Are they? It is now again almost too late to put force to the test. On the whole, I think that up to date it has been wise to use force so judiciously, in fighting against a legitimate political cause, albeit one using illegal methods. But for this argument to be correct it is essential to get set in motion efforts at a settlement. Almost any attempt to negotiate would do, but in the absence of such an attempt the odds are heavily against a preservation of 'peace'. The move at this stage must come from the strong side –

i.e. Government. The difficulties are obvious to the leaders (on both sides). We must use the dangers of the Punjab troubles as a lever of persuasion on our Ministers – but we must also find new leaders on the other side who can negotiate decently.

The leadership might also have come from the Centre, as it was to do six weeks later. But for the moment the new Viceroy had not had time to assert his initiative, and it was near the end of April before he got Gandhi and Jinnah to agree on a joint appeal to their communities to desist from violence. In the Frontier, in the meantime, Dr Khan Sahib and his colleagues fulminated against the Governor and all his officers, the Governor kept sending ominous and despairing messages to Delhi but seemed to us on the spot to be floundering helplessly in face of unfair attacks on his hard-pressed colleagues. Every day the risks of open intervention by the Red Shirts as a sort of private pro-Government army seemed to grow, and the evidence was not lacking that the Muslim League would be ready for them. Under the Minister's orders, more and more decent Muslim League members were arrested and detained. It was becoming an urgent duty for honourable men to acquire the mark of political martyrdom, the badge of imprisonment in the cause of Pakistan. My respected friend, Ghulam Haider Khan of Sherpao, who had helped so much with the weekend parties of British soldiers and airmen in Sir George Cunningham's day, came to me one day with tears in his eyes and said his turn had come; he must be arrested tomorrow. Yet the scheming went on underground, in secret, working steadily towards a deadly climax.

Almost daily there were episodes in the progress of the campaign, and regularly, at least once a week – not always on a Friday – there was a major incident. The first of them, on 10 March, only three days after the meeting I have been recording, proved to have a symbolic influence on the civil disobedience campaign. It was the day of the Budget debate in the Legislative Assembly. The Assembly building was in a triangle of ground at the edge of the cantonment. The apex of the triangle was a junction on the Grand Trunk Road, one leg of which continued through the cantonment along North Circular Road past the military lines towards the aerodrome and Islamia College. The other leg of the road turned parallel to the railway, on the cantonment side, and ran up the hill past the Secretariat and the jail towards the Cantonment Railway Station. Not far from the jail it was joined by another main road which ran outside the city wall and linked the main exits from the city to the civil secretariat part of the cantonment by a bridge over the railway. Back at the junction near the Assembly building, the trunk road from the Punjab passed under the railway, having on its left skirted the city's eastern wall and the old Sikh fort, Bala Hissar, and on its right a large and beautiful public garden, the Cunningham Bagh. The railway was carried on a long embankment for several hundred yards, well clear of any buildings. The rail bridge over the road had a parapet from which there was a clear view over the Cunningham Garden, down the trunk road, over to the old fort, and up towards the city and the Lady Reading Hospital. Behind was the Assembly Building, a couple of hundred yards away, beyond the barbed-wire barricade of the cantonment.

The Muslim League declared that they intended to picket and interrupt the Budget Session of the Assembly. The Ministry directed the Deputy Commissioner to prevent this – there was on no account to be a repetition of the incursion of 21 February when armed demonstrators had invaded the cantonment and the Chief Minister's garden. Given the mood of the people and the dispositions which the DC had to make to fulfil the ministers' orders, the stage was set for a major trial of force. The military were available to back up the police – a whole company of infantry was posted near the Assembly building. I had at my disposal a subaltern in command of a jeep with driver and signaller with a wireless set. We did not of course know from which direction a procession might march towards the Assembly. It might cross the railway near the jail, perhaps branching off towards the Secretariat, or Government House, or the Chief Minister's residence. Or it might come under the railway by the Grand Trunk Road.

Magistrates had been posted at several important points. We were well aware that on this day the order to fire might have to be given. On the main bridge over the road I found my old Miranshah friend and colleague, the fat and cherubic Mohammed Jan, now an Extra Assistant Commissioner in Peshawar. I knew of nobody more staunch and steadfast, or more reliable in judgment, among the young political officers of the provincial service. He was not, however, in his usual cheerful mood. When I asked what was wrong and whether he was unwell, he begged me to move aside with him. As we walked alone he dissolved into tears, confessing that if the worst happened he knew he would not bring himself to require the Army to fire. The victims would be innocent demonstrators – people he knew and loved. It was quite different from Waziristan, where the tribesmen expected us to trade violence for violence, and deserved whatever they got in open battle. I am afraid that I was soft, as I do not think I would have been with any other junior officer; but Mohammed Jan was a well-tried friend. I said that I would relieve him early, certainly at the first sign of trouble in his sector, and that whatever happened I would stand by him. I do not think I could have said less. If I had been tough with him, I suspected – knowing him – that he would openly refuse to cooperate, and that I would be unable to protect him from ministerial wrath.

In the event the trouble came, not long after, from the other direction. Not along the Grand Trunk Road, but – to our surprise – along the railway line, from the direction of the City Station. The crowd no doubt had clambered up on to the line from the far reaches of the Cunningham Garden, which with its trees and shrubs provided a good deal of cover. At that point the magistrate on duty was Abdul Rashid, the City Magistrate – senior to Mohammed Jan. As the crowd advanced, police officers went forward and warned them to halt. Soon they pressed forward again. The time came for the magistrate to intervene with a clear warning. There had been a clash with the police, and stones had been thrown – the ballast on the embanked line provided ample ammunition. The stage had been well chosen for it could be viewed from a distance by plenty of spectators who did not wish personally to get involved. The City Magistrate became very nervous and I went forward with him in a final attempt to harangue the crowd and dissuade them from advancing. They were warned that the soldiers would fire if they crossed a line which we indicated clearly behind us. I remember being shaken to see in the front ranks a number of young students from Islamia College. Amongst them was an agitator from the Punjab who had been reported by police intelligence sources as very active at the College and in other potential trouble spots.[3] There were several others near the front whom police officers identified to us as active troublemakers. Suddenly there was a rush and a hail of stones before which Rashid and I beat a hasty retreat. The crowd stopped, not far short of the forbidden line, and I went back to the jeep, fifty yards away on the roadside, to send a report to the DC. When I got back to the line the company commander told me that he was having trouble in getting Rashid to sign his card. Rashid was standing some distance away, his head down, the picture of wretched misery. There was no escape: I told the officer that I would sign the card authorising him to disperse the demonstrators. He filled it in – and the duplicate for the Magistrate, which I still have. It reads:

> I, F. Noble Esq. IC.S. Joint District Magistrate of Peshawar, acting under Section 130 of the Code of Criminal Procedure, required No: A11150 Rank: Capt. Name: J.G. Collins of the 'D.' Coy Unit 1st B[ln] The Royal Garhwal Rifles to disperse an unlawful assembly at 09.40 o'clock (approximately) on the tenth day of March 1947 at Peshawar.

Countersigned by J.G. Collins, Capt, my signature, inscribed with a very nervous hand on a military notebook, is clumsy and barely decipherable. Underneath, more firmly and clearly, I had written '09.40 hours'.

Four sepoys moved forward to within twenty paces of the forbidden line, and took up firing positions and waited. The crowd wavered and I thought they were going to retreat. Suddenly more stones were thrown, and there was a rush forward – not from the front ranks but from further back. Four shots were fired on command;[4] an extraordinary silence followed; for several seconds the scene seemed to freeze; then a backward movement started and in a minute the line was clear, except for some men carrying others behind the running mob. All the shots had struck low, below the knee as the manual prescribes. But at that range, the damage was severe. Two of those who were hit subsequently died. As Mohammed Jan had foreseen, they were elderly *zamindars*, not active political agitators, who had probably come into town for the *tamasha*. The mob's leaders had discreetly melted away when the soldiers took up firing positions, perhaps to cast the stones that caused the crucial last flurry of movement over the line. Thankfully, the young students also had retreated or turned aside.

I was too busy at first to feel unduly concerned, relieved that the threat to the Assembly had been repelled, as the Ministers had ordered, but preoccupied by the inevitable consequences that followed at once in the city – looting and burning of Hindu property, and stabbing and beating of anyo e who looked as if he might not be Muslim. But the horror of the experience stayed with me, for the order to shoot had been given, not to stop a communal riot, but to save the face of an unpopular Ministry and to fulfil their expressed instructions. I did not find it easy to argue with myself that if we had stood aside and let the crowd advance, more men would have died at the gates of the Assembly, perhaps even some of the elected representatives of the people.

In the tense weeks that followed the Army was active in aid of the civil power in Peshawar. But that was the only instance when its firepower was brought to bear. There was an irony in that, for the Royal Garwhal Rifles was the regiment which had refused to obey an order to fire at the very start of the 1930 riots in the city, and consequently there had been months of martial law and administrative chaos throughout the district. In 1947 the regiment did its duty with economic efficiency and may have saved a great deal of bloodshed in consequence. Though there were days and weeks of at least night curfew in the city and tear gas had to be used frequently by the police, the army patrols were not challenged, and their coordination with police activity was a superb demonstration of fine planning and first-class training.

Best of all at this job were the British regiments. During the worst period we had a battalion of KOSB (King's Own Scottish Borderers) frequently in the city, and it was a joy to watch their platoons cheerfully clear a street of potential troublemakers just by the perfection of their well-drilled movements. The battalion had had a long and arduous campaign in Burma. Their CO (Lieutenant Colonel Payton-Reid) had won a DSO at Arnhem so they could have been excused for longing for demobilization and Blighty. But they rather enjoyed exploring the narrow lanes of Peshawar and they won the approval of keen Pathan eyes, always quick to appraise good soldiering. The Peshawaris decided that they had no quarrel with the British and equally treated the Indian battalions of the brigade with respect. It is worth mentioning that I personally was able to walk about the city fairly freely, without special escort. I owned a service revolver but I never carried it. To have done so would have shown insecurity and tempted someone in a crowd to take it from me and shoot me with it – or use it against his communal enemies. The streets were usually crowded and I found it far more helpful to carry a heavy walking-stick, cut from Himalayan oak, very thick and hard at the end, so that just a gentle swing as I walked ensured that anyone jostling me moved smartly aside to save his shins.

The cooperation of the army staff was magnificent. The Brigade

Commander was H.E. Cubitt-Smith, a Frontier Force officer with much experience, calm and steady as a rock and very tolerant of my fussy requests. When I sometimes felt lost in an alien world of mysterious politics, I found his friendly sympathy a source of reassurance. It was part of my regular duties to convey to him the wishes of the DC for the following day, to interpret the political situation, explain the police dispositions and to arrange the magistrates local postings and 'shifts' whenever trouble calling for military help was anticipated. One evening, after several tense days, when I called in on the DC for our usual conference he dismissed me quickly, but without explanation, saying only that he would make no request for military help next day. It was time they had a day off and he and the SSP were going out shooting game birds.

An hour or so later I felt very uneasy. I had had no report of a change in the situation. I saw the Brigadier: he agreed with me that we could not afford to take risks and said that he would issue orders for a battalion to be available at locations we agreed. Later still I rang the SSP, and quizzed him about the shooting expedition, hinting that I thought it was a poor show that they should plan to be absent without making any preparation for the sort of contingency that had been preoccupying us. He was astonished that the DC had not told me the reason. He had agreed with the Muslim League War Council that everyone was tired and in need of a break; in reply, they had promised a whole day of peace. But Shah had not disclosed these machinations to me. I went to the Brigadier to explain and apologize. He saved me any further embarrassment by his straightforward reactions, expressed as pungently as always, and by reassuring me that 'notwithstanding' the DC's contrivance, the Army would be ready to back me up if any trouble did break out. The next day was entirely quiet. I realized that I still had a lot to learn and that perhaps Sir Olaf Caroe had been right when he told me he wanted me to keep an eye on what the DC got up to.

An interesting aspect of the civil disobedience movement was the part increasingly played in it by Muslim women. Participation by women in public events was in those days anathema in Islamic eyes; but some of the educated women had begun to want to play their part and apparently groups had been preparing for this for some time. Perhaps the male activists wanted physical relief from daily demonstrations and conceded occasional days when it would be the womens' turn to keep the police on their toes. The first time they marched over the railway bridge towards the cantonment provided the police with a tormenting test. They closed every possible gate and pulled barbed-wire barricades across the path of the marching women whose features were of course hidden by their all-enveiling *burqas*. But determined women found ways through and round the barricades and the police became helpless, for they were unable to lay hands on their female tormentors. After this first trial the women were emboldened to go for specific objectives. The first was the cantonment railway station where they quickly exploited the normal state of chaos on the crowded platforms and for a time prevented any trains from moving. This so exasperated the pious DC that he instructed the police to turn hosepipes on the women if they were afraid to push them back or use their *lathis* on them. After a rather half-hearted onslaught on them with water, they withdrew, furious at the unfair tactics of the authorities, and proclaiming that these tactics were as serious a violation of their modesty as if they had been manhandled personally like male demonstrators.

A day or two later their objective was the Civil Secretariat. Once again they brushed aside the large body of policemen guarding the entrance gates and flooded over the gardens and courtyards into the corridors and verandahs of all the different offices. I had just been informed of their arrival when I got a petulant and somewhat worried call from Mehr Chand Khanna, the Finance Minister, who was locked in his office and demanded that I should do something about it. I could hear the shrill cries of the demonstrators as he spoke on his telephone. My office was well over a mile away so I got on my autocycle and proceeded to the rescue. At the Secretariat gates I found the police mustered in force, but looking helplessly inward, instead of to the outer world. Their officers, however, had been sensible enough to ensure that none of the Muslim League men – who invariably escorted their womenfolk on these adventures – had been allowed past the gates. Feeling that a European officer was safer from attack by these Amazons than any Pathan policeman, I felt brave enough to walk through the crowd towards the Minister's office. Most of the women, in fact, were resting from their exertions, huddled in the garden and roadways like large flocks of broody hens crouching in characteristic posture on their heels, almost the only movement throughout the massed ranks of little white tents being the nodding of the tiny little hard tops of each *burqa* as one head chattered through a little barred vent in the cloth to its neighbour. It was a comical sight and as I reached the verandah I was grinning and chuckling in a manner not at all appropriate in such a serious situation.

Perhaps that explains, if it does not excuse, what followed. On the verandah there was a busy group, not crouched, but standing round a ladder. I realized that there was a lady on the ladder and, looking up, discovered another on the roof. Surprised, I called, in English, 'What on earth are you doing up there?'

Instantly the reply came – in impeccable English – 'We, the women of free Pakistan are raising the flag of our country!' I suddenly realized that the Union Jack, which normally flew above the Secretariat, had come down.

Without pausing to think, I called up, 'Do you require my help?' 'No thank you!'

'Very well,' I said, 'I will leave you while I go to see the Minister, if you will promise me that when you come down the ladder you will march away with all these ladies. Otherwise I shall have to take the ladder away and leave you up there indefinitely.'

The promise was given at once, and without delay I went along the corridor and knocked on Mehr Chand's door. When he let me in, he was in an uncertain mood. He was angry and irritated by the noise and threat of the demonstration, and by the fact that nobody had stopped the crowd from getting to his door. Almost certainly he was at least a little frightened. I think he was quite a brave man; he was assuredly a very intelligent one, and he was acutely aware of the communal tension and the high risks of his personal position. There was clearly danger in a situation where a cloaked and anonymous figure, unidentifiable afterwards, might produce a knife or even a revolver in the rage of religious fanaticism. And if the women were there in such numbers, how was Mehr Chand to know that the police had managed to keep their menfolk out of range?

But I was still light-hearted with the humorous side of the incident, and gaily told him that his worries were over, for soon they would all be marching away. When I explained about the flag, he affected to be furious, but I could not take that seriously either, for he too belonged to a political party which had long sworn to pull down the Union Jack, and often used much more violent tactics to attack it.

'But how can you trust them to do what they have promised?' he demanded.

'I accepted the word of a lady,' I replied. I would have been hard put to it if he had asked me to justify my belief that the leader was a lady.

I suppose some instinct had told me that she must be, to have engaged in such a conversation on the instant in such circumstances – and in English too, albeit in quite sharp and querulous tones. At any rate, within five minutes, the women were all gone; Mehr Chand had nothing more to say. In no time at all the Union Jack was back at the top of the pole. But in tribute to the women's enterprise, I ordered the police to allow the other flag to fly for the rest of the afternoon. If I had been a military officer, I might have been cashiered. But I heard no more about the matter, either from the Congress Ministry, or from the Chief Secretary or the Governor. As for the DC, I suspected that he was glad not to have had to face the women himself. He would have been tempted to turn the hosepipes on them.

I was lucky that day, and so were the Muslim League women activists. Weeks later I discovered that the lady on the roof had been Begum Kamalud-din, a well-to-do emancipated widow who had been prominent in the social life of the Bedi circle in Abbottabad. She had the advantage over me because I had no hope of identifying her from her voice, while she could identify me both by sight and by voice, for I do not suppose she had met many European officers with a northern Scots accent. It was reported that her companion on the ladder was Begum Firoz Khan Noon, wife of the distinguished politician who had been for long a member of the Viceroy's Executive Council. He was now a committed proponent of the cause of Pakistan, but unhappy about direct action and the trend towards lawlessness, and he was left with less immediate influence over the policies of the League than his wife had in the development of the women's movement.[5]

The women were not so lucky another day when so far as I know neither of the ladies I have named was present. On 14 April a procession of women, accompanied by a considerable escort of men, left the city for the spot on the railway line near the Assembly building which marked the martyrdom of the victims of the shooting on 10 March. Crouching on the line, they stayed immobile while the Bombay Express ran downhill towards them. They assumed that the train would stop because they were there.

The driver, a Hindu, not unnaturally thought that human beings would give way to the train – after all, the sacred cow unfailingly did – and only at the last moment applied the brakes. In fact, he had been travelling quite slowly, but even so his engine passed the spot where most of the women were congregated before it stopped. Had the train been moving even a little faster, the accident would have been disastrous. As it was, several were hurt, some badly, one very seriously; but nobody was killed. The evidence showed that probably only one woman had been struck by the engine. Most of the rest were injured by falls as they flung themselves aside on the steep embankment amidst the stony ballast of the track. The spectators at once bombarded the train with stones. The driver started up again, but somebody pulled the communications cord. Fortunately for the passengers it was the driver that the enraged crowd was after. He escaped by luck, scrambling down the other side of the bank, snatching a bicycle and pedalling furiously to the city railway station, where a kindly railway policeman locked him in a lamproom and told the pursuit that he had escaped in a train. The crowd's wrath turned inevitably to the city where shops were burned and Hindus stabbed. An hour or two later, while the DC and I were busy on the aftermath, word reached us that the driver had been brought secretly to a little police station in the cantonment not far from my home in North Circular Road, and I was sent to take a statement from him. Next day, I was appointed special magistrate to conduct an enquiry into the whole episode.

I laboured on this for several days, examining a large number of witnesses, seeking to establish why the train had been allowed to start – when police officers and the City Magistrate had been on the spot when the women's intention to squat indefinitely on the line had become apparent – and whether the Hindu driver should be charged, as the League demanded, with attempted murder and various other offences. I took part in a dramatic reconstruction of the incident, riding in the cab of the engine of a goods train while policemen wearing white sheets enacted the part of the women, and others took the places and imitated the actions of spectators – including the police officers and magistrates who had tried to 'wave down' the oncoming Bombay Express. The injured women in hospital declined to cooperate by giving formal evidence, though I did get from them some insight into their view of the affair.

The magisterial enquiry presented me with considerable

problems, not least because of the speed with which it had to be carried out in an atmosphere of tense public excitement. Both political parties were anxious to secure maximum advantage from my findings. I was anxious only to elucidate the truth in establishing the causes of the accident and allocating responsibility or blame. I spent four days examining twenty-nine witnesses, some of whom had to be re-examined later as the details of the story were filled out. The evidence ran to sixty pages of typescript, and there were nineteen pages of exhibits, including formal answers to specific questions put to an expert of the North-West Railway. My final report, which ran to about 8,000 words, almost certainly pleased nobody of importance. The train driver was exonerated, the organizers of the demonstration were criticized, and a number of officials were probably embarrassed by comments on their failure to prevent the accident. As I proceeded with my task, my despair about the Indian situation grew. In itself the enquiry was important: but its true significance was submerged in the thorny thickets of the political struggle – and public interest ceased as soon as it was realized that my findings would not contribute to the cause of either party. That was quite a healthy lesson for me, for at the start my inflated ego had imagined my investigation to be central to the course of the political struggle. After all, in Peshawar its public focus had been on that railway embankment since the riot of 10 March, and the accident to the women was inflicted by a train which was seen as an instrument of Government whose operations the League wanted to halt. There was an intriguing symbolism about the affair which it became my duty to shatter. But in doing so, I felt deflated. Even as I worked on the report, I realized how trivial any single event in the struggle had become – however central apparently for a day or two in a local context in relation to the hugeness of the upheaval that confronted the attenuated number of those who served the Crown in India.

Notes

[1] In order to emphasize the significance of this Muslim League victory I ought to explain that the by-election had been caused by the resignation of the Khan of Hoti. He was by far the richest and

most cultured landowner in the district, and might be said almost to have a feudal right to the constituency. But he was fiercely independent, very pro-British and unhappy at the League's policy of civil disobedience. He declared that he was neutral during the election campaign and this handicapped the League's cause.

The result of this important by-election was frequently referred to in Mountbatten's discussions with Nehru and other political leaders in April and May 1947. The verdict on it by Sir Olaf Caroe was that it had been a significant result pointing to a decline in the influence of Abdul Ghaffar Khan and Congress. Nehru relied on the smallness of the increase in the League's majority to conclude that the result showed no marked change in the positions since Congress won the 1946 General Election. (Letter to Viceroy dated 4 May 1947).

[2] Iskander Mirza was destined to become President of Pakistan, 1956-8. A.S.B. Shah became an Ambassador in Pakistan's diplomatic service.

[3] This was a man called Khurshid Anwar, whose continuing role in the worst aspects of the League's campaign led the Viceroy to make a specific protest to Jinnah in a letter dated 1 May 1947.

[4] This is my recollection. The Chief Secretary's report to the Government of India said that approximately nine shots were fired, causing about fifteen casualties. The injured were removed by the demonstrators, so the number of casualties is uncertain. My memory is that there were about seven.

[5] Sir Firoz Khan Noon became Prime Minister of Pakistan for a short time in the mid-Fifties.

CHAPTER XIII

Viceregal Drama

Two weeks after the accident, the railway embankment was the scene of another dramatic event. This time the Viceroy himself was the central figure, and what happened was of incalculable importance to the outcome of his efforts to negotiate the transfer of power in India. I shall describe what I saw of events on the occasion of his historic visit to Peshawar. There have been several accounts of it by different writers, some of them participants, including the Viceroy himself. I saw it from a different angle and some of what I record is new. But first, I must set the scene.

By the beginning of April it had become apparent that the problems of the Frontier Province were going to play a far bigger part in the Viceroy's negotiations than the size of its population seemed to justify. To some extent one might have expected this because of the geography of the Frontier, its strategic role in all historical studies of the defence of India – prior to the threat of invasion by Japan – and the unsolved problems of law and order in the tribal borderland. The independent tribes, who had separate treaties with the British Government, had for generations been the chief preoccupation of the Indian Army in a series of hard-fought campaigns. Even in times of comparative quiet, like the present, agreements with them to maintain the peace of the border cost the Government of India a large annual subvention of several crores of rupees. Yet these were not the matters which drew the attention of the politicians to the Frontier in the spring and early summer of 1947. Even the British Government, in its statement of 20 February announcing the intention to transfer power by June 1948, curiously omitted all reference to the Frontier tribes. This was a source of anxiety to the Governor, Sir Olaf Caroe, who constantly reminded the Viceroy of his special responsibility for tribal affairs, under the instrument of Instructions in his appointment by the King. There was a growing conflict between his interpretation of this responsibility, discharged direct to the Viceroy, and his responsibility as Governor towards the duly elected Provincial Government, constitutionally responsible for the settled districts. This conflict had been highlighted during the ill-advised tour of tribal areas which Pandit Nehru had made in November 1946 in company with the Chief Minister, Dr Khan Sahib, and his brother Abdul Ghaffar Khan.

Misled by A.G.K., whose understanding of tribal matters was slight, Nehru had formed a prejudiced view of the Frontier and its political officers, which clouded his judgment throughout the 1947 negotiations – Caroe later went so far as to attribute the ultimate need to partition India to the disastrous mistakes of Nehru's 1946 tour and its aftermath. Shortly before Wavell handed over to Mountbatten, he had to stall over a renewed demand from Nehru that Caroe be removed from office. The demand was reiterated to the new Viceroy and supported by a vituperative campaign in the Hindu press, aimed against Caroe and his officers. Relations between them and the Provincial Ministers deteriorated just when the Muslim League's campaign of civil disobedience put them under strain. Although Peshawar was the nerve centre of the province, and the civil administration, with the support of the Army, succeeded in that district in preventing large-scale rioting and heavy loss of life, serious communal trouble in Hazara was followed in mid-April by unprecedented disturbances in Dera Ismail Khan and Tank. The destruction of property and loss of life were on the same huge scale as in several districts of northern Punjab and it looked as if the whole of north India was on the verge of civil war and anarchy. Thousands of Hindus and Sikhs were already refugees from Frontier districts.

One of the Governor's greatest anxieties was that if the troops had to use their firepower freely against Muslims in the settled districts, the tribes would rise in a mass revolt. Fortunately, they kept their heads. The Faqir of Ipi seemed uncertain what he should proclaim: his enemy had always been the British – should it now be the Congress Government of the province? When he kept silent, tribal voices influenced by the Pir of Manki hinted that he was in the pay of Congress all along. The Afridis decided to stand back and prepare to drive a hard bargain after Partition, confident that the Hindus could not now prevail. Their lead influenced the other tribes and there was more consultation between them than there had been for many years. But in mid-

April this was still all uncertain, and the Governor's fears of the tribal dimension of the problem were fully justified.

In the six settled districts of the province, the constant pressures of the League's campaign began to tell, both in terms of growing violence and in undermining the claims of the Ministry to an unshakeable right to govern. The anomaly of the Frontier became clearer. The general election a year earlier had given a clear majority to the Congress Party in the Frontier. The Viceroy had been unable to return to the abortive plan of the Cabinet Mission, and the partition of India had become inevitable. The provincial Congress Ministry was linked to Hindustan, opposed to Partition. Did it still have a valid mandate to keep the people of the province out of Pakistan – even if what Jinnah achieved was but a 'moth-eaten version' of what he wished? Nehru and his colleagues at the centre insisted that Dr Khan Sahib's position, democratically decided at the polls, was unassailable. Jinnah and the other League leaders argued that the unrest in the province proved otherwise: now that the issue was clearer and partition inevitable, nobody could brook the wishes of the Muslims, who were over 90 per cent of the Frontier's population. The ominous silence of the tribes, who had clearly demonstrated their rejection of Nehru and of Hindu dominance in November 1946, could scarcely be misinterpreted, except perhaps by Abdul Ghaffar Khan.

Throughout April the question grew more urgent. The Governor's early advice to the Viceroy was that there should be a fresh election. Should the Ministry be dismissed so that the election would be held under Governor's rule, under section 93 of the Government of India Act? Gradually he drew back from that: constitutionally, it was hard to establish a legal case for dismissing the Ministry. Nehru and his colleagues, under pressure from Mountbatten, stayed adamant that there should be no election under the duress of the Muslim League's civil disobedience and disorder, although they were prepared to admit that after the British Government had made its final decisions about the transfer of power the views of the Frontier people might have to be sought through the electoral process. Meanwhile, there must be no question of section 93 rule, particularly under a Governor whose impartiality they challenged implacably.

Early in April the Viceroy sent the senior member of his private staff, General Ismay, to Peshawar to see what he could make of the situation. Ismay's appraisal was shrewd; as a young cavalry officer he had been 'brought up' on the Frontier. But he found no solution. The Governor was summoned to Delhi, where on 16 April he took part in an intense discussion with Mountbatten, Nehru, Liaqat Ali, Baldev Singh, the Sikh leader, who was Minister for Defence, Auchinleck, the Commander-in-Chief, and Ismay. The official record shows how confused their discussion of these difficult matters was, in the wake of the destruction of D.I.K. and Tank; even the Viceroy seemed to be reduced to uncertainty. While violent disturbances were continuing, no decisive action could be taken that would not seem to have been forced by rebellion and law-breaking.

Dr Khan Sahib was summoned to Delhi, and two days later Mountbatten told him that the Frontier situation was likely to prejudice the wider problem and that he would have to find a temporary expedient to restore peace until the overall solution for the whole of India had been decided. Apparently with the Viceroy's encouragement, there was a remarkably frank confrontation between Khan Sahib and Caroe – perhaps a sort of experiment in blood-letting. Mountbatten had just very cleverly manoeuvred Jinnah into signing a joint declaration with Gandhi appealing for the renunciation of the use of force for political ends, and Dr Khan Sahib was persuaded to issue an announcement, linked to that appeal, calling for a response to it by the Frontier factions, and undertaking to release all political prisoners who had not been charged with specific offences involving violence – the jails were overflowing; even the revered Pir of Manki had recently been arrested. The statement was to make no reference to any proposal to hold an election; but the Viceroy felt free to discuss it with Jinnah, on the basis that it could not be undertaken while the League engaged in direct action against the Government.

One thing in which all participants in this dramatic meeting were agreed was thankful acceptance of the Viceroy's offer to visit the Frontier personally. Meanwhile, while the absolute ban on processions was to be enforced, no police action against meetings would be undertaken, however freely the right of freedom of speech was exercised on such occasions. The Frontier Government's announcement was issued on 19 April; the Viceroy's visit was scheduled for 28 and 29 April. On 24 April, Jinnah appealed publicly 'to all Muslims to maintain peace, law and order... so as to give the Viceroy every opportunity to fully understand the situation'. Helpfully, he added 'I feel that the Viceroy is determined to play fair.'

Apart from the published official statements, I knew little about these matters at the time, though I regularly glanced through the reports and comment in the *Civil and Military Gazette* and the *Statesman*, the most accessible English language newspapers, and I picked up a rough idea of what the vernacular press was saying, both locally and nationally, either from these main daily papers or from All-India Radio broadcasts. I certainly did not realize at that stage how threatened the Governor's personal position was. I was well aware of the dangers in the Peshawar situation and disturbed about the spread of violence in the south of the Province, but too absorbed, and exhausted, by my own narrow field of experience to dwell consciously on the wider background. At that stage, in spite of the riot at the Chief Minister's house on 24 March, life in the cantonment itself was little disturbed, except occasionally by the noise from the jail, and I did not feel acute anxiety for the safety of my family, whose move to the hills for the summer was near.

On the Saturday before the Viceroy's visit – 26 April – Major Shah, the DC, held a long conference of senior staff to agree on dispositions for the protection of Mountbatten and the security of the cantonment on the 28th. His aeroplane was scheduled to arrive before nine o'clock so that movements of police and troops had to be completed very early. At the meeting, I felt that the plans were carefully thought out. The chief worry seemed to be the protection of the aerodrome where it was expected that a large crowd would assemble, with several possible lines of approach. I was uneasy about the protection of the cantonment in the neighbourhood of the Assembly building and the railway line, at the back door so-to-speak of Government House – particularly when the Brigade Major said firmly that that sector had been allocated to a Sikh regiment. By then, we all knew the risks of communalism affecting discipline in the Army and I would have preferred to have the Sikhs tucked away less provocatively further from the front line.

On the Sunday, however, I spent a quiet day at home with time for reflection, growing steadily more uneasy about what might happen. It seemed to me that the dispositions we had made stemmed from the tacit assumption that confrontation with the Muslim League was inevitable, and from whatever angle I viewed the prospect I could see no way of avoiding the use of the Army's firepower if the crowd was as determined as recent events conditioned me to expect. In itself that conclusion was bad enough, but what made it unacceptable was the thought that bloodshed during the Viceroy's visit could have a disastrous effect on his efforts to procure a peaceful agreement on the transfer of power. Everyone accepted that he had already won unprecedented trust and confidence from all the contending parties and the thought that that might be lost in the violence of a Peshawar riot appalled me.

About seven in the evening I was so restless that I decided to call on the DC. Although I arrived without warning, his orderly took me straight to him. He was sitting in his dining room with Sir Firoz Khan Noon. That was the first surprise of many that evening. They had just finished their meal; Shah asked me quietly what I wanted; embarrassed by the presence of Firoz Khan Noon, a former member of the Viceroy's Executive Council and a very prominent Punjab politician who was rather on the sidelines of the Muslim League at the time,[1] I stammered out my anxieties about the next day. Calmly, Shah said, 'That is exactly what we have been discussing and we don't know what we should do about it.' After some discussion, Firoz said that some effort must be made to prevent the crowd assembling at the aerodrome: he seemed to be sure that a demonstration there was intended by the League. But he opted out of any part in pursuing his suggestion, implying that his own influence with the Provincial Muslim League War Council – so it was designated – was so negligible that representation by him would be counterproductive.

So it was left to the DC to make a move. To my surprise he picked up the telephone and asked for a number, explaining to me that it was the number of a phone in a *hujra* (a meeting place) in the city. After a short conversation, he turned to me and said, 'Let's go.' We drove straight to a place just off the Grand Trunk Road, about half a mile outside the city wall, which he explained was the headquarters of the League's 'War Council'. Without delay we were admitted to the main room where about a dozen men were clearly engaged in a meeting. I had thought that most of the real leaders of the League were in prison; though I knew of the existence of this War Council, I had no idea that it was still functioning so effectively. But the biggest surprise was the presence of Sardar Abdur Rab Nishtar, whom I had known as a minister in

Aurangzeb's Government in 1943. He was now a League nominee in the Viceroy's Interim Government and I was shaken to find him engaged in this cabal, which was clearly responsible for arrangements that might threaten the Viceroy's whole mission to India.

Nishtar took charge of the discussion at once. Shah explained our anxiety that a demonstration at the aerodrome might become uncontrollable. Nishtar agreed, clearly sharing our anxiety, but asked what was the alternative. The League had already made its dispositions and parties of men were believed to be already on their way to camp at the aerodrome. In the exchanges which followed it became clear that the *sine qua non* for the League was to set up a situation in which the crowd was assured that the Viceroy personally had seen them and assessed the strength of their numbers. I suggested that this might best be achieved in a relatively confined space, like the Cunningham Garden, which had the further advantage that it was neither in the cantonment nor in the military environment of the aerodrome, but conveniently near the city from which no doubt many would wish to join the gathering. The aerodrome was several miles away to the west – a long trek across country from the main centre of population. Some members of the War Council emphasized how difficult it would be at such a late hour to alter instructions that had already gone out to various units or groups of League volunteers. They insisted that no change could be made unless they had an assurance that the Viceroy would review the gathering in the Cunningham Garden. It was not acceptable to them to say that he would see them from the air as his plane approached the landing ground. When Shah said that in any case he had no means of providing such an assurance that night, Nishtar at once intervened to say that all that was required was a telephone message to Delhi. He knew the Viceroy's working habits, and we could be assured that if the Governor rang Delhi at any time before midnight he would be put through to Lord Mountbatten.

There appeared to be no alternative. It was already nearly eleven o'clock. Shah undertook to ring the *hujra* with the answer before midnight, to give them time to put out new instructions to their followers. When we left, however, he was very depressed and hesitant about approaching the Governor on this basis. I suggested that in any case, since the proposal would have important implications for the Army's arrangements, we should call on

Brigadier Cubitt-Smith and seek his support in approaching Caroe. As always, the Brigadier was quick in his appreciation of the situation. He agreed that if the scheme worked, it might provide the best chance of averting a clash of arms. He was very perturbed by the prospect of having to deal with a large crowd at or near the aerodrome. But the matter was one 'for the civil power' not the Army, at this stage, and he declined to accompany us to Government House.

Encouraged none the less by his reaction, we went off to Government House. HE had gone to bed, and his ADC (David Bivar) was understandably unwilling to disturb him. Shah became insistent, and the reluctant David disappeared, to return five minutes later with a dishevelled and sleepy-looking Governor in his pyjamas, his normally immaculate grey hair tousled and his eyes heavy and tired. He sat on a settee in the hall outside the drawing room and listened patiently to what Shah had to say. He showed no sign of surprise and scarcely interrupted with a question. After a time he sat with his head bowed, resting on his hands, and I wondered if he was going to fall asleep. Suddenly, he got up, and saying, 'You can tell Nishtar to go to hell,' he stamped out, back to bed – I assumed.

My heart was in my boots. David Bivar bade us an embarrassed goodnight and we went out onto the portico at the top of the steps leading into the house. On one side there was a telephone for the use of the Governor's orderlies and the military guard. Shah picked it up and asked for the *hujra* number, which he clearly had in his head. The conversation was in Persian or some form of Peshawari dialect which I did not understand. But I listened intently, picking up some recognisable words and phrases, and when he put the phone down, I challenged him at once.

'You told Nishtar it is all right.'

'Yes, I did.'

'What will he do now?'

'That is up to him, isn't it?' He was despondent and exhausted and we drove back to the DC's house without another word.

Riding home on my autocycle I was revived by the rush of cool air and lay for a long time pondering what would happen. At dawn, I went down to the city gates on my machine and was surprised by the number of people already on the move. I rode through the Cunningham Garden and saw that large numbers had spent the night there and on the open spaces beyond. I spotted

Gilbert Grace, the Inspector General of Police, and rode over to greet him. Like me, he was making a scouting expedition of his early morning walk, anxious to know what was going on. I told him briefly about the League's apparent plan and asked if he would be prepared to advise Caroe to request the Viceroy to visit the scene if all went well with his arrival. He not only agreed, but suggested that I should go straight to the Chief Secretary with my account, and ask him to approach the Army Commander, General Ross McCay. My good friend Norval Mitchell had recently taken over as Chief Secretary when Colonel de la Fargue went on long leave. I found him at breakfast, told my story, and got his immediate response – he would speak to HE, and I was to go to GHQ to see the General. Ross McCay said that he would like to have a look at the ground and took me in his staff car with his G1. I thought that it might not be a good idea for us to be seen too close to the crowds on the move, and suggested that the driver go into the old fort Bala Hissar. From the heights of its ramparts we could see over the Cunningham Garden and observe the crowds moving out of the city across the Grand Trunk Road. Away in the distance people were coming in from the villages in the other direction – probably some of them having been recalled from the aerodrome. Already the numbers on the move were impressive and the park itself was very busy. As on my earlier perambulation I was struck by the apparent calm and relative quiet of the scene. As yet, there was none of the angry buzz that one had learned to associate with a hostile procession or demonstration. From the fort, it all looked like a crowd assembling in anticipation of an exciting football match.

I was on duty at Government House, not at the aerodrome, but when the plane was due I went down to the railway embankment overlooking the park. As it flew overhead, there was a distinct ripple of excitement in the crowd. The plane was fairly low, its speed on approach slow, and one felt that the Viceroyal party would get a good idea of the crowd if they had been alerted to look out.

I learned afterwards that nothing about the demonstration had been said to Lord Mountbatten during the formalities of his arrival, but that in the car on the way to Government House the Governor had told him about the crowd, making it clear that he had been advised by all the senior officers, and by the military commanders, to recommend that the Viceroy should agree to see the crowd himself. As I was given to understand the Governor himself declined to make such a positive recommendation, possibly on the grounds that it savoured too much of playing the Muslim League's game. But he did explain the fears, which everyone shared, that if the Viceroy did not go to see the crowd, they would try to force their way to Government House to see him.

When the party entered Government House, Mountbatten and Caroe were still discussing the position, and stood within earshot of me at the door. Suddenly the Viceroy said, 'I must go, but not unless I have the Chief Minister's agreement. What is his view of the matter?' Everybody had forgotten to think about that.

I was despatched to fetch Dr Khan Sahib, pretending that I knew nothing of the reasons for this hasty summons so soon after he had greeted the Viceroy at the aerodrome and left him in the Governor's care. When I ushered him into their presence, the Viceroy said very briskly that he had been advised to see this Muslim League crowd to avoid a serious risk of violent disturbance, and for that reason alone, provided the Honourable Chief Minister had no objection, he proposed to go – though as Dr Khan Sahib would appreciate, he was not in the least impressed by crowds or by numbers, and would not be influenced by them. It seemed to me that Dr Khan Sahib was taken completely aback. He was never particularly quick in oral debate, and spluttered, 'Your Excellency must just do whatever you please.' Without hesitation, Mountbatten said, 'Very well; thank you. Now tell me how is your brother – I quite forgot to enquire when we met...' I feel sure that it was not at this stage, but later in the day when the Viceroy met the Ministers officially, that Khan Sahib remarked that he would be aware in any case that it was the Governor who had arranged for this Muslim League demonstration of numbers, and that he himself had cancelled a similar demonstration of Congress supporters in order to avoid the risk of a clash.

It took a few minutes to escort the Premier back to his house. When I returned, the party at Government House was almost ready to leave. When she heard about the expedition, Lady Mountbatten insisted on going with it. The cars were left where the trunk road widened after emerging from the railway over-bridge, at the junction near the Assembly building. There they were out of sight of the crowd in the Cunningham Garden –

screened by the railway embankment. There was a line of policemen across the road at the other side of the bridge and a considerable party of police around the cars. The troops were in position well back from the bridge, and of course out of sight from the demonstration. We scrambled up the rough, steep bank and walked along the line to the bridge over the road which was clear of onlookers. The crowd in the park was impressive – much more densely packed than when I had last seen them. They had spilled over onto the railway, in the direction of the city station, so that although the vast majority were below us in the park, several thousands were on the embankment level with us, the nearest no more than twenty yards away. We were standing only a few yards from where shots had been fired on the advancing crowd on 10 March and from the scene of the railway accident involving the women's demonstration on 14 April.

The early morning silence had been replaced by a considerable noise, which was hard to interpret. It was not the angry sound of a mob about to riot but it was not reassuring either. The Viceroy moved forward to the parapet – a low wall hardly more than a foot high – then stood erect on it. Suddenly one was aware that the noise was dying away; seconds ticked past in a strange silence, then perceptibly, the sound increased to a gigantic murmur swelling almost to a roar. One sensed at once that this was not a note of anger, but of amazed approval. The Viceroy must have known at once that he had won the day. Turning to face the crowd on the line nearest to him, he called out, 'Get the people nearest to sit down so that others behind can see better'. A senior police officer and I entered their ranks, calling out in Pushtu that the Lat Sahib wanted them to sit so that more could see better. Some of them did; the feeling I got from them all was one of amazement and bewilderment. They were not noisy or elated, but respectful and a little overawed. Near the front I stopped in astonishment as I came face to face with a Tori Khel *malik* called Sanobar Khan whom I had known well three years before in Waziristan. We greeted each other warmly, as Pathans do, but when I asked him what he was up to he was uncharacteristically reticent. Perhaps he did not want to admit that he was now on the Muslim League side. Men had certainly come long distances to join this demonstration.[2]

It has been said that the Viceroy's green Burma bush shirt and trousers captured the crowd's approval. It may have helped; all I can say is that the colour of his clothes made no difference to me, but that I was captivated by a demonstration of personal magnetism unique in my experience. After a few minutes, the party withdrew down the steep bank to the cars. There, I had some uneasy moments. Looking up the road under the bridge I saw the line of police gazing fascinated at the Viceroy and his party, their backs to the crowd which was now advancing quickly down the road towards the bridge – and the cantonment gates. I ran towards the police swearing at them for falling asleep; a police officer ran up with a platoon of reinforcements and their ranks closed, just in time to keep the crowd from bursting through below the bridge. It probably had no hostile intent, but the exuberance of spectators can provide an opening for any group intent on mischief.

I was not involved in the remainder of the Viceroy's visit, in the course of which he interviewed a number of my senior colleagues, seeking to assess the morale of a service which was under great pressure. He himself has recorded the tragi-comedy of his meeting with the Provincial ministers, and his interview with Muslim League representatives, some of them out of jail 'on parole'. The record also shows how the Afridi *jirga* next day gave a characteristically impressive performance for him – politically subtle but responsible, missing no tricks. There can be no doubt, from the decisions and action that he subsequently took, that his visit enabled him to grasp the complexities of the Frontier problem, which had previously left him unusually unsure and hesitant, if we are to judge from the record of his meetings in Delhi in the weeks before he arrived. From the end of April he knew far more clearly how he was to attain his objectives and how to deal with the Congress and Muslim League leaders; if anything, his worst problem was to manipulate everything within a shortened time-scale, and to meet the difficulties that occurred to the Cabinet in London. Those too were resolved by a personal visit – in which of course he was helped by the determination of the Prime Minister (Attlee) to get to the solution quickly.

If this interpretation is correct, it adds to the significance of the events of the morning of 28 April, which I have just described. I have always been convinced that if something had gone wrong that morning, the effect on Mountbatten's negotiations might have been irretrievable. That nothing did go wrong was partly an enormous fluke, partly the product of the Viceroy's peculiar genius and flair. Reading the official documents now published, I think that one new element has emerged. Late on the Sunday evening in Delhi, Jinnah told the Viceroy that there would be a procession to Government House in Peshawar to impress him with the strength of the League. The Viceroy telegraphed to the Governor immediately afterwards, at 10.35 p.m, saying that he had made it plain to Jinnah that any procession would be 'completely contrary to assurance I had given to Khan Sahib'. He would have no objection to a meeting or gathering from which not more than six delegates would be allowed to go to Government House to see him. I think that it is clear from this that Nishtar had been in touch with Jinnah on the Sunday evening – probably before Shah and I saw him, though quite possibly immediately after we went on our way to see the Brigadier and the Governor. It is not clear when the telegram reached Caroe. If he had it before we saw him, it is strange that he should not have said so. In any case, it is clear that Mountbatten was not altogether taken by surprise by the Governor's news that a crowd had gathered and wanted to see him.

Although the events of these days were to prove to have been such a dramatic turning point, it was some time before life became more peaceful in the Frontier. On that Monday night, Barbara and I were wakened by shots being fired nearby. Going out onto our verandah I saw tracer bullets flying past our garden. General Ross McCay's official residence was about a hundred yards away. A party of miscreants had crept over the golf course onto a little hill less than a hundred yards from the wire, from which they fired bursts from a light machine-gun straight into the General's bedroom, having first apparently demoralised the guard by throwing hand grenades in the direction of the guard room. The General luckily was unscathed, but very angry with his Gurkha guard. The culprits of course escaped over the golf course and the cantonment wire impeded the belated pursuit. Intelligence reports tentatively identified them as a group of Red Shirts from a notorious village near Peshawar. They were alleged to be henchmen of the Minister for Revenue, Qazi Ataullah.

Although the Viceroy went back to Delhi on the Tuesday after his visit to the Khyber, Lady Mountbatten was determined to visit some of the refugee camps and devastated towns in the south of the Province. Having accompanied her husband on the first stage of his return journey, to Rawalpindi, where they saw for the first time the results of appalling communal conflict, she then flew to Dera Ismail Khan and Tank, spending most of two days on her feet in the heat and discomfort of refugee camps, smouldering ruins and overcrowded hospitals. In Peshawar, she had visited the Lady Reading Hospital, which was by far the best that the province could offer, and an institution of which we were rather proud. Her inspection revealed operational deficiencies which she insisted should be rectified, and she declared that she would be back to make sure that this had been done. I was on duty to escort her on her return to Peshawar on the Thursday. Her plane was late, no doubt because she had kept it waiting while she saw what she wanted in Tank. The day had been very hot and I suggested that she cut out her return visit to the Lady Reading Hospital. 'Nonsense: I promised to go back, and I must. All I need is a cup of tea.' That was easily provided by Lady Caroe as soon as we got to Government House – and drunk standing; then we were off to the city, to check on the hospital's efficiency.

It was almost eight o'clock when I got her back to Government House and there was to be a dinner party, for which the guests were invited to be present at 8 p.m. for 8.30. Somehow I got home, changed, and presented Barbara within the time limits. Lady Mountbatten was standing with the Caroes, receiving the guests, immaculate and dust free – probably for the first time in two days. At dinner, during the main course, she suddenly rose and left the room, followed by her lady-in-waiting, who returned after a few minutes to convey her apologies, explaining that the Vicereine had been suffering from acute toothache for two days. When the ladies withdrew, the men felt sure that we would not be seeing her again that evening – but when we rejoined the ladies in the drawing room, she was sitting beside Barbara, deep in conversation about her experiences with the Girl's Training Corps during the War. The courage, determination and endurance that these two days called for were remarkable.

Notes

[1] Malik Sir Firoz Khan Noon was Member for Defence, Viceroy's Executive Council, 1942-5, and India's representative, British War Cabinet, 1944-5.
[2] There have been various published estimates of the size of the crowd, ranging from 50,000 to 100,000.

CHAPTER XIV

Referendum and Retreat

Soon after the Viceroy's visit, Barbara and little Hilary went to Nathia Gali for the summer. She was to share a bungalow called *Moonrising Cottage* with Mary Mitchell and Betty Latimer – an arrangement that I was happy about, for they got on very well together. Betty was expecting her first child, Barbara was nursing Hilary, Mary was temporarily separated from her family, so they needed mutual support – but each was ideally equipped to provide it. When Norval Mitchell drove us up to Nathia in his big Chevrolet station waggon, loaded to the gunwales, he chose the longer but less precipitous route via Rawalpindi and Murree, thence along the ridge by Khanspur, Changla Gali and Dunga Gali to Nathia. It was an exceedingly hot journey. I clearly remember that we had to make one stop, for Hilary's sake, not far along the road from 'Pindi, before it began the steeper part of its climb. As we slaked our thirst I looked over the scrub-clad hills towards the mountains of Hazara and told Norval how I used to tour the villages in the valleys when thousands of their *jawans* (young men) were serving in the Army and the people wanted to hear about our progress in the War, and were not interested in the politics of Congress or the League. Many years later, a mile or two from the same spot, I sat with the British Ambassador at tea in the garden of his embassy in the new capital of Pakistan – Islamabad, an urban concept which even as late as May 1947 could scarcely have been envisaged by either of us.

At that date we thought that we had another year to go before the Raj ended, and that we could leave our families in peace in the hill station for the months of the hot weather. We felt some anxiety about leaving them, for, a couple of thousand of feet below Nathia, pockets of Sikh habitation near Malach had been burned that winter and their occupants slaughtered. Although the culprits' quarrel was not with the British, any serious disturbance in their villages might leave Nathia Gali cut off, and its wooden bungalows at risk from conflagrations in the forest started by arson lower down the ridge.

Less than a month later these suppressed fears surfaced in an acute form. Dr Khan Sahib was determined to spend some time in the bungalow allocated to the Chief Minister in the summer headquarters at Nathia. The other ministers generally disliked the high altitude, preferring a midway base at Abbottabad, at about 4,000 feet. But Mrs Khan Sahib, the Premier's English wife, was already in Nathia, and characteristically he ignored the pleas of the Deputy Commissioner Hazara (now Oliver St John) and set off up the hill to join her. Villagers promptly blocked the road by felling trees, and threatened that if he carried out his intention they would set fire to his house which was very close to Moonrising. The British families were alerted to be prepared to be evacuated at twenty-four hours notice and for a couple of days there was great unease, while the stubborn old man persisted with his claim that the whole thing was part of the British plot against his Ministry, and that the villagers really bore him no ill-will. When I next saw her, Barbara told me that shortly before this excitement, the *chowkidar* of their bungalow, who slept on the verandah at night to keep prowlers away, whether two-legged or four-legged – the disturbers of the peace were usually jackals, whose howls would upset any baby – had asked her for a chit to give to the Deputy Commissioner. He explained that he had to appear in a court case in Abbottabad and might be delayed overnight if she did not ask the DC to be sure to hear his evidence early, to ensure his timely return to duty. She complied, and the *chowkidar* turned up as usual the next evening, but when she next saw Oliver, she thanked him for his help and asked whether her request had inconvenienced him. 'Oh, no, the fellow was only one of the accused in the Malach arson case, and he was on bail anyway.' She was slightly perturbed to realize that the residents of Moonrising were protected at night by a man charged with arson and murder, but by now she knew enough about communalism in India to be philosophical, realizing that his loyalty to his employers was not in doubt, and that his background probably made him a reliable watchman.

In Peshawar the previous high pitch of tension changed to a persistent atmosphere of general unease and anxiety. There were fewer specific instances of violence; but there was an almost routine expectation of trouble and a monotonous inability to overtake arrears of normal administrative and magisterial work. I found this induced a sense of helplessness and even hopelessness that was alien to my whole philosophy of service in India. The feeling that the struggle in which we were engaged was no longer one in which the role of Britain was pre-eminent became oppressive; far from manipulating events, as Congress persistently accused, I felt that we were being pushed onto the sidelines. The Ministry was liberally issuing gun licences to its supporters. A new elite body of Red Shirts (the Red Guard) had been formed, armed and uniformed as a private army. It almost seemed as if Khan Sahib really was contemplating replacing the official police force with his own civil militia. Inevitably the Muslim League followed suit, and though their Greenshirt private army (the so-called National Guard) was smaller and apparently less well armed, the possibility of civil war grew ominous. Gradually in Peshawar – though not elsewhere in the province – the tension eased a little. Jinnah's restraining directives did seem to produce some quietening effect. But most of the political prisoners obstinately refused to accept the amnesty and leave jail, and about the middle of May the Government withdrew certain privileges they had been allowed – like having charpoys to sleep on. There was a wild riot that evening in the jail. The din was so loud that I heard it at home over a mile away and had left for the prison before any message about the riot was telephoned to me. The hero of the night was the veteran Colonel Shelley Smith ('Haripur' Smith) who flung himself unsparingly into the fray and succeeded in rallying some of the more prominent League leaders to help in restoring order. I have a vivid recollection of him, stripped to the waist, with a wet kerchief round his neck – used to protect his eyes from bursts of tear gas, for, like the crowds in the city, the prisoners were adept at returning the smoking canisters to the point of origin. My other memory is of meeting by his side Abdul Qayum Khan, who had switched his allegiance a few months before, having been the most effective Frontier representative on the central committees of All-India Congress for several years. Now he was the acknowledged leader amongst the politicians of the Frontier Muslim League – less influential in the rural and tribal areas than the priestly Pir of Manki but far more experienced politically. He had been a political prisoner since February. He seemed to have been revelling in the heat of the jail battle and teased me jovially for arriving late. I felt glum and no doubt looked grimly at him, for I was upset by the violence even though by now it was spent. It gave me no pleasure to think that this clever but aggressive man might soon be Chief Minister of the Province. Meeting him in these circumstances made me more convinced that there was going to be no future for me in India after the transfer of power.

Back in Delhi, in conversation with his staff, Mountbatten had made up his mind about the Frontier. He substituted for the proposal to hold a new general election – with all the constitutional difficulties – the novel proposition that there should be a referendum. The issue to be put to the electorate would be simple and straightforward – in effect, do you wish the Frontier Province to be part of India (Hindustan) or of Pakistan? The organization of the referendum would be established by the Governor-General himself, working through military officers specially chosen and appointed. In this way nobody could say that the result would be prejudiced because of manipulation of the voting machinery by the Provincial Government, or because of the alleged partiality of the civil administration.

It did not take long to persuade Jinnah to accept this proposal. It would be decided on the principle of 'one man, one vote' and this avoided the obstacle that confronted the League in an election – namely, the reservation of a disproportionately large number of seats for the minority communities – the Hindus and Sikhs had nearly a quarter of the seats in the Legislative Assembly, though they were only about 5 per cent of the population. After protracted negotiation, Jinnah eventually issued an appeal for a return to moderation – although Mountbatten could not allow him to make public reference to the referendum proposal. Its point was submerged in a lengthy preamble in which there was a denial that there had ever been a campaign of 'direct action', and the 'civil disobedience' campaign was justified – though acts of violence and communal hatred were deplored. But for those who read or listened to the end, there was a plain enough message – to cool the temperature of the Frontier, and by the middle of May I certainly thought the results were discernible for I was actually finding time to resume court work.

The Viceroy had far more difficulty with Congress. Gandhi, the man of the people, told him that the 'Referendum is a dangerous thing in itself,' and said that 'nothing should or can be done over Dr Khan Sahib's head.' As always, Nehru was the key figure.

Having put up a stubborn resistance in principle, he was constrained to admit that 'intellectually, he was in favour of a referendum'. His argument then was for delay, because of the risks of further disturbance. When the Viceroy pointed out that the timing of the referendum must be related to the date of the transfer of power, Nehru was cornered It was not possible to transfer power before a settlement of the NWFP issue. The sooner the referendum was held, the sooner could be the date of transfer. Nehru could not resist that argument; but there were still serious doubts in the minds of the British Cabinet's India and Burma Committee, which were not eased by the hesitation of Ismay about the proposal – he had been sent to London as the Viceroy's intermediary. When Nehru suddenly resiled from previous agreement to the terms of the draft Plan in the Cabinet's hands – not of course on the Frontier issue, but on broader grounds – the Prime Minister invited Mountbatten to London for the ultimate decision-taking.

The final announcements were made after his return to Delhi on 3 June, and revealed for the first time the advancing of the date for the transfer of power from June 1948 to 15 August 1947. Barbara and I had already decided not to stay on beyond 1948, but the new date raised far more urgent questions, and it was not easy to discuss them. The telephone link between North Circular Road and Moonrising in Nathia Gall was invariably appallingly noisy – reminding me of frustrations endured in the hot Waziristan summer of 1944 whenever I had to seek urgent instruction from the Chief Secretary about action to be taken in the Shaktu. One thing soon became clear – the Frontier, after the announcement, was quiet at last, exhausted and almost at peace with itself. The Muslim League awaited the Referendum with quiet confidence. Congress for the time being seemed unsure what to do. There were already rumours about a campaign to form an independent Pathan state, and even suggestions of some sort of coalition between the Khan brothers and the League. What I knew nothing about was the cloud over Caroe's role as Governor. Brigadier John Booth, commander of the Wana Brigade in South Waziristan, was appointed Referendum Commissioner, and was due in Peshawar by 7 June, to be joined there by the rest of his special staff of majors and colonels seconded from units widely dispersed in India and overseas. All were to be officers who had a good knowledge of Pushtu, and who were therefore experienced in Frontier conditions.

I got a short period of casual leave and joined my family in Nathia Gali, feeling distinctly uneasy about the future of my role as Joint Deputy Commissioner Peshawar, but suddenly I was recalled to Peshawar. Mitchell, who was still Chief Secretary in de la Fargue's absence, told me that I was to be 'Civil Aide' to the Referendum Commissioner. Booth had quickly realized that he and his military staff would be sadly handicapped by their lack of knowledge of the civil administration, constitutional law, electoral procedures and such matters. Some time had been spent seeking help from Delhi, for everyone was determined to maintain the Viceroy's promise that he would keep the administration of the referendum out of the hands of the Frontier political service. But there could be no possible resolution of Booth's special requirement except by the appointment of an officer familiar with the present state of the districts and their officials. There were misgivings that such a departure from the 'purity' of the Viceroy's plan might give rise to mistrust and accusations of betrayal. But finally the Governor proposed to both Dr Khan Sahib and Abdul Qayum Khan that I should be given this special duty, and both parties agreed that I was acceptable – untainted, apparently, by suspicion of partiality for either side.

There was in fact quite a lot to do. Booth had not been given much of a local staff, either for his headquarters or for his supervising officers scattered through the six districts. This was not surprising: after the turmoil of recent months, junior officials were hard to recruit, and Deputy Commissioners, who were faced with serious arrears of court, revenue and administrative work, could hardly spare anyone. Yet inevitably the local district staff would have to be involved in the arrangements for polling stations, provision of presiding officers, and the supply of attested electoral rolls. There was not much time. It had been decided that the referendum would be held between 6 and 16 July. It was essential that it should be completed by the 17th, which was the date on which Ramadan was expected to start – the month of Muslim fasting and prayer; the date of course would depend on the sighting of the new moon.

I got on well with John Booth who was a brisk, cheerful, efficient soldier. Some of the help he needed from me was easily provided, because even if I did not know the answer I knew where to look for it, or the best person to ring up; and I could readily offer oral sketches of the personality of district officials or local politicians or the background of recent events as required by him or his military helpers. We got into deeper water when we had to probe the legal and constitutional background of what we were doing. The Government of India Act 1935 was not very helpful about the validity of the Referendum. If either political party had really set their clever lawyers to work at it, the whole exercise might easily have been challenged and delayed. In his anxiety not to offend against the constitution by dismissing the Ministry and calling a general election, the Viceroy had really invented a method of achieving the same effective result which was so novel and so persuasively orchestrated by him that nobody questioned his power to drive ahead.

The Provincial Ministry was in a quandary. They argued, for example, that if disturbances broke out during the period of the Referendum, they had the constitutional authority to suspend or postpone voting. The Referendum Commissioner claimed that such authority must vest in himself – wherever the Act provided that the judgment or discretion of the Governor became operative, it would now be for him to make decisions, just as in the districts it would be for his Special Officers to act, not the Deputy Commissioners. This all made good practical sense, and reflected the Viceroy's intentions – but it stretched his constitutional powers far beyond what the Government of India Act provided. For some time, the Provincial Congress Party was uncertain whether to boycott the Referendum or participate in the campaign. The idea that there might be a sort of unilateral declaration of independence for a separate Pathan state (Pakhtunistan) began to be canvassed. Abdul Ghaffar Khan went off to Delhi, accompanied by one of the ministers, Yahya Jan, his son-in-law, to try to persuade the Central Congress Party that the question to be put to the people should not smack of communalism – the choice between Pakistan and Hindustan. One should present Pathans with the choice between Pakistan and an independent Pathanistan. Emissaries were sent by the ministers to Kabul where the active interest taken in the whole affair by the Afghan Government called into question the notion that Pathanistan would or could be independent. Mountbatten firmly scotched the proposal, reminding Nehru that it was he who had earlier requested that the draft of the statement about the transfer of power should omit the option for other provinces of voting for independence. On this issue, there could not be one rule for the rest of India but a different and inconsistent one for the Frontier Province.

The Viceroy, however, offered Nehru important consolation. Sir Olaf Caroe was to go on leave, and be succeeded as Governor by General Sir Rob MacGregor Lockhart, whose Indian Army service had given him a good Frontier background. By the third week in June the difficult personal negotiation between the Viceroy and Caroe was completed. The announcement was made that Caroe had volunteered to go on leave, to make quite certain that no false allegation might be made that biassed or prejudiced influence over the Referendum was exercised by him. He handed over to Lockhart on 26 June and went to Kashmir. Theoretically, it might be possible for him to return, but I do not recollect that any of us expected this. It was a sad end to a career throughout which his devotion to the Pathans was remarkable, and often emotional. We all knew that he was very tired and strained. He was not universally liked and respected as Sir George Cunningham had been. He seemed to me to be an exceptionally clever man, with great verbal facility on paper – too readily exercised at length in circumstances in which Cunningham would more aptly have used a dry phrase or a sly teasing comment. But whatever our personal feelings about him, we were all shaken by the circumstances of his departure, after months of Congress propaganda against him. None of us believed that he preferred Muslim League leaders to Congress.

Abdul Ghaffar Khan returned from Delhi and at last clarified the Congress line. The party was to boycott the Referendum. The news came just in time – 23rd June – for a day or two before there had been reports of large gatherings in Peshawar and elsewhere of both Red Shirts and Muslim League National Guard; many were armed, and conflict seemed inevitable until the decision about the boycott was announced. At the same time the formalities in the Punjab were completed; the decision there to partition the Province had had to precede the formal arrangements for the Frontier Referendum – theoretically, if the Punjab had voted to join Hindustan, there would have been no option to put to the Frontier.

The Punjab decision for partition enabled the Governor-General to make formal proclamation of the powers and functions of the Referendum Commissioner, and on the initiative of Mountbatten himself Booth and I embarked on the drafting of the Referendum poster and many associated matters. The poster in basic terms reminded everyone that the plan for partition announced on 3 June had been accepted both by the All-India Congress Committee and the All-India Muslim League Council. Details followed of the provinces which were included in India, the areas which had elected to join Pakistan and the areas which had still to decide whether to join India or Pakistan. Below the text was a map showing in red the areas for India, in green those for Pakistan, and those still to decide in white. The printing on the map in two colours (other than white) in those days of poor equipment and backward technology gave us a great deal of trouble; but the Viceroy's instructions were specific. The poster then posed in simple terms the issue for the voters, explaining that a vote to join the Indian Constituent Assembly was in effect a vote that NWFP should be a part of India – rendered in the vernacular as Hindustan – and a vote to join the Pakistan Constituent Assembly was a vote that the NWFP should be a part of Pakistan. At the end, it was firmly proclaimed that there was no other alternative at issue whatsoever, and a simple explanation of how to express the voter's individual preference through the ballot paper ended the text.

When Lockhart took over on 25 June he had plenty to absorb his attention. A day or two later I was invited to dine with him. Only his Secretary was present (Jack Lowis) and the occasion reminded me of my evening with Sir George Cunningham and Oliver St John just after my transfer to Peshawar in 1944. When he discovered that I had been born in Cromdale we had a relaxed conversation about Strathspey; his mother was a MacGregor of Balmenach, a family well known to my parents. Within a few days he was consulting the Viceroy anxiously about the lack of a legal or constitutional basis for intervention in possible malpractices by Congress during the Referendum. For example, what was he to do if the Ministry forbade officials who were responsible to the Provincial Government to play any part in the arrangements? Sensibly, the Viceroy's advice was, for the meantime, do as little as possible. In fact, though there were rumours that the Red Shirt mafia was threatening to make things difficult for some officials, the Provincial Government generally observed the spirit of Gandhi's message to stay out of the whole affair. Threats that polling stations would be picketed came to nothing, possibly because during the campaign the League mustered very large numbers at its rallies. The Ministry's official line was to decry the Referendum and deplore the communally-inspired partition of India.

One of our anxieties was the risk that firearms would be used during polling and special orders were issued prohibiting weapons being carried within a certain distance of polling stations. So many Pathans carried guns ordinarily, even in settled districts, that such an ordinance might be useless; but in fact there was little interference and less violence when polling went on. I recollect an early report that voters had been fired on somewhere in Charsadda subdivision, but that was a fairly normal occurrence when the crops were high and opportunities, or excuses, were available to pursue a blood feud. The incident proved to be isolated. Booth and I toured around, generally together, during the days of polling, and saw little to disturb us, except perhaps some evidence in Hazara that more votes were being cast than the number on the electoral roll would justify. The special officers were efficient and alert, however. At each polling station Congress as well as the League was entitled to have three agents present at the clerk's table, to challenge any bogus voter, or check anyone from voting more than once. Very few challenges were made under the procedures provided, and this greatly weakened the effect of the vague, generalized complaints of malpractices with which Congress subsequently challenged the result of the Referendum.

This was that 289,244 votes were cast for Pakistan, only 2,874 for Hindustan. The vote for Pakistan was 50.49 per cent of the total electoral roll – and Congress, having boycotted the poll, challenged the significance of the result, implying that an almost equal number of votes might have been cast for Hindustan. In fact, out of the total electorate, there were 84,781 Hindus and Sikhs on the roll – with a weighting of political power greatly in excess of their proportion of the population. So the percentage of votes cast for Pakistan was considerably more than 50 per cent of the Muslim electorate. At the general election in 1946 the total votes actually cast had been 375,989, compared with which 289,244 was a very significant majority. In spite of the Congress tactic of avoiding the battle, there can be no doubt that the League won a clear victory.

At the time it was not so very difficult to interpret what was happening. But behind the battle there was a campaign in which Congress was still playing a full part, determined still to find a way to still higher stakes. This was something I could only dimly sense. The attempt to introduce the Pathanistan issue was in itself understandable enough, but what precisely the objective was, or the working definition of the slogan, was most obscure. Gradually the bonds that united the Frontier Party to the All-India Congress came apart, as the Centre realized that the Provincial Party could not win the Referendum, and Abdul Ghaffar and Qazi Ataullah realized that they had been abandoned and must recover ground by fighting for an 'independent' Pathan state within Pakistan. Dr Khan Sahib seemed to be coming to terms with reality in July. I think that after the result of the poll, if Mountbatten and Lockhart had decided to dismiss the Ministry, he would have accepted the position, and would have prepared to fight an election on a new platform, accepting the need to come to terms with Pakistan. But the British Government resisted such a move as unconstitutional, and Sir George Cunningham, who was reluctantly persuaded in July to accept the insistent invitation of Jinnah and the British Prime Minister to return to the Governorship on 15 August, the day of Partition and the transfer of power, wanted to delay the dismissal of Khan Sahib till after the *roza* (the month of fasting) – that is, till about 20 August. But Jinnah's authority as the first Governor General of Pakistan could not be denied; and he was adamant that Khan Sahib and his Ministry be removed at once. The new Chief Minister was Abdul Qayum.

Early in June I had applied for release under the terms of compensation for loss of career announced by the British Government. I was very disappointed to have to make this decision, but I stayed firm over it because I felt that I could not expose my wife and baby daughter to the risks of staying on. I was sure then, and I am still sure that if I had still been a bachelor I would have wanted to stay for a year or so, but now family considerations mattered more than anything else. I put my name forward as a candidate for transfer to the Home Civil Service, but as the weeks went by doubts about this grew. There were two reasons. The more important and definite one was that I felt I could not endure the sort of family life I imagined a junior London-based civil servant must lead in those austere days – commuting from some soulless suburb. The other reason was that I suspected that, after the excitement, responsibilities and challenges of the last six years, the next ten years in the Home Civil Service would be dull. I enquired whether I could be guaranteed a posting in Scotland – but soon realized that my yearning to get home amongst my own people was, for the present, so strong that I could not be content with the promise that my preference for the Scottish Office would be noted.

I began to feel that what I would really like would be the sort of position my father had had as a village schoolmaster, respected and influential in a small community of his own folk. I knew that Sir William Fyfe, the Principal of Aberdeen University, was Chairman of the Scottish Advisory Council on Education, and I wrote to tell him about my position and my feelings. Quickly he replied with the news that I could get a place on a shortened course for ex-service graduates to train as teachers, starting at the end of September. I accepted; and withdrew my other enquiries and applications – which included the possibility of going to Australia, first mooted by a party of Australian industrialists who had come to the Frontier when I was Director of Industries in 1946.

When I joined the Referendum Commissioner's staff, and the dates were agreed with the objective of getting the result declared before Ramzan began (about 20 July), I applied to be released as soon as the clearing up operation had been completed (about 27 July). I had no fancy to return to my post as Joint Deputy Commissioner, Peshawar for an awkward fortnight. About a week before I was due to leave, de la Fargue, who had returned from long leave to resume his post as Chief Secretary, sent for me to say that the Chief Minister had been looking at the list of officers who were intending to leave and had been surprised that I was one of them. He did not wish me to go and I was to be told this at once. All I could think of saying was that I was grateful for his kindness, but feared he might not be in office to keep a benevolent eye on me much longer. He was more likely to be in jail.

On the long, hot summer evenings I had sadly packed and crated most of our personal possessions, occasionally trying on a crackling telephone line to talk to Barbara about our plans. She must have been feeling as depressed and frustrated as I was. As soon as I could, I went up to Nathia Gali for the last time. Morale there was low. The exigencies of the summer had disrupted the normal calm hill station routine. Most families were preparing to pack, some had already gone. We made the long drive to Peshawar in a hired car, packed to the roof, with a driver sleepy from the effects of fasting in the hot season. In the next week in Peshawar, Hilary – only 8 months old – developed prickly heat and could get no rest. I felt conscience-stricken about having brought her and her mother downhill during the most humid part of Peshawar's hot weather. But the die was cast. Because of Ramzan, I escaped the ceremonial farewells that were the normal lot of a departing officer, yet when the day of departure came, there were a surprising number of friends and well-wishers to see us off, and our compartment on the Bombay Mail was filled with flowers, besides the garlands piled round our necks; their fragrance was overwhelming in the confined space. After a time we had to cast most of them out – an action which filled me with sad regret, as though I was symbolically rejecting the country and the people whom I had loved and wanted to serve.

CHAPTER XV

Postscript

As we travelled through the Punjab, the province was in turmoil, but our passage was unimpeded. By leaving at the beginning of August, we escaped the disruption of rail traffic which was to be one of the tragic features of the appalling massacres which followed the partition of the province and the mass movement of refugees in both directions. At Lahore station, during the long scheduled halt, Brian Williams sat with us in our compartment, the last parting in India from a close friend of the years since November 1940.

In Bombay we stayed expensively in the Taj Mahal Hotel, where we could engage one of the hotel's ayahs to take care of the baby when we were out or at meals. We missed our own ayah who had coped admirably during Hilary's restless week after leaving the cool of the hill station. Our days at the Taj, for all its grandiose reputation, were uncomfortable and uneasy. My most vivid memory is of the horde of maimed and disfigured beggars who clustered round the hotel doors, ceaselessly importuning guests for alms, relentlessly pursuing anyone who ventured abroad on foot. We made one or two pleasant sightseeing excursions under the care of a young Muslim textile wholesaler, Mohd Shafi, who had a big trade with the Frontier. But we were thankful to get on board our ship, and to shed our responsibilities for our vast amount of luggage.

The ship was the *Franconia*, a Cunarder built for the Atlantic, and not for the Indian Ocean and the Red Sea in August. We were lucky to have a tiny cabin on an upper deck to ourselves – a single cabin into which a second bunk had been fitted, with a baby's hammock slung in the cramped space between the bunks. There was no porthole to the sea, but at least we had privacy. Most of the passengers slept in big dormitories, the sexes being segregated, for the ship had been fitted as a troop-carrier, and not yet been reconverted. A rope, stretched across the boat deck aft, marked the boundary which the 'other ranks' could not transgress to enter the 'cabin class' accommodation. It seemed to be one of the pastimes of the troops to congregate at the rope and watch the antics of their compatriots who were favoured with lounging chairs. The heat greatly troubled little Hilary, and whenever she seemed inconsolable, one of the British soldiers could be relied on to reach out and take her in his arms and soothe her cries. The heat in the Red Sea was ferocious and the forward motion of the ship just cancelled out the slight following breeze. By now the ship's news bulletins had shifted their focus from reports of the celebration of partition back in Bombay and the rest of India to events in Britain. As always, the main preoccupation of the British seemed to be with the weather. We were constantly being informed that the long heatwave in London was unbroken – a matter which seemed laughable after what we had endured and what bore down on the suffering millions in the Punjab.

Back in Scotland, recollections of an aborted career were soon relegated to the background, as in our new life we struggled to establish ourselves and our family in the challenging conditions of post-war shortages and controls. It did not take long to find out that my memories of a country schoolmaster's career had ceased to be relevant to post-war Scotland. I looked at a number of alternatives, and was on the point of going to Bristol to be interviewed as a potential agricultural economist by the university when my old teacher at Aberdeen, Professor Henry Hamilton, offered me an opening in his department. I accepted, having stipulated that I would complete the teacher-training course before starting my duties at the university. From April 1948, about the time that my leave pending retirement from the ICS expired, I began a spell lecturing in Political Economy which was to last nearly ten years. One of my interests was in the economic problems of underdeveloped countries. Through that interest, I kept alive many memories of India which might otherwise have been allowed to fade.

I was lucky in the sense that I found congenial and challenging opportunities to build a fresh career, and soon lost any bitterness that I carried home in the summer of 1947. Disappointment, frustration, even anger were manifest on board the SS *Franconia*. Many of the civilian passengers were leaving behind the career of a lifetime, unhappy about the state of Britain, uneasy about the prospects ahead. Amongst them were men whom I had known and admired for the distinction and efficiency with which they had served India – Gerald Curtis, Alastair Low and Norval Mitchell. It was interesting to observe how each in his different way was facing up to the need for adjustment. Gerald had perhaps come nearest to breakdown and rebellion in his despair after the madness of Nehru's Frontier excursion at the end of 1946 – he had requested to be allowed to retire in January 1947. On the ship he sought us out for a chat each day, assiduously plying us with his humorous version of the ship's gossip, bolstering our morale with his unfailing wit and stable philosophy. Alastair, who had had an outstanding success in his prolonged tenure of the post of DC Bannu, with all its responsibility for watch and ward at the most disturbed interface between the settled districts and the tribal areas, and equal distinction in the Secretariat as Finance Secretary, sat with us in the dining room and regaled all around with his views and comment – at the next table sat the ship's nurses, who eavesdropped on his conversation, trying to resolve the question of Alastair's profession: one of them was sure that he was a naval captain, so knowledgeable was he about the navigation of our vessel and all matters relating to the sea. Norval had only recently completed an exhausting spell as Chief Secretary and was perhaps the most frustrated of all of us at that stage, but also the best prepared in his plans for the future. He was immersed in his reading for a new venture into hill-farming, and stayed self-contained and silently withdrawn from the shipboard commonplaces of the voyage.

These men represented a generation of ICS officers who left a proud legacy in India and Pakistan. That more than anything explains the staunchness of the relationship between Britain and each of these countries through the strains and stresses of the long years that have followed independence and partition – a relationship often hidden beneath the formalities of official postures and policies, but surviving sturdily for all that. It is a strange feeling to have been part of the death of a great empire, and I believe that for many years after the trauma of 1947 the British were unduly reticent about their achievements in India, and guilt-ridden about their failures. Yet those who were members of the ICS, 'the heaven born', have no reason to be ashamed. I always regarded my own service, not as a career in imperialism, but as devoted to the Crown and the people. If that seems too subtle a distinction, the reader may be asked how else to explain the curious institution of the Commonwealth, of which India remains a proud member, an independent republic acknowledging the Sovereign as Head of the Commonwealth family of nations. It is surely true that Pakistan's decision to withdraw from the association has been generally regretted, and may be remedied. (Since this was written Pakistan has rejoined the Commonwealth.)

Our service was truly one of which to remain proud over a lifetime. In the early years of my university career I often had good cause to visit St Andrews and stay with Sir George and Lady Cunningham, who made a beautiful garden there just as they had in Peshawar and Nathia Gali. On one of my visits Sir George showed me correspondence he had been having with Sir Olaf Caroe and Lord Hailey about the proposal to erect in Westminster Abbey a tablet commemorating the Civil Services of the Crown in India. The Dean of Westminster at the time, the Very Rev. Alan Don, was an old personal friend of Sir George. It seemed to be Caroe who had proposed to the organizing committee the passage from the scriptures which was to be inscribed in the tablet. It was from the prophet Micah:

> He hath showed thee, O man, what is good; and what doth the Lord require of thee, but to do justly, and to love mercy, and to walk humbly with thy God?

Sir George felt that, with the other phrases of explanations essential to the dedication of the inscription,[1] the inclusion of the whole of this text made the whole thing too wordy. He had been pondering for some time how to put this most tactfully to Caroe, and asked me for my ideas. I could offer no alternative to Micah, so I suggested that his point might be met if part of the verse were to be omitted. Finally, he said 'Yes, we did justly and we loved mercy, but did you ever think of Roger or Packy as walking humbly with their God?' His proposal to Caroe and Alan Don was accepted; the abbreviated passage engraved on the tablet is:

> O man, what doth the Lord require of thee, but to do justly and to love mercy?

That was not, however, the end of the story. Dr Don's successor as Dean of Westminster took exception to the mutilation of the holy scripture and insisted on fresh work by the stonemason, but Lord Hailey, and many others including Lord Mountbatten and

Lord Attlee, joined successfully in the protest against the alteration of the tablet from the form unveiled by the Queen and duly dedicated and blessed on that occasion. The visitor to the West Cloister of the Abbey can see the plaque today as it was meant to be, and only the closest scrutiny will reveal the faint trace of the stonemason's repair in the restoration.

The history of the ICS is a proud story, about which there is no need for false humility; and I have always been glad to have been a tiny part of it – to have been 'something in India'.

> There are in our existence spots of time,
> That with distinct preeminence retain
> A renovating virtue, whence our minds
> Are nourished and invisibly repaired;
> A virtue, by which pleasure is enhanced,
> That penetrates, enables us to mount,
> When high, more high, and lifts us up when fallen.
>
> Wordsworth, *Prelude*

Notes

[1] The complete text of the inscription, headed by the Royal Arms, flanked on one side by the badge of the Order of the Star of India, on the other by that of the Order of the Indian Empire, is:

1858–1947

HERE ARE COMMEMORATED THE CIVIL SERVICES OF THE CROWN IN INDIA

LET THEM NOT BE FORGOTTEN FOR THEY SERVED INDIA WELL

WHAT DOTH THE LORD REQUIRE OF THEE BUT TO DO JUSTLY AND LOVE MERCY?

Glossary

Badal	Revenge, blood feud.
Barampta	Collective action against a village or a particular section of a tribe.
Burqa	All-embracing outer garment concealing a woman in purdah from public gaze.
Burra	Big, great. The opposite is chota (e.g. chota peg – small whisky).
Chae	Tea. *Chota haziri* is early morning 'wake-up' tea.
Chalak	Cunning, clever but untrustworthy.
Chatti	Large earthenware water container.
Chowkidar	Night watchman.
Dak	Literally post or mail. A dak bungalow is a resting place for travellers a day's march away.
Dhobi	Washerman, responsible for the laundry.
Gadi	Throne.
Ghasht	A patrol from a Frontier Scouts post.
Hamsaya	A refugee under protection of another tribe.
Hujra	A meeting place, in a village often next to the house of the local chief.
Ilaqa	District or area.
Jawan	Young man. Often applied to junior soldiers or members of the Frontier Scouts.
Jirga	An official meeting between political officers and a tribe, or a small group trying cases under the Frontier Crimes Regulations.
Jehad	A holy war.

Kacha	Temporary, impermanent, poor quality.
Khud	Steep slopes, on either side of a mountain track.
Kanungo	Junior revenge official (senior to the village *patwari*).
Khassadar	Tribal levy (recruited to keep open a stretch of public road).
Kharif	Autumn crop.
Kor	Household, extended family.
Kot	House, property.
Lashkar	Hostile force, likely to move on the warpath. Sometimes starts as a small gang of outlaws, growing rapidly as hostilities attract recruits.
Mali	Gardener.
Malik	Headman, a recognized leader.
Man Bap	Literally, 'father and mother', a term of great respect for an individual like the District Magistrate, or DC.
Mandi	Market, group of warehouses.
Maund	Measure of weight, varying in different areas, usually rather less than a hundredweight.
Mela	A grand fair or festival.
Mujahidin	Participant in a holy war (*jehad*).
Mulakat	Petitioner, who presents himself in person before the political agent, often the source of information, not often reliable.
Muzri	Grey cloth, produced from a plant.
Pukka Ishtunt Sahib	A 'proper' assistant commissioner no longer a junior trainee probationer or apprentice, now holder of an 'established' post.
Pukhtunwali	Code of Pathan conduct and honour.
Pattar Rakh Bhai	'Put down the stone, brother', shouted by the driver to the boy apprentice at the back of the bus, instructing him to block the spinning back wheel as he tried to propel the bus round a hairpin bend.
Patwari	The most junior revenue official charged with maintaining the records of ownership, tenancy, etc. of village land.
Pugree	Headgear, often just a turban.

Rabi	Spring crop.
Riwaj	Tribal custom.
Saman	Baggage.
Sangar	Rought stone shelter from hostile fire.
Serai	Market place, collection of shops.
Shariat	Islamic law.
Sharif	Gentle, well-mannered, cultivated.
Sirkar	Government (usually the British Raj), often personalized in addressing a District Officer.
Spingiray	Grey-beard, a venerable old man.
Tahsil	A division of a district, for purposes of land revenue collection.
Tamasha	Fun and games, a large-scale party.
Taqleef	Troubles, cause of pain.
Tikala	Food, a feast.
Urz	Petition.
Zabardast	Tough, strong, perhaps a shade too firm.